BEYOND
NEIGHBOURHOOD PLANNING
Knowledge, Care, Legitimacy

Andy Yuille

D1612591

P

First published in Great Britain in 2023 by

Policy Press, an imprint of
Bristol University Press
University of Bristol
1–9 Old Park Hill
Bristol
BS2 8BB
UK
t: +44 (0)117 374 6645
e: bup-info@bristol.ac.uk

Details of international sales and distribution partners are available at
policy.bristoluniversitypress.co.uk

British Library Cataloguing in Publication Data
A catalogue record for this book is available from the British Library

ISBN 978-1-4473-6283-8 hardcover
ISBN 978-1-4473-6284-5 paperback
ISBN 978-1-4473-6285-2 ePub
ISBN 978-1-4473-6286-9 ePdf

Cover design: Lyn Davies Design
Front cover image: alamy/Allsorts Stock Photo
Bristol University Press and Policy Press use environmentally responsible
print partners.
Printed and bound in Great Britain by CPI Group (UK) Ltd, Croydon, CR0 4YY

FSC
www.fsc.org
MIX
Paper | Supporting
responsible forestry
FSC® C013604

Contents

List of figures and table

Figures

Table

Acknowledgements

I would like to express my gratitude and appreciation for the help and support that I have had in assembling this book. First, to the two neighbourhood planning groups who participated in the research, and to their consultants and Local Planning Authorities, who generously let me work alongside them (for a lot longer than any of us expected!), and whose persistence and resourcefulness were a lesson in themselves. All names and other identifying features have been anonymised as an original condition of conducting the research, but they will know who they are. Second, to the supervisors of the doctoral research on which much of the book is based, and my mentors in the subsequent fellowship which developed the ideas arising from that research, for their inspiration, commitment, wisdom and good humour: Claire Waterton, Vicky Singleton, Noel Cass, Gordon Walker and Rebecca Willis. Particular thanks go to Noel for his tremendous dedication in doing this outside of the formal system, unable to be formally appointed as a supervisor because of the short-term nature of his research contracts. Third, to the colleagues who made it all more colourful, sociable, intelligible and, dare I say it, sometimes even fun. Special mention to the various permutations of Write Club and particularly Jess Phoenix, Rebecca Willis (again!), Cath Hill, Cosmin Popan and Lula Mecinska.

Thanks to my wife Anna for her unstinting support and encouragement, reminders that it's supposed to be hard, comments on the final drafts, and for organising writing weekends for the two of us so that I could enjoy it as well as get it done. Thanks to my parents for not throwing up their hands in despair at my wanting to 'go back to school' in my 40s, and for being as wonderfully understanding and supportive of this as they have been for everything else ever. Thanks to my friends who pretended to be interested, bought me wine, and mostly refrained from asking if I've got a real job yet. And thanks to the sociology department and the Lancaster Environment Centre at Lancaster University for hosting this adventure, and to the Economic and Social Research Council for funding it through PhD studentship grant 1539678 and postdoctoral fellowship grant ES/V01112X/1.

Preface

From 2006 I have led policy and campaigning work for a variety of environmental non-governmental organisations (NGOs) and community groups – primarily the Campaign to Protect Rural England. I often represented these groups in the planning system and other forums that were ostensibly intended to widen public and stakeholder participation in decision making and incorporate a wide range of knowledges and values. I found that much of what I was doing was acting as a translator, taking the lived experiences of individuals and groups and transforming them into technical jargon and instrumentalised arguments that would fit into particular policy pigeonholes: turning them into something other than what they were presented to me as, to enable them to have traction in formal and sometimes intimidating settings.

I also observed members of the public and community groups representing themselves, particularly in formal spatial planning settings. They often expressed themselves eloquently and passionately, to apparently sympathetic planning inspectors who listened carefully, ensuring that everyone felt that they had had the opportunity to fully contribute. However, that testimony would often then be all but discarded because it didn't fit easily into the scales with which the 'planning balance' was weighed. Even in these theoretically inclusive forums, the things that really mattered to people were often excluded and made invisible: what Science and Technology Studies scholar John Law describes as being 'othered'. Representing community groups and NGOs in other technocratic locations, such as the North West Regional Assembly, Regional Development Agency and Government Office, I found debate foreclosed because the questions and problems to be considered were framed in particular ways, and there were unofficial but taken-for-granted restrictions on the types of knowledge and value considered valid.

Then, in 2011, the government introduced neighbourhood planning through the Localism Act, enabling community groups to write their own land use planning policies, to decide what evidence was needed to support them, and to produce that evidence. The discourse of neighbourhood planning emphasised local, experiential knowledge – people were portrayed as being qualified to plan for a place because of their experience of living there. It emphasised people's affective, emotional connections with place, something that the planning system (and planning scholarship) has previously disparaged. It was claimed that it would shift the focus of hyper-local planning from a bureaucratic, technical, expert-led process to a more democratic, community-led one. It promised to make translators like me, at least in some circumstances, effectively redundant. This book explores these claims through ethnographic research conducted between 2015 and 2018, and examines ways in which its findings might be extended beyond neighbourhood planning to other sites of participatory democracy.

Andy Yuille
November 2022

1

Introduction: Neighbourhood planners and the turn to participation

> Neighbourhood Planning is about letting the people who know
> about and care for an area plan for it.
> > Planning Advisory Service (2013)

Introduction

This is a book about neighbourhood planning, a 'community right'
introduced to England by the Localism Act 2011, which allows community
groups to write their own land use planning policies for their towns, villages
or parts of cities. This means that they can now do what previously only
credentialled experts working within the machinery of government could,
a move which has been described as 'arguably the most radical innovation
in UK neighbourhood governance in a generation' (Wargent and Parker,
2018: 379). As the opening quotation from the Planning Advisory Service
(a government-funded programme providing support to Local Planning
Authorities [LPAs] to help them understand and respond to planning
reform) highlights, neighbourhood planning emphasises the importance and
centrality of the knowledge and care that local people have for the place
where they live, derived from their experience of living there.

Portrayed as an antidote to a planning system that was too complex,
technical and exclusive, proponents of neighbourhood planning claim that
it promotes local democracy by widening and deepening participation in
planning, one of the most controversial aspects of local life in the UK. As
the government's flagship initiative for local engagement with planning,
and for localism and community control more widely, it was intended to
extend and pluralise the range of voices and sources of knowledge that can
be influential in planning: enabling the people who know and care about a
place to make their own decisions about how it changes. This book charts
some of the challenges faced by two neighbourhood planning communities
and how they responded to them, told from the perspective of someone
working closely with them.

But it is also a book about the dilemmas and potentials of participatory
governance more widely, in the context of an increasing, international
perception of democratic deficit, in which citizens feel disconnected from
and distrustful of those who make public decisions on their behalf (Foa

1

et al, 2020). It explores how processes that are established with the purpose of enabling communities to have their say on issues which affect them can result in those communities feeling that the things that matter to them have not been adequately addressed. But it also emphasises how, at the same time, those processes can and do make material differences, bringing about changes that would not have happened otherwise. It maintains this 'both/ and' focus throughout, on how neighbourhood planning and participation more widely can simultaneously disrupt and reproduce existing power relations. It does this by using resources from Science and Technology Studies (STS) to explore the ways in which knowledge and power, and subjects and objects, are co-produced and entangled through participatory processes (Jasanoff, 2004a; Chilvers and Kearnes, 2016). And it asks, and proposes some tentative responses to, the question of how marginalised knowledges can be worked with better.

Because it's *also* about what is described in STS as 'ontological politics' (Mol, 1999). This refers to the decisions that are made *before* the decisions that are recognised as political are made, such as during the production and presentation of evidence. These processes are not generally recognised as political, and in fact are often framed precisely as being *not* political. They deal with questions about what there is in the world, how things fit together, what causes might have what effects, and what is relevant and important to the situation under consideration. These are questions that can be described as 'ontological'. Answers to these questions tend to be presented as value-free knowledge, hard evidence, statements of fact. Then, once we have the facts, we can make our political decisions. But what knowledge to trust, which voices to listen to, what evidence to produce, what assumptions and simplifications to make, what to foreground as important and what to background as marginal – in other words, what to make visible to politics and political decision making – are all highly political choices. Political not in the sense of party or even personal politics, but in the sense of an ongoing struggle to define what the world is like, what matters, what elements of complex situations are relevant and important. So this book is also about care: what people care about, how that care can (or can't) be articulated, and the effects that has.

This book is highly specific in its focus on neighbourhood planning and its detailed analysis of two case studies of community groups preparing neighbourhood plans. But I also hope to show how the ideas and insights generated here can travel and help to understand and interpret other cases of place-based participatory democracy. And, in turn, I hope to show how this can open up possibilities for intervention, to help enable particular instances of participatory democracy come closer to realising their promise and to resist the traps of co-option, governmentality and tokenism. But before briefly reviewing this wider landscape, I'd like you to meet the people whose work and commitment to shaping the future of their neighbourhoods over more than three years animate these pages and constitute the stories I'm going to tell.

Meet the cast

Arriving in Oakley

On a cold, dark night in February 2015 I was walking around a small coastal town in northern England, trying to find a place I'll call Elizabeth Hall.[1] The banners on the wall and posters in the window of the building in front of me, saying 'Oakley Neighbourhood Plan: We need you to vote YES', confirmed that I'd come to the right place. I was about to meet the Oakley neighbourhood planning group (NPG) for the first time, to ask them if they'd be willing to take part in an ethnographic research project. They had started work on a neighbourhood plan in the autumn and, I learned that evening, were consulting the neighbourhood on the broad issues the plan should tackle and general principles that should underpin it.

The main entrance was locked for the night, so I followed the light from a side door around the corner, and headed upstairs. The NPG were meeting in the Council Chamber, where the town council also held their meetings, a room dominated by a huge wooden boardroom-style table in the middle of the room and heavy wooden panels on the wall listing past mayors. There were ten of them here tonight, four of whom were also town councillors, along with the council's deputy clerk. They seemed, on the whole, reasonably well off, confident, comfortable in themselves and in this situation, and welcoming to me as a stranger. The discussion that evening included the group auditing their skills and experience to see what they might be missing, which revealed that they were mostly retired, from professional backgrounds. Stephanie, the Chair, was very self-deprecating about her title, but chaired the meeting efficiently and professionally, skilfully managing both those members who wanted to talk a lot (primarily Robert and Andrew), and drawing out those who seemed less confident or comfortable about contributing (most notably Sarah, Paula and Henry). After swiftly dealing with actions arising from the last meeting, Stephanie, supported by interjections from around the table, filled me in on some brief background to the town and what they were doing.

Oakley is a small coastal town of just over 4,000 people. It grew from a cluster of fishermen's cottages to a popular seaside resort almost overnight with the arrival of the railway in the mid-1800s. This boom of tourists seeking the health-giving benefits of the sea air shaped the architecture, character and development of the town, with a strong orientation towards the sea, several large hotels, public gardens and attractive public realm. Oakley did not suffer the precipitous decline of many British resort towns, but rather stagnated, catering to a small and sedate visiting public (Walton, 2000: 42). Its population is now old and ageing, with over 40 per cent of the population over 65, compared to around 16 per cent of the population nationally. There are relatively low levels of deprivation in the town overall, but this conceals some distinct social and spatial inequalities. There are few economic opportunities for young people in the town, and the group were concerned about the lack of housing that could be suitable and affordable both for younger people and for older people looking to downsize.

Oakley's location just outside a national park, where the type and scale of development is limited, leads to increased pressure for development in and around the town. However, a slew of housing developments over the past few years had been strongly opposed locally as they didn't meet these community-identified needs, but rather tended to be intrusive, large, executive homes which did not respond to or respect their built and natural surroundings. They were widely regarded as the wrong development in the wrong places. Conversely, there had been strong support for a large new social housing project led by a housing association near the town centre, in terms of its design, location, integration with the built form of the town, and type of housing it provided. The group wanted to make sure that future development in the town actually met the needs of the local community for jobs and housing, while also ameliorating (or at least not worsening) existing problems with flooding and traffic, and maintaining Oakley's distinctive character.

Resentment, peripherality and disconnection

One of the main themes that came out of that first meeting, and that haunted much of the next few years as I worked with them to produce their plan, was a sense of resentment towards and betrayal by the district's LPA. In briefly outlining to me why they had chosen to produce a neighbourhood plan, they explained that as well as permitting the alienating developments already mentioned, the LPA had adopted a new development plan just over a year earlier, allocating several sites in and around the town for development that had been strongly resisted locally, including the last remaining green space between the town and two nearby settlements. Widespread engagement by individuals, self-organised action groups, and the town council in consultations over the plan and individual development proposals seemed to them to have been ignored. On-the-ground knowledge about local conditions was, in their view, passed over in favour of remote technical assessments which, as far as they were concerned, bore little resemblance to the place where they lived.

Some, but not all, of the NPG had been involved in these consultations in one way or another. But even those who had not been involved agreed that this reflected a wider, ongoing pattern: of not having their voices heard, their needs acknowledged, their knowledge recognised, or what mattered to them taken account of. This ranged from local warnings about flood risk in relation to new development going unheeded, to being passed over for investment in, or even maintenance of, basic infrastructure in favour of other, more central places in the district, particularly the main town where the LPA's offices were located. There was a strong feeling of being marginalised, of existing geographically and figuratively on the periphery. Making a neighbourhood plan was seen by the town council as an opportunity to gain some statutory power that would mean that their voice would have to be heard. They were also attracted by the promise of additional funding that it would bring.[2] Four town councillors agreed to establish a NPG, and then invited other residents to join the group via their website, Facebook page and the local newspaper, leading to a 14-strong NPG.

Connecting disconnections

This sense of disconnection from and distrust of the LPA was shared by the second NPG I came to work with, in Wroston, a small rural village of around 500 people, in another northern county. I met them for the first time the following week, on another dark night, in the village hall. There were signs directing people for the neighbourhood plan meeting to the first door on the left; the room opposite was piled high with a seemingly random collection of things. The room was small, with a trestle table that four chairs could just about crowd around, more folding chairs set out around the edges of the room, and a shelf-like work surface along one side. It clearly served several purposes – as a storeroom, general meeting room, the Wroston computer centre (as declared by an A4 sign, a couple of large laptops, and a server continuously emitting a high-pitched whine) – and as the neighbourhood planning hub, with A4 laminates on the walls describing the village's 'assets and issues' as identified in the group's first community consultation.

The setting was much more informal than Oakley, and the people were too, although they appeared to share a broadly similar social and cultural background, and they were again friendly and welcoming to me. They were markedly younger overall; although a small majority of the eight people there that night appeared to be over 50, most were still in work. None were parish councillors. A planning consultant, Scott, and the very part-time parish clerk were also present. Simon, the Chair, entered and called the meeting to order. He attempted to follow quite a formal style of chairing, but many of the group acted much less formally, particularly Anne (who turned out to be the group's unofficial Vice Chair), who regularly laughed, joked, swore and interrupted. However, she clearly had a lot of respect from the group, was a well-known figure in Wroston and appeared to be a woman who could – and did – get things done. The atmosphere in general was more relaxed than in the formal council chamber at Oakley. They laughed a lot.

But despite the laughter and the informality, discontent and distrust were readily apparent here as well. The LPA for the district that Wroston is in was in the process of preparing a new local plan that would allocate sites for development. At a packed public meeting in the village the previous year, the agent for a local landowner had proposed developing the fields surrounding the village on the north and east sides for housing, which could triple its size (from around 200 to around 600 houses). The LPA, under pressure to find enough land to meet housing targets that were widely perceived as being externally imposed and excessively high, appeared inclined to include the sites in their plan, despite very widespread local opposition, and very limited accessibility to services or employment by any means other than driving. At this meeting, a parish councillor proposed producing a neighbourhood plan so that residents could have more control over how the village developed, and after a couple of initial meetings with parish councillors and other residents, this was taken forwards by a group of resident volunteers.

Wroston lies just inside the boundary of a sparsely populated Area of Outstanding Natural Beauty, and is still largely based around a linear medieval street pattern, with buildings fronting the roads one deep. The built-up areas are of a surprisingly high density, with many older houses in terraces where gaps between cottages have been filled in over the centuries, and with newer developments largely on sites that had previously been used for industry. However, the village is surrounded by open countryside with networks of footpaths and green lanes, and contains plenty of public green space. From its original role as an agricultural settlement, by the 19th century it had become a minor industrial centre, and although the traditional industries that thrived there have all declined to zero, it is still a working village, with 44 businesses ranging from farming to therapy operating there. It is also a lived-in place, with over 95 per cent of homes being permanent residences – it has not been hollowed out like other villages in scenic locations by second homes and holiday lets. However, in common with many rural places it has suffered from a stark loss of services, losing a GP surgery, two pubs and several bus services in the past few years.

As in Oakley, the NPG felt that their community was very peripheral: that they were 'off the radar' of the LPA as anything other than now a place to 'dump' extra housing to achieve excessive targets. They believed that the LPA had no real knowledge of or engagement with their village, or interest in the needs, wellbeing or knowledge of the local community. This group were also concerned that there was not enough housing locally that would be suitable or affordable for younger people. But at the same time, they were determined that the village should grow organically to primarily meet local needs, and in ways that preserved its historic character and sense of place and community. Their knowledge of recent developments permitted by the LPA nearby, and their sense more generally of the LPA as a remote institution with little interest in them, led them to believe that this would not happen without their active intervention.

Optimism and scepticism

But despite these rather negative beginnings in both cases, both groups at this stage were full of energy, optimism and hope. The government had promised them 'direct power to develop a shared vision for their neighbourhood and shape the development and growth of their local area' (DCLG, 2014b). Early and extensive consultation throughout their neighbourhoods had garnered widespread public support and given them some clear indications about the priorities of their communities. The task before them was daunting but do-able: to produce a statutory framework that would shape the growth and development of the places where they lived for the next 10 to 15 years.

Both groups agreed to let me join them while they worked towards that as a participant observer – someone who would work alongside them while simultaneously conducting research on the processes that we were working in and on – with a mixture of enthusiasm and scepticism. In both groups there was an overall agreement that it could benefit them, as I would become a part of each group and pitch in with the work of producing the plans, both as an extra pair of hands and also drawing on my previous experience of working with community groups in the planning system. Most of them were curious about the idea of becoming the subjects of a research project, but there was some initial hesitance about the focus and methodology. When I first talked to him about an interest in different ways of knowing and valuing place, Simon, Chair of the Wroston NPG, had tersely warned me that neighbourhood planning is "not about that wishy-washy sort of stuff, it has to be based on hard evidence". However, he was particularly keen for me to help them with consultation data analysis for confidentiality reasons, reasoning that the village is so small that people could be readily identifiable, even though surveys would be anonymised. Having (unpaid) outsiders involved at this point was seen as a big bonus. Stephanie, Chair of the Oakley NPG, was particularly sceptical of the idea of ethnography, saying that that, at least in the early days of ethnography, "us colonial types went off to study 'tribes' and wrote down all sorts of nonsense that had nothing to do with anything, then came back home and reported it as facts". She was, understandably, worried about being misinterpreted, and about these misinterpretations being used to further political agendas that she did not share. Conversely, she and several others were excited at the idea that they could be involved in research that might, just possibly, help to shift government policy in favour of further empowering local communities.

I say this to very deliberately locate myself within the study, as a member of the cast as it were, as well as an observer and interpreter of their actions and circumstances. I worked within and alongside these groups for over three years, sharing their enthusiasms, challenges, victories and disappointments. This book is not a detached record of events viewed at a distance, but rather an engaged account in which I am entangled with the participants, enabling me to witness and experience their practices in situ as they unfolded: to both watch and participate in the process of producing a plan. Ethnography is a situated practice that locates the observer in the world, and which is grounded in a commitment to the first-hand experience and exploration of the realities of everyday life in a particular setting (Atkinson et al, 2007; Denzin and Lincoln, 2008). And so, acknowledging that 'knowledge is always mediated by pre-existing ideas and values, whether this is acknowledged by the researcher or not' (Seale, 1999: 470), rather than vainly striving for an unattainable 'view from nowhere', I attempt to be clear about my own positioning (Haraway, 1988).

The international turn to participation

The people described in the previous section were embarking on one very specific journey of participatory democracy. Enhancing public participation in policy and decision making has been a subject of central concern for the English planning system for over 50 years, since the Skeffington committee published its report on *People and Planning* in 1969. This makes the planning system one of the longest-standing arenas in which the dilemmas and potential for participatory democracy have been played out, and in which they are frequently revisited (Inch et al, 2019). At the time of writing, radical reforms to the English planning system proposed by the Conservative UK government in 2020 are in the process of largely being quietly dropped after years of delay. This was primarily due to concerns voiced by professional planning associations, non-governmental organisations (NGOs), local councillors and backbench MPs that they would drastically reduce the opportunity for citizens to have a say on material changes to their environments, demonstrating the continuing centrality of participation in planning.

But English planning does not operate in a vacuum, and these ebbs and flows reflect and are embedded in broader international social and political tides in a widespread 'turn to participation' (Bherer et al, 2016b). The ground-breaking Skeffington report was published in the same year as Sherry Arnstein's seminal paper introducing the idea of a 'ladder of citizen participation' (Arnstein, 1969), a metaphor still frequently drawn on today to analyse the differential degrees of empowerment that initiatives described as 'participatory' might achieve. Public access to policy and decision making, for citizens to have a meaningful say on matters that directly affect their lives across a broad spectrum of issues, has been at the forefront of public discourse for many years. Indeed, the manifold appeals of and rationales for extending participation have become so deeply embedded in governance arrangements at all scales that citizen participation and community empowerment have arguably become a new orthodoxy (Stirrat, 1996).

Beginning in the 1960s, an extraordinarily wide variety of methods of widening participation in governance have proliferated, with a view to enabling affected stakeholders and publics to scrutinise, debate and influence decision making from diverse perspectives (Polletta, 2016). This still-unfolding movement towards expanded and pluralised involvement in decision making takes in much of both the 'global North' and the 'global South' (Beaumont and Nicholls, 2008), and authoritarian as well as liberal regimes (Yan and Xin, 2017). In a context of pervasive claims of democratic deficits (Norris, 2011), where the diagnosis of 'democracy in crisis' takes on many different forms and meanings (Ercan and Gagnon, 2014), and some analysts even contend that globally we have entered a period of 'democratic recession' (Diamond, 2015), the demand for such experiments in democracy, which promise to reconfigure relations between citizens, civil society and the state, is only accelerating.

Formal, institutionalised participatory practices are increasingly common in areas as diverse as land use planning in general (Innes and Booher, 2004) and urban planning in particular (Stewart and Lithgow, 2015), rural development (Chambers, 1994b), public spending (Shah, 2007), transport planning (Bickerstaff et al, 2002), natural resource management (Halseth and Booth, 2003), waste management (Petts, 2005), social and welfare services (Pestoff, 2006, 2009), infrastructure provision (González Rivas, 2014), environmental management (Reed, 2008; Luyet et al, 2012), health care (Franchina et al, 2020), climate and energy policy (Sandover et al, 2021), and a wide array of other issues. Participatory mechanisms are increasingly utilised by national and local governments, public agencies, private companies, unions, NGOs, community groups and social movements (Bherer et al, 2016a). At an international level, they have been central to the operations of the World Bank for decades (World Bank, 1996, 2014) – albeit with very varied opinions on their effectiveness – and they underpin several of the UN Sustainable Development Goals and elements of the New Urban Agenda and the Paris Agreement on climate change. The Organisation for Economic Co-operation and Development hosts a handbook on 'Citizens as Partners' which 'offers government officials practical assistance in strengthening relations between government and citizens' (OECD, 2001). And in 2021 the European Commission established a Competence Centre on Participatory and Deliberative Democracy, providing 'services, guidance and tools to support the development of socially robust policy through citizen engagement practices' (European Commission, 2021).

There is a long list of reasons why these diverse participatory projects have been developed (see, for example, Fiorino, 1990; Beierle, 1999; Fung et al, 2003; Innes and Booher, 2004; Irvin and Stansbury, 2004; Stirling, 2006). These can be summarised as: informing and educating the public; enabling a wider range of knowledge, skills and values to be brought to bear on matters of public interest; enabling decisionmakers to learn more about public perspectives and priorities; enabling disadvantaged groups to be heard, thus promoting fairness and justice; enabling citizens to have some influence over decisions that would otherwise be taken in political, bureaucratic or expert institutions that are physically or figuratively remote from the people and places they would affect; securing legitimacy for public decisions and institutions; ensuring that the knowledge relied upon to make decisions is fit for purpose; improving the quality and effectiveness of decision making and delivery; making elected leaders and governments more accountable, transparent and responsive; empowering citizens to 'take control of their own destinies'; and being simply the right thing to do in a democratic society.

Individual participatory democratic projects seek to deliver on some (but rarely all) of these rationales, to greater or lesser extents, and in different combinations of emphasis – and some analysts have highlighted that some of these rationales may in practice be incommensurable or contradictory (for example, maximising participation versus targeting assumed holders of specific knowledge or experience) (Wesselink et al, 2011). However, despite some efforts to establish a framework for doing so, actual instances of participation are rarely explicitly evaluated to assess which, if any, of these aims have been achieved (Beierle, 1999). Indeed, there have been trenchant critiques of actual instances – and the very idea – of participation, highlighting practical and conceptual flaws and the ways in which participation can in practice co-opt participants and reinforce and reproduce existing inequalities and power relations.

That said, one of the key ways in which participatory projects have been distinguished is the extent to which they invest participants with real power over decision making. The best-known example of such a heuristic is, as mentioned earlier, Arnstein's original 'ladder of citizen participation'. This charts degrees of possible community engagement in participatory processes, ranging from the public simply receiving more or better information, through consultation and partnership, to significant levels of citizen control. Many authors over the intervening decades have suggested ways in which the ladder should be complexified to respond to the complicated dynamics of actual participation (Wilcox, 1994; Tritter and McCallum, 2006), and other typologies of participation have been developed, analysing, for example, the depth and breadth of participation (Farrington et al, 1993), how people participate (Pretty, 1995), and the interests involved (White, 1996). However, Arnstein's ladder remains a central reference point in academic, policy, and practitioner communities, with both supporters of participation and critics of particular processes advocating positions higher up the ladder as more desirable (Ianniello et al, 2019).

Interventions to involve citizens in decision making have been described variously as participatory democracy, inclusive governance, civic engagement, community empowerment, citizen control, coproduction, localism, deliberative democracy, stakeholder inclusion, interactive decision making and double devolution, among a wide range of other labels and combinations. They take a wide variety of forms (Bherer and Breux, 2012), with well-known examples including 'mini-publics' such as citizens' assemblies, citizens' juries and consensus conferences, participatory budgeting, community councils, deliberative opinion polls, consultations, citizens' advisory committees, service coproduction, town hall meetings, referendums, collaborative governance, and many digital equivalents and extensions. Smith (2005) details 57 typologies of such experiments in democracy from around the world, from the now-routine to the more radical, covering various forms of electoral, consultative, deliberative, co-governance, direct democracy and e-democracy innovations. Rowe and Frewer (2005) highlight over a hundred different types of participatory practices focused on the UK and US, and emphasise how very incomplete this extensive list is even in relation to those countries alone. Elstub and Escobar (2021) have more recently compiled an overview of current research on experiments in democracy, exploring different types of innovations, their potential and uses in different thematic and geographical areas, the actors involved, and the methods used to research them. And many instantiations and typologies of democratic experimentation and innovation have their own dedicated literature. Deliberative democracy, for example, is the subject of dozens of books spanning several decades (for example, Elster, 1998; Fishkin and Cran, 2009; Bächtiger et al, 2018), two journals (the *Journal of Public Deliberation* and the *Journal of Deliberative Democracy*) and thousands of peer-reviewed articles.

These terms and practices imbricate with but do not replicate each other. For example, not all localist governance is participatory, although localism generally seeks to bring decision making closer to affected citizens (Ercan and Hendriks, 2013); and not all participatory practices are local or place specific (for example, patient associations affected by a particular disease can span countries and even continents [Callon and Rabeharisoa, 2008]). Likewise, not all practices of deliberative democracy are particularly participatory (such as expert appraisal panels), and not all participatory practices are deliberative (such as referendums). The theoretical or ideological context for different interventions may differ profoundly, for example, a localist paradigm that requires power to be devolved to communities, who are defined as being better off without the 'dead hand' of the state, as against a community empowerment paradigm that advocates communities deciding the level of empowerment that is appropriate for them, working in partnership with the state (Rolfe, 2018). Public engagement can serve many different purposes, which requires different concrete modes or models of participation (O'Faircheallaigh, 2010). However, here I will use the phrase 'participatory democracy' as an umbrella term to capture the wide variety of methods, purposes and ideologies intended to enhance citizen engagement in decision making, without in any way intending to flatten out or negate the multiple differences between them.

But the movement towards participatory democracy does not stop there. Beyond this wave of formal participation, organised and sanctioned by the state and other powerful actors, the past few years have also seen the emergence of significant social movements. Prominent examples include Black Lives Matter and Extinction Rebellion, alongside a grassroots social response to COVID-19 which included a surge of informal mutual aid and self-organised community groups. These movements build on long traditions of community organising and campaigning for rights and the redistribution of power in society. Indeed, as Della Porta points out, the idea that 'democracy' is done purely through delegation of powers to elected representatives does not reflect the actual functioning of any democracy at any point in history. There is always a 'circuit of surveillance, anchored outside state institutions', made up of critical citizens, social movements, mass media, independent experts and authorities and so on, that challenges, makes claims on, and holds elected representatives to account, and without which the idea of democracy would be extremely hollow (Della Porta, 2013: 5).

Faranak Miraftab (2004) distinguishes between 'invited' spaces (which are legitimised and often orchestrated by states or other powerful actors, to engage citizens or other stakeholders in processes of consultation, deliberation and sometimes decision making) and 'invented' spaces (which are initiated by citizens, communities or social movements themselves, and may be more directly oppositional to state or other actors' proposals or practices, such as local action groups, protest groups and self-organised community groups). Bua and Bussu (2020) provide an alternative characterisation of these distinctions, contrasting top-down 'governance-driven democratization' – which aims to enhance the dwindling legitimacy of institutions and experts and improve policy making by engaging wider voices, interests and knowledge – with more critically oriented, bottom-up 'democracy-driven governance', which has more transformative ambitions to advance social justice and deepen democracy. Important work can be done in both kinds of spaces in relation to the rationales given earlier for encouraging participatory democracy. Furthermore, these different kinds of space and process are not mutually exclusive, but rather often have individuals, collectives, knowledge, values, and so on circulating between them (Miraftab, 2006).

Other authors have called attention to the fact that participatory democracy is not in practice separable into such neat categories, despite their analytical usefulness, and have suggested the existence of spaces beyond (Smith and Rubin, 2015) and between (Bussu, 2019) invited and invented. These spaces are not static but dynamic: for example, citizenship practices in invented spaces may lead to new opportunities in invited spaces, and the perceived failure of invited spaces to engage with 'what matters' to citizens may ignite, strengthen or renew invented spaces (Bua and Bussu, 2020; Miraftab, 2020). There are growing demands from social movements for the creation of participatory institutions with real powers, for example, Extinction Rebellion's demands for citizens' assemblies to drive governmental climate policies (Sandover et al, 2021). On this basis, I argue that both formal and informal spaces should be included in an expansive definition of participatory democracy, as well as those groups operating between these spaces (Fischer, 2006). This is particularly the case given that the establishment of invited spaces, while offering the potential for greater citizen input and/or control in highly specified ways, may have the effect of delegitimising other forms of citizen engagement and action (Cornwall, 2002).

So when I talk about participatory democracy – or indeed participation in planning – I don't just mean the formal, institutionalised, 'top-down' instances in which citizens can participate in decision-making activity through mechanisms defined and controlled by the state or other powerful actors, but also the self-organised, autonomous, 'bottom-up' spaces and methods that grassroots movements have carved out for themselves in order to influence decision-making processes that they are excluded from, and the ways in which these spaces and methods interact (Aylett, 2010). Although this understanding is not universally shared (for example, radical democrats and liberal democrats may disagree about the democratic legitimacy of a protest that occupies a busy street and prevents traffic flow [Ercan and Gagnon, 2014]), this expansive definition will be used here.

As Andrea Cornwall emphasises, analysis of any individual instance of participation requires careful attention to 'what exactly people are being enjoined to participate in, for what purpose, who is involved and who is absent' (2008: 281). Neighbourhood planning is very specifically situated. It is limited to England. It deals specifically with land use planning – although work on neighbourhood plans also tends to catalyse and provide a focus for other place-based community activity (Parker et al, 2020). It has to date been heavily concentrated in more rural and affluent areas (Parker et al, 2020), although with some notable exceptions, and recent government initiatives have made efforts to encourage and support it in more urban and deprived areas (MHCLG, 2021). It can only be initiated by specified 'qualifying bodies' – a town or parish council if there is one in the area, or a specially constituted Neighbourhood Forum if there is not, and there are specific hurdles that a group must clear to get a plan adopted, which will be outlined in the following chapter.

However, despite the relatively privileged position of many neighbourhood planning communities, as already highlighted they are still often peripheral to decision making that affects their lives, and in particular marginalised from policy and decision making in planning, which is widely accepted as being 'complex, remote, hard to understand, difficult to engage with, slow and unpredictable and, generally, "not customer friendly"' (Baker et al, 2007: 80). And despite the procedural constraints on the neighbourhood planning process, it is intended to be citizen-initiated and community-led, with considerable freedom for groups to determine their own membership, boundaries, issues and processes: 'this was not "participation" in a state-led initiative. ... It was up to citizens to construct the process' (Vigar et al, 2017: 425). This locates it as a hybrid of invited and invented space, in continuous tension between processes of 'governance-driven democratization' and 'democracy-driven governance' (Bua and Bussu, 2020). Neighbourhood planning is intended to pluralise the voices and knowledges that could be effective in the planning system, to give weight to that which had previously been marginalised, appealing to and empowering people's lived experience, sense of place and place attachments (Bradley, 2017a), resonating strongly with the wider participatory turn. Its advocates claimed that it situated NPGs on the highest rungs of the metaphorical participatory ladder, giving communities 'the greatest possible opportunity to have their say and the greatest possible degree of local control' (The Conservative Party, 2010: 1).

Ideas that travel: diverse settings of participatory democracy

In the following chapters I explore how NPGs achieve their legitimacy to act as intermediaries between state and community, how particular kinds of knowledge and voice are produced and suppressed, and how their relations with professional actors both enable and constrain them. These findings are all specific to these case studies, and are intended to be of use in the practice as well as the study of neighbourhood planning. However, I also suggest that there may be insights from the study of one form of participation that can travel to other sites, notwithstanding their manifold and manifest differences. This is not, of course, to say that such insights are generalisable, or (even worse!) universal – given the vast array of actual and potential instantiations of participatory democracy, it would be absurd to claim that the study of any one of them could yield results that would be directly applicable to others.

Ideas generated in one site can however be used as sensitising concepts to suggest possibilities for the attention, analysis and intervention of researchers and practitioners elsewhere (Blumer, 1954). They may suggest new questions to ask of situations, new techniques for interrogating what is going on, a different lens to look at the object of study through, a different way to think about similarities and differences (Mol, 2010). This may produce results which resonate with a particular study, or which are in tension with it – but either result is worth having. Despite the fragmented nature of participatory democracy and its vastly different experiences in different contexts and places (Brownill and Parker, 2010b), there remains scope for ideas developed in one specific context to be adapted to and tested in very differently situated locations.

Attempts to make ideas travel between sites should do so with a decolonial sensibility – an awareness that assumptions have often been made about the transferability of knowledge about or from the global North to the global South without adequate regard for the specific situatedness of those sites, and of the tendency for paradigms, methods and theories from the North to predominate and present themselves as universal. In this vein I will offer tentative suggestions as to how observations of neighbourhood planning might generate ideas that can usefully travel elsewhere (and vice versa), with full regard and respect for the social, cultural and historical differences between those sites. I will illustrate this with reference to three international cases drawn from across the participatory democracy spectrum – participatory rural development and community organising in informal settlements in the global South, and environmental justice movements in the US.[3] These sites have been chosen precisely because of their differences to neighbourhood planning in setting, context, participants, structures and so on. But what they do share is an explicit intention to pluralise the range of voices and knowledges that can be effective in decision making. I am particularly interested in how and why, in such situations, some things get 'lost in translation', some kinds of voice and knowledge remain marginalised, and how such marginalised knowledges can be worked with better. The following sections provide some broad background to each of these situations of participatory democracy, and sketch out some of their main similarities and differences with neighbourhood planning.

Participatory rural development

In the years following the Second World War, development, reconstruction and economic recovery became key policy preoccupations for national governments in the global North and South alike, and for major new multinational organisations, the International Monetary Fund and the World Bank. Despite a first wave of participatory development projects that reached over 60 countries in Latin America, Africa and Asia by 1960, responding to the UN's call to 'create conditions of economic and social progress for the whole community with its active participation and the fullest possible reliance on the community's initiative' (United Nations, 1955: 6), development at this time was primarily seen in terms of generating rapid economic growth, often via support for rapid industrialisation, increased international trade and large-scale undertakings such as infrastructure or extensive centralised housing provision. Due to perceived failings in achieving their stated objectives, support for small-scale community development projects dwindled by the end of the 1960s (Mansuri et al, 2013).

Mainstream development approaches were characterised by top-down methods, driven by the assumptions, knowledge and decisions of detached experts and institutions. These were dominated by White men from the global North for whom 'development' meant becoming more modern, rational, industrialised and 'westernised', and who thus perceived communities and (often newly independent) countries in the global South to be deficient (Escobar, 1995). Development was largely considered to entail the transfer of knowledge, practices, technologies and economic models from North to South, growing national economies so that the benefits would trickle down to all communities. But as mainstream development theory and practice moved in this direction, more critical and radical thinkers (such as Fanon, 1965 [1961]; Freire, 1970) developed a renewed interest in processes that were more inclusive, democratic and empowering.

By the 1980s, the poor performance of many large-scale, centralised development programmes and their negative social and environmental impacts led to a resurgence in interest in approaches which enabled the values, knowledge and skills of local communities to play a more central part (Mansuri et al, 2013). Alternative approaches which sought to both change the practices and redefine the goals of development gained traction. Participatory and community development, as more people-centred approaches to development, moved from the fringes back towards the mainstream. This was primarily directed towards rural communities in the global South who were perceived as being left behind by technological, social and economic advances. Community participation became seen as an important element in making development programmes successful, and the goals of development shifted from a relentless focus on gross domestic product growth to incorporating human and social development and wellbeing as more appropriate measures (most prominently enshrined in the UN Sustainable Development Goals). Development became more oriented towards the agency of local actors, and advocacy and requirements for community participation became an almost ubiquitous theme for all aid agencies and development-oriented organisations, from small NGOs to major multinationals (Pieterse, 1998; Mohan and Stokke, 2000). This shift of the idea of participatory development from the critical fringes of development discourse to a central pillar of mainstream orthodox practice has been described as a profound revolution in development theory (UNDP, 1993).

One particularly prominent variant of this movement, alongside Participatory Action Research (with which it shares many key concepts and principles [Fals Borda and Rahman, 1991]), was Participatory Rural Appraisal (PRA, also now known as Participatory Learning and Action). PRA was championed by Robert Chambers, and heavily influenced by Paulo Freire's insistence that poor and marginalised people can and should be enabled to determine and analyse their own problems, needs, capacities and solutions. It grew out of 'Rapid Rural Appraisal' (RRA) – itself an attempt (likewise championed by Chambers [Chambers, 1984]) at developing non-prescriptive, flexible ways to get at local knowledge. RRA, however, was a more 'extractive' process in which an external professional development worker would collect data about the circumstances of a place in order to assess and propose options for development. In PRA, by contrast, the emphasis was on the local community (including its most marginalised members) owning, analysing and using the information generated, with professional support to facilitate this, with the end goal of communities empowered to decide on and drive their own developmental trajectories (Chambers, 1994b).

PRA itself is deliberately non-prescriptive, offering a wide-ranging toolkit of visual and experiential activities and interventions through which participants can articulate, define, refine and investigate issues and ideas (for example, matrix scoring and ranking, seasonal calendars, mapping and modelling, transect walks, trend and change analysis, diagramming). It emphasises a shift in the subjectivity of the development professional, away from an identity as an independent expert who is best placed to produce and analyse evidence, make decisions, and develop strategies, to one which facilitates these capabilities in the local community (Narayanasamy, 2009). It was arguably largely through adaptation of and inspiration from this work 'that "participatory development" rose to the mouths of seemingly everyone in the development industry by the year 2000' (Kelty, 2020: 216). One particularly influential example of this was the World Bank's 'World Development Report 2000/01: Attacking Poverty', which marked the first time that their understanding of poverty was informed by the experiences and opinions of ordinary citizens living in poverty (World Bank, 2001).

Participatory rural development, then, refers to a broad range of approaches that enable communities to act collectively to improve their life circumstances. In theory at least, these approaches adapt to local social, cultural, economic, environmental and political realities; incorporate and prioritise local knowledge, skills and resources; and ensure that development programmes and projects respond to people's actual needs. In essence, it posits that poor and marginalised people should be able to influence the decisions that affect their lives, which will lead to materially better outcomes by improving connections between development and aid programmes and their intended beneficiaries (Kyamusugulwa, 2013).

However, there have been trenchant criticisms of both the theory and practice of participatory development approaches. Critics claim that these methods can reinforce rather than challenge local power relations and inequalities, centralised bureaucratic control of decision making and resource allocation, and the dominant imaginaries, goals and values of development and participation. This reinforcement is however concealed both by the rhetorics and concrete practices of participation, which serve to legitimise decisions, trajectories and understandings which are imposed upon the most marginalised, extending colonial and patriarchal logics. The most well-known articulations of these critiques are marshalled in Cooke and Kothari's edited volume, *Participation: The New Tyranny?* (2001). However, advocates of participatory development, while rarely directly contesting these critiques, dispute their universality and insist on its potential, if engaged with critically and creatively, to genuinely empower communities (Hickey and Mohan, 2004; Williams, 2004; Cornwall and Pratt, 2011; Meade et al, 2016a).

There are therefore some clear similarities and differences in the characteristics of participatory rural development (PRD) and neighbourhood planning. Like neighbourhood planning, PRD is often sponsored by the state, but may in contrast also be jointly or wholly sponsored by other powerful actors (such as aid or development agencies or NGOs at a range of scales). It is similarly ostensibly intended to invert relations of power and control in favour of local communities, placing trust in local people and their lived experience. Both are facilitated by certified experts. Both are, in more or less subtle ways, steered towards delivering growth in some form. Neighbourhood planners retain more freedoms to determine their own membership and boundaries, but participatory development has more scope to determine their own issues (that is, they are not thematically tied, as neighbourhood planning is to land use planning). And most obviously, neighbourhood planning is concentrated in relatively affluent communities in England, while PRD takes place in impoverished rural communities across the global South. While acknowledging the vast social, cultural, material and political differences between sites of PRD, and the differences in the challenges facing them, the contrast between such projects collectively and neighbourhood planning in terms of such differences could hardly be more stark.

Environmental justice movements

Environmental problems such as land, air and water pollution affect us all. However, they do not affect us all equally, and some groups of people are disproportionately harmed by them, a situation increasingly referred to as environmental injustice. These groups are often marginalised or disadvantaged in other ways as well, for example, by social structures relating to race, ethnicity, class, age and gender. Environmental injustice is thus usually experienced as a part of a wider tapestry of injustice. Communities that experience environmental injustice – from neighbourhoods to nations – are often also those with limited resources or capacity within formal systems of governance to resist or solve these problems. Different injustices are experienced differently in different places and different communities (for example, between White, Black and Indigenous communities in the US), and what environmental justice looks like or means will vary from place to place and situation to situation (Gilio-Whitaker, 2019).

'Environmental justice movements' thus refer to a diverse range of grassroots social movements, activists and NGOs that draw attention to these issues, usually in relation to locally specific situations (Walker, 2012; Holifield et al, 2018; Coolsaet, 2020). They tend to focus on local impacts and experience, inequitable vulnerabilities, the importance of community voice, and demands for community empowerment – where, again, community may stretch from a neighbourhood to a nation (Schlosberg and Collins, 2014). Their emergence broke with the tendency of the mainstream environmental movement to be primarily concerned with 'pristine' or 'wilderness' environments, to insist on a focus on the environments of everyday life, work and play (Novotny, 2000).

The origins of these movements are usually traced back to the efforts of activists in low-income neighbourhoods in the US to publicise and challenge the negative health impacts on their communities of nearby toxic waste dumps, with the first flashpoint at Love Canal in New York (Levine, 1982). In the 1940s and early 1950s, the partially built Love Canal was converted for use as a chemical waste dump, then capped off as a landfill site and sold to the municipal authorities. In the late 1950s, a working-class neighbourhood was built at and around the site. In the late 1970s, grassroots health surveys and investigative journalists revealed that the community around Love Canal were suffering from abnormally high rates of illnesses such as epilepsy, asthma, migraines and nephrosis, and of birth defects and miscarriages. After initially being ignored and dismissed, and fighting battles that went on for several years, these first environmental justice activists eventually achieved the relocation of hundreds of families.

The public controversy caused by these events led to the establishment in 1980 of the federal 'Comprehensive Environmental Response, Compensation, and Liability Act' (better known as 'Superfund'), intended to hold polluters financially responsible for cleaning up their toxic waste sites. Alongside other high-profile cases in the following years involving majority Black communities in Houston, Texas and Warren County, North Carolina (who met considerably harsher responses from the authorities than the majority White Love Canal community [Murdock, 2020]), they also helped lead to the emergence of widely dispersed grassroots activism, academic research and official investigations, which collectively highlighted that the presence of environmental hazards such as toxic waste dumps were highly correlated with low-income areas and, even more so, with higher populations of people of colour (Bryant and Mohai, 1992; Bullard, 1993; Ringquist, 2005). An early and enduring focus of environmental justice movements thus revolved around environmental racism.

From these beginnings, focused on the specific spatial distributions of environmental hazards, their impacts on local populations, and their relationship to particular population characteristics, a diverse and overlapping set of environmental justice movements has developed. Collectively, these have evolved into a new 'paradigm' within (or possibly alongside) the wider environmental movement – a new way to identify, interpret and express social and political grievances (Taylor, 2000). Various groups from disparate backgrounds such as the civil rights and anti-toxics movements, academics, Indigenous and labour rights activists that would coalesce into the environmental justice movement were deliberately brought together for the first time in 1991 at the First National People of Colour Environmental Leadership Summit (Cole and Foster, 2001). Since then, local groups and environmental justice support and advocacy networks and organisations have expanded to cover issues such as biodiversity loss, resource depletion, transport, energy, flooding and other environmental disasters, patterns of consumption, deforestation, access to environmental amenities such as green space – and of course climate change – that unequally affect marginalised or disadvantaged populations (Benford, 2005).

These groups highlight the lack of attention paid to issues such as race and class in the mainstream environmental movement. This poses a counterpoint to the still-common idea that worry about environmental problems is a luxury that can only be afforded by predominantly White, middle-class people in high-income countries, by foregrounding that it is precisely those populations that this framing excludes that are often worst affected by environmental problems (Sze and London, 2008). More recently there has been an increased focus on inequalities experienced by Indigenous peoples and the legacies of colonisation, most prominently with the Standing Rock Sioux Tribe spearheading the resistance against the Dakota Access Pipeline (Gilio-Whitaker, 2019) – although of course Indigenous people have been fighting these injustices for centuries. While they have often made alliances with scientists, lawyers, academics, organisers and other professionals, environmental justice movements tend to privilege the voices, experiences and expertise of those directly confronted with issues of environmental injustice, embodied in the maxim 'We speak for ourselves' (Cole and Foster, 2001). Environmental justice movements have spread across the globe, and indeed the UN declared in 2021 that access to a safe, clean, healthy and sustainable environment is a human right (United Nations, 2021).

The diverse environmental justice movements across the US started to achieve some scattered but significant local impacts in the 1980s and 1990s in addressing the siting of environmental hazards such as landfill sites, chemical waste dumps, petrochemical installations and incinerators. However, they were perhaps more effective in raising awareness of environmental injustice as an enduring and widespread problem, and mobilising groups and networks to challenge it (Newton, 2009). Through separate and collective campaigning and lobbying they also achieved national impact, most significantly in the mid-1990s through the creation of the Office of Environmental Justice within the Environmental Protection Agency (EPA), and the requirement (through Executive Order 12898, signed by President Clinton) for federal regulatory agencies such as the EPA to incorporate environmental justice principles into their work. This included the active participation of marginalised and disadvantaged groups and environmental justice organisations in developing plans and policies. In 2003 the EPA began developing national and regional Environmental Justice Action Plans to address what they identified as key environmental justice priorities.

However, the operation of these federal functions in incorporating the concerns and communities of environmental injustice into formal governance structures has been patchy and has varied significantly over time (Holifield, 2012). This is witnessed by Executive Order 13990, signed by President Biden in 2021, which acknowledges that '[w]here the Federal government has failed to meet that commitment in the past, it must advance environmental justice' (US Executive Office of the President, 2021: np). Significant influences on the effectiveness of the implementation of environmental justice principles include the political orientation of the federal administration, with Democrats generally being more supportive of state engagement with these movements and Republicans less so, leading to varying levels of resourcing; effective lobbying from industrial bodies and local and state governments; and incorporation of neoliberal economic imperatives into the ideologies and programmes of both major political parties (Faber, 2008).

The differences between environmental justice movements and neighbourhood planning as instances of participatory democracy are more evident than the similarities. Environmental justice movements are essentially autonomous, invented rather than invited spaces, constituted by local communities independently reacting to material situations and/ or proposals. Often, initially at least, they operate outside and frequently in conflict with formal governance arrangements, mobilising the tactics of campaigning and protest rather than committees and policy making. Unlike neighbourhood planning, there are no rules or regulations about who can start a movement, or how, or what to focus on – they are generated organically through bottom-up, grassroots concerns and processes. They are predominantly found in areas with higher concentrations of people of colour and working-class, lower-income populations, quite the opposite to the distribution of neighbourhood planning areas. The outcomes of a successful environmental justice movement are far less clear than the neatly bounded policies of a neighbourhood plan – having successfully drawn attention to a localised case of environmental injustice, it is often not immediately obvious what should be done in response (Mohai et al, 2009: 407–408). And where environmental injustices are not tackled, the outcomes for those communities can be far more severe.

However, there are similarities as well. Both tend to be locally specific, with a focus on place-based impacts, local experiential knowledge and care, and the voice and embodied expertise of the community. Both represent attempts to pluralise, widen and localise the kinds of voices and knowledge that can be effective in decision making, in response to a sense of having been excluded from important decisions by powerful remote actors that are not adequately aware, or do not adequately care, about the things that matter to the community. Although tending to begin as organic, 'invented' spaces, environmental justice movements and their advocates may move into invited spaces by participating in the formal structures and programmes of local authorities, the EPA or other governmental agencies (Wilson et al, 2007; Bruno and Jepson, 2018; Harrison, 2019). NGOs and networks from local to international scales provide support, projects, campaigns, tools and models which local groups can adopt and adapt (Faber and McCarthy, 2001; Harrison, 2011), shaping local groups and movements. And, of course, both are underpinned by making knowledge claims that need to be supported by compelling evidence.

Community organising in informal settlements

The world's urban population has grown rapidly, from 751 million in 1950 to 4.2 billion in 2018 (United Nations, 2019). This astonishing rate of urbanisation has seen alongside it an associated increase in the number of people, particularly in the global South, living in informal settlements. More than half of the population in cities such as Mumbai (India), Nairobi (Kenya) and Mexico City (Mexico) live in informal settlements (UN-HABITAT, 2003). Although defining precisely what constitutes an informal settlement is not easy (Samper et al, 2020), they can be broadly understood as areas of housing which are generally unplanned, unauthorised, not in compliance with building regulations, on land which occupants often have no legal claim to, and which lack protection from the state (Roy, 2009). They are known by many names, including slums, shanty towns, favelas, homegrown neighbourhoods, and bustees. From 2000 to 2010, the number of people estimated to be living in informal settlements in the global South increased from 767 to 828 million (UN-HABITAT, 2011). Occupants of informal settlements generally lack security of tenure and often lack access to civic infrastructure, services and amenities such as sanitation, potable water, gas and electricity, waste collection, road building and maintenance (UN-HABITAT, 2016), and the state is typically unable to claim rent or land taxes in these areas.

It is important to recognise that informal settlements are highly heterogeneous in terms of their living conditions, relations with the state, cultural and historical roots, and other forms of situatedness. Likewise, occupants within and between informal settlements are diverse groups of people with different interests, means and backgrounds (Gilbert, 2007). However, occupants of informal settlements often share particular vulnerabilities associated with insecurity, overcrowding, inadequate access to services, poor housing and living conditions, and 'informal' (unsettled, insecure and unprotected) relationships with the state and with other organisations such as utilities providers, leaving them subject to risks such as poor health, a cycle of poverty, discrimination, eviction and displacement (Ezeh et al, 2017; Peirson and Ziervogel, 2021). Across national and cultural boundaries and different historical situations, this has led to a rise in community-organised movements attempting to secure justice for their communities and address issues of poverty, insecurity, inequality and political voice. These are not necessarily formally constituted organisations, but also include 'more nebulous, uncoordinated and cyclical forms of collective action, popular protest and networks that serve to link both organised and dispersed actors in processes of social mobilisation' (Mitlin and Bebbington, 2006: 1), with groups and networks advancing the democratic claims of their members both inside and outside formal political processes.

Recognising that the physical and socioeconomic conditions in informal settlements were unacceptably poor and often hazardous to health – and that the presence of such conditions could be a barrier to investment (Weber, 2002; Baeten, 2007) – various different types of top-down intervention have been attempted by national and local governments. From the 1950s to 1980s the most common response was to attempt to rehouse occupants of informal settlements in public housing or on land zoned for regulated self-building elsewhere, but there was often little attempt to match the characteristics of the resettlement programmes to the needs of the occupants. From the 1980s, there have been more attempts to upgrade the quality of housing and provision of services and infrastructure in situ, at first as a series of imposed programmes, but increasingly with recognition that a key factor for success is an element of self-determination, with active involvement from citizens, community groups and NGOs alongside local authorities and businesses (Wekesa et al, 2011). This also led, in principle, to a shift of focus to integrate physical, social, economic, organisational and environmental improvements, delivered cooperatively between these multiple stakeholders.

This more or less coproductionist model in principle delivers not just improved access to services but also a greater level of local community control, capacity building and political voice (Imparato and Ruster, 2003). However, this ideal, championed by states, donor organisations and multinational institutions alike, often fails to live up to its theoretical promise and upgrading is often perceived as being as much of a threat as (and sometimes tightly aligned with) forcible displacement, eviction or resettlement, all of which can disconnect communities and individuals from the social and economic networks necessary for survival (Uysal, 2012; Dupont et al, 2013). Self-organised community groups have therefore often come to act as intermediaries between citizens and the state in invited spaces. They may act as formal negotiators on behalf of their communities, or become even more closely integrated into state structures as community panels, or members of forums or boards (Guimarães et al, 2016; Ziervogel, 2019), although these can be used as tools of co-option as well as emancipation (Bhan, 2014). These broad-based grassroots community organisations often revolve around or have grown out of urban poor federations, community-based savings and credit groups, cooperative groups and housing groups, often led by women (Holston, 2009).

However, while governments feel able to engage with forms of mobilisation that align with their own concepts of progress, rights and democratic participation, other forms of mobilisation which they feel less comfortable with are likely to encounter strong state resistance (Mohanty et al, 2011). There is also a long history of protest and other forms of resistance in informal settlements, and of communities generating invented spaces and methods to assert their claims of needs and rights (Atia, 2019; De Geest and De Nys-Ketels, 2019). Indeed, the very concept of an informal settlement suggests self-organised modes of production through which the urban poor assert direct democratic claims through the production of affordable housing and urban infrastructure (Dovey et al, 2021). Many of these groups and actions can be described as 'an attempt to marry the politics of protest with the politics of delivery' (Bradlow, 2015: 133). They do not just demand their rights from the state, but also actively coproduce or independently seek to deliver them, often combining their demands on the state and other powerful actors with advancing or exemplifying workable solutions for issues such as providing improved shelter or basic services such as sanitation (Mitlin, 2008). In doing so, they blend and alternate a variety of approaches from contestation to collaboration to subversion (Lines and Makau, 2018; Mitlin, 2018).

Networks of local self-organised community groups have grown into social movements, from local to international scale. They often work closely with NGOs which coordinate, support and/or act as intermediaries on their behalf with governments and other powerful actors. Transnational networks of NGOs and social movements such as Shack/Slum Dwellers International, which brings together community-based urban poor federations from across Africa, Asia and Latin America, enable community organisers to learn from each other to develop their strategies for confronting the challenges they face around issues such as evictions, economic exclusion and lack of political voice (Bradlow, 2015). Such transnational and translocal networks have also come to include other actors such as local government officials, enabling them to learn collectively with community groups and improve relations between urban poor federations and local authorities, as well as producing tangible policy changes, including for better inclusion of community groups in planning processes.

Community organising in informal settlements in the global South is literally and figuratively half a world away from neighbourhood planning in England. Informal settlements include the most extreme cases of urban poverty and exclusion, in contrast to generally relatively affluent neighbourhood planning communities. Community organising in these sites is driven by a need to survive, to improve living conditions sometimes to a barely acceptable minimum (in terms of the UN Sustainable Development Goals). Its issues are wider ranging than those of neighbourhood plans, although there is often overlap in terms of land use, affordable housing and, albeit at different ends of a spectrum, local service provision. Unlike neighbourhood planning, community groups tend to initially generate their own invented spaces, although these do often morph into formal, invited spaces as relationships with the state and others (such as utilities companies) develop over time and the state attempts to accommodate their demands – and their existence – on its own terms. The NGOs which support, network and coordinate community movements tend to be independent, while those that provide most support and assistance to neighbourhood planners are funded by the state to perform that role. And where neighbourhood planning produces policy, participatory rural development guides decision making and strategies for development investment and interventions, and environmental justice movements seek to influence public and corporate decision making, these community organisers (while also perhaps seeking to achieve any or all of these ends) are often directly involved in the delivery of the rights, recognition and services to which they are staking a claim. However, again in common with neighbourhood planning and the other instances of participatory democracy outlined earlier, they focus on amplifying the voice, knowledge and lived experience of local communities and finding ways in which they can influence material changes to place.

Beyond neighbourhood planning: knowledge, care, legitimacy – an overview

The rest of the book develops an argument about alternative ways to conceive the people, places and issues of participatory democratic practices, and why such alternative approaches might be desirable. It focuses on neighbourhood planning as a central illustrative case, and considers how insights arising from the study of neighbourhood planning might be made to travel to other situations.

Chapter 2 provides a concrete and practical grounding in neighbourhood planning. It sets out the rationales behind its introduction, the procedural requirements on communities producing neighbourhood plans, and how neighbourhood planning connects with other reforms to the planning system introduced at the same time. It goes on to discuss the dilemmas and contradictions of the turn to participation, with a focus on how they play out in this particular initiative.

Chapter 3 sets out the theoretical underpinnings of the book, which is grounded in STS. It explores how this approach can bring a new and nuanced perspective to the issues at the heart of neighbourhood planning and participatory projects more widely. It outlines some of the concepts and ways of thinking that are central to an STS analysis and relates them to the specific case of neighbourhood planning. In doing so it problematises some of the key notions invoked by the discourse and practices of neighbourhood planning and participatory democracy more widely, facilitating alternative ways of understanding both the ways in which we represent the world, and the world itself.

Chapter 4 turns to the empirical case studies to explore one of the central questions in participatory democracy – in the absence of the formal representative authority bestowed by elections, what legitimises the actions of citizens or groups that make (or are implied to have) some claim to represent others? It challenges the framing of neighbourhood planning as a straightforward transfer of power from state to communities in a series of steps. It then advances the proposal that neighbourhood planners achieve their legitimacy by enacting a set of three distinct identity relations with their neighbourhoods. Each of these identities provides access to different knowledge practices and forms of authority, and all are necessary to establish legitimacy. However, they are sometimes contradictory and come into conflict with each other. It concludes by considering whether and how the performance of these identities can be seen in other instances of participatory democracy.

Chapter 5 focuses on the production and use of evidence in neighbourhood planning, as one of the central mechanisms through which the identities described in the previous chapter are enacted and come to dominate or be suppressed. It outlines the evidentiary requirements of neighbourhood planning, and suggests why the kind of evidence produced to support a neighbourhood plan might be expected to be more expansive, inclusive and diverse than is traditional in planning. It documents two instances of evidence production, one from each case study, exploring how the NPGs interpreted what can count as evidence. It discusses the ways in which these interpretations act to restrict the promised pluralisation of ways of knowing in neighbourhood planning. It concludes by reflecting on similarities and differences in the production and presentation of evidence in the other cases of participatory democracy considered.

Chapter 6 further problematises the description of neighbourhood planning as a transfer of power from state to communities. It explores the idea of power not as a property that can be possessed or given, but rather as an effect that is produced through particular practices. It shows that while neighbourhood planners have been able to have material effects and to shape their neighbourhoods in ways that would not otherwise have been possible, their ability to do so is both fragile and precarious. They remain reliant on various types of certified expertise and the professionals that embody them, and as such are subject to displacement by those professionals from their notional position at the heart of the neighbourhood planning process. The chapter concludes by considering similar processes of reliance upon, and displacement by, external expertise and authority in the other cases of participatory democracy.

Chapter 7 addresses some of the neglected things in neighbourhood planning: the experiential knowledge and care for place that previous chapters have shown often get excluded. It begins by describing some of the attempts that neighbourhood planners made to engage with these knowledges and cares, and the difficulties they encountered in articulating, capturing and translating them into evidence. It draws on the concepts of matters of concern (Latour, 2004b) and matters of care (Puig de la Bellacasa, 2017) to develop a speculative reflection on ways in which these neglected things could more effectively be included. It reviews some examples of initiatives intended to incorporate such marginalised knowledges in planning and related processes, and considers how adapting a narrative approach to the production and presentation of evidence could facilitate this. It also considers the barriers and constraints to such innovation, and concludes that if it is to succeed on its own proclaimed terms, neighbourhood planning can and must do better at including the excluded things that matter to people.

Chapter 8 draws together the key themes from the previous chapters. It starts by summarising the argument made throughout the course of the book. It then goes on to discuss the implications of that argument for the practice of, and research into, neighbourhood planning and participatory democracy more widely. It explores how these findings can contribute to the STS-inspired project of 're-making participation' (Chilvers and Kearnes, 2016): making participatory democratic processes more transparent, accountable and responsive, by reconceiving how we understand the people, places and issues at stake.

Planning, participation and democratisation

The problem with the current planning system is that it is not seen to be fair to local communities. It seeks to drown out their voices rather than to amplify them. Despite the clear wishes of local communities and local councils, the local view is that developers eventually ram through inappropriate developments on appeal ... pitting local residents against the might and resources of developers.

Alok Sharma MP (Hansard, 2011)

Introduction

In this chapter I introduce neighbourhood planning in more detail. I sketch out how the English land use planning system is intended to function regarding public participation in decision making. I then highlight some criticisms of the system, contrasting the participatory ideal with people's experience in practice, as exemplified by the opening quotation. Alok Sharma, the speaker, was at the time a Conservative MP and had been Minister for Housing and Planning in 2017–2018. This quotation is from a debate in the House of Commons on the Localism Bill, the legislation that brought neighbourhood planning into being, and exemplifies the rationales given for the introduction of neighbourhood planning. I then set out some of the reforms introduced by the Conservative–Liberal Democrat Coalition government of 2010–2015, which, in part at least, were intended to address these criticisms. Prominent among these reforms was the introduction of neighbourhood planning. I provide an overview of the requirements for preparing a neighbourhood plan, and some of the key aspects of the wider suite of reforms introduced at the same time, in relation to how they affect the abilities of the public to participate meaningfully in the system.

I then go on to situate neighbourhood planning in relation to the wider turns to participation and localism. I explore how it is subject to criticisms levelled at participatory and localist initiatives more widely, while also recognising a counter-current to this critique which suggests that it does introduce potential for real progressive change. I note that neighbourhood planning looks set to remain a significant part of the English planning system for the foreseeable future.

Planning in principle, planning in practice, planning reform

According to the Town and Country Planning Association, 'planning remains one of the most controversial aspects of local life, generating more political heat than almost any other local policy issue' (TCPA, 2017a: 1). Neighbourhood planning is one of the most recent in a long series of reforms of the planning system (see TCPA, 2017b for an overview). The contemporary planning system was instituted by the 1947 Town and Country Planning Act, in a climate of rising concerns about public health, poverty, inequality, spatially imbalanced economic growth and employment, environmental quality, countryside conservation, and agricultural self-sufficiency. Its purpose was to regulate the development and use of land in the public interest: to determine what kind of development is appropriate, how much is desirable, where it should be located, how it should look and function. The Act established 145 Local Planning Authorities (LPAs), based on district and county councils, that would be responsible for preparing comprehensive development plans and for granting (or refusing) planning permission for most proposed development. While there have been many changes to the system over the intervening years, this remains its cornerstone.

The public were initially expected to have a passive role: evidence would be gathered by expert planners and decisions made on the basis of that evidence, and consultation was very limited. However, following the Town and Country Planning Act 1968, and the *People and Planning* report from the Skeffington Committee (1969), public participation in the decision-making process became a central tenet of the system. While the emphasis on inclusiveness has varied over time, with public participation being alternately characterised as causing delay and uncertainty as well as providing necessary legitimacy, the principle of participation has been consistently sustained by governments of all political persuasions, on the basis that 'planning shapes the places where people live and work. So it is right that people should be enabled and empowered to take an active part in the process. Community involvement is vitally important to planning' (ODPM, 2004: 1).

The planning system is thus one of the longest established participatory decision-making arenas in the UK. Anyone is able to make comments on plans and planning applications, but the terms of engagement – what is considered to be a 'material consideration' and the forms of argument and evidence that hold weight – are simultaneously heavily regulated and ambiguous, favouring those with greater experience of the system.[1] The knowledge and views of affected communities are, in principle, central considerations in these processes. Indeed, at public inquiries and 'Examinations in Public' (the formal culminations of plan-making processes), planning inspectors tend to be at great pains to ensure that members of the public and other 'non-expert' stakeholders feel that they have been able to 'have their say' and that their points have been listened to. However, the automatic privileging of some forms of knowledge over others (Aitken, 2009) means that although they can 'have their say', they may not necessarily be effectively heard.

In contrast to the rhetoric about community engagement, as noted earlier, in practice the experience of non-expert participants in the planning system is often that it is 'complex, remote, hard to understand, difficult to engage with, slow and unpredictable and, generally, "not customer friendly"' (Baker et al, 2007: 80). As the UK government department responsible for planning observed in a briefing note on neighbourhood planning, '[i]n theory, planning was always supposed to give local communities a say in decisions that affect them. But in practice, communities have often found it hard to have a meaningful say' (DCLG, 2012b: 3). The system can be complicated and make specific and highly ritualised (although not always obvious) requirements of participants, maintaining a degree of exclusivity and inaccessibility to ordinary citizens (Abram, 2000). It requires a degree of specialised knowledge to have an impact, including membership of particular epistemological communities and use of the languages and assumptions that are associated with them (Davies, 2001b). It 'pre-frames' problems and solutions in a relatively narrow way, rather than permitting free-ranging consideration of future options for development (Allmendinger and Haughton, 2012).

Publics are often perceived to be in 'deficit', with the assumption that if they only had access to the relevant facts and could understand them properly, they would think more like the 'experts' (Burningham et al, 2014). Technical knowledge is privileged as evidence, while experiential knowledge is often sidelined as mere opinion. And while the things that matter to people are, by definition, emotive issues, things they feel strongly about, planners

> focus on the 'rational' analysis of mostly quantitative data, with the implications that emotional concerns are not a source of information, emotional thinking is not a method of understanding, and interaction is typically a diversion from methodical planning. In the end, there is something about planning that actively ignores and resists emotion. (Baum, 2015: 512)

While there are legal and policy requirements to engage stakeholders and publics at various stages of plan-making and decision-taking, the points at which participants are able to 'have their say' are often not those at which significant decisions are made, with communities consulted on proposals formulated behind closed doors and excluded by both developers and planning authorities from 'real' decision making (Civic Voice, 2015). The outcomes of engagement frequently appear to communities to not be in their interests, and the terms of engagement with LPAs are not reciprocal, often seeming solely designed to achieve the aims of the more powerful actor (Gallent and Robinson, 2013).

Promises of empowerment confront 'the reality … of a planning system that seems difficult to input into and causes frustration' (Gallent and Robinson, 2013: 165), a system that is remote, technocratic, top-down and dominated by powerful actors. Even initiatives that had enabled local communities to plan collaboratively to produce formal documents – such as Parish Plans and Village Design Statements which could be adopted by LPAs as supplementary planning documents – often led to frustration when decisionmakers gave them little weight as they did not have the statutory force of local plan policies.

This gap between rhetoric and reality is a well-known story, and the planning system has undergone numerous reforms in order to tackle it, alongside participatory and localist reforms of governance structures more generally (Brownill and Parker, 2010a; Connelly, 2015). The Skeffington report prompted a surge of participatory experiments in the 1970s (Davies, 2001b). In the 1980s, driven by the neoliberal Conservative government, reforms emphasised deregulation and reducing burdens on business, while calls for enhanced public participation focused on appeals to consumerism and efficiency (Home, 1991). The New Labour administration elected in 1997 then sought to introduce a more inclusive process of participation and consultation, alongside more effective collaboration with policy makers and stakeholders in other sectors (Nadin, 2007).

In 2001, the foreword to a government Green Paper on planning reform – entitled *Planning: Delivering a Fundamental Change* – observed that:

> What was once an innovative emphasis on consultation has now become a set of inflexible, legalistic and bureaucratic procedures. … People feel they are not sufficiently involved in decisions that affect their lives. So it is time for change. … We need a better, simpler, faster, more accessible system that serves both business and the community. (Department for Transport Local Government and the Regions, 2001: 1)

But despite concrete moves towards increasing participation in the system under the New Labour government, critics drew attention to their contradictory relationship with other changes which increasingly centralised power and control (Bailey and Pill, 2015). In fact, the seemingly never-ending series of reforms themselves – resulting in constant change and increasing fragmentation of the system – arguably made the system more inaccessible and obscure.

In the mid to late 2000s the Conservative Party mobilised this criticism alongside many of the arguments outlined earlier to mount a sustained attack on the Labour governments of 1997–2010 for being top-down, target-driven and bureaucratic (Haughton and Allmendinger, 2013). Particular targets included:

- Regional Spatial Strategies, which set out strategic policies for the eight English regions and London, to which local plans had to conform, and which were viewed by some as lacking democratic accountability and imposing unpopular decisions upon local areas.
- The Nationally Significant Infrastructure Projects regime, introduced in 2009 – whereby particularly large or significant projects would be decided by a new Infrastructure Planning Commission rather than by LPAs, under a 'fast-track' system that reduced opportunities for public and local council involvement.
- A planning inspectorate that the Conservative Party viewed as overly powerful, with power concentrated in the hands of centrally managed officials rather than (locally or nationally) elected politicians or communities.
- The perceived inability for local people to influence decisions which would have major impacts on the places they lived, due to the inaccessibility, complexity and sheer quantity of planning policy, which acted as a barrier to participation and could only be taken advantage of by well-resourced development interests.

In response to these framings, in February 2010 the Conservatives published a Green Paper, *Open Source Planning*, which set out their vision for a planning system that would be more accessible for local people, with greater local and public influence over decisions. It proposed 'radical change', stating that their

> conception of local planning is rooted in civic engagement and collaborative democracy as the means of reconciling economic development with quality of life. … Communities should be given the greatest possible opportunity to have their say and the greatest possible degree of local control. If we get this right, the planning system can play a major role in decentralising power and strengthening society. (The Conservative Party, 2010: 1)

This paper included the outline of a system of locally determined neighbourhood planning, which would 'create a new system of collaborative planning by giving local people the power to engage in genuine local planning through collaborative democracy – designing a local plan from the "bottom up", starting with the aspirations of neighbourhoods' (The Conservative Party, 2010: 2).

After forming a Coalition government with the Liberal Democrats in May 2010, the Conservatives quickly enacted a variety of planning reforms (Rozee, 2014). This included abolishing Regional Spatial Strategies; merging the Infrastructure Planning Commission into the planning inspectorate and reserving decision-making powers on 'nationally significant' infrastructure projects for the Secretary of State; replacing (almost) all national planning policy documents with a single, simplified National Planning Policy Framework (NPPF), which was less than 5 per cent of the length of the policies it replaced; and introducing neighbourhood planning as a 'community right' in the Localism Act (House of Commons, 2011).

Neighbourhood planning enables communities to draw up their own spatial plans for how their areas will change: where new homes, shops, offices and so on will be built; how new development should be designed and connect to existing settlements; and which areas should be protected from change. Once adopted, neighbourhood plans become part of the development plan for the area and have statutory force: all planning decisions must be made in accordance with them, unless material considerations indicate otherwise. This puts them on an equal footing with local plans made by LPAs, which establish the higher-level, strategic policies for the LPA area. This is the first time that lay people have been able to produce such plans themselves.

LPAs have a 'duty to support' communities undertaking neighbourhood planning, and government made (limited) funding available for communities to engage consultants and specialist contractors, so certified professionals are not excluded from the process. However, the stated intention of these reforms was to reverse the situation in which 'people have been put off from getting involved because planning policy itself has become so elaborate and forbidding – the preserve of specialists, rather than people in communities' (DCLG, 2012a: ii). With neighbourhood planning, plans would be written not by remote technical experts but rather 'written by the local community, the people who know and love the area' (Locality, 2017). This would, the government claimed, have the effect of 'taking power away from officials and putting it into the hands of those who know most about their neighbourhood – local people themselves' (DCLG, 2010).

Neighbourhood planning is thus represented as an inversion of existing relations between citizens and state: offering not mere public participation in a state-led initiative or consultation on state-driven proposals, but rather '[i]t was up to citizens to construct the process', of which they would be in control, and which the state would support and endow with independent authority (Vigar et al, 2017: 425). Certified professionals were to play a subordinate role by providing support on request, thus promising to overcome the 'double divide' between experts and laypeople and between ordinary citizens and decisionmakers (Callon and Rabeharisoa, 2008). It is framed as a particularly strong form of participatory democracy, with citizens having a powerful, in some ways determinative, influence over the future of their neighbourhood – a very strong claim and set of rights over public authorities and over private interests (Sorensen and Sagaris, 2010), putting neighbourhood planners near the top of the notional hierarchies of participation (Arnstein, 1969; Tritter and McCallum, 2006).

In August 2020, the Conservative UK government published the *Planning for the Future* White Paper, setting out proposals for fundamental changes to the planning system. These promised 'radical reform unlike anything we have seen since the Second World War' (MHCLG, 2020: 6). However, concerns from a wide range of stakeholders, including the government's own backbench MPs and Conservative councillors, that the proposals would limit citizen's opportunities to participate in the system led to the proposals in large part being abandoned. The proposals initially seemed to suggest that neighbourhood planning would be retained, but with a somewhat more limited role (Yuille, 2022). However, by 2022 the government was instead looking for ways to strengthen and extend neighbourhood planning, especially among urban and deprived communities (DLUHC, 2022).[2]

Doing neighbourhood planning

Despite the claims made for neighbourhood planning, neighbourhood planning groups (NPGs) are not free to plan for whatever they want, however they want. There is a legally prescribed set of procedural requirements that must be complied with, and a set of basic conditions that a plan must meet to be 'made' (adopted by the LPA as part of the statutory development plan). I describe these briefly in the following sections – see Chetwyn (2013) or DCLG (2014b) for more detail.

Establish a 'qualifying body'

Only two types of organisation can initiate a neighbourhood plan. In areas where there is a town or parish council, they are automatically the qualifying body. In non-parished areas (including most urban areas), a Neighbourhood Forum must be formed. A self-organised community group submits an application to become a Neighbourhood Forum to the LPA, who may allow or refuse it. A Forum should reflect the character and diversity of the area's population and meet a number of other criteria, but it is up to them how they achieve and demonstrate this (Chetwyn, 2013: 21). There have been a number of refusals, for example, due to the LPA considering that the proposed Forum is not adequately representative or does not cover an appropriate area, or where two Forums-in-the-making compete to represent the same or overlapping areas (Colomb, 2017).

However, the qualifying body will not necessarily do or be closely involved in the work of preparing the plan; it is merely necessary that it initiates and takes overall ownership of it. The day-to-day work is often done by a separate group, which may be a subgroup of the qualifying body, or may be made up of other local residents with or without members of the qualifying body. The names used for these groups vary, but I will describe them throughout as NPGs.

Designate a neighbourhood plan area

The qualifying body must apply to the LPA to designate the area it wants its plan to cover. There is some guidance as to what might make a suitable area, but it is entirely up to the qualifying body to propose a boundary (Chetwyn, 2013: 19) – although in practice many opt for existing administrative areas such as parishes or wards. The LPA must run a six-week public consultation on this application. It may then decide to approve the proposed area, reject it, or designate an area with different boundaries that it believes are more appropriate.[3]

Plan preparation

Once an area has been designated, NPGs can begin their main body of work – preparing the plan. There are no prescriptions on the process for doing this or for the issues that a plan should address, other than that it must contain policies for land use planning, be based on evidence, and involve the local community. Content, preparation process and level of detail in plans can vary enormously. In general, plan preparation will involve community engagement at various stages to identify and agree issues, aims, options and proposals; gathering and analysing evidence; and eventually writing policies (Bailey, 2017). But within these broad parameters, there is very considerable scope for creativity, experimentation and innovation.

LPAs have a legal duty to support NPGs in this, but implementation of this duty is extremely variable (Parker et al, 2014). Limited funding is available for all NPGs to contract specialist support, especially to assist in areas where they feel they lack technical expertise, and a government-funded technical support programme provides specific services (such as site viability assessment and Environmental Impact Assessment) to groups facing more complex issues. There is also an ever-increasing raft of formal and informal guidance and advice, toolkits, workshops, templates and so on available online, face-to-face, and via phone and email from both from government-supported sources[4] and private contractors. Once it has a plan that it is content with, the qualifying body must conduct a formal six-week consultation on it with the community in the plan area and with statutory consultees.

Plan submission

After making any changes it considers necessary following the consultation, the qualifying body submits the plan to the LPA. The LPA then publishes the plan and its supporting documents, which set out the evidence on which the plan is based, and invites comments in a further six-week round of public consultation. Comments at this stage are sent to the independent examiner (see next section). The LPA must also satisfy itself that the plan is legally compliant: that the aforementioned steps have been carried out properly and that all required documentation has been submitted and is in good order.

Examination

Following this second formal consultation, the LPA arranges an independent examination of the plan; they must agree who will conduct the examination with the qualifying body. The examiner may be any suitably qualified and experienced independent person who does not have an interest in any land that may be affected. Senior and retired planning inspectors, consultants, and academics are common choices. The Department for Communities and Local Government[5] supported the establishment of a referral service by relevant professional organisations to 'broker' examiners (Neighbourhood Planning Independent Examiner Referral Service), but there is no requirement to use this service.

The examination consists of the examiner reviewing the draft plan, the evidence and supporting statements submitted, and the comments from the second formal consultation. If they consider it necessary, they can hold public hearing sessions, although these are not normally called. They may also ask the LPA and/or the qualifying body questions, most often via email, which may then be published on the LPA's website, along with their responses and all the other documentation. The purpose of the examination is 'limited to testing whether or not a draft Neighbourhood Plan ... meets the basic conditions' (DCLG, 2014b: np). This means whether it:

- has regard to national policy;
- contributes to the achievement of sustainable development;
- is in general conformity with the strategic policies in the local plan;
- is compatible with human rights requirements; and
- is compatible with EU obligations.

The plan must have policies that deal with the use and development of land, and must not plan for less development than is set out in the local plan prepared by the LPA, most prominently in relation to housing numbers. But within these very broad parameters, there is very little prescription regarding either the content of the plan, or the evidence put forward to support and justify it, other than that the evidence should be 'robust' and 'proportionate' (DCLG, 2014b: np).

These 'basic conditions' represent a very different and much lower bar than the 'tests of soundness' that a strategic local plan is required to meet in its examination. One of the very few clear and direct prescriptions regarding the examination of neighbourhood plans is that the examiner 'is not testing the soundness of a Neighbourhood Plan or examining other material considerations' (DCLG, 2014b: np). This policy prescription has been repeatedly validated in the courts, which have 'confirm[ed] that examination of Neighbourhood Plans is less rigorous than is required for local plans and that examiners can apply a "lighter touch"' (Carter, 2014, cited in Bailey, 2017). However, more recently, examinations have become more rigorous, due to a litigious development industry seeking to overturn neighbourhood plans in the courts, which has increased pressure on plans to be litigation-proof and on their examiners to identify and correct any potential vulnerabilities (Bradley, 2017d; Parker et al, 2017b).

Following examination, the examiner must recommend that the plan:

- meets the basic conditions and so should proceed to the next stage, a local referendum; or
- should be modified in specified ways which would enable it to meet the basic conditions and then proceed to referendum; or
- should not proceed to referendum, as it does not meet the basic conditions and is not capable of being modified to do so.

The majority of plans are modified in some way, ranging from minor changes to policy wording to the wholesale deletion of policies (Parker et al, 2016). The examiner reports to both the LPA and to the qualifying body, but the LPA is responsible for making any recommended changes to the plan. The examiner's recommendations are not binding (unlike those of a planning inspector examining a local plan), but not following those recommendations would increase the plan's exposure to legal challenge. If the qualifying body is not happy with the modifications, it can withdraw the plan – meaning that, if they still wished to produce a plan, they would have to go back to the 'plan preparation' stage. In one extreme case, the LPA modified the Swanwick neighbourhood plan as recommended by the examiner and put it to a local referendum – but the NPG campaigned against the plan (and won) because they felt that it no longer reflected what the community wanted (Bradley, 2017d).

Referendum and adoption

Assuming the plan passes examination, either as submitted or with modifications, the final stage is a local referendum, arranged by the LPA.

Eligible voters will usually be all residents of the plan area, but the examiner can recommend that this area is varied (for example, to included adjacent areas if they will be significantly affected).[6] If support for a plan achieves a simple majority, the LPA will formally adopt or 'make' it – it will become part of the statutory development plan, and it will (alongside the local plan) be the starting point for deciding all planning applications in the area. Neighbourhood plans may – and usually do – also have other uses, such as to set out actions for the parish council, Neighbourhood Forum or others, shape negotiations about land management or use of public spaces, catalyse and coordinate community activity, or provide recommendations for infrastructure spending, but their only legally binding function is in relation to land use planning.

As is evident from these procedural requirements, while official discourse around neighbourhood planning promises to deliver power to the people, and legislation and policy provides NPGs with substantial freedoms and flexibilities as to how they go about developing plans and what they can contain, they do so within a quite tightly drawn and heavily constrained framework. Far from being freed from the top-down influence of officials, specialists and technical experts, there is 'substantial influence being exerted at each stage by the local authority and the examiner' (Bailey, 2017: 12).

Neighbourhood planning in context – associated planning reforms

The introduction of neighbourhood planning must also be seen in the context of other planning reforms introduced at the same time, in particular the revision and simplification of national planning policy and abolition of Regional Spatial Strategies. While the rhetoric around these reforms was similarly focused around inclusion, democratisation and empowering local communities, their effects in practice often served to make many communities feel more disempowered and unable to influence decision making (Bailey, 2010; CLG Select Committee, 2014) – which, paradoxically, may have driven the uptake of neighbourhood planning as a means of gaining some control in an environment perceived as being increasingly uncontrolled.

The central reasons given by the Conservatives for wanting to abolish Regional Spatial Strategies was that they were produced by the Labour-created Regional Assemblies, which they characterised as unaccountable. They claimed that the Assemblies imposed unnecessarily high and unpopular housing targets on democratically elected LPAs, and that due to the resentment this generated, these targets actually led to more objections and less housebuilding (Pickles, 2013). This, they alleged, often meant that LPAs would be forced to allocate more land for housing than they or the communities that they represented wanted. Regional Assemblies and their strategies were therefore represented as doing undemocratic, top-down, technocratic planning (Gallent and Robinson, 2013: 3–4).

The NPPF (DCLG, 2012a) was the new, simplified and ostensibly 'public-friendly' statement of national planning policy. It was far shorter than previous planning policy (around 50 pages as opposed to over 1,000), condensing many separate Statements, Guidance Notes and Circulars into one document, and was intended to be understandable to the general reader, not just to planning experts. It required LPAs to set their own housing targets, and not to have regard to the soon-to-be-abolished Regional Strategies.[7]

This appears to represent a substantial move towards inclusiveness, devolution of power, and increased flexibility for LPAs and their communities to make their own decisions. However, the NPPF also introduced a series of new or redefined policy 'artefacts', which, taken together, had the effect of giving greater priority to the national agenda of increasing economic and housing growth than to local self-determination. I outline the most significant of these in what follows, to provide the immediate context within which neighbourhood planning was situated.

The presumption in favour of sustainable development

In paragraph 14, the NPPF established a 'presumption in favour of sustainable development', which was described as 'the golden thread running through both plan-making and decision-taking', and which meant, specifically, that:

- When making development plans, LPAs should plan to meet the *objectively assessed needs* of their area, unless other policies in the Framework indicate that development should be restricted (for example, because of environmental designations), or unless the adverse impacts of doing so would *significantly and demonstrably* outweigh the benefits.
- When taking decisions, permission should be granted for applications that accord with the development plan; and permission should also be granted for applications where the development plan is *absent, silent or relevant policies are out-of-date* – unless other policies in the Framework indicate that development should be restricted, or the adverse impacts of doing so would *significantly and demonstrably* outweigh the benefits. (DCLG, 2012a)

The concepts emphasised in italics have become significant challenges for communities who want to shape their own surroundings. They formally embed '[t]he hegemonic position of pro-growth planning [which] means that development is effectively synonymous with the public interest, the primary good that the planning system should seek to promote' (Inch, 2015: 411). This has led to many LPAs and communities perceiving national policy as taking power and influence out of their hands and concentrating it in the hands of developers and planning inspectors. I explore how these concepts operate to favour growth over democratic participation in the following sections.[8]

'Objectively assessed needs'

LPAs are required to 'objectively assess needs' for housing and other forms of development in their area 'based on facts and unbiased evidence' (DCLG, 2014a: np), and then to set targets in their local plans to meet those needs. But there was no further guidance on what this meant for several years, and the means of 'objectively' assessing needs remained open to interpretation. In 2018 the government introduced a standard method for assessing housing need, using projected household growth data from 2014 as a baseline to identify a minimum number of homes that an LPA would be expected to plan for. Following a consultation on changes to this standard method, it was updated in 2020 to add a 35 per cent 'uplift' to the 20 largest urban areas in the country (Barton and Grimwood, 2021). However, variations from this baseline due to factors such as projected employment growth or environmental constraints are still fiercely contested. LPAs and interested parties undertake widely varying approaches to this technical assessment, producing, deploying and manipulating a variety of demographic, economic and other evidence, and making divergent assumptions. The better-resourced parties (LPAs and developers) usually utilise software models that 'black box' the material process of assessment, that is, render it opaque and conceal internal uncertainty, ambiguity, contingency and complexity, making it difficult for non-specialists to understand, let alone critique (Latour, 1999; Holly, 2017).

The intended objectivity of these processes is belied by the fact that it is not uncommon for numerous assessments, conducted on behalf of different parties (such as developers, landowners and/or their professional representatives; local residents; and campaign groups), using different methodologies, and in many cases different computer models and software simulations, to indicate wildly varying levels of need. This is often the main controversial issue in local plan-making (Bailey, 2017). Competing assessments are put forward to the planning inspector responsible for the local plan's 'Examination in Public'. Considerable amounts of time are spent debating different figures and the assumptions and tools used to construct them. A debate which is inherently highly political and contested is translated into – presented as – technical argumentation (Boddy and Hickman, 2018).

Great weight tends to be given to institutional authority and technical credentials, and to 'black-boxed' results. Figures which are materialised from computer models, the technical operations of which are not transparent, are often given more weight and greater respect than verbal discussion about, for example, the assumptions used to reach or to support particular results. Technologically mediated and technically accredited evidence is used to shut down debate and contestation about the quality or robustness of underpinning assumptions, for example, about future conditions or causal connections (see Aitken, 2009 and Rydin et al, 2018 for parallel findings in other planning contexts). And better-resourced parties, in particular from the development industry, often employ professionals (consultants and barristers) whose expertise lies more in persuading inspectors of their case than in the 'coalface' work of planning. After hearing the arguments and evidence, the inspector will have to decide which assessment of need is more likely to be 'objectively' correct, and, if necessary, to advise the LPA to amend their targets or to do more work to establish the evidence base for new targets.[9] Inspectors are, of course, experienced and qualified professionals, but they are not necessarily experts in assessing housing need, and the exercise of their professional judgement on these matters can also be something of a black box.

Even the (then) Secretary of State responsible for planning described this system as resulting in 'an opaque mish-mash of different figures that are consistent only in their complexity' (Hansard, 2017). A common outcome of this process is that LPAs are compelled to increase their housing targets, sometimes very significantly, and often to levels well above the targets previously set by Regional Spatial Strategies. This is often against the wishes of the LPA and of local communities, and is seen as an imposition from a remote centre, despite the absence of any specific 'imposed' target (Goodchild and Hammond, 2013). The 2018 revision of the NPPF additionally requires that 'objectively assessed needs' are met as a minimum, and that unmet housing need from surrounding areas is taken into account when setting targets, putting further upward pressure on supposedly locally determined targets.

'Significantly and demonstrably'

The requirement that the adverse impacts of development must 'significantly and demonstrably' outweigh the benefits before plans may cater for less than their area's 'objectively assessed needs', or before a planning application may be refused, raises the bar of proof significantly. It does so both in terms of the degree of harm that must be caused, and the evidence that must be marshalled in support of any such claim. Previously, national policy generally required permission to be refused if the adverse impacts outweighed the positive. The 'planning balance' has therefore been tipped significantly in favour of new development, and 'the emphasis on economic growth is overshadowing the wider social and environmental goals of sustainability'

(Rozee, 2014: 130). This is explicitly acknowledged by decision takers in justifying their decisions: 'It is necessary to aggregate all the adverse impacts and weigh them against all the aggregated benefits, but applying the tilted balance' (Hill, 2017: para 109). The balance is tilted not just in favour of allowing considerably more harm to be caused, but also in favour of those actors with the resources to produce more and 'better' evidence; both of which tend to disadvantage public participants. By permitting greater levels of harm to be caused by new development, and imposing a heavier burden of proof in relation to that harm, it 'effectively elevates a conception of the good [that is, economic and housing growth] above democratic rights to decide where the public interest lies' (Inch, 2015: 412).

A further problem arises in that neither of the terms 'significantly' nor 'demonstrably' are further defined, leaving it open to various participants in the system to interpret them in different ways. And this in turn points to a pre-existing issue: where the 'planning balance' lies in individual cases, whether the positive impacts outweigh the negative, is also inevitably a matter of judgement and interpretation, particularly because the positive and adverse impacts tend to affect different dimensions of 'sustainable development' (economic, social and environmental) and are therefore difficult to compare directly. Planning inspectors and LPA planning officers are assumed to have the expertise and training to make this judgement effectively, consistently and impartially. Other participants' ability to make such judgements is often 'pre-judged', positively or negatively, with reference to their imputed level of expertise, rather than the actual quality or content of the conclusions that they reach or the premises that they are based on (Petts and Brooks, 2006; Aitken, 2009).

'Absent, silent or relevant policies are out-of-date'

The requirement to grant permission for applications where the development plan is 'absent, silent or relevant policies are out-of-date' leaves the door open for much development to be permitted that would not previously have been considered acceptable. In January 2019, only 44 per cent of LPAs had a local plan in place that was recognised as being up to date (National Audit Office, 2019). There are several reasons for this:

- Many LPAs simply do not have an up-to-date local plan in the common-sense meaning of the phrase, with plans having been adopted many years ago without being reviewed or revised and circumstances having changed in the meantime.
- As one requirement for a local plan is that it conforms to national policy, it has been argued that any local plan adopted before the NPPF (or

subsequent substantial revisions) came into effect could be considered out of date (Goodchild and Hammond, 2013: 87).

- Crucially, the NPPF specifies a set of circumstances regarding housing development, where 'relevant policies' may be considered out of date, even if the local plan would otherwise be considered up to date. This is known as the 'five-year supply rule', and I outline this in the following section.
- In 2018, the government also introduced a Housing Delivery Test, which specified that if less than 75 per cent of an LPA's housing target had been built out over the past three years, the presumption in favour of sustainable development should be applied to decision making, effectively rendering their local plan housing policies out of date.

The five-year supply rule

A local plan usually covers a period of 15–20 years. It is required to provide for the 'objectively assessed' development needs of its area for the whole of that period. But in terms of housing 'need', the NPPF also imposes a shorter-term time horizon. It requires LPAs to identify enough specific 'deliverable' sites to provide five years' worth of housing, plus a 'buffer' of either 5 or 20 per cent, depending on past performance. Deliverable sites must be available now, offer a suitable location for development now, and have a realistic prospect that housing will be delivered on them within five years. In practice, deliverable sites tend to be considered to be some proportion of sites that already have planning permission, although the issue is complex and contested (Cannon, 2020). This list must be updated at least annually. If an LPA is not able to demonstrate such a five-year supply of housing land (plus buffer), then the housing policies in its plan (and any neighbourhood plans in its area) are considered out of date, and the presumption in favour of sustainable development is triggered, giving an LPA 'relatively little room to manoeuvre when faced with planning applications which it might otherwise seek to refuse ... undermining the general move towards planning decentralisation which the government has otherwise been claiming to promote' (Sibley-Esposito, 2014: para 10).[10]

As highlighted previously, the 'objectively assessed need' for housing for an area can be strongly contested. Whether an LPA has a five-year supply is also often strongly contested when planning applications are made. Furthermore, the courts have repeatedly ruled that the weight given to development plan policies (in or out of date), the tilted balance, a lack of five-year housing land supply and the deliverability of sites are matters for the professional planning judgement of the decisionmaker, and they are also strongly contested (Green et al, 2020). These contests favour developers who can usually support their claims with more technical and financial resources than are available to communities (and often to LPAs). Where an LPA is found not to have a five-year supply, planning permission is very often given for applications that would have been refused otherwise. Research by CPRE (2014) showed that at least 39 out of 58 major housing applications – 67 per cent – were given permission at appeal in the year to March 2014, after having been refused by the LPA, double the number in the previous year. And the same study indicated that in at least 14 additional cases, LPAs felt obliged to grant permission for developments that conflict with their local plan, for fear of having a decision to refuse taken to appeal (with all the resource implications that has) and losing on the basis of lack of a five-year supply, which could also result in costs being awarded against them.

In summary, the combined effect of these policy artefacts is that development plans, which are the outcome of processes (however flawed) that are undertaken by democratically elected LPAs and which invite public participation, are increasingly being overturned through a technocratic system that favours growth over a democratically decided public interest, and favours the resources and expertise at fighting examinations, appeals and legal battles of developers over under-resourced LPAs and minimally resourced community groups.

Permitted development rights

At the same time, since 2010 the government has also dramatically extended the scope of permitted development rights, that is, development for which planning permission is not required. Alongside allowing the conversion of barns to residential use, doubling the size of extensions that householders can build, and allowing the upwards extension of some buildings for residential use, the most notable new rights allowed the conversion of first offices and subsequently a wide range of other commercial, business and service uses (such as shops, cafes, restaurants, nurseries, gyms and day centres) to residential use. As these rights remove the need for planning permission to be granted, they remove the scope for the public or the LPA to have any say on whether or how they should take place. This led to trenchant opposition from the planning profession and civil society organisations due to fears both that town centres and high streets would be hollowed out, and that inappropriate conversions would create 'the slums of the future' (TCPA, 2021: 1).

The overall impact of this interconnecting matrix of policy artefacts has thus been to put the rhetoric of community empowerment strongly at odds with national policy imperatives of deregulation and increased housing and economic growth. Neighbourhood planning was explicitly introduced as a means of enhancing public and local participation in decision making, as part of a wide-ranging commitment to 'localism' and the devolution of powers. But it was also explicitly intended to reduce opposition to new development and to promote growth, on the basis that if people were more in control of development in their area, they would be better able to identify what development was needed, and less inclined to see it as an unwelcome imposition. Yet it was set in a context where changes to national planning policy were leading to many people feeling less empowered and less able to influence those decisions than ever before.

Wider context and critique

So, neighbourhood planning is situated in the broader ebb and flow of the English planning system. And as set out in the previous chapter, the English planning system does not exist in a vacuum, but is located in much broader circulations of concerns about citizen empowerment. The international turn to participation and localism, in which planning is embedded, has played out in the UK in a variety of modalities over several decades. Steve Connelly has tracked the increase in public participation in local governance in England over the past three decades and beyond (Connelly, 2015). He begins by highlighting initiatives in the late 1960s and 1970s which bloomed from influential reports on public involvement in planning (Skeffington, 1969) and social services (Seebohm, 1968), and from experiments with community development in Labour-led urban areas. These largely faded out by the 1980s with the changes brought in by a neoliberal Conservative government, but had a legacy influence on the shift, starting in the mid-1980s, from governmental domination of policy making and implementation to 'governance' involving stakeholder collaboration in more flexible and less formal structures. This was epitomised by local government responsibility for service provision and policy development across a wide variety of issues increasingly becoming shared across a range of new and existing actors from the private, public, voluntary and community sectors, in an increasingly complex set of marketised, contractual and/or partnership relations (Rhodes, 1996).

From the mid to late 1980s the public were also more frequently consulted by local authorities on various matters, and invited to participate in initiatives that could inform decision making, but were rarely directly involved in governance. There was some limited public involvement in urban regeneration and renewal programmes. Community/civil society/local government partnership working accelerated under the banner of Local Agenda 21, the programme to drive sustainable development from a local level with a focus on public and community participation, which emerged from the 1992 Rio Earth Summit (Lafferty and Eckerberg, 1998).

The election of the New Labour government in 1997 saw efforts to 'modernise' local government to focus more strongly on tackling social exclusion, building social cohesion and giving communities a direct voice in local governance. Citizen participation and community leadership, either directly or through civil society organisations, became a key feature of regeneration and renewal, public health, social services, environmental improvement, and the pursuit of sustainable development in its broadest terms. Public participation in governance and service delivery was encouraged at local authority level, especially through Local Strategic Partnerships and their role in producing Community Strategies to improve the social, economic and environmental wellbeing of the area (Geddes et al, 2007). There was also an increasing focus on targeting hyper-local areas described as 'neighbourhoods', especially where these were seen to be suffering from particular disadvantages (Smith et al, 2007). The government espoused a policy of 'double devolution', devolving power from central to local government, and from local government to their constituent communities (Hilder, 2006) – although this was also criticised as merely a new way to centralise power (Davies, 2008).

The emphasis on localism and devolving power to communities was retained through the election of the Conservative–Liberal Democrat Coalition government of 2010. The focus on targeting disadvantaged areas was however abandoned, and replaced with a voluntaristic approach in which entrepreneurial individuals and communities – the 'Big Society' – would be freed from the dead hand of the controlling 'Big State' and invested with new powers to drive change from below. Being thus liberated, according to the governmental narrative, would enable them to revitalise and reorganise public services and the management of civic space from the ground up, ushering in an era of civic empowerment and democratic renewal (Buser, 2013) – albeit one framed by deep public spending cuts (Kisby, 2010). Neighbourhood planning was one of the flagships of that Big Society movement.

Participatory planning in the UK is thus thoroughly embedded in the wider turn to participation. The claims made for this turn were discussed in the previous chapter. However, as Quintin Bradley puts it, '[t]he spectre of hierarchical power continues to elude all attempts to deepen democratic participation in land use planning … participation still eludes its anticipated empowerment' (Bradley, 2017c: 39). Despite the ubiquity of rhetoric and practices ostensibly aimed at community empowerment, many authors contend that the same applies across the board of participatory initiatives (Cooke and Kothari, 2001; Swyngedouw, 2005; Wilson and Swyngedouw, 2014; Baiocchi and Ganuza, 2017) – although often also holding out hope that a critical approach to participation can still potentially reap rewards (Reed, 2008; Legacy et al, 2019). So before looking at the empirical detail of the case studies, it will be useful to have an overview of the critique that has been levelled at neighbourhood planning, and to locate that in the analysis of the wider participatory turn.

Post-political governance?

First, as set out earlier in this chapter, there is a fundamental conflict between two of the central aims of English national planning policy: to empower communities collectively to exert more control over development, and to 'roll back' planning to prevent its interference in markets that are assumed to be capable of delivering 'better' outcomes, in particular more economic growth and more housing (Haughton and Allmendinger, 2013). It is 'a political culture that paradoxically encourages engagement but also defends against its disruptive effects' (Inch, 2015: 405).

This apparent contradiction may be resolved, from the perspective of the government promoting it, if another aim and assumption of neighbourhood planning is operationalised. While the rhetoric of neighbourhood planning focuses strongly on its supposed transfer of power from LPAs to communities, it also has the explicit aim of increasing growth. If communities have genuine control over the specifics of development in their area, it was assumed that 'growth would be regularly embraced rather than rejected' (Gallent and Robinson, 2013: 21). Communities with new, real planning powers are framed as more likely to accept and promote increased and accelerated rates of development: 'if we enable communities to find their own ways of overcoming the tensions between development and conservation, local people can become proponents rather than opponents of appropriate economic growth' (The Conservative Party, 2010: 1).

'The local' is frequently represented as the best, if not the only scale at which these tensions can be resolved (Bailey and Pill, 2015), reflecting a 'dominant consensus ... that equates good policy-making with the local scale' (Raco et al, 2016: 217) and local communities as 'those best placed to find the best solutions to local needs' (Hansard, 2011: 14). The apparently conflicting aims of the reforms – more community control and more growth per se – no longer conflict if it is correct that resistance to development is generated largely by resentment of the imposition of development by external forces, and that local communities will want to promote more development if it is better quality, more appropriately sited, and fulfils locally identified needs. On this reading, government is 'merely' enabling communities to meet their own needs, which they would recognise and want to meet once freed from the stifling imposition of state planners.

Critics suggest that this indicates that neighbourhood planning functions as a particularly blatant example of neoliberal governmentality. This refers to 'the conduct of conduct', the subtle ways in which modern states and other institutions conduct (guide or govern) the conduct (action or behaviour) of their citizens (Burchell et al, 1991). It suggests that while citizens are not explicitly forced to act in certain ways, they are nevertheless pressured to do so through pervasive and non-obvious techniques of control that, paradoxically, are often manifested as aspects of individual or collective autonomy and self-determination. In this case, neighbourhood planning communities are being empowered to make decisions in a specific overall direction. As responsible citizens they are expected to make particular choices, and are 'nudged' in that direction through the ways in which they engage with the policies and practices of neighbourhood planning. These practices require certain types of rationality, reasoning and action, which combine to make the citizens who undertake them act in particular ways and incline towards particular decisions (Davoudi and Madanipour, 2013; Haughton et al, 2013). This enables states to govern through communities, in the guise of allowing communities to govern themselves (Rose, 1996). Many analysts insist that this is a common feature of participatory democracy – the particularly blatant aspect of it in neighbourhood planning is that the state has announced in advance the direction that communities will be disciplined into, that is, increasing rates of development.

However, even if more subtle attempts at directing the outcomes of neighbourhood planning were to fail, the basic conditions wrapped around it constrain the autonomy that NPGs have to restrict new development. While it is certainly arguable that alignment with higher level strategies and principles is necessary to maintain a focus on the wider public good over narrow parochial interests (Gallent and Robinson, 2013: 49), the requirements to conform to national and strategic local policy severely limit room for manoeuvre. In particular, the explicit requirement that neighbourhood plans 'should not promote less development than set out in the local plan or undermine its strategic policies' (DCLG, 2014b: np) means that communities may be obliged to sanction development allocations that they would otherwise oppose. Many commentators have claimed that neighbourhood planning largely functions to deliver the centrally determined objectives of economic and housing growth (see, for example, Allmendinger and Haughton, 2012; Parker et al, 2015).

Neighbourhood planning is also inextricably a part of the Coalition government's 'embarrassing and outdated' Big Society logic (McKee, 2015: 6), which has resonances with other transnational projects of participatory localism under the imperatives of fiscal constraint (Featherstone et al, 2012). While presented by the government as advancing an agenda of community empowerment, the Big Society concept and related projects have been denounced as a cynical drive to impose neoliberal policies of austerity: shrinking the state and outsourcing its accountabilities; burdening communities and individuals with responsibilities, risks and costs without (sufficient) additional resources; coercing them to volunteer time and effort in order to secure outcomes that were previously theirs by right; obscuring and marketising state responsibilities; prioritising cost-cutting over the availability, consistency and quality of service provision; and replacing skilled, paid professionals with amateur, unpaid volunteers, and replacing state employees oriented towards the public good with private contractors driven by the profit motive (Kisby, 2010; Lowndes and Pratchett, 2012; Lord and Tewdwr-Jones, 2014; Lord et al, 2017). In contrast to the often-claimed progressive aims of localism and participation, Coalition localism has been branded a 'straightforward conservative force' (Clarke and Cochrane, 2013: 10).[11]

All of this taken together means that, for some analysts, all neighbourhood planning empowers communities to do is to enact decisions which have already been taken elsewhere (Allmendinger and Haughton, 2012). It merely allows tinkering with the finer details of those decisions, and does 'not necessarily give communities greater leverage over the principal changes that they are most concerned about' (Gallent and Robinson, 2013: 160). It can thus be characterised, as participatory initiatives often are, as a 'post-political' form of governance. This implies that such processes have the effect of avoiding controversy rather than enabling genuine alternatives to emerge (Marris and Rose, 2010) and closing down and co-opting resistance and dissent (Mouffe, 2005), thereby cultivating consent or legitimacy for decisions and practices that are not in the interests of the communities concerned (Swyngedouw, 2009). This would therefore effectively reinforce rather than reform (much less reverse) existing structural power relations (Huxley, 2000; Bailey and Pill, 2015: 289).

As noted in the *Open Source Planning* Green Paper, the participation envisaged in neighbourhood planning is based around 'collaborative democracy'. It draws on Habermas' theories of deliberative democracy and communicative action, based on inclusive, formal debate between all those affected by an issue with the aim of reaching consensus on the best decision (Habermas, 1996). This theory has been developed specifically in relation to planning by scholars such as Patsy Healey (1997) and Judith Innes and David Booher (2000). Critics claim that this central insistence on consensus building negates the possibility of a more agonistic form of debate in which genuinely irreconcilable differences can be engaged with (Mouffe, 2005), either within the territory of the neighbourhood plan, or between the neighbourhood and higher levels of governance. Rather than any real opportunity for communities to shape their own destinies, then, it is 'an example of participatory design which attempts control from a distance and represents a linked effort to de-politicise planning' (Parker et al, 2017a: 455). This reflects a long-standing critique of the participatory turn more broadly:

> Far from being a transformative process in which local people are able to exert control over decision making, participation becomes a well-honed tool for engineering consent to projects and programmes whose framework has already been determined in advance – a means

for top-down planning to be imposed from the bottom up. (Hildyard et al, 2001: 59–60)

As discussed earlier in this section, the government openly states that the purpose of empowering communities through neighbourhood planning is so that they will make particular choices, that is, to embrace higher levels of development. It is therefore not simply a project of empowering communities, but of producing communities that will make those choices. According to Brownill, four distinct aims can be identified in the overall project of neighbourhood planning, including precisely this identity-shaping work on citizens who 'are encouraged to participate in the spaces of neighbourhood planning in a particular way … turning "the folks" into local citizen-planners who accept the need for development and who willingly engage to deliver this' (Brownill, 2017b: 32).

Empowering the powerful?

The project of neighbourhood planning reflects the assumption that not only can communities engage in planning, they can lead it. This cultural change reallocates roles and responsibilities from officials and specialists to citizens. Lord et al (2017: 359) point to the 'host of requirements relating to the skills and implicit code of semi-professional practice that will be made of private individuals in order to transform them into citizen planners', while Inch (2015: 409) highlights the need for 'the cultivation of specific civic virtues, including particular conceptions of how the common good should be understood and what constitutes legitimate political behaviour'. He emphasises that the subjectivities required for collaborative and agonistic planning are antithetical, and so a process that shapes individuals and communities to be fit for one kind of engagement simultaneously makes them unfit for the other, and that only certain types of citizen and of participation are legitimate in the model of planning that underpins neighbourhood planning.

This leads to concerns that neighbourhood planning (and the localism and participatory agendas more generally) will entrench privilege and further empower the already relatively powerful who are most able to take advantage of opportunities for participation in governance – who are most able to enact themselves as those types of citizen and engage in those types of participation. This would then increase inequalities and insider/outsider dynamics both within and between communities, such that those with access to the greatest social, cultural, symbolic and economic resources would become even more dominant (Bailey and Pill, 2015; Hastings and Matthews, 2015; Matthews et al, 2015; Wills, 2016). Existing power relations among 'the public' as well as between 'the public' and other actors (such as national and local government, developers and landowners) would be reinforced rather than countered. The democratic accountability and representativeness of NPGs has been questioned, suggesting that they favour existing 'elites' and/or the views of only a limited segment of the community (Davoudi and Cowie, 2013; Gallent and Robinson, 2013; Vigar et al, 2017).

Studies repeatedly show a trend towards 'an uneven geography of representation in favour of the more affluent, better educated and more vocal social groups who often have time, resources and knowhow at their disposal' (Davoudi and Madanipour, 2015: 185; see also Parker et al, 2014, 2020). Despite this, governmental rhetoric has tended to downplay asymmetries within and between neighbourhoods (Parker, 2017), although some small steps have been taken to address this imbalance. The year 2015 saw the launch of a short-lived fund for Community Organisers to support groups in deprived areas to take up neighbourhood planning and other community rights, and a pilot project aimed at capacity building for community organisations in deprived areas to engage with neighbourhood planning. In 2020 additional funding and technical support packages were made available to urban and deprived neighbourhoods, and pilot programmes were launched in 2021 for LPAs to help establish Neighbourhood Forums in urban and deprived areas and to trial 'light' versions of neighbourhood plans with communities that lacked the capacity to produce a 'full' plan. However, these efforts to address inequalities between neighbourhoods does not necessarily address inequalities or the potential for elite capture within neighbourhoods – and by late 2022 had not delivered significant increases in neighbourhood planning in more urban and deprived areas.

'Not In My Back Yard' neighbours?

Another issue raised in relation to place-based participatory democracy is the potential tension between parochial local interests and the wider public interest. Ludwig and Ludwig (2014) argue that even though neighbourhood planning is intended to smooth the path to more development, in practice it is often likely to give ammunition to those who want to stop development and to stir up inflammatory anti-development feeling. Samuels observes that 'the big defect with this system is that our lives are not constrained within the medieval boundaries of parishes' (2012: 41), and argues that the relentless focus of neighbourhood planning on the very local is bound to lead to narrow, parochial concerns being given priority over wider strategic objectives. Any such resistance to the policy objectives of increased housing or economic growth tends to be characterised as 'regressive, place-bounded, small-world self-interest' (Mace, 2013: 1144), and there have been concerted efforts to characterise neighbourhood planning as a 'NIMBY's Charter' (Orme, 2010; King, 2011).

As Wolsink (2006: 87) observes, NIMBY (Not In My Back Yard) is not a well-defined concept, but rather is 'used as a pejorative to imply selfish behaviour on the part of opponents', consisting of the irrational obstruction of reasonable proposals that, by implication, the objectors would be happy to see built elsewhere. The derogatory label functions as a negation of the labelled subjects' capacity to engage in collaborative efforts and to see the bigger (and implicitly more important) picture. It implies the clouding of rational judgement by emotion (Cass and Walker, 2009). It seeks to dismiss all and any arguments the labelled subject might present as irrelevant and ill-founded; 'a by-product of subjective vested interests and/or ignorance and mis-understanding of what it is that experts are seeking to do' (Raco et al, 2016: 223).

This labelling of any resistance to the neoliberal growth agenda as NIMBYism further reduces the scope for agonistic approaches from NPGs. The association of neighbourhood planning with NIMBYism threatens to construct an imagined identity for NPGs that is likely to generate responses from other actors (such as LPA planners and landowners) that would compromise the capacity of NPGs to function (Walker et al, 2010; Barnett et al, 2012). To be successfully labelled as a NIMBY in the planning world is effectively to have one's identity spoiled: to be discredited and stigmatised (Goffman, 1968). However, Matthews et al (2015) suggest that by virtue of misconceptualising the roots and reasons behind resistance that is characterised as NIMBY, the new localism agenda, especially neighbourhood planning, is likely to fail to overcome such resistance and actually lead to an increase in effective oppositional action. Parker et al (2015: 530) summarise both horns of these dilemmas, with resonances for place-based participation more widely: 'the danger is that the plan and its content simply results in performing national agendas, or conversely in reflecting the predilections of a small group of people residing in the neighbourhood'.

Countering the critique

These critiques are deep and wide-ranging. But some authors – including some of those providing the warnings of danger – also see the potential for real change to be achieved through neighbourhood planning, and participatory democracy more broadly. The extent, nature and outcomes of participation are contested and complex, and the foregoing critiques are evidence of complexity, not dichotomies. As Wargent (2021) points out with respect to neighbourhood planning in particular, actual attempts to 'govern through communities' are never totalising and monolithic, but messy, incomplete, and tend to fall short of their intended realignment of citizens' agency to serve externally imposed objectives. Indeed, Foucault himself recognised that the enactment of governmentality, of subtle disciplinary control of citizens, always contains within itself the seeds of resistance and the potential for subversion (Burchell et al, 1991). Community empowerment, on this reading, always 'contains the twin possibilities of domination and freedom' (Cruikshank, 1999: 2). So while the localism and participatory agendas clearly need to be viewed critically, the possibilities that they introduce also need to be explored (Parker et al, 2017a). The literature suggests that some of the concerns raised by commentators are borne out in the practice of neighbourhood planning, but others are not (Sturzaker and Shaw, 2015).

Despite claims that neighbourhood planning essentially continues existing patterns, whether of entrenching privilege or subjecting communities to post-political governance at a distance, a number of authors have suggested that neighbourhood planning represents radical change (Bradley, 2017c; Bradley and Brownill, 2017a; Lord et al, 2017; Parker et al, 2017a), or at least has novel elements that make it quite different from previous initiatives (Sturzaker and Shaw, 2015; Sturzaker and Gordon, 2017). Indeed, Vigar et al (2017: 425) suggest that the central role of 'ordinary citizens' 'renders much of the planning literature on collaboration and participation – with its assumption of a "planner" at the heart of the process – only tangentially useful' in understanding neighbourhood planning.

One aspect of this novelty is that it enables the construction of a new collective identity or planning polity with the ability to determine its own membership, boundaries and issues – 'the neighbourhood'. 'The neighbourhood' becomes a significant new actor in the planning system, where previous participation tended to aggregate consumer preferences from 'outside' and cast organised collective action as self-interested and NIMBY (Bradley, 2015). A clear boundary line is drawn between autonomous polities – the neighbourhood and the LPA – which enables agonistic encounters both within the new polity (in an alternative discursive forum away from the modulating influence of officials and their specific framings and rationalities), and between it and the LPA and other actors (Bradley, 2017c). While the politics within neighbourhood planning may be constrained, the existence of a neighbourhood plan is inherently political. While in its present form, neighbourhood planning does not wholly meet the demands of either agonistic or collaborative planning theory (and indeed, what concrete form of participation does?), it arguably opens up spaces for both kinds of engagement (Bond, 2011; Parker et al, 2017a; Vigar et al, 2017).

While neighbourhood planning may have been intended to tame the antagonism between communities and the planning system and smooth the way for the achievement of neoliberal objectives, instead it has displaced this antagonism, allowing communities to produce policies that conflict with the corporate interests of the liberalised housing market (Bradley and Sparling, 2016). Instead of producing communities that were acquiescent to the requirements of speculative housing developers, it produced communities that became differently attuned to the needs of the area and the community, and the different ways in which these could be met, favouring models for meeting local needs that conflict with those of the volume housebuilders (Bradley et al, 2017).

The literature on neighbourhood planning shows the potential for NPGs to 'work the spaces of power' (Newman, 2012) and to assemble neighbourhoods around distinctive and progressive priorities, subverting the implicit intentions of the processes of governmentality. It is 'constituted by and constitutive of the statecraft of localism… [but has] … already exceeded its boundaries' (Bradley and Brownill, 2017a: 263). It repeatedly describes examples of NPGs that are prioritising local distinctiveness, place identity and protection of green space (Bradley and Brownill, 2017a: 260). As well as (re)assembling and (re)configuring neighbourhoods, these NPGs begin to open up spaces to reconfigure the purposes and aims of planning itself (Brownill, 2017a), with 'the neighbourhood emerging as the proponent of sustainability and social purpose' (Parker et al, 2017a: 458).

To the extent that this may appear to cast neighbourhood planning precisely in the role of a 'NIMBY's charter', Matthews et al (2015: 57) note that 'the literature which interrogates and criticizes the NIMBY concept recognizes that much of the opposition is valid and linked to broader societal concerns such as sustainability and social justice' (see, for example, Devine-Wright, 2009; Sturzaker, 2011; Burningham et al, 2014). Far from being parochial and self-serving, the caring-for-place motivations dismissed as NIMBYism often relate to concerns that are much more expansive than the relatively narrow act of calculation performed in the planning balance. It has been suggested that neighbourhood planning could offer a site where these much-derided concerns could be 'reframed as legitimate attempts to assert a local narrative of place over external versions' (Mace, 2013: 1144). Traditionally, both planners and planning scholarship have tended to steer away from the emotional realm and the attachments that people feel to place (Hoch, 2006; Baum, 2015), despite their central role in driving participation (Porter et al, 2012), while the policy of neighbourhood planning explicitly invokes and relies upon these commitments (Bradley, 2017a).

Neighbourhood planning, then, represents a cat's cradle of contradictory relations simultaneously supporting and undermining each other. Indeed, as Brownill and Bradley observe, '[i]n no other case study of devolution, across a broad international canvas, do we see so vividly the liberatory and regulatory conflicts that arise from the assemblage of localism, or the tangled relations of power and identity that result' (2017: 251).

Whatever the intentions of this particular brand of localism, such conflicts are likely to open up spaces for the unexpected and unintended, where difference can be achieved (Levitas, 2012; Newman, 2014). It has also been suggested that focusing solely on indications of 'post-political' regimes not merely ignores, but may also contribute to the suppression of other possible outcomes (Williams et al, 2014). Regardless of the powerful critiques outlined earlier, localism and participation remain central narratives worldwide. Their differing manifestations and the different effects of these manifestations cannot be ignored (Parker et al, 2017a), and before dismissing them outright, it is important to get a detailed understanding of their operation in practice, and the practices implicated in their operation (Parker and Street, 2015). The rationales for participation remain valid, despite the failings of individual instances and the deeper, structural critiques of its 'dark side': 'participation is not always desirable in practice. … Yet at the same time the idea of participation … must ultimately be desirable' (Brownill and Parker, 2010b: 281).

Impacts on the ground

However it is theoretically characterised, neighbourhood planning has had significant practical and political effects, becoming established as 'one of the most widespread community initiatives in recent years' (Brownill and Bradley, 2017). A briefing paper by No. 5 Chambers, one of the country's leading planning law practices, described it as 'one of the most important issues in land use planning today. It sits at the epicentre of the seismic tension between Localism and the national policy imperative of significantly boosting the supply of housing' (Young and Burcher, 2014: 1). Vigar et al note that neighbourhood plans 'have come to exert much greater authority over land use policy than initially thought' (2017: 423) and 'been shown to exert real power in decisions over land use' (2017: 439).

By autumn 2019, over 2,600 communities had formally applied to begin the process of developing a plan, and 865 had been formally adopted by their LPAs, although rates of take-up have slowed considerably (Parker et al, 2020). Far from being unwillingly or unwittingly coerced into the government's neoliberal agenda of increased growth and less control, a report from planning consultancy Turley found that over half of the first 75 published neighbourhood plans focused on preservation and protection of the local area (Turley, 2014), while a 2020 survey of planning consultants found that 73 per cent believed that neighbourhood planning had increased residents' ability to resist development (Khan, 2020). Regardless of the rights or wrongs of development decisions in any particular area, this suggests that neighbourhood planning has given communities a degree of autonomy and independence that does not align with governmental intentions or developer ambitions.

In many cases, neighbourhood plans have had a real impact on decision making, both in terms of the effect that they have in individual cases and the wider impact that decisions involving them are perceived to have.

Their impacts were assessed by the 'Impacts of Neighbourhood Planning in England' report (Parker et al, 2020), commissioned by the government and based on research conducted independently by a team, of which I was a part, led by the University of Reading. It found that both LPAs and NPGs considered that neighbourhood plans improved the quality and design of new development – poor quality and design being major issues driving public resistance to development, the erosion of local distinctiveness, and the unsustainability of housing stock (Carmona et al, 2020). It also showed that neighbourhood planning has delivered a modest uplift in the amount of housing delivered compared to that set out in local plans, although due to the constant cycle of updating and reviewing plans this calculation is difficult to make and should be treated with caution. At any rate, it seems unlikely that this has met the government aspiration that neighbourhood planning would significantly increase housing development – but neither does it point to neighbourhood plans being used to block development. This suggests that NPGs have in practice been at least to some extent successful in resisting the disciplinary intent of neighbourhood planning.

And in any case, this uplift does not take the form of acquiescence to the corporate interests of the housing market or the (perceived) government imperative to indiscriminately 'build, build, build'. Rather, there is evidence of neighbourhood planning communities drawing on their intimate knowledge of local spatial relations to propose locally tailored, socially inclusive and sustainability-oriented ways in which their needs can be met (Bradley and Sparling, 2016). This enables them to place greater emphasis on locally responsive and locally supported locations, mixes, affordability, local occupancy and design of housing (Bailey, 2017), tailoring development to meet the specific needs of the local area, for example, for young families starting out or older people wanting to downsize. They have been described as having 'demonstrated a different way of "doing" planning' (Field and Layard, 2017: 107).

This 'different way of doing planning' extends beyond the government's main concern with planning (delivering housing) to cover the whole range of planning matters as they manifest at a very local level. Neighbourhood plans tend to approach these matters with a particularly strong focus on environmental quality, sense of place and social wellbeing (Bradley and Brownill, 2017a). Many of them have designated places of particular community value for protection, for example, as Local Green Spaces, green corridors, separation zones or assets of community value. They prioritise the use values that motivate their communities over the exchange values that guide private development markets and much professional planning (Bradley et al, 2017). They seek to emphasise the concrete characteristics and qualities of lived place alongside the substitutable calculations of abstract space, mobilising care for and ways of knowing place that are not accessible to remote professional planners (Yuille, 2021). As a result, they have become an important tool for asserting locally determined priorities.

Parker et al conclude that, despite the strong conservative forces that operate through neighbourhood planning, there are examples in which 'policy innovation ... is being applied that can improve quality and sustainability' (2020: 18). Although these may be the exception rather than the rule, it demonstrates that with the right structures and support in place, there is scope for neighbourhood planning to achieve much more in terms of unlocking the creativity of local communities to better address local priorities. The majority of neighbourhood plans also catalyse wider place-based activity, becoming important vehicles for stimulating and coordinating placemaking beyond land use planning (Parker et al, 2020).

This highlights both that communities lack a formal arena for placemaking projects that imbricate with, but go beyond planning policy, and that 'the public' sees place and placemaking holistically and in much broader terms than conventionally conceived planning practice (Layard et al, 2013a). Communities can be more effectively and creatively involved – and local democracy thus enhanced – if their engagement extends beyond 'merely' planning matters to include overlapping and adjacent issues such as environmental and public realm improvements, traffic management and highways improvements, green space management, improving community assets, affordable housing and community renewables. This also often acts to stimulate wider debates about community actions and issues, which can further reinvigorate local democracy (Parker et al, 2020).

Combining projects with planning policies can help to maintain public engagement with a plan, both during preparation and after adoption. Successful neighbourhood planning is not a one-off event, but an ongoing revival of civic engagement. Much to some groups' surprise, after their plans are adopted, they are most effectively implemented if they interpret and apply their own policies by commenting on individual applications. In some cases, NPGs have acted as a new locus for community engagement in masterplanning and preapplication discussions, and in early stages of local plan preparation such as site identification – with frustration and resentment evident in communities where this has not happened (Parker et al, 2020). Neighbourhood planning engagement with the local democracies of planning can go much further than 'simply' producing a plan.

Early neighbourhood plan policies were strongly defended at appeals by successive Secretaries of State, who regularly emphasised the importance that they placed on them in their decision letters, not infrequently disagreeing with appeal inspectors' recommendations in order to do so (DLP Planning, 2014; Bailey, 2017). In some cases, where LPAs could not show a five-year housing land supply, and the presumption in favour of sustainable development was therefore triggered, they nevertheless gave sufficient importance to neighbourhood plan policies to outweigh the presumption, where the appeal inspectors had given priority to the presumption (for example, Javid, 2016: para 16). In others, where inspectors considered the absence of a policy about a particular parcel of land to mean that a neighbourhood plan was 'silent' about it, therefore triggering the presumption in favour of sustainable development, the Secretary of State interpreted the plan in a more 'muscular' fashion, determining that the plan taken as a whole did contain a sufficient body of policy to indicate that permission should not be granted on such a site (for example, Javid, 2017: para 18).

However, as the housing crisis became an increasingly important political narrative, over time relatively more weight has been given to LPAs' lack of housing land supply (McDonnell, 2018). Early victories for NPGs at appeal have begun to be overshadowed by an increasing number of appeal decisions which have allowed developments that conflict with them. These decisions are, in the main, due to LPAs being unable to demonstrate a sufficient supply of housing land, or neighbourhood plans being found out of date due to changes to local plans to which they have not had an opportunity to adjust – factors entirely beyond the control of NPGs themselves (Burns and Yuille, 2018). However, while this is a significant and widespread cause of dissatisfaction and disillusionment among NPGs, there is also evidence to suggest that neighbourhood plan policies are often supported and upheld at appeal (Bishop, 2018; Parker et al, 2020).

In some cases, developers unhappy with the outcome of neighbourhood planning processes have brought legal challenges against them. However, a series of legal judgments have taken a 'generous approach' towards neighbourhood plans (Sturzaker and Gordon, 2017: 1335), giving them 'considerable leeway' such that 'very few have been successfully challenged in the courts' (Parry, 2020: np). This appears to indicate that the courts have attempted to interpret the law in a way that maximises the power of NPGs to make decisions, and to minimise the ability of traditionally more powerful actors to use their more substantial resources to overrule them through judicial review. The courts have affirmed the flexibility that neighbourhood plans have with regard to higher level policy, ruling for example, that the need to be in 'general conformity' with local plan policies does not require conformity with every policy, and that the requirement to 'have regard' to national policy allows for more flexibility than the requirement on local plans to 'be consistent with' national policy. They have confirmed that neighbourhood plans can come forward before local plans, despite the conflicts this can produce (such as if the local plan seeks to allocate more or different sites), that neighbourhood plan policies that are out of date (for example, for falling foul of the five-year supply rule) can still carry very significant weight, sufficient to overcome the presumption in favour of sustainable development, and that conflict with a neighbourhood plan can in itself significantly and demonstrably outweigh the benefits of proposed development (Morgan, 2017). They have taken a restrictive interpretation of the timescales within which neighbourhood plans can be subject to legal challenge, confirming that strict time limits apply with regard to each stage of the process, and clearly stating that the need to avoid public disaffection with neighbourhood planning informed their reasoning (Dehon and Fitzsimons, 2021).

However, despite these often 'generous' legal interpretations, a limited number of neighbourhood plans have also fallen foul of legal decisions, and in these cases the courts have clarified the need for neighbourhood plan policies to be based on robust evidence, and that there are definite limits to the flexibility and to the weight that neighbourhood plans can bear (Morgan, 2017; Parry, 2020). Despite the relative infrequency with which neighbourhood plans are successfully challenged in the courts, the propensity of developers to do so has led to the examination process becoming less 'light touch' and requiring more of the kind of technical evidence that is usually associated with local plan examinations, in order to improve the chance of plans withstanding aggressive legal challenges (Parker et al, 2017b). The judgments in these cases affirm that while 'evidence for neighbourhood plans does not need to be as technical as that for local plans, the court has clearly found that qualitative evidence, which can be acceptable to support a policy with, must be supported by research and not simply guessed' (Donnelly, 2016: np).

The drives towards localism and participation that neighbourhood planning embodies remain central narratives worldwide (Legacy, 2017). The very existence of increasing numbers of appeals and court cases (and the associated resource implications) that revolve around neighbourhood plans indicate the impact that they are having. The government has used several different mechanisms to strengthen the role and powers of neighbourhood planning since its introduction, through legislation, policy, guidance, and funding and support arrangements (Grimwood, 2018). Both the Conservative government and the opposition Labour Party remain committed to 'Neighbourhood Plans being central to a new streamlined system of plan making' (Blackman-Woods, 2018). After early indications that the proposed reforms of the early 2020s might shrink the role of neighbourhood plans (Yuille, 2022), they seem instead likely to remain a significant part of the system (Parker et al, 2022). Neighbourhood plans are having substantial consequences and appear to be here to stay for the foreseeable future.

Conclusion

Neighbourhood planning has enabled local communities to set statutory planning policies and produce the evidence needed to justify them, an ability previously reserved for technical specialists within local government, in processes that were perceived as remote and inaccessible. While there are legally prescribed stages that neighbourhood plans must pass through, there is great flexibility in the content and processes for producing them. This is presented as a significant transfer of power which enables communities to plan collaboratively. However, it is set in a context of wider neoliberal planning (and other) reforms that aim to drive growth through deregulation and to enable governance through, rather than by, local communities. Research on neighbourhood planning provides contradictory messages, with both positive and negative impacts being theorised and observed. The context-specific experience of participation leads to a rather fragmented tapestry of encounters that do not easily lend themselves to universal claims. But however fragmented the landscape, neighbourhood planning appears highly unlikely to disappear from the English planning landscape any time soon.

There has been a call for research to focus more on specific, situated episodes, and on issues left unexplored by a focus on the 'bigger picture' of universal claims such as entrenching privilege, post-political governmentality, or agonism versus collaboration. These calls seek 'more nuanced analyses of the conflicting rationalities underlying planning practice and the dynamics and contradictions often found at the micro-level' (Brownill and Parker, 2010b: 276), or, as Polletta puts it, in order 'to adjudicate between the champions and critics of contemporary exercises in citizen democracy, we need careful studies probing the operation and impacts of particular initiatives' (2016: 234). In the following chapter I set out how this book contributes to these calls by using theoretical and methodological resources drawn from Science and Technology Studies.

3

Knowledge, politics and care: perspectives from Science and Technology Studies

> Planning documents, from maps, to models, to GIS, to plans
> themselves, do in fact all tell a story ... there is no such thing
> as mere description, or pure facts. There is always an author ...
> who is choosing which facts are relevant, what to describe, what
> to count, and in the assembling of these facts a story is shaped.
>
> Sandercock (2003: 21)

Introduction

It is frequently repeated that planning is much an art as a science. So why look at it through the lens of Science and Technology Studies (STS)? In brief, and as I will develop throughout this chapter, STS concepts and approaches are particularly well-suited to help us think through the kinds of issues raised by planning scholar Leonie Sandercock in the opening quotation. Sandercock highlights that 'the facts' are never just that, never simply objective truths standing apart from interpretation or value judgements. And by the same token, evidence and policy are never as clearly separated as conventional models of planning would have us believe – as a minimum, because the evidence is always shaped by an author telling a story, when other stories could also be told, and policy is shaped by which stories are made visible in policy-making processes. STS methodologies open up questions of fact and value, of how facts are made and how stories are told with and about them, of whose knowledge is trusted, of how decisions about what is relevant and what is important are shaped, of what and who should be counted and how.

As discussed in Chapter 1, interest in participatory processes and deliberative democracy has flourished over the past decades. STS scholars have made a significant contribution to this 'participatory turn', both as advocates and critics (such as Fiorino, 1990; Latour, 2004a; Wynne, 2007; Callon et al, 2009; Marres, 2012; Chilvers and Kearnes, 2016). They have mobilised powerful arguments for increasing public engagement and plurality in making evidence and policy, in order to 'uphold the standards of democratic society; test the framing and direction of expert-led processes; subject institutional interests to public scrutiny; establish cultural bases for knowledge and decision making; and enhance civic capacity to reflect on the challenges of modernity' (Leach et al, 2005: 38).

But despite apparent increases in local, bottom-up and democratic participation, these same STS researchers have shown that practices of decision making in public policy have proved remarkably resistant to incorporating lay people's understandings and knowledge. Indeed, they have suggested that participation can be ritualistic, manipulative and harmful to those that it is notionally intended to empower; can reproduce social identities and relationships in ways that both conceal and perpetuate existing power relations; and often insist on reductionist simplifications and assumptions about the power and agency of participants and the knowledge, experience and skills that they can contribute (Jasanoff, 1990; Wynne, 1992; Stirling, 2006; Welsh and Wynne, 2013).

STS scholars have highlighted that understanding participatory democracy requires not just asking who gets to participate and how, but how those participants, the issues at stake, and the processes themselves are constructed and framed through particular encounters. They have tried to generate social change and more inclusive, transparent and plural processes by first calling for greater public participation in making knowledge (or evidence) and decisions, and then by drawing attention to concealed elements of actual participatory practices: elements that are not seen or shown, but which have powerful and often determinative effects (Wynne, 1982; Johnstone and Stirling, 2020). They have also begun to actively intervene in reworking both the theory and practice of participation (see, for example, Lane et al, 2011; Tsouvalis and Waterton, 2012; Chilvers and Kearnes, 2016).

The field of STS has grown largely out of questions about knowledge, such as what counts as knowledge, who can produce knowledge, and how knowledge is made and represented. It analyses and interrogates assumptions that are often taken for granted about knowledge, evidence and accepted practices of 'how things are done'. These issues are central to planning in general, and to neighbourhood planning in particular, given its focus on the local knowledge of non-experts and its claims to represent a new way for citizens to engage with planning. For the same reasons, they are also central to the operation and analysis of participatory democracy more widely.

While STS originally developed to understand and reconceive the making of scientific knowledge and technological innovation, over the past few decades it has arguably become 'a generalised study of expertise' (Roosth and Silbey, 2009: 466). Its tools and terms have proved useful for the study of knowledge practices in many other fields (McNeil and Roberts, 2011). Furthermore, the knowledge practices of the natural sciences have extensively informed the norms and conventions of knowledge production in 'Western' culture in general, and specifically 'the Enlightenment foundations of modernist planning, anchored … in an epistemology that privilege[s] scientific and technical ways of knowing' (Sandercock and Attili, 2010: xx). Planning is not a science, but tools that help to understand the production and use of scientific knowledge can certainly help to understand the production and use of planning knowledge.

In this book I draw particularly on two elements within STS: feminist technoscience studies, and Actor-Network Theory and its 'successor projects', but I will use the generic shorthand of 'STS' throughout (Law, 2009). By this, I don't mean to imply an artificial unity within this highly diverse field, but to recognise that what is of use here is what might be termed a 'core STS sensibility' (Law, 2008: 630). This sensibility provides 'a range of tools for understanding, problematizing, and undermining the naturalisation' of many of the things we take for granted (McNeil and Roberts, 2011: 33), and brings a new and nuanced perspective to some of the issues at the heart of neighbourhood planning. It is concerned with the ways in which the social world (of language, social practices, policies, ideas, institutions and so on) and the material world (of human bodies, physical objects, spatial arrangements, technologies, natural and built environments and so on) are inextricably intertwined. It is thus sometimes described as 'material semiotics', that is, it has to do with both physical, material *stuff*, and the *meanings* that that stuff is imbued with. It is interested in how those meanings are created and communicated, and how the relations between meaning and materiality develop.

It traces how particular connections between elements of the social and material worlds (or 'sociomaterial relations') become established and durable, and how they then act to support or suppress other such connections. In doing so, it challenges naturalised dualisms such as nature/culture, fact/value, emotion/reason, subject/object, and tends to suggest that the sharp separations that we assume between the two sides of these supposed dichotomies are not as absolute or as obvious as they may at first appear. It starts from the position that all subjects, objects and knowledge claims are historically, culturally and materially situated – that they come *from* somewhere – and that this situatedness is always worthy of attention. All of this in turn problematises notions, such as community, power, knowledge and care, invoked by the discourse and practices of neighbourhood planning. It allows us to look at these things from new perspectives and understand them in new ways.

This chapter introduces some of the key concepts drawn from STS that can be useful in generating new ways of understanding both neighbourhood planning in particular, and planning and other arenas of participatory democracy more generally. These concepts inform and underpin the analysis in the rest of the book. They provide a set of valuable lenses with which to examine the practices and outcomes of planning. From the outside, however, they can at first seem counterintuitive and complicated. They are most easily understood through observing how they play out in specific empirical examples, so it may be worthwhile returning to this chapter as you move through later chapters where these concepts are applied to concrete situations. As a bundle of resources to think with, they allow us to develop new perspectives on old problems – and therefore possibly new ways to intervene in those problems. They can be briefly summarised as:

- *Situated knowledge* – the idea that all knowledge comes from a particular perspective. All knowledge is produced through particular methods, theories and frameworks. It is therefore in important ways inseparable from the 'knower' and the ways it is known. All knowledge is necessarily a simplification of reality, and there is never just one obvious or necessary simplification to make.
- *Imaginaries* – the idea that the way that we act in and understand the world is conditioned by cultural frameworks that permeate all aspects of our lives. These 'imaginaries' make shared practices and collective meanings possible, and at the same time are reproduced and reinforced by those shared practices and meanings.
- *Assemblages* – the idea that everything (such as objects, places, identities, and institutions) is made up of heterogeneous (that is, diverse and dissimilar) elements, both material and social, human and non-human, physical and intangible. The specific ways in which these elements relate or connect to each other generates 'emergent' effects that are more than the sum of their parts. Furthermore, these relations could always be otherwise, so assemblages are always to some extent precarious.
- *Performativity, translation and inscription* – the idea that when we represent something, we do not merely describe it, we bring it into being in a particular way, by foregrounding some characteristics and relations and backgrounding others. By making choices (conscious or otherwise) about what is relevant and important about the thing described, we actively shape how it can be interacted with and thus how it is in the world. And there are always different choices that could be made. This is a process of translation – of generating representations that can meaningfully stand in for things – and these translations gain strength and durability by being inscribed in certain ways.
- *Co-production* – the idea that we bring order to the material world through science and other means of generating knowledge, at the same time and through the same processes that we bring order to the social world through institutions, policies, laws and power relations. Neither of these precedes or is separate from the other. They unfold together simultaneously – they are coproduced. Science and politics, knowledge and power are thus inseparable.

- *Multiplicity and ontological politics* – the idea that, as a consequence of the concepts outlined previously, the act of description and analysis – of generating knowledge – is always 'political'. It makes some realities visible, prominent and available to be engaged with; it makes others invisible, marginalised and hence unavailable. This is the politics of 'ontology' – the struggle to define what there is in the world, what is relevant and important in the current situation. Public institutions can only see and act upon that which is made visible. Representing and acting on particular versions of reality will tend to be more benign for some interests than others. There is, at least, always a choice to be made about which realities we make visible, and those choices have material consequences.
- *The 'turn to care'* – the idea that care is crucial to every dimension of human life, and yet is under-researched. Care is conceived of as complex and multifaceted, combining affective states and attachments, material activity, and ethical and political obligations. The 'turn to care' focuses both on paying attention to the workings of care in the world, and to being 'care-full' about the ways in which research is done and reported.

The rest of this chapter will explore these concepts in more detail, and relate them specifically to the world of neighbourhood planning.

Situated knowledge

Knowledge in planning

In the UK planning system, 'generally greater weight is attached to issues raised which are supported by evidence rather than solely by assertion' (Planning Aid, nd: np). The closer this evidence appears to be to 'scientific' knowledge, the more weight will generally be attached to it. As Rydin (2007) observes, all participants in the planning system tend to present their claims, as far as possible, as representing this kind of objective knowledge, as this increases the status of those claims. Planning is susceptible to a generally perceived hierarchy of knowledge in which lay, local knowledge rests firmly at the bottom (Eden, 2017: 51–53) and institutionalised and scientifically framed claims are at the top (Ockwell and Rydin, 2006). Rydin and Natarajan highlight that 'the way that community experience of the environment is conveyed explicitly combines values with knowledge' (2016: 2), reducing its status by 'tainting' the objectivity of knowledge with the subjectivity of values. They explain that such 'knowledge-value hybrids' have to be reframed or translated before they can be considered relevant to or hold weight in the planning process. In particular, 'affective' elements of such hybrids are removed.[1]

In other words, what local people think they know about the place in which they live, and the things that they care about in that place – the bases of neighbourhood planning – are often treated as not-knowledge, not capable of being evidence or of being given weight. Indeed, Anna Davies describes 'a widespread popular culture of silence about emotive environmental issues in the face of apparently unquestionable scientific or utilitarian values that dominate political decisions' (2001a: 87). Based on these culturally dominant assumptions about knowledge and evidence, what local people know about an area through their experience of living there tends to be valued less highly than what remote experts know through their application of computer models, economic and demographic forecasts, schematic or formalised assessments, and quantitative surveys.

Broadly speaking, representations of abstract space (knowledge about a locality produced from a physical or metaphorical distance through technical methodologies and technologies, which focuses on what can be categorised, quantified and substituted between locations) tend to be automatically privileged over representations of lived place (knowledge about a locality produced from within that locality through direct engagement with and experience of it, which focuses on its particular concrete characteristics and qualities and their meaningful and symbolic dimensions) (Massey and Thrift, 2003; Agnew, 2011). This automatic privileging of some types of representation over others occurs because the epistemology of modernist planning values scientific and technical ways of knowing over others. And this valuation rests on a series of assumptions – a story – about the functioning of scientific methods, so deeply ingrained that they are rarely even noticed, let alone exposed to a critical gaze.

Stories about science

The story that we have been telling ourselves about science, and knowledge more widely, begins with the absolute separation between matter and mind, the world 'out there' and our knowledge of the world 'in here': the objective and the subjective. This separation tells us that the world is what it is, passively waiting to be discovered, a singular, definite, independent, pre-existing entity (Law, 2004). But, the story goes, as subjects we experience all sorts of interference that gets between us and this world: affective, somatic, perceptual, intellectual and cultural biases, assumptions, and distortions. To produce genuine knowledge about the world – descriptions of the world as it really is – we must therefore strive towards objectivity. In effect, we must get out of our own way, by carving out a space into which our own subjectivity, our cultural biases, do not intrude. That is the function of the scientific method: it produces a 'culture of no culture' that eliminates such subjective distortions (Traweek, 1988: 162). This allows us to become 'the legitimate and authorized ventriloquist for the object world, adding nothing from [our] mere opinions, from [our] biasing embodiment' (Haraway, 1997: 24).

After this division of the world into the radically separate categories of objective and subjective, the story then requires a second strong separation to be made, between reason and emotion: 'the splitting of affective matters from the researcher's experience' (Puig de la Bellacasa, 2011: 97). Reason, although subjective (it is 'in here', not 'out there') enables us to minimise affective and other distortions. Scientific methods engage reason while distancing us from our affective states – from our capacity to be affected by things. This enables them to mechanically filter out noise from signal and to make correct and accurate interpretations of the world. These separations (between subjective and objective, and reason and emotion) can be achieved using what are described in STS as 'technologies'. While this may refer to what we commonly understand as 'technologies' – machines, devices and other engineered physical objects – in STS, it can also refer to any other socially constructed tool or technique for achieving a particular end. It may refer to a practice, a way of doing something, as much as to a physical object.

Shapin and Schaffer (1985) describe the development of three such 'technologies' that came to define the scientific method, and by implication, all 'objective' knowledge-making: a material technology (the scientific apparatus and method); a literary technology (a 'naked' way of describing or representing the experiment); and a social technology (a set of conventions determining how scientists' claims could be validated by direct or indirect public witnessing, and who was capable of such witnessing). Insofar as planning practices seek to produce objective knowledge, they reproduce these technological categories, with material technologies ranging from housing need surveys to demographic software packages such as POPGROUP; literary technologies such as maps and Housing and Economic Land Availability Assessment reports; and social technologies such as consultations, planning committees and Examinations in Public.

Generating objective knowledge requires the use of such technologies to efface the subjectivity of knowing subjects. They must become transparent: 'unmarked, disembodied, unmediated, transcendent' (Haraway, 1988: 586). The adoption of scientific methods is alleged to enable knowing subjects to transcend their own viewpoint, to see and to represent the world as it is, beyond subjective differences of perspective. The closer that any knowledge claim can position itself to this 'gold standard', the weightier its claim to be good evidence.

Alternative understandings

However, STS studies have shown that such assumptions about what legitimate knowledge is and who can produce it, despite having become so ingrained as to be taken for granted, are in fact contingent (that is, they could be otherwise), contestable and saturated with concealed value judgements. They have also demonstrated that the views of institutionally certified professionals are often privileged in situations where other ways of knowing the world are equally valid, but are suppressed and delegitimised (Wynne, 1996). This reflects a *scientistic* (as opposed to scientific) approach, which excessively valorises scientific methods as the only valid means to acquire reliable knowledge, as being capable of describing all relevant aspects of reality, and of being the only proper basis for decision making (Stenmark, 1997). In contrast, an STS reading insists that scientific facts are constructed rather than discovered, and that the processes of construction inevitably combine social norms, political values and pragmatic issues with epistemic concerns (Latour, 1987). This is particularly relevant to land use planning, where the 'soft' experiential knowledge of communities is juxtaposed with the 'hard' technical evidence produced by LPAs, developers and consultants. An STS approach would require both sources and types of knowledge to be evaluated more symmetrically, without making automatic assumptions about the validity of either.

Through detailed empirical and theoretical work, STS scholars have unpicked the stories that have been constructed around science,[2] and that have subsequently been used as a yardstick against which all knowledge claims in 'Western' culture have been measured – and which have been imposed on other cultures as well, to the detriment of other ways of knowing and being in the world (Mignolo, 2011). They have also proposed alternative explanations that, they claim, not only give better accounts of the world, but can also enable better, more liveable worlds to flourish (Puig de la Bellacasa, 2011; Haraway, 2016).

To start with, the very idea of objective knowledge produced through a distinctive scientific method or rationality has been challenged. Early STS studies of the actual practices that take place in laboratories and other key sites of scientific activity demonstrated multiple ways in which the production of scientific knowledge is a thoroughly social and cultural process (Latour and Woolgar, 1979; Knorr-Cetina, 1981; Lynch, 1985; Traweek, 1988). They found that the processes, practices and choices that characterised the production of knowledge could not be explained by a distinctive form of rationality or scientific procedure. Science was described as a process of producing material culture through social negotiation embedded in specific, local, material contexts and practices. Scientific facts and realities were shown to be created in specific social and material situations, which embedded contingent decisions and assumptions within them, rather than being revealed or discovered truths about the world. Latour (1987) described the creation of facts as a rhetorical process of progressively deleting the evidence of the social origins – the process of construction – of the fact.

All 'raw data' has been shown to be already theorised, that is, with value judgements and assumptions imposed upon it. Indeed, it would be unintelligible as data without some contingent framing assumptions about both the nature of the object and the techniques and technologies of study. Latour suggested that to recognise this always-already-present entanglement of theory and data, facts and values, 'one should never speak of "data" – what is given – but rather of sublata, that is, of "achievements"' (1999: 42). Data – facts about the world – are created (or 'achieved'), not discovered, and this process of creation requires the embedding of value-laden assumptions. The assumed rigid division between facts and values is thus artificial, and the ambition of transcendental objectivity impossible: values and interests are 'inseparably constitutive of the judgments that frame the choices scientists make about which questions to ask and their assumptions about what data are relevant and how they are to be interpreted' (Millstone et al, 2015: 24). Scientific knowledge is not transcendent but specific to the material practices, conceptual frameworks and institutional structures in which it is produced. In order to understand what knowing is, and what it is that we know, we have to also consider *where* we are knowing from (Haraway, 1988). Science as the 'culture of no culture' turned out to be a socially and historically situated culture after all (Traweek, 1988: 162).

Donna Haraway describes the idea of an objective perspective as 'the god trick' (Haraway, 1988: 581) – the reassuring fiction that we can extract ourselves from our situated position to become a disembodied observer capable of viewing the world from no position. This trick is a literal impossibility, which conceals and naturalises the value-laden assumptions of the knowing subject, privileging their perspective by creating the illusion of value neutrality which in fact embeds their values and assumptions (Haraway, 1997). Maps are a classic example of such a god's-eye view of particular relevance to planning, which 'pretend merely to record knowledge, but in fact help to shape it through choices about what to leave out, what to include and how to represent it' (Davoudi et al, 2018: 118).

The early men of science were described as 'modest witnesses' for their ability to efface themselves from accounts of the production of stand-alone, universal knowledge. Haraway (1997) contends that appearing to succeed in attempts at this impossible trick is inevitably, albeit perhaps unwittingly, a form of epistemological con-artistry. She proposes that by instead recognising all knowledge as being situated, refusing the possibility of self-invisibility, we can construct better, more reliable knowledge through a different kind of modest witnessing. The 'modesty' of this position comes not from self-effacement, but precisely from the limitedness, positionality and specificity of its claims, and from its recognition that 'knower and known cannot be separated in any meaningful way' (Massey and Thrift, 2003: 290). This kind of modest witnessing is 'about telling the truth, giving reliable testimony, guaranteeing important things, providing good enough grounding ... to enable compelling belief and collective action' (Haraway, 1997: 22).

Haraway and other STS scholars are adamant that this account is not intended to undermine the validity of scientific knowledge – she retains 'a no-nonsense commitment to faithful accounts of a "real" world' (1988: 579). However, for many in the natural and social sciences, as well as in the worlds of policy and politics, this insistence on the fundamental entangledness and mutual embeddedness of science and politics, facts and values, knowledge and institutions, appears to be a form of damning criticism – it cuts at the heart of their assumptions about the rigid separation of these domains. But from an STS perspective, the problem with scientific accounts of the world is not that they *are* situated in this way. They could not be otherwise. The problem is rather that they are presented as *not* being so, thus obscuring information crucial to a full understanding of the claims in question. Rather than attempting to subvert scientific and other 'objective' knowledge, this is an attempt to redescribe more carefully the conditions by which it comes to be known. This is not relativism, but 'partial, locatable, critical knowledge' (Haraway, 1988: 584).

A corollary of understanding knowledge in this way is a requirement that knowledge which does not fit standard 'Western' models of objectivity and rationality be taken seriously and critically engaged with, rather than simply marginalised or dismissed a priori (Wynne, 1996; Verran, 1998, 2001; Yeh, 2016). This may include traditional Indigenous knowledges, hard-to-articulate skills or craft-based knowledges, and the local knowledges of neighbourhoods in the global North. It means, for example, taking seriously the first-hand experiences of residents, and finding ways in which they can be articulated so that they become legible to the planning system, rather than discounting them because they do not fit easily into established pigeonholes.

There is an increasing recognition (at least in theory), from the very local to the global scale, that it is not only right, just and fair to pluralise the sources of knowledge available to decisionmakers, but that this also leads to more complete and fully rounded knowledge about the world (San Martín and Wood, 2022). It is not suggested that these other ways of knowing should replace the technical, technologised modes of knowledge-making associated with more scientific approaches, but that they should complement each other, be critically analysed side by side, without automatically privileging or marginalising either. There are some things that science is very good at but others that it is not. The problem with a *scientistic* approach arises when it colonises or suppresses other spheres of knowing and being. The same applies to the domination of abstract space over lived place in planning: it obscures important dimensions which are, in the end, what planning is supposed to be all about – the interaction of people with place (Metzger, 2014b). The problem arises when first-hand accounts from, for example, children who (want to) play in the streets and people who have witnessed a place changing over decades compete with computer models and algorithms, rather than complementing them.

Sandra Harding (1986) developed these notions of the partiality and situatedness of knowledge, calling for knowledge claims to be subjected to a test of 'strong objectivity'. This would include analysis of the positionality of the knowledge claimant alongside analysis of the knowledge itself, as this situatedness is inevitably caught up in the knowledge produced – in the algorithm as much as the children's account. It shapes what kind of claims are intelligible, who can be heard, and what kind of justifications are acceptable. This connects with feminist standpoint theory, which suggests that thinking from the perspectives of marginalised groups and suppressed ways of knowing may help to produce better knowledge because they literally experience a different world than those in more privileged positions, enabling different questions to be asked (Smith, 1987). STS thus requires us to look at the entanglements of power and knowledge: the specific ways in which power shapes knowledge as much as the ways in which knowledge generates power (Stirling, 2006, 2015) and to recognise 'the imprints of power in what is seemingly true' (Stirling, 2016: 263).

Questions have been asked, quite reasonably, about whether the unpaid, unqualified amateurs preparing neighbourhood plans are able to produce sufficiently robust and credible evidence to adequately justify their plans, whether this will adequately engage with the needs of the whole community, and whether it will stand up to independent examination and scrutiny by hostile barristers in subsequent public inquiries and court cases (Parker et al, 2015, 2016; Lord et al, 2017; McDonnell, 2017). However, seen through an STS lens, the issues about knowledge practices in neighbourhood planning – what counts as evidence, how it can be produced and presented, and who gets to decide – change markedly. A new set of questions opens up. If the purpose of neighbourhood planning is to allow people who know and care about a place to take responsibility for its future, it must enable them to demonstrate what they know and how, and what they care about and why. The focus shifts from how their knowledge and attachments can be crammed, if at all, into conventional evidentiary and policy boxes, to how they can be better articulated and represented in ways that are intelligible to an external audience – how the boxes can become better adapted to them.

Neighbourhood plans are required to be based on 'robust' and 'proportionate' evidence, but there is very little guidance on what this might consist of, and government guidance explicitly states that 'there is no "tick box" list of evidence required for Neighbourhood Planning' (DCLG, 2014b: np). This is therefore a partially open, experimental space, without prescription, in an arena where care and experiential knowledge are explicitly valued and given as a rationale for the project. Neighbourhood planning, for reasons that I explore in Chapter 5, appears to offer a set of conditions that could be particularly conducive to articulating and acting on more qualitative, affective, 'meaning-full' knowledge, of a kind that the planning system has previously tended to render invisible.

Can the practices of neighbourhood planning enable more modest, situated knowledges to be presented as robust evidence? Can it be a practice that 'makes understood as discourse what was once only heard as noise' (Ranciere, 1999, cited in Sagoe, 2016: 3) – a practice that enables the often-erased concerns of communities to be made visible to decisionmakers? Given that the definition of legitimate knowledge often involves contestation over who has the right to determine what counts as knowledge or evidence in specific situations, can neighbourhood planning enact new legitimate holders, producers and types of knowledge? STS perspectives are particularly well-suited to analysing the emergence of such knowledges and their interactions with other, more conventional, forms of planning knowledge.

And it is the interactions with more conventional forms of planning knowledge that are particularly crucial. It is right, of course, that neighbourhood plans must be based on sufficiently robust technical evidence to ensure that they can pass examination and stand up in court. But it is also right that such technical evidence is not sufficient to capture the aspects of neighbourhood that communities want to plan for, the neighbourhood of lived experience. The argument from an STS perspective is not that we should cast aside or deny the validity of technical evidence. It is rather that we need to acknowledge that there are vital aspects of neighbourhood that elude detached, technical ways of knowing, but which are central to the very concept of planning, about the relations between people and place. These aspects require other ways of knowing in order to be better represented, ways which need to be critically appraised alongside more conventional methods, not subsumed into or marginalised by them. All forms of knowledge are situated and partial. The argument is not for replacing one kind of evidence with another, but for pluralising the kinds of knowledge that can be counted as evidence, for bringing them together differently to work together in more productive ways.

Imaginaries

One prominent way in which knowledge is situated is in an overarching 'imaginary'. Imaginaries can be understood as the overarching frameworks which provide a structure for us to think and act intelligibly, and which permeate our ways of understanding and doing things in the world. They consist of the sets of beliefs, assumptions, orientations, metaphors, norms and conventions that underpin practices, discourses and experiences in particular spheres (McNeil et al, 2017). In other words, they are the ways of thinking that mean that we understand and do particular things in particular ways. They are what makes doing those things, and understanding in those ways, make sense.

They may operate on many different levels, for example, national, cultural or specific to a field of practice or activity. They can therefore also be 'nested' inside one another. So, for example, a specific early 21st-century English planning imaginary – the practices and ideas that define what planning is and how it is done – sits within the broader modern/Enlightenment imaginary of knowledge practices outlined in the previous section. Imaginaries enable shared practices and meanings, and simultaneously both legitimise and are circulated and reinforced in those practices and meanings. So doing particular things in particular ways reinforces the ways of thinking that make doing those things make sense. Imaginaries are thus not (just) located in the mind, but in practical doings – it is in 'the everyday messing around with mucky, obdurate stuff, and in the conversations and other texts – official and unofficial – that imaginaries are enacted and enact' (Verran, 1998: 252).

Imaginaries are both representative and performative – that is, they both describe how things are, and bring into being the things they purport to merely describe (Gond et al, 2016).[3] They do this by providing a framework within which to think, describe and interact with things, thus shaping how we understand and relate to those things. They are generally tacit and taken for granted, structuring the way we think and act rather than being thought about or questioned themselves. As such they tend to become naturalised both as the way things are, and the way things should be – our 'common sense' assumptions about what makes legitimate knowledge provides a good example. However, they are also always contingent and (at least in principle) contestable, despite the strong hold they have over our understandings (Davoudi et al, 2018).

For example, while it is commonly acknowledged that planning is as much an art as a science, the tropes and metaphors used to describe the activities of planning belie this, and create an imaginary in which planning decisions, and the evidence on which they are based, are scientific, quantifiable and precise. The more 'objective' evidence is, the more weighty it can be considered. Numbers derived from a software package, say, are automatically seen as more credible than the eyewitness, experiential testimony of the grandmother who has spent 40 years observing the flows and changes of a place. The more removed evidence is from human fallibility, and the more closely associated it is with mechanistic, technological processes, the closer to the gold standard it can be considered: 'robust and credible [evidence] is interpreted as quantifiable and measurable' (Davoudi, 2015: 317). Decision takers then 'weigh' this evidence on both sides in 'the planning balance'. Arguments are metaphorically quantified to be made measurable, and assigned, for example, 'great' or 'limited' weight. Judgements are often described as 'finely balanced', implying a degree of computable precision.

In this imaginary, the figure of the decisionmaker is the figure of the expert, innocently (that is, without bias or preconceptions) revealing and assessing the objective facts from an Archimedean point (the hypothetical 'view from nowhere') and calculating the appropriate answer on that algorithmic basis. These linguistic turns, figures and tropes do not merely inflect the discourse of planning: they shape its practices and constitute its realities, 'hold[ing] the material and the semiotic together in ways that become naturalized over time' (Suchman, 2012: 49). The extent to which the tropes of measuring and weighing have become naturalised and come to dominate actual practices and understandings is forcefully illustrated by recent High Court and Court of Appeal decisions. The years 2018 and 2021 both saw legal challenges which turned upon the degree of precision which could be attributed to the weighing exercise of determining a 'planning balance'. The judges were forced to assert in their judgments that planning decision making should not be (as it clearly was being) interpreted as a 'mechanical, or quasi-mathematical activity' (Lindblom, 2017: para 50) or one which required 'a particular mathematical exercise' (Eyre, 2021: para 34). Both judges concluded that determining a 'planning balance' in the light of differently weighted harms and benefits was a metaphor that planners and others should avoid taking an 'excessively forensic' approach to (Eyre, 2021: para 32) – but the fact that the metaphor carries so much power that such questions are required to be repeatedly determined in the courts speaks volumes.

Imaginaries both underpin and are reinforced by concrete practices: they enable us to take part in shared or common activities, which have shared or common meanings, and the repetition of these meaningful activities embeds the enabling imaginary ever more firmly in our social and material worlds. This iterative process strengthens ways of knowing and acting that cohere with the dominant imaginary, and undermines and weakens alternatives. Because they both co-constitute (are an essential part of) and are in turn co-constituted by material practices and the people who participate in those practices, imaginaries have very real, material effects (Jasanoff and Kim, 2015). They are the glue that holds societies, or groups within societies, together in a common world. Recognising the power of imaginaries helps to explain how a particular community (for example, of planners), and the practices they perform and the understandings they have that make them a community, do not just exist, are not natural givens, but rather only exist in the way that they do because they are collectively imagined and performed in certain ways (Taylor, 2004).

Assemblages

STS often considers its objects of study (such as a neighbourhood, or a particular instance of neighbourhood planning, or the practice of neighbourhood planning in general) as 'assemblages' (or, in a closely related concept, as 'actor-networks' [Law, 2009]). Translated from Deleuze and Guattari's original (French) notion of 'agencement' (Deleuze and Guattari, 1988), an assemblage is a coming-together of multiple parts, in which the elements combine to generate something that is more than merely the sum of its parts. Crucially, the elements of assemblages (or actor-networks) are both social and material – they include the human and the non-human, material things and immaterial concepts and ideas. This might include, for example, the individuals in a neighbourhood planning group (NPG), national and local planning policy, the physical places in the neighbourhood, the techniques and tools used to produce evidence and engage the public, and the professionals that support the NPG. The relations between the different elements of an assemblage, the specific ways in which they are arranged, produce emergent effects. These include 'producing' the assemblage itself as a whole in a particular way which, were those relations different, could be otherwise. These relations may stabilise and become durable for a while, but they are always precarious, always subject to being unsettled (Müller, 2015).

Each element of an assemblage will itself also be assembled from heterogeneous sociomaterial components, and each assemblage will in turn be connected to and a part of an interconnected web of other assemblages. Where an assemblage starts and finishes, then, is in large part an analytical heuristic: as analysts we can describe something as 'an' assemblage, but we need to remain aware that it is simultaneously constituted by and is partially constitutive of an ever-ramifying array of other assemblages (Law, 2004). What is background and what is foreground, what is the object of study and what is context, is therefore largely a matter of analytical choice, rather than an externally imposed reality.

Sue Brownill (2016) highlights three particular advantages of assemblage thinking in examining the practices of localism and participatory democracy. First, it insists on a focus on actual unfolding empirical instances, without assigning them to predetermined categories or assuming causal factors or explanations. It thus enables researchers to explore the fragmented landscapes of participatory democracy through careful and nuanced studies of particular cases, beyond the 'grand narratives' of empowerment, privilege or governmentality (Brownill and Parker, 2010b; Polletta, 2016).

Second, it prioritises relations between the material and the social. This fits particularly well with the notion of 'the neighbourhood' as an entity that is quintessentially hybrid, inherently defined by both social and material relations. The *Oxford English Dictionary* online gives, as its first three definitions of 'neighbourhood': 'The people living near to a certain place or within a certain range; neighbours collectively'; 'A small sector of a larger urban area, provided with its own shops and other facilities'; and 'A district or portion of a town, city, or country, esp. considered in reference to the character or circumstances of its inhabitants'. Even in an everyday way of talking, then, the neighbourhood is thus social (the people and their collective relations to each other) and material (the physical territory and its built and natural features) *and* the relations between the two: a sociomaterial assemblage. With this as a starting point, it becomes easier to consider other entities – such as groups, individuals, institutions, places, policies, plans – as heterogeneous assemblages that are in some ways unintelligible without accounting for the relations between both their social and material elements.

Third, it understands power as an emergent effect rather than something that is possessed by groups or individuals. That is to say, power is not something that one *has*, but something that is generated as a result of the way that the elements of the assemblage(s) under consideration are arranged in relation to each other. This enables different readings of how power relations come to be established and stabilised, and how they might be changed, by paying attention to relations between different social and material elements of the network that may not be immediately obvious as carriers of power. It can thus capture the complexities of shifting power relations, and explore the opportunities that actors have for 'working the spaces of power' (Newman, 2012). This is particularly important for examining instances of participatory democracy, like neighbourhood planning, that claim to empower citizens but which have their roots in neoliberal, post-political intentions. Assemblage thinking is interested in two kinds of power. First, the *power to do*, or agency – the capacity to act, to have effects and make a difference in the world. And, second, in *power over* other actors – to 'make' them have the effects and make the differences you want. But it always starts with the former, and with how that power (or agency) grows out of networks of relations and practices (Law and Singleton, 2013).

Performativity, translations and inscriptions

Thinking in terms of assemblages suggests a sense of instability and emergence; of subjects and objects as impermanent and variable, in a process of continually becoming rather than simply 'being'. As discussed further in Chapter 4, governmental discourse on neighbourhood planning assumes a coherent, static, unified version of 'neighbourhood'. But from an STS perspective, neighbourhoods are assembled, not already given. They are represented and understood through particular practices, such as specific techniques of producing and presenting evidence on specific topics, all of which could be otherwise (Brownill, 2017a). They are presented as being subject to particular issues or problems (for example, lack of affordable housing, loss of green space, need for economic regeneration) that are framed in particular ways, all of which could be otherwise (Bradley, 2020).

These processes of assembling *perform* or *enact* neighbourhoods. They bring particular versions of them into being in particular ways. They put boundaries around them, spatially and conceptually establishing where they start and finish. They determine what their relevant and defining characteristics are. They draw attention to some aspects of 'the' neighbourhood, which diverts attention from other aspects. This brings particular versions of neighbourhood to presence, and makes them available to be acted upon, while other versions of neighbourhood are concealed. And which versions are made visible could always be otherwise. Like all assemblages, neighbourhoods are always in the process of being made and remade, defined and redefined: they are not natural or inevitable (Law and Singleton, 2014). And neighbourhood planning is just one of many practices through which neighbourhoods are continuously being assembled. These practices may be more or less formal, and they may compete with or complement each other.

Performing or enacting things in particular ways can support or subvert their enactment in other ways (Moser, 2008). The more that a description of a neighbourhood as being 'like this' becomes accepted and normalised, the less possible it becomes to describe it as being 'like that'. This applies both to the form of the description (what kinds of things matter about neighbourhoods in general) and its content (what this particular neighbourhood is like in terms of those criteria). Assembling neighbourhoods through neighbourhood planning thus does two types of 'boundary work' (Gieryn, 1995). It sets the boundary of specific neighbourhoods, defining their territorial location and their relevant and important characteristics. And in doing so repeatedly for many neighbourhoods, it marks boundaries as to what is and is not legitimate (important and relevant) knowledge about neighbourhoods, what are valid ways of representing them, and who can legitimately make those representations. Objects (such as neighbourhoods) and subjects (such as neighbourhood planners) are not just being described but being made through this process – and they could always be made differently. As Donna Haraway puts it, 'who and what are in the world is precisely what is at stake' (Haraway, 2003: 8).

From this perspective, assemblages exist, out there in the world. But they are also enacted through description. All 'things' are complex combinations of social and material elements that are connected to the rest of the world through multiple sets of relations. Context is not easily separable from an object, or background from foreground, once you start looking at the relations of assemblages. They spread out everywhere with no obvious cut-off point (Law and Singleton, 2014). But all knowledge production requires this expansive network to be cut somewhere, a boundary to be drawn that counts some things in and some things out of the object of study. Decisions must be made (Strathern, 1996). So while the object of study exists 'out there' in the world, its precise nature – its boundaries and defining characteristics – are determined 'in here' (Law, 2007). It is translated from a complex thing out there, to a simplified thing in here (Law and Mol, 2002). It is enacted in a particular way.

For example, some attributes and relations of objects can be foregrounded as significant and be abstracted – such as by being reduced to a number or classified as a category – while other attributes and relations are obscured (Jöns, 2011: 160). Think of a Sustainability Appraisal of a local plan. The attributes of various potential development strategies and sites are assessed in terms of, say, impacts on biodiversity, health, social exclusion and local economic regeneration. Each strategy and site receives a score for each criterion. The set of criteria as a whole includes some relevant things and excludes others. The indicators which are intended to represent performance against each criterion further include some relevant things and exclude others. This renders the assemblages comparable as wholes (in this case, as strategies and sites which are more or less sustainable), while also rendering those wholes partial and incomplete (because of the simplifications and abstractions that were necessary to make them comparable) (Callon and Law, 2005; Callon and Muniesa, 2005). These processes of abstraction and transformation enable the exercise of the calculative rationality that is so central to the tropes and metaphors of planning, based around measuring, weighing and balancing.

These decisions about how to cut the network – what is to be counted as relevant and important – shape the nature of the objects being studied. But the modernist framework of objective knowledge insists that these cuts were already there, given in the world: that the facts correspond directly to singular, pre-given objects. It thereby erases the traces of the process of cutting. This 'purifies' the knowledge produced into objective facts, and the objects produced into 'real things': 'black-boxing' them in a way that erases the messy traces of their sociomaterial production (Latour, 1987). Black-boxing is 'the way scientific and technical work is made invisible by its own success' (Latour, 1999: 304), concealing internal complexity and historical contingency behind an opaque veneer of naturalised simplicity.

All of this is a process of translation, of enabling one thing to stand in for another, so that we can say that one thing (such as a report back from a consultation event, or a Sustainability Appraisal report) is in some way equivalent to something else (such as the views of the community, or the relative sustainability of different strategies or sites) (Latour, 1995). Translations thus enable things to travel – to have effects beyond their original context. However, they also necessarily, to a greater or lesser extent, result in betrayals, because something is always lost and gained in translation (Latour, 1999; Galis and Lee, 2014). So, translation is also about transformation – about performing things in new ways rather than producing perfect equivalences.

Translations can become durable, but they are also precarious (Callon, 1999) – they are never done once and for all but require continuous enactment. They can, however, become more stable by being inscribed. Indeed, inscription is often a crucial stage of translation, in planning as much as in the natural sciences. Inscriptions – reports, maps, graphs, plans, surveys, templates, pictures, diagrams, software and so on – enable action at a distance. They give material form to particular translations (and not to others) and allow them to circulate, thus propagating particular interpretations of meanings and situations (Latour and Woolgar, 1979; Latour, 1987). The circulation of inscriptions across and between networks, and their capacity to combine with other inscriptions, enables their re-enactment. This strengthens the versions of reality that they represent and, as a corollary, weakens other versions.

Specific translations and inscriptions, while themselves contingent (that is, they could have been otherwise) become sedimented into ways of knowing and doing things, and come to limit which futures are apparently possible. Knowledge practices such as neighbourhood planning are therefore 'path dependent': assumptions, practices, materials and so on that become established early on in any one instance of neighbourhood planning, or in the career of neighbourhood planning as a practice, shape and constrain what can be done later (David, 1985; Arthur, 1994; Urry, 2004). An STS perspective helps to unpack these dependencies and to make visible the processes of assembling, enactment and translating that underpin them.

Co-production

This all suggests that 'the ways in which we know and represent the world (both nature and society) are inseparable from the ways in which we choose to live in it' (Jasanoff, 2004a: 2). Knowledge, and the ways we produce and represent it, act to stabilise and support particular ways of acting and being in the world. Specific institutional forms, social practices, norms, conventions and so on in turn act to support and stabilise particular ways of knowing. This process is always already ongoing and has consequences: it shapes what we (can) know and how we (can) live, as these consequences sediment down over time and become more stable, more apparently fixed, natural and given (Lovbrand, 2011). Sheila Jasanoff coined the term 'co-production' (Jasanoff, 2004a) to describe this relationship between how we know the world and how we live in the world, in a challenge to the everyday, positivist portrayal of science and society as strongly divided, separate realms with different aims, norms, methods, standards of success and sources of authority.

As discussed in the earlier section on situated knowledges, this rigid separation distinguishes 'nature, facts, objectivity, reason and policy from ... culture, values, subjectivity, emotion and politics' (Jasanoff, 2004a: 3).

In this 'standard' model, if the latter class of item interferes with the former this is seen as a failure of the system, an illegitimate blurring or crossing of boundaries between two spheres which must remain clearly divided in order for each to function properly according to their own norms and standards. Science will tell us objective facts about the world, and politics will decide how we live in the world, using those facts as necessary evidence to inform choices, and requesting specific scientific or technical information as necessary. Choices should be made on the best available evidence, which strongly implies that there are objective standards by which evidence can be measured. Political choices are often couched in terms of being courses of action that are a logical consequence of what the facts tell us – exemplified by the varied responses in different countries to the COVID-19 pandemic, which all claimed to be 'following the science'. There is therefore a flow of information between the two spheres of facts and values, knowledge and policy, but this model understands the factual (producing knowledge, gathering evidence) to remain separate from the value-laden (making choices), even though the value-laden relies heavily on the factual.

However, on a co-productionist reading, science and other methods of knowledge production are always jointly produced with particular ways in which society is ordered. It suggests that knowledge, and the processes of knowledge production, emerge together with the broader institutions, norms, conventions, identities and relationships that make them possible, and that they are mutually stabilising. Knowledge is produced through contingent and particular practices (that cut networks and enact assemblages in particular ways), and is also at the same time constitutive of those practices. Structures of knowledge help to produce, stabilise and/or change structures of power and authority, and vice versa. Matters of concern come to be understood as particular types of problems, about which particular types of inquiry are appropriate, and which will generate particular types of fact (Latour, 2004b). In turn, the facts produced shape what can be considered as appropriate responses to those facts (for example, what kind of problem they represent, and how that kind of problem can be tackled).

There are therefore social and material consequences of knowing in a particular way, seeing the world through a particular lens, and acting on it with a particular set of tools. And simultaneously, the specific ways that we categorise, manage and control the world shape what we can know and the kinds of knowledge and knowledge-making that are seen as legitimate. The ways we live shape the ways we know, and the ways we know shape the ways we live, and so on – the consequences of our past co-productions are our present and future co-productions. It is clearly not possible, on this account, to accept the rigid separations of fact/value, nature/culture and so on that underpin the modern Enlightenment imaginary. Drawing on STS resources therefore draws attention to neighbourhood planning as a knowledge practice, and to how the knowledge generated within that practice supports some ways of acting and organising and undermines others – and also how those ways of acting and organising support some forms of knowledge production and undermine others.

Multiplicity and ontological politics

To recap some of the key points that emerge from discussion of these difficult and complicated ideas: the processes of assembling and translating objects and facts enact the world in specific ways. Different methods of making knowledge make some things selectively visible, and in doing so necessarily make other things invisible by directing attention away from them or otherwise silencing them. John Law (2004) contends that, contra to our common-sense realist view of the world, when we generate representations of the world, we generate worlds along with them. When we attempt to find some sort of meaningful pattern in the messy complexity 'out there' – which we do when we make representations of the world, in academic research as much as in neighbourhood planning – our methods impose order, rather than discover it. So an STS sensibility 'suggest[s] a reality that is *done* or *enacted* rather than observed … Rather than being seen by a diversity of watching eyes while itself remaining untouched in the centre, reality is manipulated by means of various tools in the course of a diversity of practices' (Mol, 1999: 77, emphasis in original).

And if realities are enacted or performed through particular practices, this implies that different practices can make different realities: overlapping, entangled, distinct but not separate realities. The neighbourhood as experienced by a resident is not the same as the neighbourhood represented in the charts and maps of a planner, or the profit and loss accounts of a developer. But, from this perspective, these different neighbourhoods are not aspects of a single unitary object, but rather different versions of the object. They are different but related objects, objects-multiple, more than one but less than many (Mol, 2002).

On this account, the 'tools' used to represent a neighbourhood – such as land surveys, community surveys, spreadsheets, memories, conversations, maps, cameras, theodolites, GPS, the census, assessments of housing need and growth potential – actually help to bring into being different versions of the neighbourhood. These multiple realities depend upon, support and/ or undermine each other in complex ways. Worlds (or neighbourhoods) cannot be made on a whim. Realities require constant re-enactment; they do not just get built and stay built. They are precarious even when stable and dominating. They take a lot of work both to make and to un-make. Not just any worlds are possible – the material world resists and accommodates our engagements with it (Hacking, 1999), and 'there is a backdrop of realities that cannot be wished away' (Law, 2004: 31). Nevertheless, from this perspective, realities emerge out of our practices: the world is enacted in the practices through which we interact with it, and different practices enact different worlds.

Classic STS studies by Ann-Marie Mol (2002) and Ingunn Moser (2008) have shown how diseases (atherosclerosis and Alzheimer's, respectively) are enacted differently in different locations and through different practices (for example, in Moser's study, through an international Alzheimer's patients' movement; a medical textbook; laboratory science; daily care practices; an advertisement for anti-dementia medication; general medical practice; parliamentary politics; and a conference on dementia). The practices in each of these locations produce different versions of the disease. All the different versions hang together in a variety of ways, but are not the same, single object. The different versions of the disease that emerge in different locations require different kinds of response. I suggest that the same is true of the neighbourhood. The specific neighbourhood that is enacted through specific practices of evidence production enables some specific responses to be made in policy and constrains others. A neighbourhood enacted differently, through different or additional knowledge practices, would require different responses.

Processes such as neighbourhood planning thus do not just produce plans and evidence, but also produce identities for individuals, communities and places. They produce subjects as well as objects. In planning practice it is usually assumed that 'the community' has something to say, as an aggregated or fragmented set of individuals. But from an STS perspective those individuals and communities are not just given, with an opinion that is fixed and that can be straightforwardly extracted. Rather, the kinds of knowledge that they can express – the kinds of worlds that they can represent – depend on the framings of the process, on the kinds of identities and issues that are created by and for them through that process (Marres, 2005).

So, the business of producing knowledge or evidence is not a distinct domain isolated from the rest of social and cultural life. Instead, it 'both embeds and is embedded in social practices, identities, norms, conventions, discourses, instruments and institutions' (Jasanoff, 2004a: 3). There are social and material consequences of knowing the world in a specific way and acting on it with a specific set of tools. If knowledge practices shape realities as well as representations of realities, questions about knowledge and evidence are not just empirical, but also political. The versions of reality – the neighbourhoods – produced by different knowledge practices may be more or less desirable from different perspectives.

(Neighbourhood) planning policy can only respond to the world made visible to it through its evidence base. So which versions of the world are enacted through that process, through which practices, using which tools and techniques, is a matter of vital, if constrained, choice. And this is a highly political choice, despite this aspect of plan-making tending to be presented as being before, or beyond, politics. From an STS perspective, this is the case for all knowledge practices. The very idea of being beyond the political is an impossibility. So given this, it is critically important to draw attention to and to reflect on the versions of reality that are being enacted through processes of evidence production, and those that are concealed or suppressed, and how this is done.

Ontological politics, then, is about the power to define and contest what there is in the world, and what its relevant and important characteristics are. After this, the 'conventional' politics about what we should do in response to these facts is highly constrained. If things are excluded from becoming evidence, they are excluded from policy. In other words, it suggests that 'ontology' – what there is in the world, the baseline conditions of possibility – is not given beforehand, but rather is in part generated through our practices of knowing, describing and analysing. Our knowledge practices do not merely describe pre-existing conditions of possibility, they are actively implicated in generating those conditions. If this is the case, then, at the very least, there are choices to be made about which versions of neighbourhood (for example) we can and should be bringing to presence, enacting and making visible. There are questions about which versions matter, to whom, and why – and who gets to decide, and how. There are questions about the ways in which these versions relate to each other: whether and how they might support or undermine each other. And there are also questions about what the implications of 'doing' different versions of neighbourhood might be for different subjects (like planners, or residents, or homeless people, or developers) and other objects (like local plans, or national housing targets, or adjacent neighbourhoods). These are the questions of ontological politics.

The 'turn to care'

Given that what we choose as our objects of study and the ways that we study them have the kind of implications outlined earlier, there has been a recent upsurge in STS research and beyond revolving around the theme of care. This 'turn to care' (Lindén and Lydahl, 2021) relates both to the care which scholars enact in their relations with the worlds they study, and that which circulates within those worlds. It requires research to be 'critical and attentive to the situated workings of care in the world' and ask 'questions about the practices of care in sites not traditionally associated with care' (Martin et al, 2015: 627).

Local community care for place is one of the central assumptions underpinning the rationale for neighbourhood planning. However, as Martin et al (2015) note, care is hard to pin down. It is necessary for life but multivalent and extremely problematic once one tries try to define, legislate for, measure or evaluate it. Care for place can be of vital importance to self-identity, wellbeing, and for flourishing places (Knez, 2005; Manzo, 2005; Hernandez et al, 2007; Church et al, 2014), and is a central driver for community action such as neighbourhood planning (Devine-Wright, 2009; Devine-Wright and Clayton, 2010; Vidal et al, 2013). Although there is an established literature on place attachment and place identity from an environmental psychology perspective (Lewicka, 2011; Devine-Wright, 2015), there is little work on the ways in which local residents enact care for place through the practices of spatial planning (Metzger, 2014a). One aim of this book is thus to pay more careful attention to the cared-for dimension of place in spatial planning (see also Yuille [2021], where I develop ideas about the caring components of neighbourhood planning further).

Planning scholars, like planners in practice, tend to have an aversion to the emotional and the affective, with a few notable exceptions (such as Davies, 2001a; Hoch, 2006; Porter et al, 2012; Baum, 2015). As something of a bastion of positivism, planning tends to insist on 'objective' facts, and shy away from the 'taint' of subjectivity. The difficulties inherent in making 'care for place' an object of evidence frequently lead to its neglect in a reductionist, positivist culture dominated by the crude but practical assumption that 'if you can't measure it, it can't (be shown to) matter'.

Martin et al, drawing on Lorraine Code (2015), call attention to one particular formulation of care that positions it as the rhetorical opposite of knowledge, underpinned by the Enlightenment norm that affective involvement can only muddy rational knowing. Those who care are disqualified from producing objective knowledge: 'to be an advocate is to be partial and thus to compromise or taint knowledge claims' (Martin et al, 2015: 630). If planning policy must be based on robust evidence, and caring compromises one's ability to produce such evidence, this suggests a paradox at the heart of neighbourhood planning. How can neighbourhood planning empower communities 'if caring and knowing, or caring and clout, are opposed' (Martin et al, 2015: 631)?

This cuts to the heart of the previously discussed, unspoken but problematic assumptions about knowledge production which dominate public policy spheres, including the English planning system. Neighbourhood planning, by insisting on the relevance of the affective dimensions of people's relations with place alongside the cognitive, appears to offer a way towards more inclusive planning practices (Bradley, 2017a). Like neighbourhood planning, the loose research programme around care in STS also re-entwines knowledge with care: rather than declaring them as incompatible, as in the dominant model of objective knowledge, it posits them as inseparable (Code, 2015). It therefore provides a critical tool with which to analyse the implied shift generated by neighbourhood planning in whose knowledge can count and how it can be constituted.

Many authors draw on Maria Puig de la Bellacasa's article 'Matters of care in technoscience: assembling neglected things' (2011) as the wellspring for this new current. In it, she picks up on Bruno Latour's worry that STS critique has 'run out of steam' (Latour, 2004b) because it has become corrosive, merely deconstructing knowledge practices without reconstructing anything in their place, leading to cynicism about and disbelief in objective knowledge. In response to this worry, Latour proposed thinking and talking about things (assemblages and the knowledge produced about them) as 'matters of concern'.

'Matters of concern' would explicitly include all the social and material elements that constituted those things, unlike 'matters of fact', which, he argues, are created precisely by stripping away the evidence of their production. This would, he hoped, clarify that the role of STS analysis was not to deny the reality of the facts, but rather to render them *more* real by tracing the (contingent) pathways that lead from the complex sociomaterial world to the abstract simplifications that represent it. This would in turn enable a more inclusive vision of knowledge and its production. For Puig de la Bellacasa, the affective connotations of 'concern' are helpful, but she finds Latour's overall formulation – a move to respect all views – as shrinking too far back from the critical edge that is necessary in a world of inequalities and injustice. She proposes drawing attention to care as a means of avoiding the pitfalls that Latour identified, while retaining a critical perspective that is also geared to generating new caring relations.

Puig de la Bellacasa's paper rehearses many of the central concerns of the STS sensibility outlined in this chapter: that '[w]ays of studying and representing things can have world-making effects' (2011: 86); that facts and things are 'not just objects but knots of social and political interests' (2011: 86) and that 'interests and other affectively animated forces – such as concern and care – are intimately entangled in the ongoing material remaking of the world' (2011: 87). She agrees with Latour that '[t]he purpose of showing how things are assembled is not to dismantle things, not undermine the reality of matters of fact with critical suspicion ... [but] to enrich and affirm their reality by adding further articulations' (2011: 89). She argues that where Latour's formulation of 'matters of concern' helps to resist the bifurcation of nature (into subjective and objective), thinking in terms of 'matters of care' also resists the bifurcation of consciousness (into affective and rational) – and, as set out earlier in this chapter, both of these dichotomies are strongly present in planning practice. Puig de la Bellacasa also emphasises the active and multivalent nature of care as a practice, signifying 'an affective state, a material vital doing, and an ethico-political obligation' (2011: 90). Each of these aspects is highly relevant to neighbourhood planning – the emotional state of caring for place, the material work of care (through making a plan), and decisions and beliefs about what should be cared for and why. Studying (with) care leads us to ask not just 'who benefits?' from a process, decision or structure (Star, 1990), but who cares, for what, how, and why – and how could things be different if they generated care differently?

However, care cannot be taken as a self-evident good (Metzger, 2014a; Murphy, 2015). It has a dark side – it is a selective means of drawing attention to some things, which necessarily requires withdrawing it from others; and it is already embedded and circulating in the worlds we wish to study, often associated with domination, exploitation and inequalities. Valorising care for place in one neighbourhood by one specific group of people may lead to injustice and harm to other people and/or places, for example, by excluding the knowledge of people who care for this place in a different way, damaging other places whose residents cannot or will not demonstrate care in legitimised ways, or excluding potential future residents or other interests from consideration.

Crucially, the STS turn to care requires that we 'pay attention to the workings and consequences of our "semiotic technologies"' and their 'consequences in the shaping of possible worlds' (Puig de la Bellacasa, 2012: 199). As well as paying attention to how care is manifested or marginalised in the situations we study, we must also be attentive to the ways in which we ourselves make caring relations more or less possible. By choosing particular objects of study, defining and representing them in particular ways, and using particular tools and techniques to produce knowledge about them, we are doing ontological politics. The turn to care urges us to do so in ways that foster caring relations and which strengthen the conditions of possibility for a more caring world.

Conclusion

Neighbourhood planning presents itself as a site which is appropriate for analysis using STS resources. It is underpinned by the principle of letting the people who know and care for a place participate in its governance, legitimising the presence of subjectivity and values in an arena where the power to act has traditionally been legitimised by appeals to objectivity and fact. Despite having been in existence for over a decade, neighbourhood planning is still not yet stabilised as a practice, in that there is still substantial indefiniteness about its boundaries and possibilities. Reforms to the planning system proposed in 2020 and still unresolved at the time of writing appear likely to secure the place of neighbourhood planning within the system, but unlikely to provide any further clarity on these issues, and indeed have the potential to unsettle them further.

Neighbourhood planning is a process that revolves around the production, interpretation, presentation and validation of knowledge. It brings together a variety of expert knowledges – of planners, economists, demographers, landscape architects and so on – with deliberative democracy, public participation and diverse practices of knowing and valuing. It holds the potential for making various things visible and invisible in different ways, and STS analysis may cast some new light on the mechanisms through which this happens. It also promises to put local communities in control, in theory valorising their claims to knowledge rather than marginalising them as 'polluted' knowledge-value hybrids, and consigning experts to be 'on tap, not on top'. As a practice and an object of study it resonates strongly with STS interest in participation, knowledge, care and ontological politics.

As researchers, planners or citizens, we have to fight for the value of facts in a world where facts and expertise are increasingly disputed and depreciated. This is a particularly crucial point to make in an era when UK Cabinet ministers can claim that we've 'had enough of experts' (Mance, 2016) and the president of the US and his spokespeople can assert 'alternative facts' and 'fake news' solely on the basis of personal authority (Swaine, 2017). In an era when a future UK prime minister could win a major constitutional referendum, in part, by repeatedly making claims that the UK Statistics Authority branded as 'a clear misuse of official statistics' (Norgrove, 2017). When the entire world is struggling to grapple with the twin crises of climate and COVID-19. The facts, the knowledge about the world generated by scientific and other rigorous methodologies, have arguably never been more important.

But we also have to widen our understanding of what facts are, and deepen our understanding of how they are made, while at the same time fighting back against the idea that we can all have our own facts. There can be – there always are – multiple facts/facts-multiple about any given situation, produced by engaging with that situation through different practices, from different positions. There is never just one logical or correct simplification of the world. And different kinds of facts will be suitable for different kinds of purpose. But this does not justify alternative facts in the 'Trumpian' sense: facts-multiple do not make fake news real. While many knowledge claims about a situation can be right, including apparently incommensurable ones, claims can also be demonstrably wrong. An STS approach requires that all knowledge claims and the processes by which they are arrived at are engaged with fairly and critically – the sort of approach under which 'alternative facts' wither and die. But the sort of approach under which facts-multiple can be fostered, and better dialogue between technical expert knowledge and lay/local/peripheral knowledge promoted.

This is important because the knowledge, the evidence that we produce makes some things visible in specific ways, and conceals others altogether. It shapes realities in particular ways. Policy and decisions can only be made on the basis of what has been made visible. And because there is never just one logical or correct simplification of the world, just one way to produce or present the evidence, then how knowledge is produced, and by whom, and using what practices, is of vital importance. If certain knowledge-making practices are a priori marginalised, then the knowledge that they produce cannot be considered in policy making or decision taking. Certain versions of the world will not receive consideration. This is the stuff of ontological politics – the politics of what there is, and what can be said to matter, in the world. If the versions of neighbourhood that communities want to plan for are not being enacted through neighbourhood planning practices, then new, innovative, creative ways must be found that enable the enactment of those versions.

However, there are major risks with attempting to operationalise such innovative approaches in an established practice such as planning. In the first place, innovation is not effortless. Generating new and creative ways of producing and presenting knowledge is no easy task – especially as the very need for such innovative approaches suggests that the knowledge sought is not easily articulated or captured, at least not in ways that will be considered as legitimate evidence. It can be difficult, it can take time, and it can take resources, even in the most open of conditions, which is a significant burden for unpaid amateurs and overstretched professionals alike.

But conditions are not that open – there is an existing planning imaginary, in which established norms and conventions operate which are, at best, very difficult to extend or diverge from. How things are done becomes how things must be done, and ways of doing things that are 'merely' custom and practice acquire the weight of definitive rules. Indeed, many of those norms and conventions exist for good reason, even if their operation has unintended consequences. I am not for a moment arguing that planning policy should not be based on robust evidence. I am merely suggesting that the definition of what might be considered robust evidence can, and should, be widened. But the tendency of current practice to reproduce itself means that there is a strong force of inertia pushing back against any such widening. And this is even more the case for outsiders to the system, non-experts such as neighbourhood planners, who can easily be persuaded by their expert advisers that the way that they have done things before is the way that things must be done now.

Any process that departs from the tried-and-tested norm is also more vulnerable to challenge. As is frequently pointed out, neighbourhood plans and the evidence that supports them must be able to withstand challenges at appeal and in the courts. They need to stand up to attack in judicial and quasi-judicial settings, under fire from professionals who are highly skilled in the art of finding vulnerabilities. And any newly created assemblage, any new way of doing things, will tend to be weaker than one that is established, tried and tested. The dangers of being more creative, of reflecting more fully the neighbourhoods of experience that communities want to plan for, are very real.

To restate a key point, I am not arguing that 'anything goes'. I am arguing, rather, that everything should be critically appraised. Means of producing and presenting knowledge should not be automatically accepted or rejected without working through what it is they represent, and how, and how that fits with the needs and ambitions of the neighbourhood, as defined by the neighbourhood. I am also arguing that there is a need for neighbourhood planners, and the professionals that support and assess them, to embrace more creative and innovative methods in producing evidence and policy – and that resources drawn from STS can play a useful role in enabling that to happen. But I acknowledge the need for a great deal of care in doing so, in the face of a practice that is permeated with conservative tendencies and a culture that is increasingly litigious (Parker et al, 2017a).

4

Neighbourhoods, identity and legitimacy

> The neighbourhood has emerged as a precocious new actor in the contested production of space.
>
> Bradley et al (2017: 71–72)

Introduction

Neighbourhood planning is framed by its promoters as a straightforward transfer of power from state to existing communities. In this chapter I examine the experience of two case studies in order to problematise this framing, drawing on some of the approaches outlined in the previous chapter to ask questions about identity, representation and legitimacy. As planning scholar Quintin Bradley observes in the opening quotation, 'the neighbourhood' has become a significant participant in the world of English planning. And as he says, this 'precocious actor' is *new*: it is not simply the case that 'the neighbourhood' is straightforwardly equivalent to the community to which the state is supposedly devolving power. This chapter thus engages with one of the central dilemmas in participatory experiments in democracy – in the absence of formal representative democracy, what legitimises the actions of citizens or groups that claim, or are implied, to represent others? How do they come to be legitimate intermediaries between community and state? And, given that the landscape and experience of participatory democracy is diverse and fragmented, is there anything that can be learned from the situated construction of legitimacy in neighbourhood planning that might be made to travel to other locations – and vice versa?

In this chapter I describe how neighbourhood planning produces two new, mutually dependent 'actors': local communities as 'neighbourhoods' and neighbourhood planning groups (NPGs) as their spokespeople. I then focus on the fluidity and multiplicity of the NPGs' identity, tracing their performance of three distinct identities or versions of themselves in relation to the neighbourhood.[1] I draw attention to the ways in which each identity confers a different kind of legitimacy on the NPG, by enacting different relations with the neighbourhood through different kinds of knowledge practices and modes of representation. However, there are also tensions and conflicts between the different identities. I suggest that holding these identities together in different ways will lead to different enactments of neighbourhood – will make different worlds visible to be acted upon. I then consider the ways in which the enactment of these multiple identities can also be seen in the other modes of participatory democracy described in Chapter 1.

Much governmental discourse and much of the literature uses 'the community' and 'the neighbourhood' as interchangeable terms in relation to neighbourhood planning. However, the referents of these terms are slippery. While 'the community' may refer to some, or all, of the people resident in a given area, 'the neighbourhood' may refer to either these social actors, or to the physical territory and features within the plan area's boundaries, or to the heterogeneous, sociomaterial assemblage of the two. These relational social and material overtones of 'neighbourhood' make it especially fitting as a term for participatory land use planning. I tend to use 'neighbourhood' when referring to the communities of neighbourhood planning for three reasons: to draw attention to this multivalency, this sense of neighbourhood as both people and place; to highlight that 'the neighbourhood' is a new and specific instantiation of community; and to emphasise that from a Science and Technology Studies (STS) perspective, to speak of a geographical community is necessarily also to speak of the materiality of the territory which defines it – that it is the specific relations between people and place that generate specific neighbourhoods.

Empowering or enacting the neighbourhood?

In neighbourhood planning, and more generally in the wider turn towards citizen participation and localism, 'the local' is lauded as the scale at which competing priorities can best be resolved, and 'the community' are the people who can best achieve that resolution, if appropriately empowered to do so. Local knowledge (implicitly understood as deriving from lived experience) notionally becomes privileged. But who exactly are these communities? Can they be as easily and universally identified and subsequently empowered as suggested by the governmental framings discussed in previous chapters, and illustrated in Figure 4.1?

National policy and public statements indicate that 'the social and spatial imaginary that underpins parish and Neighbourhood Planning entails the idea of a relatively homogeneous, stable, identifiable and self-conscious "local community"' (Colomb, 2017: 127). This suggests that the government's imaginary of neighbourhood planning ignores the uneven distribution of time, skills and resources, which can be as pronounced within geographical communities as between them. Some communities are empowered, others are not (Figure 4.2).

But more fundamentally, this official discourse tends to assume that there is a pre-existing, stable entity with fairly well-defined characteristics that

Figure 4.1: Discourse of empowering communities through neighbourhood planning

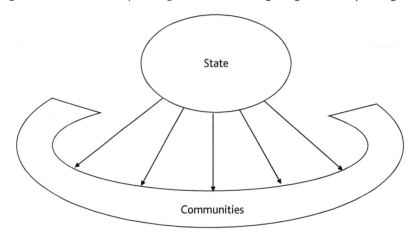

Figure 4.2: Uneven distribution of powers between communities

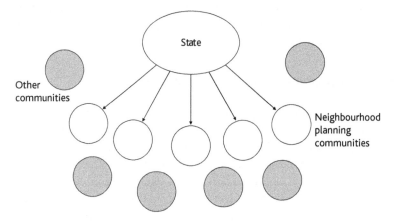

is identifiable as 'the community', to which power is to be devolved. This entity is also assumed to have an already-existing stock of knowledge about, attachments to and desires for the neighbourhood. However, the incipient NPG itself gets to propose the boundaries of its plan area, and therefore of its neighbourhood. This can be contentious, and is always contestable. In both of my cases (as in many neighbourhood plan areas), existing administrative boundaries were eventually adopted – but other boundaries were considered, debated and could realistically have been chosen. This would have enacted different neighbourhoods, counting in and out different people, places and relations between the two. This provides the first clear indication that the neighbourhood is actively assembled rather than being the kind of pre-given entity that governmental discourse suggests: that neighbourhood planning produces, not just describes, the neighbourhoods it refers to.

Claire Colomb draws attention to the 'ambiguities, tensions and conflicts that can emerge in the process of defining what and who is the neighbourhood' (2017: 134): it is not just out there as a pre-given entity. Likewise, the knowledge, values, attitudes and preferences of the neighbourhood are not already simply in existence, waiting to be drawn upon, but are generated in relation to particular possibilities (Waterton and Wynne, 1998). Nortje Marres (2005, 2012) argues that far from existing 'out there', communities are called into existence by being confronted with particular issues and by specific material encounters – for example, with participatory practices like neighbourhood planning. That is to say, the particular version of a community that responds to a particular set of circumstances is itself in part a response to those circumstances. Situated differently, the composition and characteristics – the identity – of the community would also be different. This suggests that specific communities are produced as an effect of neighbourhood planning in a more profound way than the simple drawing of boundaries. Sue Brownill has explored this process of coming into being by the 'folding in' of various actors and interests into a newly emergent space with specific reference to neighbourhood planning: 'neighbourhoods come to be "assembled" through these shifting and contentious relations [between] ... people, discourses, policies, objects, laws and the administrative measures that constitute them, and a variety of political actors' (2017a: 148).

For some scholars it is precisely this performativity, this production of a new collective identity, a new polity, that makes neighbourhood planning exciting (Bradley, 2015). Outside of neighbourhood planning, community involvement in planning tends to engage citizens as aggregations of individual commentators on expert-produced plans, and collective community action is often portrayed as obstructive, self-serving and/or 'Not In My Back Yard'. Neighbourhood planning generates the neighbourhood as a new collective identity, a 'notionally autonomous locally constituted body' (Bradley, 2015: 103) which can choose its own boundaries, membership and issues. This collective becomes an actor in its own right: it is precisely action as a collective that is empowered.

National policy, guidance and associated texts and discourse enact 'the neighbourhood' with certain characteristics. It is enacted as a knowledgeable entity: the collective experiential knowledge it can mobilise from within itself is acknowledged as being the appropriate beacon to guide local development, within the constraints of higher-level policy. It is enacted as a collective that cares: shared caring and affective relations with place are fundamental elements underpinning the very idea of neighbourhood planning, whereas in the planning system in general such affective relations are dismissed as irrelevant (Bradley, 2017a). It is enacted as a capable entity: as having the capacities necessary to perform the complex task of producing a development plan underpinned by that knowledge and care – including the capacity to resolve internal disputes. It is therefore a very specific, and novel, instantiation of 'community', with a specific orientation to the territory which establishes its boundaries, and the physical, material features within those boundaries. And how these enactments play out in practice will vary depending on the situated conditions of each individual emergent neighbourhood.

Government policy and publicity tends to imply that this collective actor incorporates all the residents of the plan area (setting aside the issue of how that area is determined). In theory, they are all entitled to contribute to the plan, and they are all entitled to vote in the final referendum. They are all in principle members of the new polity. But in practice, of course, not everyone in the area will be involved, and those who are involved will be so to different degrees. A relatively small group actively do the work of producing the plan: the NPGs (see Figure 4.3). They, not the neighbourhood at large, are the ones that take up the newly legislated powers. They are also a significant new actor. Bradley, drawing on Della Porta, describes these two actors respectively as the association (the NPG), which articulates claims about issues of public concern (including both claims about who 'the public' is and what concerns them) and about potential resolutions to those issues, and the assembly (the neighbourhood), which is the imagined constituency of the association, the subject of these representative claims (Bradley, 2020). These two actors are often conflated in governmental statements and in the media. However, while they are clearly not the same, they are mutually dependent: the specific instantiation of community that is 'the neighbourhood' could not exist without an NPG actively developing a

Figure 4.3: Neighbourhoods and neighbourhood planning groups

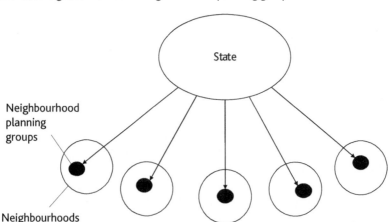

neighbourhood plan, and the NPG could not exist without the instantiation of 'the neighbourhood' as a new polity. The creation of these two new actors creates new boundaries, alignments, inclusions and exclusions. They emerge together and stabilise each other. The NPG effectively becomes the spokesperson for the neighbourhood (Callon, 1999), and its legitimacy to act depends on the relations between the two.

Legitimacy, identity and relationality

Analysing situations analogous to neighbourhood planning, Connelly (2011) concluded that the defining characteristic of such new, localist forms of governance is their reliance on a variety of different forms of representative legitimacy. In the absence of (or alongside) formal democratic representation, new forms of 'situated legitimacy' are required, and we need to understand how these forms of legitimacy are produced and interact (Connelly et al, 2006; Leino and Peltomaa, 2012). This chapter, then, explores the ways in which the specific relations that are enacted between neighbourhood and NPG legitimise the NPG as the spokesperson for the neighbourhood. No one has voted for the NPG to make a plan that will affect the whole neighbourhood. If this is an instance of participatory democracy, what makes the NPG a legitimate actor?

Several authors have interrogated this crucial relationship between NPGs and their neighbourhoods in terms of their situated legitimacy. Davoudi and Cowie (2013) contrast the claims to democratic legitimacy of Neighbourhood Forums with town and parish councils, which formally represent their communities as elected bodies. However, while town/parish councils retain formal ownership of neighbourhood plans in their area, they do not often directly take on the powers of neighbourhood planning – this is done by the NPG. Even where NPGs are constituted as sub-committees of town/parish councils, bequeathing them the legacy of representative democracy, they may develop distinct identities and outlooks from their 'parent' councils and even come to see themselves as quite separate entities, considerably weakening this claim (Parker et al, 2018). This dynamic was succinctly illustrated by a consultation response submitted by Wroston NPG to their Local Planning Authority (LPA) in July 2017, which began: 'I write on behalf of the Wroston Neighbourhood Planning Group. Whilst we are a sub-committee of the Parish Council our views are not necessarily theirs. I understand that the Parish Council will be responding separately.'

Furthermore, the essence of neighbourhood planning is as a participatory process: a new form of governance that moves beyond representative democracy even while operating alongside it. The intention to bring planning closer to the people inherently requires even NPGs constituted as town or parish council sub-committees to go beyond a nominal (and often highly flawed [Tewdwr-Jones, 1998; Gallent and Robinson, 2013]) formal claim to representativeness. The requirements on NPGs to not only produce plans and evidence that can withstand independent examination and sometimes hostile attack from well-resourced vested interests (Parker et al, 2016), but also to engage widely and deeply with the community and for the subsequent plan to be approved in a local referendum, necessitate recourse to hybrid forms of representation and legitimacy that extend beyond electoral democracy.

Other debates have also been raised about legitimacy in neighbourhood planning. As discussed in previous chapters, some commentators have argued that NPGs are little more than new vehicles to legitimise the imposition of externally decided objectives on neighbourhoods (Haughton and Allmendinger, 2013), while others suggest they will empower the already relatively privileged within communities (Wills, 2016). Parker and colleagues have pointed to the powerful influences that external actors such as LPAs, consultants and independent examiners have over the process, and the limiting effect this may have on neighbourhood ownership of plans (Parker et al, 2014, 2015, 2016). Bradley discusses the 'unsettled accommodation' (2015: 98) between participatory, representative and market models of democracy in neighbourhood planning. Sturzaker and Gordon (2017) highlight the tensions between different claims to legitimacy within neighbourhood planning, arising from direct democratic voting, direct citizen participation, and formal or informal representation.

These authors all engage with important issues about legitimacy in neighbourhood planning and the relations between NPGs and neighbourhoods. However, their discussions all appear to consider the identities (and hence the knowledge, values and preferences) of NPGs and neighbourhoods to be definite, fixed, stable and exogenous to the practices of neighbourhood planning. Adopting an STS sensibility offers an alternative understanding of these identities as fluid and temporary, rather than stable and permanent; multiple and overlapping, rather than singular and unitary; relational rather than atomistic; and continually in the process of being made, rather than simply existing (Mol, 2002). I will use this understanding to show that the practices of neighbourhood planning produce three different social and spatial imaginaries of neighbourhood-and-NPG. These give rise to three different collective identities for the NPG, in terms of how they relate to these versions of neighbourhood.

I suggest that each identity is able to draw on a specific source of authority. Each identity thus makes a crucial contribution to the NPGs' situated legitimacy, which relies on a combination of all three sources. Analysing NPGs in this way provides a new perspective on the practices through which legitimacy is achieved in neighbourhood planning. It may also contribute to new ways of understanding other experiments in democracy that rely on multiple forms of representation and participation. And, importantly, it may also open up possibilities for intervention that can help address some of the concerns raised in the literature about these experiments, such as their openness to elite capture or to post-political co-option of resistance.

Multiple identities: 'in', 'of' and 'beyond' the neighbourhood

From an STS perspective, identities should not be thought of in terms of isolated, atomistic individuals, but as being developed in relation to the social and material world around us. Rather than being fixed or pre-given, they are continuously performed through mundane interactions in everyday life. In this sense, identity is something that is *done*, and is continually being done, rather than something which simply *is*. This should not be taken to imply that these performances are deliberate (although in some cases they may be), but simply that identities are continually in the process of being made, of being enacted. And they are enacted not just by the subject of that identity, but also by others – through personal interactions, policies, laws, descriptions, practices, institutions, norms, conventions and so on. So individual identities are fundamentally relational, as well as always in the process of being done. The same can be said about the identities of groups, institutions and even material objects (such as neighbourhoods).

An NPG's identity, as a collective actor, is defined primarily in relation to the neighbourhood for which it is a spokesperson: that is its raison d'être. This identity is performed, or enacted, in a wide range of situations and locations, including the NPGs' own meetings, casual conversations, meetings with other actors, at public consultation events, and in all the work the NPG do in preparing a plan. It is also enacted in the inscriptions the NPGs produce – such as draft plans, minutes, emails, publicity, evidence documents – and in the inscriptions, discourses and practices of other actors (such as national and local government, neighbourhood planning support organisations, consultants, publics). However, in both case studies examined here, the NPGs were not enacted as a singular, unified identity, but as an identity-multiple.

Both NPGs performed the same three strikingly different identities – different versions of themselves – in relation to their neighbourhoods. While each identity was performed discretely, at discrete moments, their boundaries blurred as the NPGs slid backwards and forwards between them. While only one identity – one version of the NPG – may be enacted at any one time, 'the' NPG existed continuously in this fluid multiplicity. Different versions or identities were particularly associated with different aspects of plan preparation, so there were shifts in the relative dominance of one identity over others over a long timescale. But the NPGs also shifted between them on much shorter timescales: it would be a very unusual meeting in which all three identities were not enacted multiple times. Broadly speaking, and as illustrated in Figure 4.4, these identities could be defined as being:

- *In* the neighbourhood: socially, affectively and materially embedded in the neighbourhood – embodied and entangled in a dense meshwork of sociomaterial relations and experiences.
- *Of* the neighbourhood: arising out of the neighbourhood in order to be able to face it and engage with it reflexively on the one hand, and to mediate between it and other actors on the other.
- *Beyond* the neighbourhood: separate, different and detached from the neighbourhood, with experiences and knowledge that are distinct from the wider neighbourhood's.

Each identity relied on and enacted a different kind of material relation with the neighbourhood (embedded, engaged or detached) and generated different types of knowledge about it, by interacting with it through different kinds of practice. Consequently, each enabled different kinds of representation of neighbourhood – different versions of neighbourhood – to appear in the plan and its evidence base. Each identity thus afforded a different source of situated legitimacy: a different way of relating to and representing the neighbourhood. Being an embedded and embodied part of the neighbourhood involved the NPGs portraying themselves as an extension of it, enabling them to legitimately represent its interests as a result of their deep and intimate association with it. Being engaged but impartial conveyors of the neighbourhood's views and knowledge involved portraying the experiences of their neighbours in a disciplined and ordered form, enabling them to legitimately represent their interests as a result of robust consultation and engagement processes. Being detached and distanced from the neighbourhood involved portraying it through the use of technical devices and the production of inscriptions associated with expertise, enabling them to legitimately represent its interests as a result of the production and application of credibly objective evidence.

Each of these sources of authority was necessary for the NPGs to be enacted as legitimate spokespersons for the neighbourhood. As a new form of localist governance, unable to rely on the authority of electoral representation, they need to generate situated legitimacy in other, hybrid ways. Performing these

Figure 4.4: The multiple identities of neighbourhood planning groups

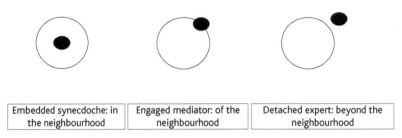

Embedded synecdoche: in the neighbourhood	Engaged mediator: of the neighbourhood	Detached expert: beyond the neighbourhood

identities in combination enabled the NPGs to come to what Chilvers and Kearnes describe as 'the often partial accommodation of competing forms of moral, political and epistemological authority' (2016: 1), achieving difficult and shifting balances between expert knowledge, popular representation and personal connection.

As each identity is only able to draw on one of these sources of authority (all of which are only partial sources of legitimation), it was necessary for the NPGs to make these three versions of themselves hang together somehow as a durable identity-multiple (see Figure 4.5). But as the ways of being in the world implied by each version are not compatible, it was also necessary to maintain them as separate and distinct. However, the different versions of NPG intersected and interfered with each other, sometimes supporting and sometimes undermining the others. The ways in which they are combined – for example, whether one becomes dominant and another suppressed – determines the extent to which each associated version of neighbourhood can be made visible in the plan or in evidence, and therefore the extent to which it can be dealt with in policy.

In the following sections I explore these identities or versions of NPGs as they were performed, following the practices and speech of the NPGs themselves. I then go on to consider how the tensions between identities play out in practice, and how identities, knowledges, modes of representation and types of legitimacy map onto each other. This approach serves to further illuminate and problematise other reflections on the plurality of representations and 'representativenesses' in neighbourhood planning (Davoudi and Cowie, 2013; Bradley, 2015; Sturzaker and Gordon, 2017) and in localist governance more widely (Connelly, 2011; Leino and Peltomaa,

Figure 4.5: Neighbourhood planning groups: an identity-multiple

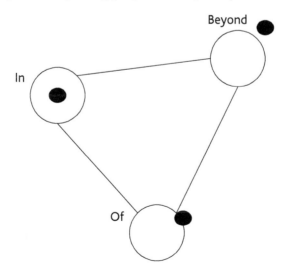

2012). The chapter finishes by considering how this type of analysis might be applied in other sites of participatory democracy.

'In' the neighbourhood

FIELDNOTES
Wroston
May 2015

The meeting finishes early, so I join Simon and Elliot for a pint in the Anvil & Hammer down the road. Conversation drifts and meanders, but what comes out most strongly is the deep sense of connectedness that both have with the village, physically and socially. They discuss in great detail who lived in which (named) houses and when, prompted by discussing when Elliot had come to the village; and this leads them in and out of other snatches of village life and times and stories: the Millennium New Year's Eve and other NYEs; the different landlords at the pub and their quirks; buildings and the works done to them to repair, restore, replace, and extend; specific detailed walks that would take them by particular trees, hedges, bits of rivers, and views; all of which make up shared reference points and which both provide and enable the construction of shared meanings. They are deeply embedded here, although both are relative newcomers compared to people like Owen, Tom and Anne who have lived here all their lives (Elliot arrived in 1998). Their lives, families, friends and identities are all deeply entwined with their sense of place.

As Brownill notes, '[t]he government's perception of neighbourhood planning is based on a spatial imaginary that sees the neighbourhood as homogeneous, persuadable and consensual' (2017b: 34). It provides no sense that either the neighbourhood might be fragmented, *or* that it is not the neighbourhood en masse who will take up these powers. In this imaginary, the people doing the planning (the NPG) *are* the neighbourhood: they are a *synecdoche*, a part standing in figuratively, practically and unproblematically for the whole. The NPG is enacted as being wholly immersed in the neighbourhood, saturated with experience of it, intimately connected to it socially and materially.

While this collective identity is the most prominent in governmental discourse about neighbourhood planning, it was seldom present in the 'formal' discourse of the NPGs themselves, such as meeting minutes, evidence documents and meetings with LPA officers. Indeed, as I explore in more depth in Chapter 5, NPG members often took care in such situations to conceal any traces of their own subjectivity and material experience, to avoid any suggestion that they could speak as or for the neighbourhood as a whole. But despite the relative absence of this identity from their formal discourse, it was constantly present around the edges, alongside, beneath and beyond this discourse, flavouring their everyday, apparently insignificant actions, conversations and decisions, the things that they do not (have to) think about, write down, or justify, the implicit and taken for granted. The fieldnote extract at the start of this section gestures towards this kind of shared spatial imaginary: the 'socially held assemblages of stories, images, memories and experiences of places' (Davoudi et al, 2018: 101) that embed and are embedded in their neighbourhood planning.

In both sites, the 'chatter' in and around the meetings (before, after, and as explanation or digression while they are going on) revealed the in-depth knowledge of people and place that the groups shared. It generated a powerful sense of being enmeshed in these neighbourhoods, with personal identities bound up with social, affective and material ties. To group members themselves, individual instances of this often seemed somewhat trivial or difficult to precisely articulate or attribute. This partially explains why they tended not to be formally recorded, but these countless concrete and lived connections informed and permeated everything the NPGs did.

A few more vignettes, taken from my fieldnotes, will help to illustrate this. At one Wroston NPG meeting, Susan showed a YouTube video about erosion in the river that runs through the village, provoking a long discussion about the changes they had all personally seen in the course and flow of the river over the years, connected to their practices of walking, driving, cycling, fishing, gardening and more. The observation of these changes anchored these practices in place and time, for example, with reference to particular floods, storms and heatwaves. In another meeting, Tom and Owen brought up the train crash of 1876, and the time when the village briefly had its own train stop, and jumped from there into tales of how their parents and grandparents and aunts and uncles used to get around, and the links between the nearby villages – who used to work and shop and go to school where and how, and how these patterns had changed over time to arrive at the present configurations.

When discussing which addresses to send business surveys to, Anne asked for suggestions of local businesses and the NPG collectively reeled off a long list, contributed to by every member of the group, of the many 'invisible' ones (such as sole traders working from home) as well as the few obvious ones. Later, in December 2015, Simon, Elliot and Ray drove Scott, their consultant, around the village to 'refamiliarise' him with the place in all its concreteness. The NPG had agreed at the previous meeting that some of the things that Scott had been saying and suggesting for policy inclusion were surprising given the materiality of the village that they were all so familiar with – its layout, location, relation and connections to the nearby city, other villages and surrounding countryside, architectural styles and materials, services and facilities. They felt that his rather generic statements didn't reflect the particular specificity of the village: as Laura put it, "It doesn't sound like he's talking about Wroston, y'know, specifically about Wroston." And as Anne said over coffee one morning in April 2015, after hinting at long-standing personal and political feuds and disagreements in the village and between NPG members, "But it's good, it's like Cheers, isn't it, the place where everybody knows your name, it's nice."

Similar accounts of shared experiential knowledge saturated my encounters with the NPG in Oakley. Everyone knew when the 'hanky tree', with its distinctive blooms, came into flower. Everyone knew, too, of the problems that Oakley experienced with drainage and flooding. It wasn't particularly liable to coastal or fluvial flooding, and so was considered by the council and the Environment Agency to be largely an area of low flood risk. But discussions at meetings frequently revolved around the problems caused by the area's sloping topography and limestone geology, combined with the impermeable barrier of the railway line at the bottom of the hill. This combination of materialities leads to sudden and powerful surface water flows (as Andrew often repeated, "It's not so much flooding, as the damage that moving water can do") and to springs appearing apparently out of nowhere. Jane told a story about discovering one that had appeared in the study room of the library overnight, filling the room six inches deep with water. Everyone had watery stories to tell: very specifically tied to the materiality of the area, and repeatedly ignored by developers and decisionmakers.

Problems with traffic and parking were another universally agreed-upon phenomenon in Oakley. The NPG brought a sophisticated, multidimensional understanding of the problems to their frequent discussions on this theme, drawing on many years' worth of their own encounters and conversations to evoke the perspectives of tourists on foot and on bikes, in cars and with caravans; residents of different parts of town and around as pedestrians, cyclists, drivers and 'dwellers'; parents of young children; older people; disabled people; lorry drivers; and through-traffic drivers. They also emphasised events such as long holdups caused by lorries and/or caravans meeting each other on narrow roads and having to reverse long distances. They claimed that such events were either not picked up or were discounted by LPA traffic surveys as being 'abnormal' – but for them such events were an integral part of the normal experience of living in Oakley.

There were disagreements in the NPG about precisely how to encapsulate the character of Oakley, and the group had focused discussions attempting to do this in July 2015. Although they could agree on the most important and relevant features of the town and its surroundings, they struggled to articulate satisfactory ways to characterise them to get across the atmospheres, meanings and sense of place that were driving them – and these disagreements became quite passionate. However, they did agree that they as a community had a much stronger sense of what mattered and why than decision takers at the council, which they perceived as remote and ill-informed.

These stories were woven into an ongoing narrative of neighbourhood. They combined personal experience with stories of chance encounters, informal exchanges and chatter in community groups. These were not 'consultation', just conversations, and obviously they only engaged specific social circles. However, both neighbourhoods had been subject to extensive consultation in recent years for various plans and initiatives. This led Oakley's NPG to talk of consultation fatigue – a generalised reluctance to engage with yet another process, when there was little evidence of previous engagement having effects. But it also led to both groups feeling that they had a sense of the mood of the neighbourhood – not from a detailed re-reading of consultation responses, but from a generalised incorporation of what they felt were the main concerns into their own thinking.

This sense of the NPG synecdochically standing in for the neighbourhood was also drawn on by their consultants. For example, when Oakley NPG's consultant Andrea said to them, "We want to find out exactly what you want for Oakley" in March 2015, '*you*' stood in for both the collective in the room with her, and the neighbourhood at large. This sense was reinforced over time, as Andrea repeatedly asserted from May 2015 that they could start drafting policies "now that we know what the community wants" – despite there having been no further consultation with the community in the intervening time. This identity was also manifest in the sheer commitment of time, effort and emotion that the NPGs invested in the project. They spent hours – sometimes many hours – of almost every week for more than three years in the process of developing these plans, which speaks to a very particular attachment to and care for the neighbourhood.

A sense emerged of the NPGs being deeply embedded within and multiply connected to their sociomaterial neighbourhoods. These attachments and entanglements were not understood or presented as evidence, acting more as background noise or context from which the groups attempted to extract, or define, a signal. But this casually intimate knowledge of the neighbourhood, which could only arise from embedded experience in place, was partially definitive of what they are as a collective. This identity was performed most clearly when the NPGs were in closed discussions among themselves, or with their consultants.

When enacting this identity, the NPGs spoke *as* the neighbourhood: *we* think, *we* want, *we* know, with no distinction or boundary between NPG and neighbourhood. Their identity derives from their positioning as an indivisible part of the lived neighbourhood, as these fieldnote extracts illustrate:

'As far as Hobson's Farm is concerned, we as a village, we as a group, what sort of things do we think ought to be being considered for that?' (Ray, Wroston, March 2016)

'I think it's for the people of Oakley, that is the neighbourhood plan steering group. ... I think it's for the people of Oakley to put it to the council: these are the ideas we would like.' (Robert, Oakley, January 2016)

This synecdochical identity broadly maps onto the moral dimension of the threefold matrix of authority (moral, political and epistemological) referred to earlier. Neighbourhood planning is a tool for people who are entangled in their neighbourhoods, who have a deep and intimate knowledge of and care for it, which has grown out of their own lived experience. It is precisely by virtue of being affected, being moved by the sociomaterial neighbourhood and what happens to it, that gives a collective the moral authority to take up the powers of neighbourhood planning. This extends beyond notions of representation based on social proximity in social movements literature (Houtzager and Gurza Lavalle, 2010; Piper and Von Lieres, 2015), and Bradley's related notion of 'nearness' that is 'conjured through face-to-face contact, regular encounters, routine interactions and local knowledge' (Bradley, 2015: 106), into material and affective embodiment. The knowledge that is expressed by this identity comes from direct lived experience and relations of both social and material entanglement and immersion.

This aligns with Lorraine Code's critique of the epistemological tradition that 'knowledge properly achieved must be objective' (2015: 1), in which she argues that knowing effectively can – and in some cases must – be bound up in affective, caring, material relations. It is an implicit repudiation of the assumption embedded in the Enlightenment imaginary that to participate in public decision making one must be free, at least temporarily, from the material entanglements of life: that only such a disentanglement enables one to become a public rather than a private actor, to engage in the public sphere, the realm of mind rather than body, of objective knowledge rather than subjective care, of rational discourse rather than emotional attachment (Calhoun, 1992; Marres and Lezaun, 2011). In the Enlightenment imaginary underpinning modern planning practice, affect and care tend to be positioned in rhetorical opposition to knowledge and to responsible public decision making. However, this dichotomy is problematised in the explicit conjunction of knowing and caring in the discourse about neighbourhood planning, and in the ways in which NPGs enact this embedded, embodied identity.

'Of' the neighbourhood

Community engagement is ... a key part of any NP. The final vision, aims and objectives need not just to reflect group views, but the views of the community so it is essential that they have a clear chance to help shape them. DH said views from previous surveys (for example from the

Parish Plan) may help provide a starting point – the group agreed. CS said that it is important that aims and objectives don't come 'top-down' and can be kept under review while they firm up – the group agreed. A working outline of *potential* objectives need to be determined asap so that the group can consider, in the light of this, how best to debate them with residents. … This is a starting point only, and will be likely to change over time and as more views and information are collected. (Minutes of Wroston NPG meeting, September 2014, emphasis in original)

This excerpt from the minutes of an early Wroston NPG meeting speaks to their commitment to deep and wide engagement across the neighbourhood. In this imaginary, the NPG is enacted as arising out of the neighbourhood in order to be able to face it and reflexively engage with it, and in turn to represent it to the state and others. They are a *mediator* between their own neighbourhood and other actors.

They gain the knowledge which they are then able to represent by making use of what may broadly be described as 'technologies of participation' (Chilvers and Kearnes, 2016).[2] These 'technologies' are the combination of material artefacts, specialist knowledge, techniques and practices for managing participatory processes to elicit information from communities, citizens and publics. They circulate between neighbourhoods in the bodies of the individual professionals that practice them, and in the inscriptions intended to reproduce and disseminate the expertise of experienced professionals. In this case, they include the array of surveys, templates, guidance, advice, workshops, newsletters, websites, roadmaps, feedback forms, activities, assessments and so on made available to NPGs by a variety of support agencies.

These 'technologies' often focus on quantification and measurement, and gathering views and information in ways that can be quickly and easily presented in forms conventionally accepted as evidence in the planning system more broadly. They are acknowledged within the community of practice of neighbourhood planning as able to distance NPGs from their own experiences and attachments, and to transform those of the wider neighbourhood into the kind of spatial knowledge that has traditionally been 'heard' within a system which privileges quantified, abstract evidence (Allen and Crookes, 2009). Stephanie, Chair of Oakley NPG, set out the advantages of such technologies in March 2017, while regretting earlier community engagement work: "The big mistake we made was asking for people's comments. You can't quantify comments. With a tickbox exercise you can easily set out what people have told you, but we had reams of people's thoughts … it really held things up."

Performing this identity, NPGs remain connected to the neighbourhood they consult and for whom they subsequently speak. The use of technologies of participation distances them from their own affectedness and enables them to represent the experience of others in simplified, codified forms (Potter, 1996). They are thus enabled to speak not *as* the neighbourhood, but *for* the neighbourhood.

The commitment to deep and wide neighbourhood engagement in Wroston illustrated in the excerpt at the start of this section was also borne out by the care they took in designing, delivering and collecting surveys in February–May 2015 (discussed in more detail in Chapter 5), in order to ensure that as many people as possible would complete and return them. The group agreed to hand-deliver surveys to every home in the parish, including the 29 homes on 'the fell', some many miles from the village. Where possible they committed to talking to the householders, not just posting the surveys. They also arranged survey collection times with each household, along with easy alternative, free and confidential methods to return them (at sealed collection boxes in the post office). The surveys were also scripted in ways designed to maximise responses. The response rate to their housing needs survey was over 66 per cent. In March 2017, the city council employed consultants to conduct a district-wide housing needs survey. They anticipated that a good return rate would be around 20 per cent, indicating the scope for neighbourhood planning to engage much more widely with their neighbourhoods than larger-scale initiatives.

Scott, Wroston NPG's consultant, suggested that the people knocking on doors should have a script, and perhaps ID badges and high-viz jackets. This idea was roundly mocked by the steering group – but similar ideas were treated seriously, and indeed acted on, in Oakley, indicating some of the differences between the two locations, among other things in terms of the relationship between the NPG and the neighbourhood, and what rituals of legitimacy might function in each place. In Oakley, the visible trappings of professionalism were perceived as, generally speaking, helpful to assert legitimacy: marked out as distinct from the community at large, while still belonging to it. In Wroston, however, the ways in which that would distance members from the community was seen as detracting from their legitimacy as it would detract from their identity as being a part of the neighbourhood, indicating how the authority conferred by these different identities and their material performances might mobilise differently in different circumstances.

Oakley NPG also demonstrated commitment to widespread engagement. The first few meetings I attended were focused on getting 'the community' to respond to their draft vision and objectives. They undertook widespread general publicity (such as posters and banners around town, an insert and full-colour double-page spread in the local paper, the town council's website and Facebook page). They also recognised that there were groups in the neighbourhood that they needed to reach out to specifically as they were less likely to get involved, and which the NPG were not themselves 'descriptively' representative of (Davoudi and Cowie, 2013). They made concerted efforts to contact specific groups – the elderly, disabled people, young parents, teenagers, and businesses – through letters, emails and face-to-face visits. They also ran pop-up stands in the town centre and at the train station to extend their reach. At an NPG meeting in July 2015 Robert said of the stands that "We got a really good response doing that, we picked up a lot of different people." This was seen as important because, as Martin insisted later that meeting, to no disagreement, "The neighbourhood plan has to include everyone." The consultants in both sites also emphasised this aspect of their identity, often repeating phrases such as: "There has to be a justification, there has to be a mandate from the community" (Andrea, Oakley, March 2015).

Members of both groups also made frequent reference to not exceeding their mandated authority. In March 2015, Anne advocated caution with the Wroston NPG's draft vision, saying "It's very contentious. … We've got nothing but our personal opinions at this point in time, I'd rather not put it in yet, we can add it after the opinion survey." In the same meeting, Tom stated "I want to know exactly what people in the village want, that's why I want this survey out ASAP." The theme was reprised at the next meeting, with Elliot reiterating that "The plan's got to be done by the village, not just by a group of people", and similar comments were made throughout the plan's development. Similar concerns were echoed in Oakley. In April 2015, while the NPG were reporting back on work that its subgroups had been doing on gathering evidence and developing potential solutions, I noted that 'the recurrent theme throughout the meeting is that the group feel that we have to test this work with the public NOW – before drafting policies'.

Both NPGs, for the first year, made ongoing efforts to communicate with their neighbourhoods through regular articles in local papers, as well as publishing agendas and meeting minutes online. Wroston NPG debated several times how open their meetings were in practice, and how they could and should publicise them to ensure that they were enabling attendance and input from anyone who wanted. The Oakley NPG also discussed this subject several times, and in May 2015 made specific plans to recruit someone to the group from an outlying part of the town – ostensibly a separate settlement – that was not currently represented. But both NPGs continued to maintain a clear line at this point between people being able to come to meetings and to joining the NPG.

In this identity, there is not a hard boundary between the NPG and the neighbourhood. The NPG remains connected to the neighbourhood who they consult and for whom they subsequently speak: a neighbourhood which is beyond their own experience, but with which they are nevertheless still associated. This soft boundary between NPG and neighbourhood is permeable – but there is a boundary. The NPGs distance themselves from their own embodied experience and knowledge in order to access those of the wider neighbourhood. They iteratively move from the outside reflexively looking in, to presenting their own neighbourhood from the inside to the outside. They explicitly recognise that their claims to know the neighbourhood need mediation via technologies of participation, that they cannot unproblematically stand in for the neighbourhood in general. In this identity, the NPGs speak in terms of 'they', emphasising the importance of hearing what *they* want before *we* make decisions; of keeping *them* engaged, of making sure it's *their* plan. They speak *for*, but not *as*, the neighbourhood.

This identity as mediator broadly maps onto the political dimension of the threefold matrix of authority (moral, political and epistemological) referred to earlier. Despite being initiated by town/parish councils, both NPGs had developed their own independent identities and operated as more or less autonomous bodies. They could thus only rely to a very limited extent on the formal democratic legitimacy of those councils. Both showed a keen awareness that their claim to represent the neighbourhood rested on their ability to position themselves as having striven to solicit and act on the views of as wide and inclusive a cross-section of the neighbourhood as possible, through technologies of participation. These technologies were assumed by the NPGs, their consultants, and the LPAs to provide a reliable method of establishing neighbourhood views. They also served to distance the NPGs from their own affective and material entanglements: their identity as being affectively and materially embedded in the neighbourhood could conflict with their perceived ability to fairly represent the cares and concerns of the neighbourhood at large.

However, technologies of participation do not simply describe the publics that they represent, but also define and organise how those publics are constituted. They shape community engagement in particular ways by determining the type of intervention that community members can make, the type of information that they can give, and the ways in which information can be articulated, captured and recorded. They ask particular questions of particular people in particular ways. And underlying this are assumptions, often tacit or taken for granted, about who constitutes (and who is worth talking to in) the neighbourhood, what they might know and care about, and how they might be willing and able to express those things, with clear implications for how the neighbourhood is represented and enacted. Thus, as well as producing knowledge from the neighbourhood, they also produce the neighbourhood in particular ways. They bring it into being as an entity with particular (social and material) boundaries, characteristics and capacities, in relation to particular issues.

'Beyond' the neighbourhood

FIELDNOTES
Oakley
April 2015

Sarah reports back for her and Paula, Paula occasionally interjects. They both seem very keen on the Shared Space concept – quite a radical option, and they show awareness that it will be resisted by the community, but they see it as the best way of achieving what the community says it wants. ... Sarah says 'I think Oakley people would be totally against it, they won't like a big change like that'. John argues that the NPG's role is to open people's minds to possibilities, look beyond 'no change' ... there is some discussion of their potentially conflicting roles as leaders/changers of public opinion versus 'channellers' of it. No real resolution, but they agree that whatever they finally come up with, they have to have the community behind them, regardless of where ideas originated.

In this third imaginary, the NPGs are enacted as different to and separate from the neighbourhood, transformed by their collective practices and experiences, with access to specialist knowledge and know-how. The requirements of neighbourhood planning oblige them to 'adopt professional methodologies' (Bradley, 2018: 31) and 'adapt ... an expert discourse' (Bradley, 2018: 38) in order to to speak for the facts of the material world. The NPGs become 'lay-experts', distanced from the sociomaterial neighbourhood and disconnected from affective relations with place in order to become self-invisible, to produce objective knowledge with no taint of their, or anyone else's, subjectivity (Haraway, 1997). While performing this position is highly problematic from an STS perspective, it is vital to achieving credibility in a positivist planning system. This aspect of enacting this identity is explored in more detail in Chapter 5. However, this detachment from neighbourhood can also be understood as a failure to perform the other two identities, to either embody the neighbourhood and 'be one of them' or to 'keep them on board'.

This difference and distance manifested itself in several ways. The fieldnote at the start of this section records a subgroup of the Oakley NPG reporting back after researching traffic problems in the town centre. They concluded, on the basis of the evidence generated and their research, that the most effective solution would be to redesign a specific area as a 'shared space' – removing pavements, curbs, road markings and so on and forcing pedestrians, cyclists and vehicles to engage more actively with each other and with the street scene. Recognising that this was beyond their planning remit, the NPG deliberated promoting it as a 'community aspiration'.

After considerable discussion and further research over several months, they decided that although the evidence they had compiled suggested that this would be an effective solution, it would be instinctively rejected by the neighbourhood more broadly.

At the same April meeting, on a different subject (a derelict public building being brought back to its original use), Andrew noted that "That is still something that people emotively want, and we need to be ready for that", marking a clear distinction between 'the people' (who emotionally want something that they can't realistically have), and the NPG (who rationally understand and accept that). Similarly, in January 2016, when Martin was reporting back to the Oakley NPG on feedback on his work on developing walking and cycling options, I noted 'much laughter as the first few [feedback forms] ask for no cycling on the prom, where the NPG are promoting shared foot/cycle paths. He concludes wryly that "I think that's gonna say that we need a bit of, uh, management of community expectations"'.

When Oakley NPG were preparing the event from which this feedback came, it was envisaged as consultation on near complete draft policies. However, following a series of 'mini consultations' on housing design they rapidly changed its nature to more of an information-giving event, as they realised that a gap had opened between their understanding of the plan and that of the neighbourhood more widely. At a meeting focused on planning for the event, I noted the following:

FIELDNOTES
Oakley
September 2015

a very long discussion involving the whole group about where the group sit in relation to 'the community' – a recognition that many, if not most people don't know what they [the NPG] are doing or who they are, what a neighbourhood plan is in general or what this one in particular can and intends to do, and what they can do to address that.

Later that month they again discussed concerns about people "resisting the plan" (Mary) and that this event might be "your last chance to get people on board" (Andrea) – and the potential consequences of this gap in terms of failing to win the local referendum, and thus having the entire plan voted down. They decided that the event should emphasise what the plan could legally and technically do, and highlight the broad areas that it tackled. They decided to seek broad feedback rather than consult on specific policies, fearing that the differences between their and the neighbourhood's understandings of the remit and purpose of the plan were too wide. And indeed, concerns about a gap growing between NPG and neighbourhood had been expressed as early as March that year by Stephanie, their Chair: "It's important that we put together some creative and plausible ideas that people can agree with … the more radical we are, the more likely it is that people will reject them, and we'll lose the whole lot." The conversion of the NPG into lay-experts – for example, by developing their understanding of the legal and technical limits of neighbourhood planning, and by deepening and refocusing their understanding of the problems and potential solutions available to their neighbourhood through the production and collation of evidence – necessarily creates a distance between the NPG and the neighbourhood. This distance can then be exacerbated when this specialist knowledge and know-how leads the NPG to consider courses of action as practical and sensible that the wider neighbourhood may consider 'radical'.

The LPA in which Wroston is located was in the process of producing a new version of its own local plan while Wroston were producing their neighbourhood plan. The LPA decided to leave white spaces on their own Proposals Map in areas where neighbourhood plans were being prepared. This effectively ceded control of what happened in neighbourhood plan areas to the respective NPGs, publicly enacting them as having the requisite skills and knowledge to produce a development plan, in stark contrast to the status accorded to any other instantiation of community. In order to perform themselves in a way that aligned with this enactment of them, the NPG utilised a range of devices and practices to distance themselves from their own sociomaterial entanglements with the neighbourhood. These included a formal housing needs survey, a landscape character appraisal, and a site assessment template previously used by the LPA in another area, and the involvement of professional consultants, as we will explore in more detail in the following chapters. This was necessary to comply with the convention that 'legitimate knowledge is that which is constituted at an epistemic distance from neighbourhoods … even though this might not correspond with experiential forms of knowledge' (Allen and Crookes, 2009: 463). Formal and informal feedback at a Wroston public consultation event in March 2017 reflected the extent to which the neighbourhood identified the expertise built up by the NPG, epitomised by comments on anonymous feedback forms such as: 'Very impressed with the extent and quality of work undertaken by the group. Very professional – well done!'

In this identity, the NPGs are constructed as being lay-experts, able to understand systems and processes that others do not, able to see matters of fact for what they are, while the wider neighbourhood is swayed by opinion and subjectivity. When performing this identity, the wider neighbourhood is often represented by the NPGs using a deficit model (Wynne, 1993): if the neighbourhood were only in possession of the information and applied the rational approach that the NPG did, they would see things differently.

This identity is associated more with calculable, abstract space than relational, lived place (Massey and Thrift, 2003; Agnew, 2011). It maps broadly onto the epistemological element of the threefold matrix of authority highlighted earlier in the chapter. Their legitimacy to act derives from their privileged access to specialised knowledge and know-how. However, as demonstrated by the fieldnote excerpt at the start of this section, they are also able to bring their relational knowledge of place to bear on this technical knowledge, showing the fluidity between the different identities – albeit, informed by this more technical knowledge, they come to conclusions that they recognise sets them apart from the neighbourhood more widely.

This identity is, like the previous one, enabled through the use of particular technologies, techniques and practices that can ostensibly detach the NPG from their subjectivity and material entanglements, which will be explored in detail in Chapter 5. This is necessary to achieve the unmarked position of the knowing subject, the view from nowhere (Haraway, 1988), from which position they can be enacted as dealing with 'unsullied' objective evidence. Although liable to be challenged by STS scholars and others who are inclined to open the black boxes of facts to reveal contingently knotted matters of concern (Latour, 2004b), this enactment is vital to achieving credibility in a positivist planning system. The boundary here between NPG and neighbourhood is hard and clear. '*We*' (the NPG) are separate from '*them*' (the social neighbourhood) and '*it*' (the material neighbourhood), so *we* can see the neighbourhood clearly. Even as *we* recognise the need to attempt to bridge this (social) gap to connect with *them*, *we* (and other actors) also recognise that *we* are now essentially different to *them*. They do not speak here *as* the neighbourhood, or *for* it, but *about* it, as something quite removed from them.

Tensions between identities

Clear conflicts emerge between these identities of embedded *synecdoche*, engaged *mediator* and detached *expert*. Legitimacy based on the grounds of specialist knowledge or know-how that is only available to those who are by definition different to and separate from the neighbourhood sits uneasily with legitimacy on the basis of representing the views of one's own neighbourhood – and even more so with legitimacy based on standing in as a synecdochical representation of the neighbourhood. Speaking *as* the neighbourhood, *for* the neighbourhood and *about* the neighbourhood require distinctly different positions or identities in relation to the neighbourhood.

But as the NPGs rely on a combination of *all* the different forms of legitimacy that are enacted through these different identities, they must somehow be held together despite the tensions pulling them apart. But at times, these conflicts came close to fatally undermining both groups, to splintering the collective identities (see Figure 4.6).

Figure 4.6: Tensions between identities

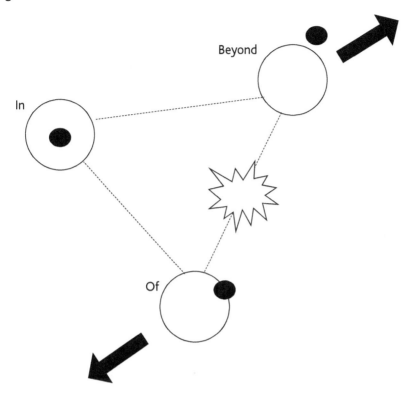

To take just one example, in Wroston, the early part of plan development up to mid-2015 was largely taken up with community consultation. But following this, there was very little formal engagement outside the NPG, as they became immersed in the technical processes of structuring the plan, assessing potential development sites, and writing policies. These processes were more difficult and time-consuming than had been anticipated, and the group (particularly Simon, the Chair), was reluctant to 'go back to the community' until there were concrete results to share. Even one-way communication via the local paper tailed off as the group's attention became focused on more technical matters.

The group discussed this growing gap with increasing frequency through 2016, with comments such as "Well, I agree wholeheartedly that we should have been putting articles in the local paper, we've been remiss ... because we've not had a lot to report to be honest" (Simon, Wroston NPG meeting, July 2016) becoming more and more common. At a meeting in August 2016 I recorded that: 'Simon and Barbara discuss whether to send the site assessments, once complete, to the planners again or to get opinions from the village. Barbara pushing hard again for more and earlier village involvement, Simon and others more keen to get the technical input from the planners first.'

This debate remained unresolved for months as the site assessment work continued. Barbara's argument was not just that they needed the views of the neighbourhood, but that they needed to be seen as acting with them, not apart from or against them. She felt that there was a risk that the NPG could end up being perceived as a remote entity imposing externally determined decisions on the neighbourhood – much as the LPA was perceived – rather than as an organic part of it. At the same meeting, Barbara emphasised that "There's a danger in leaving too big a gap between going to the planners and going to the village … If it gets out that sites have been sent to the planners, but not to the village." My notes record that 'she leaves the threat hanging tangibly in the air', but the message is clear – if the NPG is seen to be more closely aligned with the LPA than with the neighbourhood itself, and that decision making is being pushed back up away from the neighbourhood, then the plan will lose support and risk being voted down.

Tensions reached a crisis point at an NPG meeting in November 2016. Barbara was again advocating a community event as soon as possible. She felt that the NPG had become too autonomous, separated from both the parish council and the neighbourhood, risking its legitimacy. The NPG agreed that this was a problem. But Simon in particular continued to maintain that they should wait until they had a technically credible set of site assessments, vetted by external experts, before engaging with the neighbourhood more widely. He felt that their credibility and legitimacy would be at risk without this. The disagreement continued, tempers got short, voices were raised, heels were dug in, debate became argument and the group was eventually drawn into a shouting match. One member stormed out, barking "I'm not taking this!" after he and another member repeatedly, and with increasing frustration, tried to shout each other down. The situation was finally calmed, with others trying to placate the more agitated members, and a compromise was agreed – to draft a detailed timetable for the remainder of the project, including engagement with the parish council and the neighbourhood, which the group would discuss and agree at the next meeting.

This episode illustrates the tensions between the different identities that the NPGs had to adopt. Everyone in the NPG recognised the need for all the actions discussed to be done – to demonstrate technical competence and credibility with experts as well as securing widespread popular support and contributing personal experience and connections. But while some of the NPG were strongly performing the primacy of the expert identity *beyond* the neighbourhood, others were strongly performing the primacy of the mediator identity, *of* the neighbourhood.

The material entanglement of identity and legitimacy

Enacting each of these identities plays a crucial role in ordering sociomaterial relations. Different relations between different elements of the assembled neighbourhood are enacted by each identity; in other words, each assembles the neighbourhood differently. Each makes visible different versions of neighbourhood. This enables each to produce different forms of knowledge and to generate different forms of representative legitimacy.

In the first, the NPG and its members are enacted as being socially and materially entangled with the neighbourhood. Their legitimacy is derived from their direct bodily experiences of and encounters with the human and non-human elements of the neighbourhood, and the knowledge and affects generated by these encounters, particularly care for place and community. They are wholly part of the neighbourhood assemblage. In the second, they are enacted as partially disentangled through the use of technologies of participation. They are able to encounter others' experience and translate it into a form legible to external actors. They straddle the boundaries of the assemblage. In the third, they are enacted as wholly disentangled, able to encounter the materiality of the world by relying on expert techniques, 'technologies', inscriptions and professional help. This technical mediation distances the knowing subjects from the neighbourhood, detaching them from the neighbourhood assemblage, and enabling them to view it from a distance. These three positionings are illustrated in Table 4.1.

The NPGs are thus hybrid, multiple entities, relying for their legitimacy on their capacity to enact all sides of a variety of interconnected oppositions: to

Table 4.1: The multiple identities of neighbourhood planners

Identity	*In* the neighbourhood	*Of* the neighbourhood	*Beyond* the neighbourhood
Relation with neighbourhood	Embedded, embodied, entangled, lived	Technologically mediated, engaged but distinct	Technologically mediated, detached, distanced
Type of knowledge	Direct first-hand experience, informal social contact	Formally synthesised and codified second-hand experience	Technical, specialised, 'objective', 'factual'
Neighbourhood represented as	Synecdoche: speaks *as* the neighbourhood	Mediator: speaks *for* the neighbourhood	Expert: speaks *about* the neighbourhood
Type of legitimacy	Moral	Political	Epistemological
Visual metaphor			

be at once wholly embedded, partially engaged and detached and distant; experts, lay people, and mediators between the two; servants, peers, leaders and challengers of the community. They must mobilise local experiential knowledge and abstract technical evidence, engaging local aspirations and strategic priorities. Each of these different kinds of engagement with neighbourhood is necessary, and none can be reduced to any of the others. The neighbourhood may well have 'emerged as a precocious new actor in the contested production of space' (Bradley et al, 2017: 72), but it is also a fragile one, highly vulnerable to destabilisation if the balance between identities is tipped too far in any one direction, thus limiting which versions of neighbourhood can be enacted and made visible to policy making.

If the NPG is not enacted as being sufficiently *in* the neighbourhood, their plan risks becoming detached from their own lived experience, from the cares, concerns and knowledge that motivated them to act in the first place, with the likely outcome of a bland, ineffectual plan or one which gives primacy to externally derived objectives (Haughton and Allmendinger, 2013; Parker et al, 2015). If they are not enacted as being sufficiently *of* the neighbourhood, they could lose their public mandate, risking resistance during consultation and defeat at referendum, and/or risking imposing policies that unjustly favour particular interests (Wills, 2016) and disrupt their own and others' relations of friendship, neighbourliness and collegiality (Vigar et al, 2017). If they are not enacted as being sufficiently *beyond* the neighbourhood (and aligned with the expert community of practice of professional planners), they risk developing a plan that is unable to stand up to challenge by external actors such as examiners or litigious developers (Lord et al, 2017; Parker et al, 2017b).

In practice, as the following chapters explore, the first of these outcomes is most common (Bradley, 2018), as illustrated in Figure 4.7. NPGs' identities and their associated practices often become configured in a way which valorises the detached identity 'beyond' the neighbourhood (and to a lesser extent the disciplined, codified enactments 'of' the neighbourhood), at the expense of the more textured, emplaced versions 'in' and 'of' the neighbourhood. NPGs frequently feel compelled to turn their attention away from their original object of interest, the neighbourhood as experienced, in order to represent a version of neighbourhood in the 'dry as dust' forms of technical expertise (Sandercock, 2003: 21). But while this may enable NPGs to be enacted as having agency within the planning system, it generates feelings of loss, disappointment and alienation that their plans do not adequately represent the neighbourhood that mobilised them or their aspirations for it (Bradley, 2018; Yuille, 2021).

Acknowledging the differences between these versions of neighbourhood and NPG, the impossibility of reducing one to another, and nevertheless the importance of each, will not produce easy solutions for practitioners or

Figure 4.7: Imbalance among neighbourhood planning identities

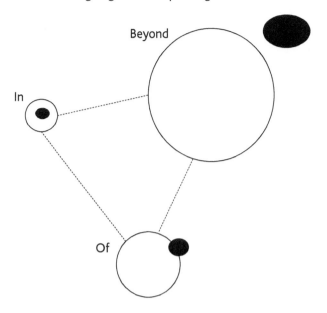

researchers. But ensuring that each is attended to, is held visibly in tension with the others, could open up possibilities for more conscious and reflexive decision making about the ways in which they are combined. This would reduce the likelihood of matters that matter to people being automatically sidelined. Richer, more textured representations of neighbourhood-as-experienced are central to understanding how people and place relate to each other. They should be considered valid and vital elements of the evidence supporting neighbourhood plans. They should neither be collapsed into technical representations of location as abstract space, nor displaced or sidelined by such technical representations. Neither should they displace such technical representations, of course, which are equally as vital to producing a robust, fully rounded plan – but this has rarely been an issue due to the importation of practices into neighbourhood planning from elsewhere in the planning system, as explored in Chapter 5. By retaining these competing versions of neighbourhood and NPG in view, policy can be developed that is more nuanced and responsive to the varied material needs of neighbourhoods. Policy can only respond to that which is made visible. Making different objects and relations – different neighbourhoods – more visible is the first step towards discussion and deliberation on how policy should respond to them.

Developing this analysis of identity-multiples and foregrounding the associations of material relations, knowledge and legitimacy sketched out here may help to better understand how groups negotiate the hybrid forms of authority that neighbourhood planning and other novel forms of participatory democracy invoke (Bradley, 2015; Sturzaker and Gordon, 2017). Different methodologies, different knowledge practices, can 'make places show up differently, so that they might be worked with differently' (Massey and Thrift, 2003: 286). But if places (or communities, or issues) do not show up in certain ways – if the knowledge practices of one identity disproportionately edge out others – then those versions of place, or community, or issues, cannot be worked with at all. The balance and combination between identities in tension determines which versions of neighbourhood get represented, and thus which get planned for.

As Law and Urry put it, '[i]n a world where everything is performative, everything has consequences, there is ... no innocence' (2004: 396). Choosing which versions of neighbourhood are represented – even if it doesn't feel like a choice – has performative consequences. It strengthens (or weakens) some versions over others, it makes some kinds of relations and knowledge visible and marginalises others, and thus shapes the possibilities for what the plan and the neighbourhood can become. Making different versions of neighbourhood visible, by making the different relations through which those versions are produced visible, enables policy to work with places differently by representing different realities to which it can respond.

Beyond neighbourhood planning

While the processes described in the preceding sections are specific to neighbourhood planning, the entanglement of identity and legitimacy can be seen in analogous ways in other instances of participatory democracy as well. Community organising in informal settlements, environmental justice movements and participatory rural development initiatives all, in their different ways, involve groups of citizens representing or acting as intermediaries between community and state and other powerful actors such as corporations and development agencies. These groups of citizens, in different ways, represent the experience and expertise, the knowledge and aspirations of their communities. Performing different identities – for example, those that are embedded in first-hand experience of community and place, that reflexively represent second-hand experience of the wider community beyond themselves, or that set themselves apart from community and place by drawing on technical, specialist knowledge and know-how – can all be crucial to performing their legitimacy to undertake this role. And understanding how different identities and the worlds that they make visible interact, how they assemble people, places and issues differently, can be of use both to researchers who seek to understand how processes function, and to practitioners who are participating in those processes to achieve specific ends.

I do not want to suggest that the three identities that I have described here are always present in all instances of participatory democracy, nor that these are the only, or the only important, identities that can be performed. Other identities may well be uncovered by using this approach to explore the ways in which relations between citizens, community groups and other actors are legitimised. These may be equally or more significant. In some cases, some but not all of the identities described here may be present. In that case, this approach may provide a useful prompt to ask why some identities are being performed and not others, and whether and how eliciting the kind of knowledge and experience – assembling the kind of world – that might be associated with other identities might add value. What I am suggesting is that mobilising the idea of making different realities visible through the performance of different identities can be a useful tool for examining participatory processes. I am also suggesting that using this as a lens can help to understand the ontological politics that is being done through those processes. It prompts us to ask who benefits, and how, from worlds being represented in one way rather than another. What does assembling people, places and issues in this particular way enable to be done, and what does it constrain? How might this be different if other identities were performed, or if the balance between identities were different?

Environmental justice

Local environmental justice movements tend to grow out of first-hand and shared second-hand experience of the local environment and its impacts on health and quality of life, for example, through air or water pollution, unwanted land uses, or direct experience of health problems. This contextual knowledge, developed through both physical embodiment in place and reflexive engagement with the wider community, is then built upon through more formal research into environmental issues and effects, for example, through health surveys or measurements of environmental characteristics such as air pollution (Wilson et al, 2018). However, all three elements of knowledge, experience and identity need to be continuously performed in order to achieve the results that environmental justice activists seek.

This can best be illustrated through an example. The residents of the small African American neighbourhood of Diamond, deep in Louisiana's 'cancer alley', on the fenceline of a major Shell chemical plant, fought for three decades for financial help to relocate away from what they claimed were the harmful health impacts of exposure to pollutants from the plant (Lerner, 2006). The early years of their struggle relied on community leaders performing identities embedded and embodied in the community (their personal experience of negative impacts), and mediating for the community (retelling the stories and experiences of other residents). They were joined in their struggle by non-governmental organisations such as Global Community Monitor, the Louisiana Bucket Brigade and the Deep South Center for Environmental Justice, who provided training, tools, techniques and expertise which enabled activists to also perform technical and expert identities. For example, a local Bucket Brigade was established – a group of local citizen activists who use a patented, Environmental Protection Agency-approved tool (the Bucket) and procedures to capture air samples for laboratory analysis and record information about them (O'Rourke and Macey, 2003). This enabled the community to demonstrate the presence of cancer-causing chemicals in the air that exceeded Louisiana state standards. Techniques like this provide evidence that official agencies may not have, make available, or analyse in particular ways. They can also draw attention to evidence that is not being gathered by official agencies.

Each of these elements is important for activist groups to secure legitimacy both among their communities and with the actors they are attempting to influence, such as governments or corporations. The production of verifiable and reliable data is central to establishing epistemological legitimacy with external actors. However, the stories told about direct lived experience are also important for raising and maintaining interest, awareness and legitimacy within the community and with the media, as well as with those actors that the groups are trying to influence to intervene in the situation and/or change their harmful practices. Connections still need to be made between air quality samples and health impacts, bridging and working together supposedly 'expert' and supposedly 'lay' ways of knowing to tell a story about how the lives of real people are being affected (Ottinger and Sarantschin, 2017). As Denny Larson, the founder of Global Community Monitor put it, 'the face of the environmental justice movement was Margie Richard's face and the faces of the residents of Diamond. … That was how to make this struggle real to other people' (cited in Lerner, 2006: 153).

The Buckets and their (citizen) scientific data only functioned in association with the textured, felt, qualitative insights into the lives of the people affected and their personal experiences of headaches, stinging eyes, allergies, respiratory problems, skin disorders and cancers: the stories that the affected residents of Diamond had been telling for the three decades prior to their eventual relocation. The ways that different identities and the different worlds that they assemble are combined in environmental justice movements can have performative effects – for example, neutralising the visceral, experienced impacts of environmental injustice if too much emphasis is placed on technical, scientific processes and results, or, more positively, aligning scientific inquiry with a vision for social change based on collective action (Ottinger, 2017). The different kinds of knowledge produced through performing different identities, and the ways in which those knowledges are valued or marginalised, also provides a new lens with which to consider what Gwen Ottinger (2018) terms 'epistemic justice' – whether people are respected in their capacity as knowers of the environment, and whether and how local, experiential knowledge can count in environmental decision making.

Community organising

In this book I talk about 'informal settlements'. However, as mentioned in Chapter 1, these are often described as 'slums', or equivalent words in other languages. These words tend to be freighted with pejorative meanings beyond the merely descriptive. In the guise of describing material conditions, they also 'homogenize and stigmatize a global urban population' (Holston, 2009: 249). They perform an identity for the urban poor who inhabit them as being 'other than' and inferior to the dominant culture and class (Gilbert, 2007; Dovey et al, 2021). Place and people are effectively conceived as an assemblage, where the lack of dignity, security and prosperity associated with slums morphs into an imaginary of the characteristics of the people who live there, people of 'low moral values and cultural backwardness' who are 'unfit for civilisation and blamed for their own misfortune' (Koster and Nuijten, 2012: 1909). Residents of informal settlements are thus enacted as an extreme case of the deficit model of publics (Wynne, 1992), 'ignorant citizens who are incapable of making competent decisions on their own and who therefore need to be led into modernity by an enlightened elite' (Holston, 2009: 258). The performance of informal settlement residents as less than full citizens – even less than fully human – also enables the exercise of government violence against them (Carman, 2015). Clearing or upgrading slums is therefore not just seen as an issue of providing better housing or infrastructure, but also 'the place where a new citizen and consumer might be forged' (Benmergui, 2009: 320) – a project of modernising the people as much as the place.

Community organising in informal settlements performs identities that resist this stigmatisation and homogenisation, at the same time as resisting the material conditions of life found in those settlements. It makes agency for these communities possible by countering these narratives and developing new forms of 'insurgent knowledge and citizenship' (Holston, 2009) or 'deep democracy' (Appadurai, 2002), in which urban poor communities are constituted as active, agential citizens with the capacities to drive change and govern themselves. These forms of citizenship and democracy rely on community leaders, organisers and intermediaries being enacted as embedded within urban poor communities, as speaking for wider heterogeneous communities, and on those communities being enacted as having the skills, knowledge and competences to reshape their own lives and their relations with the state and other actors. These identities are performed through practices within the community, with other local actors (such as government agencies and utilities providers), and translocally with local, regional, national and international networks and non-governmental organisations (Daskalaki and Kokkinidis, 2017). The combination of these identities enables a world to be made visible which bears very little resemblance to that produced by the methods of government officials, development agencies and international donors (Koster and Nuijten, 2012).

A crucial element of the success of this organising is that it emerges and is led from within the community, by people who are embedded and embodied in the situation which they are resisting and attempting to change. It is important for intermediaries between state and community to be able to draw on direct knowledge and lived experience of inequality, deprivation and discrimination, and the multiple and complex meanings and realities of everyday life for the urban poor (Ziervogel, 2019). The strength of their stories, arguments and engagement emerges from their embodied situatedness in the conditions of structural disadvantage (rather than personal moral defect) which they make visible, whether that is through protest, collaboration or negotiation (Appadurai, 2002; Mitlin, 2018). This provides a crucial component of their legitimacy both within the community and among the external actors that they are seeking to influence.

However, as a key element of much community organising is to resist the reductionist narrative of a homogeneous urban poor, first-hand testimony is clearly not adequate on its own. A repeated problem with state-sponsored attempts to upgrade informal settlements or to rehouse or relocate their residents is a tendency to treat urban poor communities as an aggregated mass with unvarying needs, whereas poverty and the experience of life conditions affect different people very differently (Gilbert, 2007). Even the segmentation of communities into categories by states and other agencies – for example, by income, gender, age, locality – can be problematic as these may not reflect the primary ways in which people experience or have a sense of themselves (Cornwall, 2008). Leaders and intermediaries thus also need to perform identities as mediators between heterogeneous communities and external actors, to enable the particularities of differential interests, needs and experiences to be expressed and understood (Koster and Nuijten, 2012). It is also important that this mediating identity remains connected to the community which it is representing (Ziervogel, 2019).

Finally, it is also vital to perform a collective identity as knowledgeable, skilled, resourceful and competent – as agential in their own right. This identity at least partially emerges from the radical collective self-reliance forced upon residents of informal settlements by their very peripherality and distance from the state. Long-term learning and development of self-knowledge is generated by the need to construct, maintain and provide their own shelter, services and infrastructure, to improvise and make do, and to challenge and/or collaborate with the state and other powerful actors to defend and improve their spaces and communities. Through necessity 'residents have turned into builders, urban planners, policy lobbyists and lawyers', adapting professional and expert techniques and discourses (Zapata Campos et al, 2022: 8). This can shift the recognised limits of practical expertise beyond professionals to include informal settlement residents and redefine the boundaries between residents and officials to counteract the asymmetries of power and agency that tend to characterise both conventional top-down and participatory design processes (Appadurai, 2002).

Performing these identities in combination can both empower the stigmatised community and enable them to negotiate on more equal terms with the state (Zapata Campos et al, 2022), reassembling the worlds of the urban poor in a way which transcends the existing limits of possibility as conceived by external actors, and 'replaces existing socialities with different ways of being in the world' (Daskalaki and Kokkinidis, 2017: 1304). These worlds include elements of structural inequality, disadvantage and discrimination; solidarity and diversity of experience, opportunity, need and aspiration; and innovation, resourcefulness, collectivity, entrepreneurship and knowledgeability, all of which are often unrecognised in official accounts (Boonyabancha, 2005).

Participatory rural development

Participatory rural development likewise requires the enactment of a series of distinct identities at different stages of the process. This requirement derives from the emphasis, formalised in processes such as Participatory Rural Appraisal (PRA), of communities themselves determining what knowledge they need in order to tackle the problems they are attempting to address, using activities from pre-prepared toolkits (and guided by a professional facilitator) to explore those issues and articulate their own experiential knowledge, and then also analysing that knowledge and shaping and managing the uses to which is put. These emphases – on translating lived experience into evidence capable of informing plans and investment decisions – closely resemble the rhetoric, if not the practice, of neighbourhood planning in England. At first glance, at least, they seem to offer a promising technique for enabling a reflexive and deliberate arranging of these identities relative to each other, such that the material relations and knowledges associated with each are able to be articulated and worked with equitably.

The activities used in PRA and allied approaches are explicitly designed to enable participants to articulate, in some way, the knowledge and values derived from lived experience, from their first-hand encounters with the sociomaterial realities of their situation. They make these everyday, non-expert forms of knowledge paramount and legible to others (Storey, 2014).

A transect walk, for example, takes participants out into the field and enables informal and naturalistic conversation and observations in response to whatever is seen (or not) along the pre-planned route, rather than trying to elicit information in more structured and formal ways at a distance from the place under consideration (Intercooperation, 2005). PRA's focus on the visual rather than the written or verbal in other activities (such as mapping, charting and diagramming) can enable participants to express and identify tacit knowledge and relations which can be more difficult to state in words, and can also reduce the problems of greater weight being given to more articulate participants or the exclusion of less literate people (Chambers, 1994a). Attempts are made to make activities informal and connected directly to lived experience, rather than being distanced from that experience through more abstract, formal processes. Activities are specifically designed to engage with and represent participants as embodied and embedded in place.

However, not all members of the community will participate in such exercises. Those that do are therefore mediators for the rest of the community – it is assumed that their experiences will to a meaningful degree reflect and represent those of non-participants, and that they will also bring their (uncodified) second-hand knowledge to bear – the experiences of others that have been shared with them or that they are aware of. A central tenet of PRA is to involve all sections of the community – including and especially the most marginalised, so participants may be considered representatives not just of themselves, or of the community more widely, but of particular sections or groups within the community (Hickey and Mohan, 2004). And in determining the questions towards which these activities will be targeted, the assumption is again made that those participating are able to also represent the interests and views of those not participating.

Participants are also involved in the definition of problems, the selection of methods, the analysis of results, decisions about what to do with the evidence produced, and the implementation, management and monitoring of the resultant actions (Burkey, 1993). They therefore also enact expert, agential identities. They are required to achieve a degree of detachment from their embodied and mediating identities, to become the decisionmakers, not merely the providers of information to external experts. Their identity necessarily shifts through the phases of the process involving differently situated knowledges, from knowing subject to known object and back again (Haraway, 1988).

It is the enactment of this third identity in particular, in specific combinations with the other two, that is relied upon for the allegedly transformative effects of PRA. Because PRA is not just about (in the terms used in this book) enacting and articulating knowledges associated with different relational identities. It is also about transforming personal and collective identities, from assumed left-behind, marginalised, 'done-to' poor communities to engaged, empowered, actively agential communities with the capacities to shape their own futures, and with different relations of identity with the state and other powerful actors (Chambers, 1984). The role of the development professional is to facilitate the development of these capacities and their realisation through the participatory development process. In the terms used in this book, this realisation would require the holding-in-balance of these three identities in arrangements in which none are marginalised by the others, enabling the articulation of knowledges and enactment of relations associated with each.

However, even as a formal process which explicitly aims at the enactment and development of these identities, achieving such balance is not guaranteed or straightforward – as it is not with neighbourhood planning. It has been suggested that those with relatively powerful positions within the community may be represented as synecdoches for the community, apparently unproblematically standing in for the community as a whole, marginalising the values and knowledge of those with different experiences (Fritzen, 2007; Balooni et al, 2010). Who participates in which aspects of the process may have determinative effects on which identities can be articulated and how they are valued, reinforcing existing relations and identities of power and marginalisation (Mohan and Stokke, 2000) – and a review of over 500 studies found that participants 'tend to be wealthier, more educated, of higher social status (by caste and ethnicity), male, and more politically connected than nonparticipants' (Mansuri et al, 2013: 5). Who exactly 'the community' is, and therefore how the collective identity comes into being, is often determined by external agents (Cleaver, 2001). Participants and non-participants alike may not feel represented or primarily identified with the categories that they are chosen to represent or be represented by, such as gender, class, caste or age (Cornwall, 2008).

The collective nature of much participatory activity may mean that embodied knowledge (for example, the experience of lower-class or female participants) that could contradict or undermine the statements or framings of more 'powerful' or higher status participants, or the expression of which does not fit with cultural norms, may be suppressed (Agarwal, 1997; Hildyard et al, 2001). Indeed, it has been argued that the imposition of a singular identity of 'the community' ignores the existing complex socio-political structures and identity relations within the group so identified, thus normalising and naturalising existing inequalities in relations of power and identity (Kothari, 2001; Farrell and Tandon, 2016). And the supposedly transformative properties of participation need to be seen in the wider context of participants' lives. Their identity relations beyond the participatory process, within and beyond the community in their everyday lived experience, need to be the focus of any genuine transformation, which will also require work to be done on identity relations with more powerful actors (such as donor agencies and the state, as well as actors within communities) (Hickey and Mohan, 2004).

Conclusion

Neighbourhood planning is framed by its promoters as devolving power to pre-existing, well-defined communities. I have problematised this characterisation by claiming that neighbourhood planning is performative. It does not merely give powers to an already existing community, but produces two new actors, the neighbourhood and the NPG: mutually dependent sociomaterial assemblages brought into being through particular practices which define them (Brownill, 2017a). In these case studies the NPGs were enacted in three distinct but fluid identities. I have argued that each of these different identities enabled the NPGs to draw on a different source of legitimacy, and that all of these are necessary to do neighbourhood planning successfully. However, these identities are always in tension and sometimes in outright conflict and holding them together requires considerable effort and skill. I have also reflected on the ways in which these identities are enacted in other locations of participatory democracy, performing similar legitimising functions.

These different identities not only perform the NPGs' relation to neighbourhood differently, they also perform the neighbourhood differently, and the same applies in other participatory situations. Each produces different versions of neighbourhood (or community, or place, or situation), different simplifications of an endlessly complex reality (Law and Mol, 2002). So, it matters in what balances and arrangements these identities are held together and which, if any, become suppressed or marginalised. This will determine which versions of people and place are enacted and made visible to policy: which versions of reality are strengthened or weakened. The following chapter examines in detail two instances through which this balance between identities both shapes and is shaped by specific practices of evidence production.

Copyright notice

A version of Chapter 4 has previously been published under a Creative Commons Attribution 4.0 Licence as Yuille, A. (2020) Performing legitimacy in neighbourhood planning: conflicting identities and hybrid governance, *Environment and Planning C: Politics and Space*, 38(7–8): 1367–1385 https://doi.org/10.1177/2399654420925823

Experience, evidence and examination

'What you're saying is we need an evidence base, that has power, if it's evidence no one can say no to it.'

Martin (Oakley neighbourhood planning group [NPG] member, March 2015)

Introduction

This chapter is about the production and use of evidence – of knowledge claims. As Oakley NPG member Martin identifies in the opening quotation, what the NPG and the neighbourhood know about their neighbourhood, and why they care about it, must be codified into acceptable material forms of evidence to justify their policy proposals. However, as observed in previous chapters, government guidance on what this evidence might consist of is loose and light-touch, stating that 'there is no "tick box" list of evidence required for Neighbourhood Planning. Proportionate, robust evidence should support the choices made and the approach taken. The evidence should be drawn upon to explain succinctly the intention and rationale of the policies in the draft neighbourhood plan' (DCLG, 2014b).

In Chapter 4 I set out three distinct identities enacted by and for NPGs, associated with three distinct kinds of knowledge and sources of legitimacy, then briefly explored how these identities were also enacted in different participatory settings. In this chapter I examine one of the central mechanisms through which these identities are enacted and come to dominate or be suppressed: the translation and inscription of particular types of knowledge into evidence. I outline the requirements on neighbourhood plans to be evidence-based, sketch out what is conventionally counted as evidence in the planning system, and then suggest why the kind of evidence produced to support a neighbourhood plan might be expected to be more expansive, inclusive and varied. Next, I document two instances of evidence production, one from each of my case studies, exploring how NPGs interpreted what counts as evidence. I discuss the implications of these findings, analysing how what counts as evidence rests upon assumptions about the legitimacy of different kinds of knowledge, illustrating the performativity of 'evidence' as a concept. I then consider how the production and presentation of knowledge claims, and their associations with different relational identities, varies across other participatory settings. This suggests different ways that identities and the knowledge claims associated with them can be combined or worked together.

The role of evidence in neighbourhood planning

As detailed in Chapter 2, there is a process that neighbourhood planning communities have to go through, focused around a series of legal requirements for becoming established as a qualifying body, designating a plan area, consulting on the draft plan, undergoing independent examination and holding a local referendum. The requirement that was of most concern to the NPGs I worked with, and the one that was seen as the highest hurdle to get over, was the public examination. This is conducted by an independent expert ('the examiner'), who must be satisfied, on the basis of the evidence put before them, that the plan fulfils the four basic conditions. So NPGs need to produce and present evidence to support their policy decisions: like all planning policy, neighbourhood plans are required to be evidence-based (Davoudi, 2015).

Specifically, they need to persuade the independent examiner that their policy choices are adequately justified by the evidence that they present. However, as the extract from the guidance in the previous section makes clear, there is no concrete definition of what that evidence should consist of. At the time my fieldwork started, in early 2015, neighbourhood planning was very much a novel, emergent phenomenon. Less than three dozen plans had made it all the way through to adoption, although well over a thousand communities were in the early stages of the process. So, as well as a lack of prescription about the type, form and content of evidence, there was little in the way of precedent. Neighbourhood planning communities, and the experts advising and examining them, were entering uncharted territory: an experimental space appeared to be open for creative approaches to evidence production and presentation.[1]

As discussed in Chapter 3, there is a tendency for 'good' evidence in planning to be associated with the positivist 'gold standard' of objective science, apparently removed from any trace of subjectivity or value judgement (Rydin, 2007; Davoudi, 2012). This approach assumes that 'cause and effect can be established between planning problems and planning solutions through the deployment of scientific methods by value-free expert planners' (Davoudi, 2015: 318) – that the relationship between evidence and policy is linear, direct and unproblematic (Davoudi, 2006). Evidence may be produced in response to areas of policy concern, but in itself it will not be influenced by policy considerations or other subjective influences, or be 'retrofitted' after the event in order to justify choices that have already been made. Rather, it will be in place first to provide the firm factual bedrock on which policy decisions will be taken (Davies, nd).

However, in practice it is widely recognised that there is a 'mismatch between notions of how the policy process should work and its actual messy, uncertain, unstable and essentially political realities' (Young et al, 2002: 218). The public narrative of the process does not reflect what happens when planning is being done. As an example of this, I reflect on my own experience engaging with a Local Planning Authority (LPA) who were undertaking a Green Belt review. I, and other stakeholders, were repeatedly told during the early stages of the process that we could not be involved yet, but that we did not have to worry: the LPA were only gathering evidence. It should not matter to us that we were unable to have an input at this point, because they were only assembling the facts, no decisions were being taken. Once those facts were in place, then there would be an opportunity to debate what the policy response to the facts should be. But once the consultation on possible options was opened, it became clear that there were very few possible responses to the facts presented, and that the only way to achieve an alternative policy response was indeed to challenge the 'facts' and how they had been produced.[2] What evidence is produced (what questions are asked, what methods are used to ask them, what sources are interrogated, and so on) determines the range of policy responses that are possible, opening some options up and foreclosing others. The production of evidence makes some things visible in particular ways, and others not visible at all (Wynne, 1996; Stirling, 2008).

As discussed in Chapter 3, in local plan-making, 'the way that community experience of the environment is conveyed explicitly combines values with knowledge' (Rydin and Natarajan, 2016: 2): the expressed encounter with place is experiential, value-laden, meaningful and affective. They explain that such 'knowledge-value hybrids' must be reframed into terms consistent with planning policy before they can be considered relevant as evidence: translated from experiential knowledge into technical 'planning speak'. However, such translations are necessarily partial and incomplete, and may betray as much as they convey (Law, 2009; Galis and Lee, 2014). Affective and practical engagement with the environment is made invisible, gets lost in translation – even though this is often what matters most to people's sense of place (Casey, 2001; Macnaghten and Urry, 2001; Thrift, 2004; Duff, 2010). People's situated, lived experience of place is replaced by an abstraction that has been sufficiently 'purified' or simplified as to be heard and understood in the terms of planning policy (Law and Mol, 2002).

Producing evidence is necessarily about making translations and simplifications. In a Science and Technology Studies analysis, all knowledge is situated, partial and value-laden, and what counts as knowledge and who counts as knowledgeable are likewise historically and socially contingent and situated (Haraway, 1988; Jasanoff, 2003). From this perspective, attempts to present the knowledge claims made in evidence as 'just the facts' is always a misrepresentation, concealing the social commitments and material processes of production embedded in those claims (Latour, 2005). On this account, what is necessary to produce good evidence is therefore not a superficial objectivity, but an attempt at transparency as to why particular simplifications were made.

Neighbourhood planning appeared to offer an arena in which different simplifications could be mobilised and where experiential knowledges could be worked with differently. It was a new, relatively open, potentially experimental space, with limited prescription or precedent, where care and experiential knowledge were explicitly valued and given as a rationale for the project. Rather than translating or reframing these hybrid encounters in which knowing and valuing are intimately entangled, neighbourhood planning seemed to offer scope to appreciate their hybridity.

Expanding the evidence base?

As Bradley observes, neighbourhood planning 'promised to widen both the sources of knowledge and the ways of knowing incorporated into local development plans' (2018: 24). The discourse promoting neighbourhood planning revolves around the idea that residents of an area are best placed to take responsibility for planning its future because, due to their experience of living there, they know it intimately, value it deeply and understand how it functions. They know what its needs are, and the best way that these can be met:

> People around the country value and love the places they live in. They want great local public services, to protect the things that make their neighbourhood special and to help their community grow and develop in the right way. To make sure that you and your neighbours have the community you aspire to, the government has given you new legal powers and new opportunities to preserve what you like and change what you don't like about the city, town or village you live in. (DCLG, 2013: 4)

The heavy emphasis on community (rather than expert) leadership and control, on care and place attachment, and on local knowledge derived from lived experience in the discourse of neighbourhood planning all suggested an opening up of what might count as evidence to a wider, more inclusive approach. This was further accentuated by the governmental insistence that the examination of neighbourhood plans should be 'light touch', and that testing of the basic conditions which neighbourhood plans must meet was intentionally less onerous and rigorous than the 'tests of soundness' which a local plan has to pass (DCLG, 2014b).

This opening up would imply a significant change for planning. Although there has been a growing recognition of the need for public buy-in for decision making in many spheres, lay knowledge remains mistrusted (Petts and Brooks, 2006). Institutional planning practices continue to maintain a deficit model of lay knowledge (Wynne, 1996), treating it with suspicion and assuming that the public are either ill-informed or misunderstand the issues, and reproducing a hierarchical structure in which remote expert accounts of abstract space continue to be privileged over lived, lay accounts of experienced place (Allen and Crookes, 2009; Bradley, 2018). This 'serves to distract attention from those expressions of lived space that are rejected and excluded from planning practice' (Bradley, 2018: 24), by framing them as irrelevant, subjective, anecdotal, or otherwise not fit to be considered as robust evidence. But there are a number of factors which suggest that neighbourhood planning might be more conducive to generating and appreciating the kinds of experiential knowledge that are usually scripted out of planning:

- *Affect:* The explicit acceptance, and indeed endorsement, of the affective nature of the relationship between neighbourhood planners and their neighbourhood. Their right to plan is officially justified as being based not just on their knowledge of the area but on their care for and emotional connection to it (Bradley, 2017a), their identity as being embedded and entangled in the neighbourhood.
- *Scale:* The very 'human', 'dwelt-in' scale of neighbourhood planning. It is concerned with the places that people are most connected with, the places in which they actually 'dwell' for most of the time, and where they are likely to have developed stronger and deeper practical, knowing and affective relationships with place through their everyday, embodied practices and experiences (Urry and Macnaghten, 1998; Ingold, 2000; Yeh, 2016).
- *Lay status:* The absence of an expert body leading the process, which has the potential to generate more of a perceived 'epistemological equality' between the people producing the plan and the wider neighbourhood:
  (a) People may feel more free to articulate 'felt', tacit and embodied knowledge and values than if they were being consulted by a body perceived as 'expert' or an 'authority' which deals in professionalised discourse. It may reduce the common 'insecurities about articulating felt or emotional responses' (Davies, 2001a: 98).
  (b) The group leading the process may indeed be more inclined to accept and acknowledge such knowledge and value as legitimate as it may reflect their own experiences, and they have not been subject to the professional disciplining of a community of practice which is taught to discount such 'subjective' responses.

- *Breadth of engagement:* The heavy emphasis in guidance on neighbourhood planning being shaped by the wishes of the whole community. This requires going significantly beyond existing interest groups who may be used to articulating their concerns in 'planning speak'. Due to the relatively small scales involved, engagement with a much wider spread of the population than at more strategic levels is at least a possibility and was certainly achieved in both of case studies presented here. Engaging with groups and individuals with no other experience of planning is more likely to elicit thoughts and feelings expressed in 'non-planning speak'.
- *Broad criteria:* The 'light touch' approach to public examination and the insistence in legislation, guidance and the courts that examination would only test whether a plan satisfied the very broadly drawn 'basic conditions', not whether it met the more rigorous tests of soundness required of local plans, or examine other material considerations.
- *Buy-in:* The requirement to pass a local referendum suggests the need to secure the 'buy-in' of the wider community, and therefore the need to address their felt relationships with the neighbourhood area. As already noted, these are experienced and often expressed in terms of knowledge-value hybrids that are 'purified' out of planning at a larger scale.
- *Containment:* The 'containment' of neighbourhood plans within existing national and local policy may reduce the likelihood of conflict with knowledge practices that suppress obvious knowledge-value hybrids. For example, disagreements at local plan level are often dominated by technical issues such as housing numbers. In theory, such 'strategic' issues are resolved outside of the remit of neighbourhood plans and provide them with parameters to work within, giving more room for different dimensions of concern, care and experience to play out. Neighbourhood planning is constructed as a 'safe space', contained by the checks and balances provided by higher levels in the planning policy hierarchy (Parker et al, 2016: 521). The boundaries of this space are firmly demarcated in the logics of abstract space which reign beyond those boundaries, notionally allowing the logics of lived place to be asserted within them.
- *Openness:* The absence of any prescribed form for the production and presentation of evidence, leaving communities free to choose for themselves what the most important issues are, how to investigate them, and how to represent their findings.

Each of the identities sketched out in Chapter 4 is associated with a different type of knowledge. Each type of knowledge contributes to the performance of an element of legitimacy. As Bradley (2018) explains, it was expected that neighbourhood planning would enable a wider range of sources of knowledge and ways of knowing to be mobilised. The need for technical knowledge of abstract space was not removed, but could be complemented by other ways of knowing – in particular, the kind of place-based, experiential knowledge that is associated with the NPGs' identities 'in' and 'of' the neighbourhood, which tends to be devalued elsewhere in the planning system.

However, my experience was that this did not happen. Indeed, the NPGs that I worked with in these case studies (and subsequently) took great pains to self-censor any manifestation of subjective experience in their evidence. This follows a pattern observed in other participatory processes, where citizens are invited to contribute based on their experiential knowledge, but have to abandon and/or suppress their personal views when actually participating (Thevenot, 2007; Lehoux et al, 2012). Evidence production strongly reinforced the dominance of their 'lay-expert' identities, as they took great care to fit into conventional evaluative structures. Their assumptions about required form and content for both evidence base and plan (structured by advice from consultants and LPA officers) compelled particular translations and simplifications to be made. The ways of knowing associated with the political/representative and especially the caring/embodied identities were suppressed, manifested in a retreat from qualitative, affective, 'meaning-full' evidence and arguments into quantitative, 'objective', technical evidence, to remove all traces of subjectivity. In the following two sections I illustrate this with stories about evidence production from each of my case studies.

Two surveys

Separating the surveys

As I started attending Wroston NPG meetings in February 2015, they were focused on producing what they then considered to be their key piece of evidence, a survey of the community. However, they quickly decided that this would be better split into two separate surveys. This was partly because they felt that a single survey would be so long and complex that people would be discouraged from responding, partly because they came to see the different elements of the survey as performing different functions, and partly so that they could progress the one they considered more important more quickly.

The housing needs survey

One survey – the housing needs survey (HNS) – was intended to objectively demonstrate the level of housing need arising within the plan area. As their plan was going to have policies for housing provision, they would be expected to have evidence about housing need and demand.[3] The assumption of the group, based on their local knowledge of the numbers of houses coming up for rent and sale, the time taken to complete sales, the formation of new households within the village and so on, was that locally generated need would be very small. The survey was intended to codify and formalise this unofficial knowledge: to translate it into a form of usable evidence. Encouraged by their consultant, they believed that if they could provide evidence that locally generated need for housing was low, they would be able to plan for relatively low levels of housing growth, and thus fend off proposals for higher levels of growth with the incontrovertible facts of hard numbers.

The other was a survey which would assess what the community valued about the area and why; what they thought needed to change and how; and what they thought was important for the plan to address. This would tap into local knowledge about the state of the area, the issues affecting it, and potential for improvement. It would build on the results of their initial consultation and on previous consultation for a parish plan.

The ways in which the two surveys figured the gulf between facts and values in this neighbourhood planning imaginary rapidly became clear (Haraway, 1997). As Scott, their consultant, said to the NPG in relation to the HNS in February 2015, "I've started referring to the other one as the opinion survey. ... This is evidence, the other one's opinion." This view of the HNS was confirmed later in the same meeting by NPG member Ray, saying "This is our really basic facts that we're trying to establish." The title given to the second survey – 'the opinion survey' – denoted its lesser importance, as NPG Chair Simon indicated in March 2015: "We need to know what people think, but it is just what they think, just opinion ... it's best to keep them [the two surveys] separate." And Scott confirmed this view later in the same meeting: "It's [the opinion survey] really just to find out what people think, you're not bound by it."

The group assumed and consequently performed a rigid and clear division between the function of the two surveys: one would produce hard facts and would be binding; the other would 'merely' canvass what people thought. While NPGs are required to consult widely with their communities, the status of the results of these consultations are ambiguous: they are seen as both separate to, and a (discrete) part of, a robust evidence base. The implication is that what can be learned from the lay knowledge and subjective values and opinions of the community is radically different to technical, objective evidence. So, for example, one popular guidebook, *Neighbourhood Plans: Roadmap Guide*,[4] provides advice separately on 'building the evidence base' (Chetwyn, 2013: 35–37) and on 'community and stakeholder engagement and involvement' (Chetwyn, 2013: 30–34). It emphasises 'the need for a robust evidence base and effective community engagement as an essential part of producing a realistic plan, which has a sense of community ownership' (Chetwyn, 2013: 5). This enacts evidence and realism, on the one hand, and community input and ownership, on the other, as quite different things. The status of the HNS, which endowed it with the purified epistemological status of dealing only with facts, enabled it to contribute to the evidence base, while the opinion survey, based on experiential knowledge, was relegated to the realm of consultation.

The NPG went to great lengths to ensure the HNS could function as a technology producing objective facts. They entrusted leadership of the HNS project to Scott, who by virtue of his qualifications and position – as a paid external consultant, a chartered planner and a member of the Royal Town Planning Institute – was considered a relevant expert. At his suggestion, they based their survey closely on one which had been produced by a housing association (also accredited experts in the field) and which had been used recently within their LPA area in an analogous situation. The LPA (one of the key audiences for this evidence) had accepted that survey's findings as valid: it was already recognised as a proven fact-making technology. They also dedicated significant time in meetings over six weeks to discussing which questions should be included and their precise wording, to ensure that the survey dealt only with factual matters and so would produce only facts.

I noted after an NPG meeting that:

FIELDNOTES
Wroston
February 2015

[T]he main topic, which takes up the vast majority of the 2 hours, was the housing needs survey. ... Their discussion around this was extremely thorough, going into great detail and often making very good points, and all giving deep consideration to points raised, and developing or countering them thoughtfully.

Tensions arose between the different sources of legitimacy that the NPG relied upon for the survey during what I recorded in my fieldnotes as 'hot debates'. For example, 'Scott recommended deleting two questions from the HNS because they were opinion, not fact (despite the fact that the survey they were taken from had been approved, and used, and that was the basis for using it as a template)' (Fieldnotes, Wroston, February 2015). The original technology – the housing association survey – while being used as a template precisely because of its proven ability to generate facts and exclude anything 'less than' factual, was itself open to criticism on this front.

However, at another point, following a particularly intricate and detailed discussion about whether a question should include reference to family members who had moved away and wanted to return to the area, they prioritised the legitimacy of the form of the template over the effectiveness of its function:

FIELDNOTES
Wroston
February 2015

At various points during the debate, not just on this point but others, Scott resorted to responses like 'This has been used already, it's imperfect but it's been used by the council' to defend not making changes [to the survey] and to get it out. So, even if it does not derive exactly the information that they want, it's better to use it because it has existing legitimacy, and if they change it to suit their purposes better there is a risk that it may be delegitimised and they are back to square one. Susan in particular also defends this line of reasoning; no-one strongly challenges it. So, they recognise (even outside of this 'returners' issue, there is long debate over many points) the inadequacies of the method, but want to use it simply because it is a recognised fact-generating device.

During these discussions the NPG also developed detailed plans for ensuring that everyone in the community would have the opportunity to complete a survey, and for maximising their rate of completions and returns:

FIELDNOTES
Wroston
February 2015

Detailed local knowledge is deployed in order to maximise response rates – surveys are planned for delivery the week after half term, to maximise the chances of people being at home, and just after the fortnightly recycling collection, to minimise chances of it being thrown away. ... Making response easy is also a strong focus. Susan suggests different coloured paper for different parts of the survey, a technique used in her school. They discuss if this could disadvantage people with sight problems, but they know the best colour combinations to use (black on yellow). They agree to delivering and collecting completed surveys from the houses by hand, providing mechanisms to get extra surveys, providing FAQs and clear instructions for completion and return, giving Simon's phone number for any queries, being scrupulous about anonymising; Simon compares it the with postal vote form and wants a similar design – clean, accessible, attractive. They really care about getting communications right.

They also included an introductory letter signed by the Chair of the parish council (adding institutional legitimacy), and clearly distinguished the two parts of the survey (part 1, to be completed by everyone, was just one page and printed on different coloured paper to part 2, which was much longer, but only needed completing by people who identified themselves or a family/household member as being in need of housing). At the next meeting I noted that 'everyone's been emailed the proposed changes [to the survey] and reasons. Still considerable debate over details – they are applying themselves with precision' (Fieldnotes, Wroston, March 2015). And this continued into the following meeting, where I noted that:

FIELDNOTES

Wroston

March 2015

There is lots of concern again about the possibility of households returning multiple forms in order to skew the results of the HNS, despite Scott's assurances that it is highly unlikely. The group are placing very strong emphasis on procedural rectitude in order to be sure that their evidence can't be challenged. Elaborate plans for distribution and collection are rehearsed and revised in order to properly involve the whole community.

The HNS became, in this imaginary, a kind of 'fact-making machine' (Latour and Woolgar, 1979), analogous to experimental methodologies used in the natural sciences, or the computer models used by planning authorities and consultants to establish housing need. It became a form of technology, a machine into which data would be fed in the front and facts would come out of the back. Its status as a technological object – designed by experts, with proven capabilities, and free from 'polluting' subjective characteristics – is what guaranteed the factual nature of its outputs (Woolgar, 1988; Potter, 1996). Any trace of the subjectivity of the NPG or of the respondents was removed, purified by its technological performance. As Law notes, this is a crucial step in being able to claim to have positivist knowledge about the world: 'statements about objects in the world are supposed to issue from the world itself, examined in the proper way by means of proper methods, and not from the person who happens to be conducting the experiment' (2004: 36).

The factual nature of the findings produced by the HNS was repeatedly asserted in the resultant report, which served not just to report but to reify them, insisting upon their objectivity both in the content and the form of the report. It emphasised, for example, Scott's credentials, the involvement of the LPA and housing associations in the production of the survey, the rigorous methods of design, distribution and collection, and the high response rate. It also stressed that a HNS report was an acknowledged material form in which facts are presented as evidence in the planning system as an important source of primary data. This extraordinary exhibition of care and attention demonstrated a strong desire to ensure the authority of the knowledge produced. The survey thus invoked the figure of detached expertise through a variety of tactics: using a proven inscription as a template (designed by experts and recognised as capable of producing authoritative evidence); having an accredited expert lead their process; extensive efforts to maximise returns and to prevent the data being biased or influenced; excluding issues identified as non-factual; and presentation in a conventionally accepted material form.

However, the central question on which the device's ability to make facts hinged, and which triggered the decision to complete the more detailed section 2 or not, was question 8: 'Do you need to move to another home in this parish now or in the next five years / Does anyone living with you need a separate home now or in the next five years?'. This question could only ever elicit contingent, situated, partial responses, and contains a whole host of hidden and contestable assumptions. The survey was not 'discovering facts', but rather constructing potential futures, based on a range of contestable and unknowable variables (including, for example, unknowable future changes in employment, relationship, health or parental status). This is not a criticism of the survey – it could not have been otherwise – simply an observation of the necessary contingency of 'factual' claims. But notwithstanding this, and despite other problematic elements in the development and deployment of this technology (such as the tensions between the different legitimising forces), this picture overall illustrates the great weight that was placed upon this technology and the (kind of) knowledge that it produced.

This mirrors the efforts by various parties at local plan level to establish their own, competing versions of 'Objective Assessment of Need' for housing. Produced through technologies such as surveys, models, statistical projections and computer simulations, these are likewise always and inevitably grounded on a host of subjective value judgements, contestable assumptions and differing interpretations of which other predictions, projections, facts and assumptions are relevant and important, and how they are likely to change and interact with each other over time. As discussed in Chapter 2, this often results in competing figures being presented to planning inspectors that may vary from each other by up to 100 per cent despite the 'purifying' technologies used to provide distance and legitimacy to such 'objective' assessments. This illustrates the argument that all evidence is constructed rather than discovered, no matter how far removed from subjective experience it appears to be. The questions asked and the tools and techniques used to answer them are never simply neutral, and are always underpinned by contingent assumptions and value judgements.

The opinion survey

In marked contrast, the 'opinion survey' was treated with far less care. Scott was not involved in its production, although he was present at the meeting that signed it off, nor was there a 'proven' template used to lend legitimacy. It was developed, instead, by the NPG agreeing the broad subjects it should cover after minimal discussion at one meeting in March, and two NPG members volunteering to write a draft which would be reviewed and finalised at the following meeting in April. However, the draft survey was only finished and circulated to members a few hours before that meeting. At the meeting, it was clear that several members had not yet had a chance to look at it; but it was also made clear by Anne (the NPG's unofficial Vice Chair and one of the two members that had prepared the draft – the Chair was not present at this meeting), that only very minor comments would be welcome. The purpose of the meeting was to agree, not to debate. At the time, I noted 'Anne in the Chair. ... It's a low turnout and she seems keen to rattle through. She chairs firmly, impatiently, with little time for discussion and a clear sense that much discussion will not be tolerated'. My notes continue:

FIELDNOTES

Wroston

April 2015

First major item – the opinion survey. It was put together by a subgroup – Anne and Rebecca – and sent out to the group just today so that it could be discussed and finalised at this meeting. But the emphasis is very much on the 'finalised'. Anne makes it clear that there will be no wholesale revision, in fact very little revision at all: 'Just a short, quick review', she says. She's really looking for 'small tweaks, typos, minor details' to be changed, if anything at all. Nothing substantive. 'We're not here to go over the whole thing again, we want to get it out'. Suggestions and questions and proposals to develop it further from around the group are largely rejected.

The tactics that were so vital to the construction of the HNS – that would enact the NPG as being 'beyond' the neighbourhood – were not considered necessary for the opinion survey. However, although this survey was 'only' dealing with 'opinions' – a category less valued by the NPG – it disciplined and ordered those opinions (Foucault, 1977, 1980). Through its structure, it made them more amenable to being considered as evidence, representable by the NPG in their identity as being 'of' the neighbourhood.

I noted at the time that:

FIELDNOTES

Wroston

April 2015

The survey has a strong focus on yes/no or numerical ranking questions. ... There is a very strong focus on gathering quantitative not qualitative evidence, partly because that is what the group perceive evidence

139

to be – numbers, measurements, quantities, statistics. Because this brings precision and objectivity. But from another perspective what this quantitative approach *lacks* is precision, specificity, detail – its very reductionist nature strips out the essence of what would, from that perspective, make it a more meaningful piece of work.

Opinions would be aggregated into numbers. Multiple choice and yes/no answers enabled the qualitative to become quantitative. The space for qualitative responses was deliberately minimised to facilitate analysis and presentation of outputs: to tame and discipline. Although the information the NPG were seeking was affective and experiential, these very qualities were abstracted by the technology of the survey and rendered invisible. The survey was trying to get at individual relations with and experiences of particular qualities of place, but its form precluded these from being recorded or carried forward. Anne was quite clear about this disciplining of the qualitative: it was necessary "so that it can be measured, quantified, that's what we need to do ... that's why we're doing closed questions, we just want to measure them" (fieldnotes, Wroston, April 2015).

My notes from the same meeting go on, 'Anne also asserts that there's no need for open-ended questions because "there's space to write in anything they want at the end"' – which there is, two lines under each of five broad themes (of 'quality of life', 'housing and development', 'protecting the environment', 'jobs and economy' and 'any other comments'). But these are only indirectly tied to the specific questions about which the NPG were seeking information. Space to write qualitative responses was deliberately minimised. The responses in this section were recorded, but only analysed insofar as they could be aggregated into previously defined categories and they were not directly referred to in the presentation of the results of the survey. The way in which the NPG discussed, designed and reported the survey made it clear that its purpose was reductionist: to order neighbourhood knowledge and views into a predetermined, quantifiable range of expressions that was perceived as usable as evidence at examination. It actively discouraged the expression of detailed affective understandings of place. In distilling opinions to aggregate them into facts, the specificity and lived experience of place that constituted the 'opinion' in question was filtered out to leave quantitative data about abstract space.

Survey effects: framing and othering

The effect of these two surveys was to render certain pictures of the neighbourhood visible. The reality of the neighbourhood is, of course, far messier and more complex – materially, socially, relationally, affectively – than that presented by these partial pictures. It is the purpose of research methods such as surveys (or ethnographies!) and their inscribed results, to impose order on these messy realities, to make them manageable by focusing attention on specific things and making them visible in specific ways. But the very action of ordering things so as to make some things visible necessarily makes other things invisible, silences and conceals them: 'others' them, or makes them 'other' than legitimate representations (Law, 2004). In this case, the lived experience of place, the specific, the affective and the relational are obscured, either entirely or through their marshalling into narrow, predefined categories.

Descriptions of what people value about place and how they interact with place were not treated as facts; distilled, numerical abstractions were. This shapes the neighbourhood made visible and the neighbourhood that can be acted upon. However, in reality neither category could be considered wholly subjective or objective, wholly social or material. Both are necessarily hybrids, entangled assemblages of human and non-human, social and material, objective and subjective. And as I discuss later in this chapter, none of this is intended in any way as criticism of the NPG or any of its members. It is simply a reflection of the power of the norms and conventions of the Enlightenment planning imaginary to shape the actions of notionally autonomous actors in notionally 'open' spaces in particular ways.

Assessing green spaces

Local Green Spaces

One of the main motivations for Oakley Town Council initiating a plan, and for the NPG in delivering it, was to protect green spaces in and around the town from future development, beyond the plan period. One of the ways in which they wanted to do this was by designating some places as Local Green Spaces (LGS). LGS is a designation introduced in 2012 by the National Planning Policy Framework. It was created because 'local communities through local and neighbourhood plans should be able to identify for special protection green areas of particular importance to them' (DCLG, 2012a: 18). LGSs can only be designated when a local plan or neighbourhood plan is being prepared or reviewed; once designated, building on them is prohibited except in 'very special circumstances'. There are a number of criteria that a site must meet in order to be designated, including that it is 'demonstrably special to a local community and holds a particular local significance, for example, because of its beauty, historic significance, recreational value (including as a playing field), tranquillity or richness of its wildlife' (DCLG, 2012a: 18).

The NPG put a huge amount of effort into identifying the town's green spaces and deciding which should be protected in this way, initially through a subgroup (consisting of Robert, Geoffrey and Andrew, of which I was also a part), and later through the NPG as a whole. This was a long, difficult and contentious process.

Conflicting approaches

There were divergent approaches from the start between the NPG and Andrea, their consultant, in how to tackle designating LGSs, exacerbated by the way meetings with Andrea were conducted (as discussed in Chapter 6). In March 2015 Andrea encouraged the group to identify their 'top' green spaces, and then to "quickly ask the community" by consulting established community groups on which they valued most and why:

> 'What I want you to do is to start looking at green space in a more realistic way. Think about what there already is and what you would never want to have built on and why. But you need to do some work in the community. A lot of work, get the community to start feeding in so that we have real justification, the community is behind us. What are their top three green spaces?' (Andrea, Oakley NPG meeting, March 2015)

However, the group did not feel this was a helpful approach: they did not believe that the 'top' green spaces were in any danger from development; they already knew which spaces were likely to be identified in this category and didn't think that it would gain them any useful information or lead to a productive outcome.

Instead, the subgroup first concentrated on painstakingly identifying and recording all the green spaces within and adjacent to the town. They used six very large-scale, A2 maps of different parts of the town as a base layer on which they outlined, shaded and numbered, by hand, each green space within and bordering the built-up area, plus one smaller-scale map to identify the larger spaces outside the town, and one 'key' map, showing what the other maps covered and how they fitted together. In parallel, they created a spreadsheet containing details about each of these green spaces – 82 in all – including map references, local plan references where applicable, short descriptions of characteristics, public accessibility, ownership where known, an estimation (from 'A' to 'D') of significance and a brief rationale for that estimation, and any existing policy or statutory designations. This was achieved through the comprehensive knowledge the subgroup members had of the town and the surrounding area, supplemented by legwork and desk-based research to check, amend and develop their records as necessary. This again indicated an inclination towards gathering evidence that is precise and technical, rather than 'soft' and qualitative.

The NPG did not intend to seek protection for the vast majority of these sites, but wanted to develop a solid basis on which to identify which sites should be protected. They were seeking to incorporate issues of both value and significance (across a wide range of issues, such as wildlife, recreation, aesthetics, and so on) and perceived vulnerability. The group wanted to work from the ground up, producing meticulously detailed information about the concrete specifics of place to develop a bespoke approach that was unique to the area, because it responded to its particular characteristics and situatedness: a fine-grained, bottom-up approach grounded in lived place rather than abstract space. However, they continued to face pressure from Andrea to simply select the three 'most important' or 'most valuable' sites, indicating an approach based on the interchangeable characteristics of abstract space, a template that could ostensibly be applied to any locality.

Progress on this exercise, and the difficulties encountered along the way, were reported back regularly at NPG meetings, at some of which Andrea was present. She encouraged members of this subgroup, as with the others, to send their findings to her as they developed, making clear the division of labour between them – that they would provide her with data, information about the baseline conditions and their aspirations, and she would produce policies that responded to that:

> 'Just send what you've got, brilliant, brilliant, you've done so much work … don't worry about the technical data, we can do all that, the policy is something that we would do for you, we wouldn't want you to do that, we're just asking you what it's like on the ground.' (Andrea, Oakley NPG meeting, May 2015)

However, despite her fulsome praise it was not clear to the NPG what, exactly, was being done with this – or any of the other evidence that they were gathering.

Being reasonable

As time moved on, the subgroup faltered. By September, Andrea was insisting that the group nominate no more than five of the most important green spaces for protection. She maintained her focus on the 'most important' spaces, and repeatedly told them that any more than five would be seen as unreasonable and would be rejected by the examiner, in various versions of the phrase: "The inspector would chuck it out … he would say it's unreasonable."[5] Through repeated references across several months, an imaginary of the examiner and examination was built up of a man (always a man) that embodied and tested a particular type of rationality and reason: the implicit model of knowledge that is committed to the scientistic ideals that the more abstract and universal, the better, more objective and more persuasive that knowledge is. This model – figured as a fully formed and already given individual with fixed views and judgements – was understood as being committed to certain ways of knowing the world, which in turn entailed a commitment to certain ways of valuing the world (Haraway, 1997). However, as Parker et al (2016) observe, due to the lack of standardised guidance, training, benchmarking or appointment criteria for examiners, and their different professional and personal backgrounds and experiences, approaches are likely to vary considerably between examiners.

Andrea repeatedly stated, verbally and in writing, that the examiner would insist upon robust evidence, for example: 'Without strong evidence to support it the plan will fail at examination so it is really important that the evidence is justifying the policies and holds up under scrutiny' (October 2015, by email); "We have to have firm evidence, particularly for something like that [designating an LGS], because a developer, the inspector, won't accept the general public's view only" (NPG meeting, November 2015). She also frequently emphasised the need to conform to this figure's standards of rationality, often repeating phrases such as: "When we put the plan together we need to have a reasoned justification for the policies, we need evidence for the inspector for what we want to do" (NPG meeting, May 2015); and "You need a nice manageable number that looks reasonable ... it's about looking reasonable" (NPG meeting, September 2015). While the insistence on robust evidence was clearly necessary, the implications as to the form that evidence could take, and the assumptions about what the examiner would consider reasonable, were clearly not.

As in Wroston, 'evidence' was consistently interpreted as meaning quantifiable, categorisable or measurable data, as only this would meet the imputed requirements of the imagined examiner. This interpretation was continuously reinforced implicitly and explicitly by the NPG and their consultant in their discourse and practices: "Yes, you really have to quantify the data, you can use the photos as a stimulus, but then separately give them a series of questions with tick boxes ... that'll give you data that you can actually use, it'll give you numbers" (John, NPG member, July 2015); "We have to somehow quantify it" (Andrea, September 2015); "That's what Andrea likes, isn't it, numbers?" (Sarah, NPG member, November 2015). The group, meanwhile, continued to struggle to work out a means of deciding which green spaces should be protected in the face of the ongoing conflict between their intuitions and their consultant's advice – the most important spaces were not threatened but nominating 'lesser' spaces without acknowledging these 'jewels in the crown' would seem incoherent. Andrea's preferred approach, a single list of ranked value or significance did not appear a productive approach to the NPG (regardless of the complexity of the ranking system), despite its attraction in providing the kind of 'hard data' that they were seeking. The figure of the examiner, exemplifying a modernist planning imaginary, mediated both the total number of green spaces they felt able to consider, and the ways in which they felt able to justify their protection.

Changing focus

This consistent pushing from Andrea to nominate only a very limited number of sites changed the operational question for the NPG from 'why might we want to protect specific sites?' to 'which are the top-ranked sites to protect?': a shift from a qualitative to a quantitative question. I was reluctant to disagree with Andrea, but I was aware of other plans in situations that seemed to have parallels with Oakley, in which many more LGSs had been designated. I brought some of these to the attention of Stephanie (as Chair) and Robert (who, by now, was undertaking almost all the work of the green spaces subgroup). Robert took one of these plans, Tattenhall, as a model for breaking the deadlock. He divided the green spaces into three categories, recreation, open space and wildlife, and on the basis of his judgement of the significance of the sites in relation to these criteria drew up a shortlist that he thought warranted protection under each category, with a short justification of each suggested site. He intended for this to be agreed by the group and consulted on with the neighbourhood.

Andrea had repeatedly tried to direct the NPG to seek community views on which green spaces were important to them and why. The NPG were likewise keen to engage the wider neighbourhood, but had struggled to find a set of justifiable proposals to do so. As discussed earlier, because Andrea didn't know the area well, the way that she framed this put her at cross-purposes with the group, who found that her instructions did not match up with their understanding of reality on the ground. Her insistence on focusing on the 'top three' green spaces that were most important to or most highly valued by the community did not fit well with the group's sense of which spaces might be at risk, and her insistence that they minimise the number of green spaces that they attempted to protect conflicted with their sense that there were a large number of small spaces that collectively made a significant contribution to the character of the town.

In November 2015 Stephanie wanted to shift the focus of the green space work from value to vulnerability, saying that there's "no point in wasting our firepower on protecting places that will never be developed in any case". She wanted to highlight the ten most vulnerable places and get the public to focus their attention on those when they were consulted. This was the third shift in the framing of the green space assessment, from most valued overall, to most important in terms of specific functions, to most vulnerable. The issue had dominated the discussions and difficulties of the group for many months, and, as Stephanie reflected, the whole process felt like "pinning jellyfish to the wall" (November 2015).

Stephanie drew up three lists of green spaces, allocating each of the 82 to one list. The A list were the most important places, which already enjoyed significant protection or were otherwise not likely to be threatened by development. The B list were those places that she thought may warrant protection by an LGS designation, including some protected by local plan policy which the group considered at risk of withdrawal when the plan was reviewed (the most controversial, largest greenfield site allocated for development in the current local plan had previously been protected as open space and a strategic gap between settlements). The C list were those places that she did not think would warrant protection – that were not threatened, or too small, or not that valuable. This was taken to the NPG and amended following their feedback. This was what the public were eventually consulted on in December 2015 as one element of a three-day drop-in consultation event in the town hall. Stephanie also extracted a selection of the B list and asked, on the general feedback form for the event, which of the listed places people had visited recently and how frequently.

The result was quite a complicated request to the public. The general feedback form was simple but gave no indication of subjective states: it showed which sites people had visited but not why, or what they felt about their experience. Everyone who visited the event was asked to fill in one of these forms, which they were given on entry. This ensured a high feedback rate from those who attended.

The specific feedback form on which green spaces people valued and would like to see protected was part of the 'environment' section of the display. It required them to look through the three lists (although their attention was directed to the B list, they were able to nominate places on the other lists as well) and eight maps, all of which were located on a desk and a display board behind it. They were asked to select the five spaces they valued most highly and would like to see protected, in the context of the list categories. They were also invited to write down why they particularly valued specific green spaces and why they merited protection. The attempts to achieve precision had resulted in complexity and nuance, but also complication. It captured elements that more simplified methods could not have done but required a potentially exclusionary amount and type of effort. However, many people who attended the event did make the effort to understand the system and to add their feedback.

Calculative rationalities

From the feedback gained through this consultation the lists were amended, and a new subgroup (Julia, Martin and James) was formed to finalise the list that would be put forward for designation. I prepared an assessment form and instructions to help the subgroup decide which sites they would put forward and to justify their choices according to national policy requirements. I emphasised the value of qualitative evidence, of describing and explaining why these places are special and important, who (or what) 'uses' them and why, and also that the nationally suggested criteria are not additive or exclusive – a site can be designated as an LGS if it is important for only one reason, or for reasons not listed in the National Planning Policy Framework. I anticipated that the subgroup might use the form to articulate why they felt that each particular place may – or may not – be worth protecting.

However, the subgroup decided to make a quantitative assessment, instead of a descriptive, qualitative one, reinforcing once again the value placed on quantitative evidence that can present a black-boxed veneer of clarity and simplicity. In effect, they adapted my inscriptions to develop their own system of multi-criteria analysis that combined deliberative and technical-rational approaches to decision making, which 'mirror[ed] or approximate[d] the decision analysis processes undertaken by the authorities themselves' (Cass, 2006). This was directed at delivering concrete answers that could be justified within the assumed evaluative framework of examination (Stirling, 2006; Wittmer et al, 2006). To make it locally specific, they weighted each of the nationally suggested criteria in relation to Oakley – for example, tranquillity was given a lesser weighting, as Oakley is a relatively tranquil place anyway; richness of wildlife was given a greater weighting, as previous feedback from the community had suggested that this is highly valued.

At the next meeting of the whole NPG (in February 2016), this multi-criteria assessment was delivered via a simple voting process, involving the whole of the NPG. In his introduction to the session, James re-emphasised that "What we want to get out of today is something that actually says this is something that we can measure." For each site on the final 'B list' (which had been amended to reflect the responses from the consultation), for each indicative criterion (such as tranquillity, beauty, and so on), the group voted on a score from one to ten, based on the information gathered by the different iterations of the green space group, the public consultation, and their own first-hand experience. Before each vote there was open discussion among the group about the characteristics and merits of the site with regard to that particular criterion. One member would then propose a score, and there was sometimes some 'haggling' as other members argued for it to be raised or lowered. Reasons were given and debated, but not recorded in any way to indicate how they contributed to the score. Once each indicative criterion had been voted on for a site, the process moved on to the next site and was repeated.

Debate was limited on each vote because, as various members mentioned at different points, they had little time and lots to get through. All the votes were unanimous or with a large majority, and there were no major discrepancies in proposed scores. The tone of the discussion was light-hearted, collegiate. There was a palpable sense of relief at finally having a resolution to this problem that had dogged them for so long, dominating the process for many months. Imperfect as it may be, they had developed a mechanism that would provide them with what they had sought – a quantitative justification for proposing designations, and a process for reaching that numerical position that could be justified (but the details of which could be black-boxed), and which also took account of the 'jewels in the crown' that were not being proposed. The rationale for making decisions and generating evidence in this way was very heavily predicated on conforming to a particular type of rationality, a type of reasonableness that relied on calculative processes, as embodied in the figure of the examiner. For example, James asked the group before the voting began, "So I guess the first question is, does that look reasonable in terms of a weighting … do they look reasonable against each other?" And Julia emphasised that they chose this method because "The main thing is we just felt this was defensible".

At the end of the process, the scores for each site were counted up and announced by Kate, giving a ranked order of sites, from which the NPG identified their top five, to comply with Andrea's insistence that they propose no more than five sites. The responses from the community consultation were then factored in (having already been used to amend the list upon which the NPG were voting), with some discussion about what weight the 'public vote' should have against their votes – the NPG were highly concerned about the potential for being seen to not pay enough attention to public responses. In the end, they selected the five sites that scored the highest in their voting exercise (which became six due to a tie in fifth place), and added two sites that had scored well in the public consultation but not in their voting. Other than these two sites, the two 'assessments' gave broadly similar results. They therefore agreed on a list of eight sites to propose for protection, based on a combination of two different scoring systems (NPG voting on contributions to nationally established indicative criteria and public voting on overall value and worthiness for protection).

As well as generating quantitative evidence and what the NPG understood as procedural legitimacy to justify decision making, this method was also seen as providing closure to the issue, as demonstrated by this exchange at the end of the voting session:

Martin: As there are quite a few people not here today, would you like me to email the email that I sent to you yesterday, about how we've done it today?

Mary: No, they weren't here and we're not going to have them arguing with us, "No, it's too weighted towards nature" or something.

Martin: Well so they are aware that's all.

Mary: You could say "We used these criteria to ...", rather than leave it open.

Martin: That's all we're suggesting, I'm not requesting anybody's feedback in terms of "No you should have done it like this".

Mary: This is what we've done. (Fieldnotes, Oakley NPG meeting, February 2016)

The perceived restriction of 'robust evidence' to that which can be abstracted, quantified and objectified had foreclosed the kinds of evidence that could be put forward in support of the NPG's decision making, and had led to a specific decision process. It was also used, for very practical reasons, to preclude any possibility of opening up what had proved to be a very difficult issue for further discussion. Despite the various different framings that the green space discussion had been through, once a process had been created that would give the kind of measurable, quantifiable data that the group considered could constitute 'defensible' evidence, all other potential framings were foreclosed (Wynne, 1996). This final process therefore served a utilitarian function for the NPG – 'closing down' an issue that needed a concrete decision. However, due to the aversion to qualitative, relational evidence throughout the development of the neighbourhood plan, the issue had never really been thoroughly reflexively 'opened up' (Stirling, 2008).[6]

Foreclosing expansion and pluralisation

The previous sections have highlighted the work done and care taken by the NPGs to present only certain (types of) representations of the world, that fit with specific models of what constitutes evidence. They illustrate a general trend across the activities of the groups, informed by the epistemology of the modernist planning imaginary: that reducing or abstracting information to numerical or otherwise quantifiable or measurable data through aggregative or distancing techniques enables that information to be presented, to be performed, as closer to the 'gold standard' of evidence. Valuing quantitative over qualitative data and taking pains to separate the known object from the knowing subject allows the preservation of the rigid distinction between facts and values.

In both examples, some things are made visible while others are made invisible (Law, 2004). Subtle, complex and diverse forms of knowledge are simplified and abstracted in order to be presented as 'evidence' in forms that participants believed would be acceptable, guided by the relevant 'technologies of participation', their advisors, and the assumptions embedded in the overarching epistemological imaginaries of Western culture in general, and modernist planning in particular (Law and Mol, 2002). The specific, the personal and the experiential are made invisible, silenced by being categorised and numerically aggregated. Meanwhile, the objectively factual is created by means that are no less subjective. The practices that produced these results are also rendered invisible, veiled by the final quantified output (Latour, 1987). While these exercises have generated one form of knowledge, another has been suppressed. As Bradley and Brownill conclude, rather than 'demonstrate the triumph of local knowledge ... neighbourhood planning has reinforced planning's arcane privilege' (2017a: 261).

These knowledge practices correspond to the NPGs' identity as being 'beyond' the neighbourhood, and to knowing and representing the neighbourhood as abstract space. They suppress their identities 'in' and 'of' the neighbourhood and translate or exclude the associated knowledges. The tensions between knowing and representing territory as abstract space and as lived place are well established (Massey and Thrift, 2003; Agnew, 2011). In public decision making, if these two kinds of knowledge conflict, 'the epistemic authority of scientists, planners and urban engineers in matters of space – their power to decree what counts as spatial knowledge – guarantees the dominance of their conceptions of space over "lived" understandings of space' (Allen and Crookes, 2009: 463). However, in neighbourhood planning these conflicts have to be managed within the same collective identity. The NPG is responsible for producing and mobilising all kinds of knowledge. They are required to be both the expert and the lay person, the detached planner of abstract space and the entangled dweller in lived place, the unmarked knowing subject and the marked known object (Haraway, 1988).

The NPGs felt compelled to represent their neighbourhoods in terms of abstract space to make their knowledge count as evidence, despite the lack of similarity of those representations to their lived experience (Bradley, 2018). This translation appeared necessary to them to guarantee the epistemological authority of their evidence, to enact the legitimacy of the expert. As Allen and Crookes observe:

> Professional planners' involvement in neighbourhoods occurs at a social and spatial distance from those places. ... Indeed, for the professional planner, 'legitimate' knowledge of neighbourhoods necessitates a 'critical "distance" between the observer and territory, as though this "taking of distance" were a necessary condition for the knowledge of territorial phenomena' (Boeri, 1998/99, 104).
>
> (Allen and Crookes, 2009: 463)

The pressures on the NPGs to take this distance, and to suppress or translate knowledges that derived from a more entangled engagement with place, were threefold. First, there was pressure from the generally pervasive positivist imaginary of knowledge and evidence and its rigid line dividing facts, objectivity and reason from values, subjectivity and emotion – and which locates expert knowledge on one side of that equation and lay knowledge on the other. Lay people as well as experts – citizens as well as planners – construct expert and lay knowledge as clearly distinguishable (Aitken, 2009).

Second, the tropes and metaphors that planners and associated professionals use to describe themselves and their work lend it a particularly scientistic, quantifiable, positivist aspect which intensifies this distinction. It is a commonly heard refrain among planners that 'planning is as much an art as a science'. However, descriptions of planning continuously evoke tropes from the practices of the natural sciences, particularly around quantification and measurement. Claims framed as objective knowledge are given more weight than other claims (Rydin, 2007). There are practical hierarchies of knowledge, with the more scientific and universal claims at the top, and the more experiential and local at the bottom (Eden, 2017). Evidence that is framed in terms of accredited technical expertise fares better in the system than less formally expressed knowledge, and evidence that can claim the distancing effect of technological production fares better yet (Rydin et al, 2018). Evidence is described as being 'just the facts', and as coming before, and being independent of, policy. 'Objective assessment' is the gold standard of evidence gathering, and subjectivity is a pejorative term. Decisions are described in terms of a rigorous cost–benefit analysis, where different issues can be quantified and assigned 'weights' with a degree of precision that allows 'finely balanced' judgements to be made. These descriptions and metaphors are not just words, they are practices, they shape the way that things are thought and therefore the way in which things are done (in both an everyday and a performative sense of 'done') (Haraway, 1991, 1997). This performs planning in certain ways and undermines other possibilities. The NPGs felt compelled to operate in these ways, despite the implicit and explicit indications that neighbourhood planning was intended to enable a new way of doing planning.

Third, and following on from this, the particular ways in which the examination and the examiner were figured by LPA officers, consultants, and the NPGs themselves, had the effect of further reinforcing this approach, inducing a 'hardening of the categories' (Verran, 1998: 241) which associate objectivity and quantifiability with reliable knowledge. As the imagined embodiment of this specific rationality of planning, the examiner functions like a future-situated panopticon (Foucault, 1977) – the NPGs shaped their actions in the present based on the imagined examiner's projected observation and assumed responses to their outcomes in the future. An imaginary figure was constructed and imbued with particular opinions, judgements and requirements – none of which exist in legislation or regulations, in policy or guidance – and these assumed characteristics functioned as a disciplinary device to control and limit the work that the group did in the present. These assumptions were essentially a distillation of the modernist theory of knowledge into the figure of an idealised expert planner (as interpreted by the NPGs, consultants and LPA officers) rather than the dispositions of any actual individual who might eventually be responsible for examining the plan, or of the rules and regulations which would guide them in that task.

These effects were compounded by the extent to which consultants constructed the conditions of possibility for the NPGs, as discussed in Chapter 6. The interpretations that consultants (and LPA officers) made of the requirements of the examination and the examiner were influenced by their own professional background and experience in the planning system outside of neighbourhood planning, facilitating the 'creep' of meanings and competences across practices (Shove, 2012). This was illustrated by the repeated reference of consultants in both case studies to the examiner as "the inspector": a planning inspector would conduct an examination of a local plan, with very different standards and requirements to the examination of a neighbourhood plan. The consultants appeared to treat the examination of neighbourhood plans in these case studies as requiring the same sort of evidence as that of local plans. This disregarded the specific intention of neighbourhood planning to pluralise evidence by valorising local knowledge.

Consultants' commitments and entanglements in the neighbourhood plan are also not the same as the NPGs: while they overlap, they do not align. The consultants' aim is primarily to get the plan through examination (rather than ensuring that it goes as far as it can to achieve the NPG's aspirations). This is again likely to lead them to promote the use of forms of evidence that are tried and tested in the expert planning arena beyond neighbourhood planning. In fact, the very openness and absence of firm guidance may also contribute to the tendency to fall back upon that which is known to be acceptable in other planning arenas rather than to experiment or push the boundaries with forms that may better reflect participants' experience of place. The technologies of participation relied upon by consultants and NPGs alike often also tend towards the production of evidence in this mould. All of this places the NPGs under very considerable pressure to adopt conservative approaches to the evidence and policies that they bring forward, either self-censoring and self-regulating in an attempt to make them fit within established norms that were never intended for neighbourhood planning, and/or to submit to their translation by consultants to fit in with those norms (Parker et al, 2015, 2016, 2017a).

NPGs must indeed show that they are in command of technical information, that they can mobilise the portrayal of place as abstract space. Successfully enacting the expert identity is one vital element to successfully doing neighbourhood planning. It is arguably enacting this identity that more than anything generates the shifts in power relations with external actors, that generates the NPGs' capacity to act and have effects. The coupling of expertise and agency is reproduced through neighbourhood planning, with

NPGs partially incorporated into the circle of 'experts'. It guarantees the epistemic authority of the NPGs and their evidence. But as these stories illustrate, this comes at the cost of suppressing, concealing and highly imperfectly translating the local knowledge and care which is supposed to underpin neighbourhood planning: of being unable to represent the world as it is experienced.

The implication of this is that NPGs cannot evidence the relations with place that motivated them to prepare a neighbourhood plan in the first place, or adequately capture the knowledge and values of the rest of the neighbourhood. This can result in apparent betrayal of their intentions by enacting neighbourhoods that are quite different from the ones that they sought to plan for. Quintin Bradley describes this as 'the alienation of neighbourhood planning' (2018: 29). Both NPGs I worked with felt that the remote, distanced knowledge that their consultants and other planners dealt in, and which they felt they had to conform to, failed to match up with their lived experience of place. Indeed, it often did not even make sense to someone who knew the place well. For example, Robert complained in September 2015 that after a year he was "sick of educating the consultants about Oakley", and as mentioned in Chapter 4, Wroston NPG felt the need to physically take their consultant out on a tour around the village to "refamiliarise" him with its material specificity. This suppression of lived experience in favour of remote abstraction results in planning documents which are:

> [D]ry as dust. Life's juices have been squeezed from them. Emotion has been rigorously purged ... they serve to perpetuate a myth of the objectivity and technical expertise of planners. In doing so, these documents are nothing short of misleading at best, (dishonest at worst), about the kinds of problems and choices we face. (Sandercock, 2003: 21)[7]

This means that neighbourhood planning, essentially, is not achieving what it set out to do. In practice, it prevents the ways that people know and care about place from being articulated or explicitly mobilised in support of plan policies. There is a need to be both more open and more analytical about all the knowledge and value claims mobilised within a neighbourhood planning assemblage. It is not the case that all claims are equal. But it is the case that all require investigation and analysis, and that requiring one way of knowing the neighbourhood to be framed in terms of another is fundamentally inimical to the intentions of neighbourhood planning. Echoing Helen Verran, we still need to find better ways of 'going on together', of working knowledges together in less dominatory and exclusionary ways that allow plural forms of knowledge to be understood and valued on their own terms (Watson-Verran and Turnbull, 1995; Verran, 1998).

This need is amplified by the recognition that planning and producing evidence is performative. It enacts multiple NPG identities, as discussed in Chapter 4, and it also enacts multiple neighbourhoods, making some aspects visible and others invisible, supporting specific ways of knowing and acting and undermining others (Mol, 2002; Moser, 2008). It 'modifies the perception and material production of place as the object of that knowledge' (Bradley, 2018: 24). Plan policies can only be justified based on the evidence presented to the examiner. Different evidences will represent the neighbourhood in different ways – will, indeed, represent different versions of neighbourhood. Only the neighbourhoods that are represented – not those that are silenced or concealed – can be planned for. The neighbourhood as depicted in the plan is the one that future decisionmakers will encounter. Decisions on whether proposals comply with the plan or not will not be taken by residents and will not be taken in the neighbourhood plan area. They will be taken by experts and quasi-judicial decisionmakers, at a social and spatial remove from the lived experience of place. Only what is made visible through policy will be accessible in these encounters, and only what is made visible in evidence can be made visible in policy.

Beyond neighbourhood planning

The production and presentation of evidence – of knowledge – is central to the practice of neighbourhood planning. It is also central to the other instances of participatory democracy we are considering. Indeed, it is central to any situations in which policy makers, corporations, investors and other powerful actors are asked to make changes on the basis of claims about how things are and how things should be. I have suggested here that different kinds of knowledge, and different ways of knowing, are associated with the enactment of different relational identities. I have also said that certain types of knowledge claims, made by certain identities or actors, are more apt to be trusted and considered reliable than others. In which case, as Walker puts it, '[i]t then becomes interesting to think about on what grounds, in what circumstances and for what reasons some claims are advocated and given more authority and respect than others' (2012: 7).

How knowledge is produced and presented – what questions are asked, who chooses, and on what basis; what methods are used to investigate those questions; how the outcomes produced are interpreted and communicated, and so on – is dependent upon the assumptions, conventions and norms about knowledge embedded in the imaginaries of the actors involved, both those producing the knowledge and those who must be convinced by it. In neighbourhood planning, the positivist, modernist, Enlightenment imaginary in which English land use planning is embedded strongly shapes the kinds of claims that are made, and how they are supported. However, across other participatory spheres, which are assembled in different ways, other assumptions, conventions and norms are also at work, which result in marked differences in the production and presentation of knowledge claims.

Environmental justice

Conventional scientific methodologies systematically marginalise the concerns of communities living with environmental hazards, as the worlds assembled through those methodologies (and the value judgements and assumptions embedded within them) often do not align with the lived experience of those communities (Ottinger, 2018). For example, the risks associated with the presence of certain chemical compounds tend to be officially assessed in terms of controlled laboratory data and model simulations that do not reflect real-life exposure pathways, including combinative effects with other chemicals. Similarly, some failures to show the statistical significance of disease clusters have been demonstrated to be attributable to problems with statistical methods or data (such as small population or sample sizes), rather than to an absence of real harm being done to a community (Tesh, 2000). Community concerns are thus frequently rejected as being merely social anxiety, rather than indicative of serious problems, and the evidence that supports those concerns framed as 'other than' and less than 'real' scientific knowledge (Aitken, 2009). As such, they are not substantial enough to warrant action or, often, even further investigation, leaving vast knowledge gaps of 'undone science', where research funding and effort is directed away from such concerns and towards the interests of economic and political elites (Frickel et al, 2010).

The role of scientific evidence is thus central to the pursuit of environmental justice: certain types of knowledge are able to mobilise action, while others are not. Local activists regularly have to produce this evidence themselves, carrying out neighbourhood health surveys, mapping pollution flows through streets and waterways, carrying out 'body burden' studies, videotaping chemical releases from smokestacks and pipelines, and monitoring air, water and soil quality (Irwin, 1995; Fischer, 2000; O'Rourke and Macey, 2003). This activity is often carried out in partnership with non-governmental organisations (NGOs) or academics, who can provide access to low-cost and/or accessible equipment and technologies, training, skills and reputation, bringing local experiential knowledge into dialogue with professional expertise (Allen, 2003; Harrison, 2011; Wilson et al, 2018).

Data produced by citizen scientists and activist researchers can be seen as 'just good enough' – while not necessarily conforming to the standards or practices of validation and legitimation of conventional scientific practice, it can be sufficient to open conversations with environmental agencies, provide provisional support for claims about excessive levels of pollution or other harms, or argue for better formal monitoring (Gabrys et al, 2016). Scientific practices can be adapted to develop new ways of generating evidence, which can in turn open new questions about what counts as evidence (Gabrys, 2017). Collecting evidence of this kind can enable groups to highlight the limitations of official risk assessment data and regulation regimes, and in some cases to overcome them (Overdevest and Mayer, 2008).

However, this evidence still needs to be associated with other types of claim – for example, evidence about concentrations of air pollutants may also need to be associated with claims about the health impacts of those concentrations, the vulnerability of particular populations to those impacts, responsibility for the pollution, why the distribution of pollution is unjust and what a fair way of addressing the situation might be (Walker, 2012). Adapting scientific methodologies, with the personal or inscribed assistance of recognised experts, can help environmental justice movements to produce and present the evidence that they need to achieve legitimacy with external actors. But if external actors are able to limit the issues at stake to such technical questions – especially ones in which evidence presented by communities can be contested or dismissed as not fitting sufficiently into conventional scientific frameworks – then this may compromise their ability to effectively articulate the complex wholes of their situations.

So while scientific evidence is crucial to identifying and solving environmental problems, including issues of environmental justice, it can also crowd out or exclude other valid ways of knowing and addressing those problems, or 'crowd in' those ways of knowing – that is, force them to be translated into technocratic terms (Bäckstrand, 2004). Claims around environmental justice necessarily also incorporate meanings, memories, experiences, values and relations (for example, of trust or mistrust of government, corporate or regulatory actors) which can be occluded by a focus on technical questions and particular kinds of evidence (Houston and Vasudevan, 2018). Technical evidence can enable the telling of some stories – the assembling of some worlds – but it also constrains others, particularly those which may involve a more thoroughgoing critique of the systems which have generated the injustices in question (Ottinger, 2017). However, this dichotomy may sometimes be worked through by making use of knowledges that have been strategically depoliticised by their reduction to technical questions in invited spaces, but re-politicising those knowledges in alternative, 'invented' spaces of resistance (Roth et al, 2021).

Community organising

In the previous chapter, I described community organising in informal settlements as (sometimes) producing new kinds of 'insurgent knowledge and citizenship' (Holston, 2009), and argued that this came about through the performance of three distinct identities. I am not of course suggesting that this applies in all cases – there are very many examples of community experience and expertise being ignored, dismissed or marginalised, such that 'the opinions of the people were completely ignored … human needs were scientifically stipulated by the planner' (Koster and Nuijten, 2012). However, partly by virtue of these communities' relative isolation from the state and from formal, official modes of governance, bureaucracy and knowledge-making, the evidence that they generate can at times more faithfully represent the experience, needs and knowledge of the community than that produced within 'invited' spaces of participatory democracy (Zapata Campos et al, 2022).

While it has long been recognised that expanding data sources to include knowledge generated by communities themselves can lead to more successful democratic innovations (Leach et al, 2005), when this is subsumed within existing formal structures, as evidenced by the cases of neighbourhood planning described in this chapter, this does not always have the desired or intended results. A crucial element of the assemblage of community organising in informal settlements that has sometimes helped avoid this problem is the support of translocal networks and NGOs (Daskalaki and Kokkinidis, 2017). These have been established to allow grassroots groups and activists to learn directly from each other, and they facilitate the changing of relations between citizens and states by enabling the articulation of local knowledge within informal settlement communities on their own terms (Bradlow, 2015). By combining awareness of formal demands for evidence, but operating outside of the constraints of formal processes, they enable and can teach a variety of methods for gathering reliable data about the community by the community, that both reflects their own lived experience and is capable of influence policy and decision making (Appadurai, 2002).

Aparacio and Blaser note a widespread process in Latin America through which, in the terminology used in this book, subjugated communities who have traditionally been enacted as identities in and of situations are developing new expert identities beyond them, which serve to challenge the conventional knowledge practices of experts by bringing them into different relations with those expert identities (Aparicio and Blaser, 2008). This challenge has two effects. First, it is generating a relative equalisation of diverse knowledge practices where previously some would be automatically privileged and others automatically marginalised. And second, by revealing 'worlds and knowledge otherwise' (Escobar, 2007) that had previously remained obscured by conventional knowledge practices, it is generating a rethinking of those practices in some areas, 'contaminating' the 'pure' modern imaginary of what counts as knowledge, who is able to produce it and how it can be represented (Aparicio and Blaser, 2008).

Such insurgent knowledge and citizenship, which 'uses the knowledge of the poor to leverage expert knowledge, redeems humiliation through a politics of recognition, and enables the deepening of democracy among the poor themselves' (Appadurai, 2002: 40) is at the heart of many of the successes of community organising, asserting alternative identities, relations and knowledges to those previously imposed upon them. It can be understood as 'de-colonising' knowledge, de-linking the legitimacy of knowledge from the imaginaries of modernity and its 'dark side', colonialism (Mignolo, 2011). It is central to models of coproduction, in which grassroots organisations collaborate with states and agencies (with varying degrees of success) to improve both the material conditions of urban poor communities, and also their political voice (Mitlin, 2008). It informs models of participatory budgeting where whole communities can participate in direct democratic voting on priorities for investment, the delivery of which is then co-managed between informal community delegates and the state (Pimentel Walker, 2016).

Moreover, it infuses the production of evidence by and for informal settlement communities, epitomised by an initiative organised by the Asian Coalition for Housing Rights, a transnational network of grassroots community organisations, NGOs and professionals. In this initiative, community organisers from informal settlements in six countries researched and recorded different aspects of poverty and their underlying causes, engaging with the urban poor themselves on their perceptions of poverty, and how to measure and address it (Boonyabancha and Kerr, 2015). This represents the production of knowledge about the poor, by the poor, with the poor and for the poor. It revealed a degree of detail and nuance not found in studies or measures of poverty by formal researchers, governments or donor agencies. As Boonyabancha and Kerr noted, '[t]he urban poor are quite capable of reflecting on how to assess and measure poverty. Because their understanding of poverty is so detailed and so grounded in actual experience, their data and conclusions can be more accurate than those of outside experts who have never experienced poverty personally' (2015: 650). The focus on multiple dimensions of poverty as experienced (instead of conventional, reductionist measures of income) then provided grassroots community organisations with a new and expanded focus for negotiations with their governments and other local institutions in their attempts to tackle urban poverty and improve living conditions for the communities that they are embedded in and represent.

So while these forms of insurgent knowledge can be deployed within invited spaces and at the centres of representative democracy and decision making, they also change those spaces and the relations that are possible within them, as they both reproduce and transform the identities of the poor and the relations between periphery and centre (Holston, 2009). And, moreover, because the production of evidence is often entwined with experience of other forms of direct self-help, such as designing, maintaining and managing their own physical improvements, it drives deeper but less tangible changes in social structures, confidence, and relations with government and other key actors (Boonyabancha, 2005).

Participatory rural development

Participatory rural development approaches go out of their way to avoid the kind of foreclosures of local and experiential knowledge that are evident in neighbourhood planning. As both are relatively formalised processes intended to enable local communities to produce knowledge which will help them to shape their futures through making plans and influencing investment decisions, some direct comparison may be helpful.

While the knowledge-generating practices of neighbourhood planning are often, in practice, geared primarily towards producing evidence that will meet the standards that are assumed to be required for public examination, leading to an emphasis on technical, abstract, quantitative evidence (which, to repeat, is *necessary* but not *sufficient* for a fully rounded evidence base), the activities of Participatory Rural Appraisal (PRA) and associated techniques are oriented to finding multiple ways to enable participants to articulate or express their knowledge, values and experience. This may in part relate to the fact that participatory rural development is often carried out in areas where there may be low levels of literacy, and significant inequalities in levels of education, meaning that finding creative, visual and informal ways to enable participants to contribute is essential to enabling full participation. However, it also reflects the explicit intention of such approaches to generate knowledge from an 'emic' embedded perspective (seen from within the context from the participants' point of view) over an 'etic' detached one (seen from outside the context from an observer's point of view) (Beals et al, 2020), and its explicit recognition of different ways of knowing and multiple potential sources and forms of knowledge (Gaventa and Cornwall, 2006).

Much of the discourse around neighbourhood planning from the government and the agencies which support neighbourhood planners revolves around local people being best placed to plan for their areas because they are the people who know it best (Bradley, 2018). However, much of the practice, and most of the effort of NPGs, focuses on the generation and presentation of 'hard' technical evidence, with the effect of marginalising the 'soft' experiential knowledge derived from everyday life. While there is thus a great rhetorical value placed on local people's knowledge, experience and values, the actual practices of neighbourhood planning subsume this beneath an assumed need to produce (only) a certain type of evidence, driven by the assumed requirements of examination and the risk of legal challenge.

In contrast, in PRA and associated techniques these everyday, informal, sometimes tacit, lived knowledges remain paramount (Chambers, 1997). The main objectives of participatory rural development are for local people to investigate, analyse and learn about the issues and situations which they themselves determine locally to be priorities, and then to plan, implement, monitor and evaluate proposals for solutions or improvements themselves (Chambers, 1994b). They are not constrained by the burden of an external examination of the evidence supporting their plans or proposals. So PRA is to a large extent free of the constraints faced by NPGs to produce technical evidence, which facilitates its focus on experiential knowledge.

PRA retains a focus on the lived, experiential knowledge of local people, while in neighbourhood planning that knowledge is in practice considered inferior to, or at best in need of translation into the terms of, certified experts and professionals. While this partly reflects the genuine demands of the English planning system for technical evidence, it is also in large part reflective of the conservative approaches brought to the potentially open and experimental space of neighbourhood planning by consultants, planning officers and, to an extent, NPGs themselves, due to the norms and conventions of the dominant imaginary in which they are situated. Consultants and planning officers in particular play a dual role as planning experts and as community facilitators, while in PRA the professionals' role is intended to be solely to catalyse, guide and facilitate the community in undertaking their own investigations and analyses, rather than to also produce or provide access to specialist knowledge assumed to be beyond the capacities of the group to generate (Mukherjee, 2002). In neighbourhood planning, as in rural development programmes that do not live up to the ideals of PRA, 'outsiders' reality blanket[s] that of local people' (Chambers, 1994b: 963), leaving the realities of neighbourhood as experienced suppressed.

While both PRA and neighbourhood planning are learning processes for their communities, for NPGs it is often a process of learning about technical, professionalised processes and procedures, and learning from consultants and planning officers about how planning is done. In PRA, conversely, the emphasis is firmly on learning from local people – their physical, social and technical knowledge – and on local people 'doing it for themselves' (Chambers, 1994a). This learning is (or should be) iterative and progressive, using methods flexibly, improvising, adapting, and cross-checking and triangulating across different methods, places, times, groups and investigators. PRA seeks to understand human experience as it is lived and felt, but it also seeks to evaluate, analyse and understand, adapt and correct for errors and biases through this use of multiple sources, methods and locations (Mukherjee, 2014). Local people generate all the evidence themselves, analyse it, decide what to do with it and consequently own it, in contrast with neighbourhood planning where crucial elements of evidence gathering and output generating (such as policy writing) are often undertaken by paid professionals. This helps to maintain an embodied, embedded perspective and the focus on experiential knowledge, while the exercises in triangulation and analysis also enact a more detached, expert identity.

Enabling the articulation of these knowledges is assisted by a focus on techniques such as diagramming, modelling, mapping and visual sharing, where participants can collectively decide what to include and discuss and modify details, and in which 'everyone can see what is being "said" because it is being "shown"' (Chambers, 1994a: 1257). This is contrasted with more extractive forms of information gathering such as questionnaires, consultation responses, feedback forms or interviews, where the information produced is transferred from community members to an expert outsider who then interprets and 'owns' it. These techniques can then be combined with others (such as timelines, trend and change analysis, seasonal calendars, transect walks, analysis of difference, multi-criteria analysis or deliberative probes) in order to develop and add depth, richness and texture to the features and issues identified (Narayanasamy, 2009).

Thus, in PRA local understandings and indigenous, lay, experiential knowledges are favoured over scientific, bureaucratic or specialist categorisations, analyses and taxonomies. Formal, mainstream ways of acquiring knowledge are explicitly rejected in favour of a focus on dynamic, visual and experiential techniques of knowledge production, emphasising the paramount importance attributed to the embodied, embedded perspective. However, despite this, PRA is nevertheless inevitably engaged in processes of translation, trying to condense multifaceted, subtle, complex knowledge into (for example) two-dimensional tables, diagrams or maps. Like all knowledge production, it necessarily simplifies lived and collective realities in order to make them legible (Francis, 2001).

While attempting to retain an embodied perspective and to represent the texture and richness of local experience, the knowledge produced is inevitably a form of reduction and purification, from which some sources of input have been omitted, ignored or sidelined (Kothari, 2001). It has also been suggested that the techniques commonly utilised in PRA may be biased against women and other disadvantaged groups, and may not be conducive to engaging with certain types of tacit knowledge embedded in community practices (Mosse, 1994). And as discussed in the previous chapter, they may even entrench or exacerbate existing inequalities (Kapoor, 2002). However, the focus on experiential knowledge, the techniques for knowledge production chosen to draw this out, and the simplifications which result from them, all mean that the picture established of the local area, issues and situations will be quite different to one generated from a detached, 'expert' perspective.

Conclusion

There are many ways that the characteristics of a place or a community can be known, valued and measured (Foster, 1997; Massey and Thrift, 2003). Examining how and why particular knowledge claims are produced through particular instances of participatory democracy, and how and why some are accepted as reliable and others are not, demonstrates the importance of social, cultural and political factors beyond the 'purely' epistemic. These factors both shape the specific nature of those claims and contribute to some claims being made rather than others. And the claims being made, by making some things visible (and others not), shape the possibilities for action that can be taken as a result.

As established in Chapter 4, NPGs need to draw on different types of knowledge to enact different types of legitimacy, and this is reflected in other sites of participatory democracy. The English planning system is an arena that brings together different kinds of knowledge and values, of varying degrees of commensurability. As Rydin and Natarajan (2016) highlight, the kind of knowledge-value hybrids that are associated with the NPG identities 'in' and 'of' the neighbourhood tend to be excluded from consideration unless they can be translated into a different type of concern. But these are often things that really matter to people. It is precisely because they have richly textured meaning both that they are important, and that public decision making struggles to find a place for them. Neighbourhood planning, by invoking local experiential knowledge and place attachment among its grounding principles, appeared to offer just such a place. The other instances of participatory democracy discussed also, to varying degrees and in different ways, offer arenas in which the knowledges associated with different identities can be combined and worked together differently.

However, neighbourhood planning as currently practised tends to reproduce the 'purification' of processes and entities that are necessarily hybrid, as the diverse knowledges drawn on by NPGs are reduced to an epistemology of abstraction. Paradoxically, it appears to reify the very kinds of knowledge that it was intended to provide a complement to, through the pressures to adopt the type of 'knowledge, understanding and linguistic resources' of the expert planner to engage successfully with the system (Matthews et al, 2015: 62). In practice, the affective and material dimensions of knowing and caring for place that are central to official discourse about neighbourhood planning tend to be suppressed. This frustrates participants even as they actively take part in that suppression, in order to conform to implicit and explicit assumptions about what kinds of knowledge can count as evidence.

By continuing to privilege the remote knowledge of abstract space over the lived knowledge of meaningful place, it excludes already-ongoing ecologies of participation in place and community: the messy, uncodified, undisciplined sociomaterial encounters from which knowledge and care about place emerge (Marres, 2012; Chilvers and Kearnes, 2016; Bødker et al, 2017). The practice of neighbourhood planning effectively becomes isolated from the countless other practices and relationships with neighbourhood which are intended to inform it. Reflecting on the experience of other modes of participation may suggest ways in which these broken connections can be remade.

There is, of course, a need for technical evidence and expert knowledge in neighbourhood planning – increasingly so, as guidance on requirements has developed, and developers have shown themselves willing to use their financial and other resources to find any technical weakness that can be exploited (Parker et al, 2017a; Bradley, 2018). But there is also a need for space to be made for other, non-conventional approaches to evidence that can deal more directly with the lived cares and concerns of residents.[8] If neighbourhood plans are produced in the same way as local plans, asking the same kinds of questions, valuing and legitimising the same kinds of evidence and the same objects of knowledge, drawing the same boundaries around facts and values, objectivity and subjectivity, then they will also reproduce the same problems and dissatisfactions. What questions are asked, and how they are asked, frame and constrain the answers that can be given. Challenging these boundaries and the practices that produce them opens possibilities for modes of planning that are more responsive to the lived experiences of local participants, based on a deeper, broader and more open understanding of knowledges as situated and hybrid rather than objective and absolute (Haraway, 1988; Sandercock, 2003; Throgmorton, 2003; Innes and Booher, 2004). The legal, policy and discursive frameworks in which neighbourhood planning is located still offer the possibility of exploring these wider understandings of what it is to plan. And while there is much in the current practice of neighbourhood planning that militates against and stifles these wider understandings, there are also indications of difference being done to relations, inscriptions and outcomes (Bradley and Sparling, 2016; Bailey, 2017; Bradley, 2017b).

Neighbourhood planning, as nationally inscribed and locally enacted, is doing politics, not only with how the material form of the neighbourhood will change over time, but with what counts as valid knowledge and evidence. The same is true of any public decision-making practices, participatory or not. A more explicitly open framing of what evidence can consist of could help to both undo the naturalisation of claims that are objectified as matters of fact, and enable a more adequate consideration of claims that are often effectively excluded as being insufficiently factual. This would do the politics of planning differently, by making different versions of neighbourhood visible and enabling different responses as a result.

6

Expertise, agency and power

> This will lead to a fundamental and long overdue rebalancing
> of power, away from the centre and back into the hands of local
> people ... as planning shifts away from being an issue principally
> for 'insiders' to one where communities take the lead in shaping
> their own surroundings.
>
> The Conservative Party (2010: 2)

Introduction

As exemplified by the opening quotation from *Open Source Planning*, the
Conservative Party Green Paper that formally established the concept of
neighbourhood planning, this was promoted as an initiative to transfer
power from state to communities. In this chapter I further problematise
this characterisation. In Chapter 4 I distinguished neighbourhood planning
groups (NPGs) from their neighbourhoods, and described them as
enactments of three distinct identities in relation to those neighbourhoods.
In Chapter 5 I reviewed one of the key processes through which those
identities are enacted, and by which one specific identity comes to dominate
the representations produced and performed by the NPG. In this chapter
I explore the effects that these enactments have on relations of power.
I consider power here not as something that is held (and can therefore be
straightforwardly transferred) but as something that is *done*. And it is done
collectively, enacted not by individuals or institutions acting alone, but by the
particular configuration of the social and material, human and non-human
elements of neighbourhood planning assemblages.

In this chapter I suggest that the creation of the two new actors – the
neighbourhood and the NPG – disrupts existing patterns of relations. I show
how this disruption enables the NPGs to have effects on policy and decision
making that would not otherwise have been possible. However, I then go on
to show that the same processes that enable this disruption also reproduce the
category of 'the expert' and the 'expert–agency coupling', which restricts the
ability to have effects to those enacted as having expertise. While the NPGs
are partially able to inhabit the figure of the expert, they are also decentred
from it by accredited professionals in a variety of ways. As the power to act
is manifested through the capacity to be enacted as expert, the NPGs are
heavily constrained as well as enabled by the disruptions of neighbourhood

planning. I then illustrate similar processes of displacement and decentring of community knowledge by a reproduction of expert categories across the other cases of participatory democracy.

Reframing power and reconfiguring relations

Reframing power

Neighbourhood planning is commonly presented as 'the redistribution of power from the centre downwards and outwards' (Sturzaker and Shaw, 2015: 604). This sense of power being held by insiders at the top or the centre (and being withheld from 'communities', at the periphery) was shared by both the NPGs I worked with. Many of the NPG meetings I attended in the first few months made reference to the individuals, institutions and practices of their Local Planning Authorities (LPAs) as being both spatially and socially remote from them – physically distant from their neighbourhoods, and also removed from their understanding of and hopes for them (Allen and Crookes, 2009). There was a feeling, which the NPGs believed was widely shared, that the LPAs were not acting on their behalf, did not take into account their local knowledge, and did not care about the neighbourhoods' wishes. They believed that the wellbeing of the neighbourhood was deprioritised in favour of abstract goals such as economic growth and housing targets that were perceived as arbitrary. This was succinctly summed up by Oakley NPG member Martin in April 2015, who said "You mention the LPA in Oakley and people just go 'thhhpt'", and mimed spitting on the ground. Stephanie, discussing the origins of the Oakley neighbourhood plan, explained that in her view "the community felt excluded, let down, betrayed by the LPA" when they produced their strategic local plan a few years previously (March 2017).

Drawing on Science and Technology Studies sensibilities (Law, 2008), I consider power not as a property that can be possessed or given, but rather as an effect that is enacted through particular practices. Power can be understood as the capacity to act – agency – and to have effects. But this capacity only arises through the complex assemblages that actors are composed of and a part of. A neighbourhood planning assemblage might include the NPG, the LPA, consultants, the wider community, the (imagined) examiner, and other humans. But it would also include legislation, funding streams, national and local planning policies, the physical place that is the neighbourhood, and the tools, techniques and processes used to produce evidence, prepare the plan and consult the public, and much more besides. If the specific relations between each of these components generated in the practice of doing neighbourhood planning were different, then the capacity of any of them (or of the assemblage as a whole) to act would be different. Agency, or power, emerges through the particular arrangements of relations between the parts of an assemblage (Latour, 1984). It takes work to maintain these arrangements, but also, once established, it takes work to rearrange them.

Framed in this way, neighbourhood planning can be considered as a practice which does some of this work of reassembling actors in new sets of arrangements. As outlined in Chapter 4, two new mutually dependent actors are produced at the same time: the neighbourhood, and the NPG as its 'spokesperson' (Callon, 1999). This is achieved by both reconfiguring the relations between the elements that come to constitute those actors (such as the individual members of the NPG and the wider community), and the addition of new elements (such as the policy, legislation and technologies of participation associated with neighbourhood planning). The production of these actors in turn reconfigures relations with other actors that have a relationship with the neighbourhood. The most significant of these is perhaps the LPA – the 'insiders' from whom power is ostensibly being redistributed into the hands of communities.

Having effects

Through these new arrangements the NPGs were able to generate effects that would not previously have been possible. In both cases, fairly early on in the process a change became evident in the approach of the LPAs and the NPGs towards each other, as the NPGs developed distinct identities that distinguished them from 'the community' at large. Their status as an expert group doing 'real' planning associated them with networks of power and expertise from which other instantiations of 'the community' had been excluded. Their new position in the reconfigured assemblage, as spokesperson for the neighbourhood, arguably enacted them as a more legitimate representation of the community than the community itself, providing them as it did with agency to shape the neighbourhood far beyond that conventionally enacted in the community. This change in relations altered the attitudes and actions of the NPGs, LPAs and other significant actors such as landowners and developers. For example, as I noted quite early in the process in Wroston, 'The LPA planners have asked to be invited to the next NPG meeting – initial enthusiasm from the NPG. ... There is markedly less animosity towards the LPA than has often been the case, they are here viewed as wanting to help, engage openly, find out what's going on' (Fieldnotes, Wroston, May 2015).

Both LPAs sought and arranged meetings with the respective NPGs, in which both 'sides' got to shape the agendas and participate in at least some ways as equals (for example, the officers' greater technical skills and the NPGs' greater knowledge of the local area were both acknowledged, and the officers explicitly recognised the NPGs as having equivalent plan-making powers). Over the course of my fieldwork I joined members of both groups in meeting with groups of LPA officers on several occasions, and they shared documents and exchanged emails outside of these meetings, all of which indicated a shift in relations between LPA and 'the community'.

At the first meeting between members of Oakley NPG and their LPA planning officers in April 2015, I noted that, after some awkward moments earlier on, by the end of the meeting:

FIELDNOTES
Oakley NPG meeting with LPA planning officers
April 2015

The diminishing barriers between the sides finally break out into expressions of collegiality when they hit common affective turf, such as difficulties in contacting the County Council, and dealing with traders' paradoxical perceptions of parking problems, who both sides comment want lots of on-street parking, but not outside their own shops. The LPA team markedly relax.

A major local landowner and developer in Oakley, Country Estates, also requested regular meetings with the NPG. Country Estates owned and were actively planning to build on the largest and most controversial site allocated for development in the local plan. The site was the last open green space separating three settlements, and its inclusion in the local plan had been vigorously opposed by the town council, local action groups and many Oakley residents, including some members of the NPG. A subgroup of the NPG met with the director of Country Estates and his planning consultant several times. It was made clear on both sides in these meetings that the NPG and the developer had different perspectives on the details of developing the site. However, there was a dialogue that appeared to be meaningful and a willingness to attempt to reach compromises. Both sides acknowledged and took into consideration the positions and statements of the other and made apparently genuine efforts to see where the gaps between their positions could be narrowed. Reporting back to the NPG after a meeting in June 2017, Stephanie said: "It was so positive I didn't really believe it ... it's the first time a developer's ever said 'We'll keep bringing it back and bringing it back until we've got something everybody's happy with'." Even the town council, the formally representative community body, had never previously been able to achieve the same level of access and dialogue with a developer.

The LPA invited the NPG to participate in the very early stages of drafting a development brief for this site, showing where housing would be built with indicative character design areas, which areas would be kept as open space, where the best access points are and so on. This engagement was far earlier than the point at which any representatives of 'the community' (such as the town council, community groups, residents in general) would normally be consulted, and the final document very much reflected their early input. Following an early discussion group, Stephanie reported to an NPG meeting in October 2015 that:

> 'We are doing the right thing. This is the first time that I have felt that the neighbourhood plan has actually had some teeth. And it felt really good. … There are very few occasions when you feel that you've actually got, not the upper hand, but at least a bit of power behind you. And it was really good to feel that.' (Stephanie, Oakley NPG meeting, October 2015)

Stephanie later continued that: "Everything that the neighbourhood plan has mentioned, practically, got mentioned and written down. It was just … it was like sitting and watching the balls line up on the jackpot on the TV and you think, hey, haha, they've written it down. It was great!"

There was much intensive discussion between the LPA and the NPG (as well as within the NPG) about the interaction between the neighbourhood plan and the development brief. When, in January 2016, it appeared that both the LPA and the developers were content that neighbourhood plan policies could directly inform the brief, Stephanie commented to the NPG, "Actually, this is a huge compliment, that the LPA think that we're capable of actually doing that." In the final development brief, the southern part of the site was allocated as open green space, which aligned with the NPG's ongoing attempt to have it designated as a Local Green Space,[1] against the landowner/developer's stated wish for it to be available for building housing. NPG members agreed that it would not have been possible for them to have these kinds of effects if they had not been preparing a neighbourhood plan. This was despite the technical relationship between the development brief and the neighbourhood plan being unclear: neighbourhood planning powers only extend to producing the plan, not specifically to wielding greater influence over other planning matters. The site was eventually allocated as a Local Green Space in the neighbourhood plan, but when these discussions were taking place the plan was at such an early stage of development that it would not have been considered to hold much weight if challenged. If the development brief had been adopted in advance of the neighbourhood plan without a clear indication that this part of the site would not be built on, it would have been virtually impossible to designate it as a Local Green Space.

The NPG were also able to produce a range of other policies that went above and beyond local plan policy. They prioritised a relatively central site for a residential care home for older people, within easy walking distance of essential services. There had been considerable pressure from developers to build such a home in other, less central locations which would have left the home's residents isolated. They required at least 35–40 per cent of homes on larger housing developments to be one- or two-bedroom houses or bungalows (not flats), suitable for first time buyers or for older people downsizing. They required new developments to show how they would provide safe walking and cycling routes internally and to key services, and to comply with a design guide intended to help new buildings respond to and cohere with the best of existing townscape character. Two key views were protected, as were dry-stone walls – a characteristic local feature – and another Local Green Space was also designated in the final plan.

The LPA in which Wroston is located was, during this time, in the process of producing a new version of its own local plan. So unlike in Oakley, where major development sites were already allocated in a statutory document, the site selection process was still underway and it was not a foregone conclusion where new development would take place. Wroston's LPA took the decision that, in areas where neighbourhood plans were being prepared, they would leave white spaces on their own proposals map (first definitively agreed with the Wroston NPG, the most advanced neighbourhood plan in the area, in May 2015). Effectively, they ceded control of what happened in neighbourhood plan areas to the respective NPGs – with the caveat that if the plans were not sufficiently advanced by the time the local plan was ready to be submitted for formal consultation and examination, they would take back control and allocate sites as they saw fit. For Wroston, given the external pressures on the LPA, this would almost certainly have resulted in two large sites surrounding the village on the north and east sides being allocated for development, and the NPG's key brownfield site in the centre of the village not being allocated.

Tony, the LPA planning officer who led on engagement with neighbourhood plans, also explicitly stated in a meeting in June 2016 that he would be willing to support the Wroston NPG in prioritising very local circumstances and ambitions over the established policy of the LPA and national government to help achieve the aims of the plan, specifically relocating a working farm from its current village-centre site to enable the site's redevelopment for housing. My fieldnotes record:

FIELDNOTES
Wroston NPG meeting
June 2016

Tony says that as building a new farm in open countryside would not normally be permitted (as departing from local and national policy which have a presumption against building in the open countryside), he strongly recommended either allocating a site for a new farm in the plan, or identifying an 'area of search' where it would be located. The policy could also include a clause making permission for a new farm conditional on gaining permission to redevelop the existing site and on continuing as an active farm for a certain period. Tony would help with wording this.

Wroston's LPA had initiated a Local Green Space designation exercise as part of their local plan development, over which they also relinquished control in neighbourhood plan areas. Wroston had put forward three sites, of which the LPA had accepted two and rejected one. Tony acknowledged in February 2017 that the NPG could take the designations forward through the neighbourhood plan instead, and he agreed to send all the documentation, including the original submissions and the LPA's reasons for approval and rejection, to the NPG. He also said that the LPA wouldn't object if all three sites were included – although he did advise them to look at their reasons for rejecting the third site, and to strengthen their arguments in response.

Perhaps most significantly, the LPA strongly objected to elements of the draft Wroston plan (the allocation of one specific site for housing, and the rejection of two large greenfield sites). They nevertheless continued to engage supportively with the NPG, attempting to persuade them to amend their policies and/or to produce different evidence to support them, but acknowledging their right to decide. In the independent examination where outstanding objections were judged, the examiner sided with the NPG. Policies which were supported by the neighbourhood (as far as this could be ascertained through the extensive consultation carried out by the NPG) but which were opposed by the LPA gained statutory status. The LPA had explicitly criticised the evidence on which these policies were based, but the examiner considered the NPG's evidence able to withstand these criticisms. As discussed later in this chapter, the key piece of evidence was a landscape character appraisal commissioned and informed by the NPG, which directly contradicted the findings of an appraisal done by consultants working for the LPA. As well as this significant achievement in terms of the allocation of specific sites, the final plan also included an overall development strategy that was based on landscape capacity, with detailed policy expressions of how new buildings should integrate with the existing built and natural environment. It also sought the maximum possible amount of affordable (subsidised) housing from new developments, encouraged small-scale growth of local businesses, and established a list of community assets and services to be protected.

The relations of the NPGs with the LPAs were thus markedly different from the relations of any other instantiations of 'the community' with the LPAs. They were trusted, supported, listened to, involved early on and meaningfully, and recognised as having the right to make decisions about their neighbourhood (within statutory limitations), even when the LPA or other significant actors disagreed with them. Documents that were central to the shaping of practices and decisions, but which were conventionally withheld from the public, were shared with them. This was almost exactly the opposite of the impression given by NPG members of the ways in which the LPAs had previously engaged with 'the community' on planning matters.

The reconfiguration of relations between actors, enabled by the definition of the NPG as possessing expertise and the introduction of specific materials, inscriptions and devices, means that agency is enacted for the NPG as a very specific instantiation of community. On this account, neighbourhood planning does not devolve powers to already-existing communities, but rather produces new actors and redefines relations between actors in ways that enable these new actors to have effects. It reconfigures assemblages in such a way as to disrupt existing power relations and engender new forms of agency. However, as well as enabling the NPGs to have these effects, these arrangements also constrained them.

Reconfiguring relations, reproducing categories

As set out in the previous section, neighbourhood planning has indeed allowed communities to have effects, to make changes that would not have been possible otherwise. But I suggest that rather than simply transferring power from the centre to the periphery, it generates new centres and new peripheries. Rather than shifting power to the community, it reconfigures the actors which can exercise agency and have effects. Far from inverting the expert–lay relation (putting experts 'on tap, not on top') and breaking the expert–agency coupling (shifting agency/power to non-experts/the community), it reproduces these relations of power, but generates new actors to which expertise can be attributed. This process is closely connected to what has been described as the 'professionalisation' of neighbourhood planning (see, for example, Parker et al, 2015): the 'becoming-expert' of NPGs.

These new centres and peripheries are most obviously enacted between the NPG and the neighbourhood, in the NPG's identity 'beyond' the neighbourhood.[2] Indeed, when performing this identity, the attitude of the NPGs towards the wider neighbourhood often seemed to reflect the 'deficit models' that are commonly performed (and resisted) between centres of expert power and their lay counterparts (Wynne, 1993). These models of the expert/public divide assume that any gap between the beliefs of experts and the public are the result of a public deficit, for example, a lack of information, or understanding, or rationality. They are also mobilised to an extent in the NPG's identity 'of' the neighbourhood, in which NPGs use technologies of participation to detach themselves from their own and others' subjective experience of neighbourhood.

It is these identities which are enacted in their reconfigured relations with the LPAs. It is not the passionate, caring, embodied 'neighbour' but the lay-expert citizen planner and mediator who is trusted, listened to and supported. At the same time as being represented as the legitimate spokesperson for the neighbourhood, the capacity of the NPG to act on the neighbourhood's behalf comes precisely from their separation from it. It is their capacity to inhabit the figure of the detached, objective expert, in possession of the facts and applying an instrumentally rational logic to them, which is strengthened by these reconfigurations. They are able to have effects to the extent that they act within the expanded boundaries of the expert planners' community of practice and mobilise its repertoire of resources (Wenger, 1998).

The expert–lay divide is therefore also reproduced through the dominance and suppression of the different identities of the NPGs. The knowledge that is gained from each identity is necessary to perform a 'complete' NPG: epistemological authority of a sort is gained from each. But the knowledge from the identity 'beyond' the neighbourhood is tacitly valorised as expertise, by the NPGs, LPAs and other actors working within the dominant planning imaginary. The knowledge from the identity 'of' the neighbourhood is tacitly somewhat denigrated as 'just opinion' (albeit opinion that gains some status the more it can be quantified and aggregated), and the knowledge of the identity 'in' the neighbourhood is tacitly denigrated as subjective and emotive (Cass and Walker, 2009). The valorisation and denigration of these categories and identities aligns with the existing states of affairs in the planning system (and more widely), which were central to the problems which the introduction of neighbourhood planning was intended to address. 'The expert' is refigured through these sociomaterial practices, and power is re-enacted in the figure of the expert, not 'given' to communities.

Decentring the new centres

Relations of power and agency are thus both reconfigured and reproduced simultaneously. The expert–lay divide and the expert–agency coupling are maintained, while the boundaries of expertise are shifted, to partially include the NPG but to continue to exclude the wider neighbourhood. The ways in which the NPG can be 'done' – the identities that it can perform – are also constrained at the same time as its agency is enacted: the 'expert' identity comes to dominate the others, which are associated with denigrated forms of knowledge. The performance of agency in the NPGs as 'lay-experts' undermines their identities 'in' and 'of' the neighbourhood, and strengthens their identity as 'beyond' it.

However, even though the NPGs are produced as new centres of expertise (and therefore agency), they are *decentred* in their relations with certified experts – consultants, LPA officers and other paid professionals. Governmental discourse – and the discourse of these professionals themselves – strongly reflects the oft-repeated maxim and raison d'être of neighbourhood planning that experts should be 'on tap, not on top'. In this section I will explore three examples where the promised inversion of power relations is itself inverted, and the reconfigured arrangements stabilise relations in ways that limit the NPGs' capacity to act by figuring them as 'not-expert'. Woven throughout these examples I also emphasise the central role played by the expertise embodied in inscriptions of various types and the consequent agency of these materials in shaping the actions of NPGs and professionals alike.

The conditions of possibility

As already observed, many of the Oakley NPG members were from professional backgrounds, and possessed the kind of skill set that is considered necessary for developing a neighbourhood plan (as they self-certified in a skills audit during my first meeting with them). Several of them had worked with, or employed, consultants in the past. However, from the outset, it was clear that control over the neighbourhood planning process was in the hands of their lead consultant, Andrea. In a meeting with the LPA in April 2015, Stephanie summed up the consultants' relationship with the NPG by saying that "They're steering the steering group ... we're providing them with lots of raw data, evidence, we prepared the vision and objectives and policy areas to consider, they're thinking about how to make that into the shape it needs to be for a neighbourhood plan."

This reflects the almost ubiquitous use of paid consultants by NPGs (Parker et al, 2015: 528), driven by the relations in the assemblages of neighbourhood planning:

> The grant drives behaviour, and that is to employ consultants, and I have not yet seen a consultant that doesn't try to work to a template ... they are targeting their offer on what they know the grant is and they can't afford to do much in that budget. We are finding communities grabbing the grant and employing consultants as they think that is the easiest way of doing it, and then finding that key issues are left out ... [the consultants] get policies from other plans that they know got through the examination process. (Bradley and Brownill, 2017b: 119)

The relationship between Andrea and Oakley NPG conformed to this pattern. One way of reading this relationship would be in terms of competing interests and a power struggle: that the power of neighbourhood planning is taken by the consultant, not by the community or their representatives. But in the relational context of an assemblage, Andrea and her apparent power are just as much an effect of the network as the NPG and their apparent lack of it. She is held in place by the relations generated by the new legislation and policy, and stabilised in the practices of doing neighbourhood planning. Her status and role as expert were not contested or disputed by the NPG but were mutually understood as being constituted by the arrangements of neighbourhood planning. This role was to explain to the NPG what they could (and couldn't) do with a neighbourhood plan and to police this boundary. It was to help them articulate what they wanted to achieve within these parameters, and to gather information from them (which they, in turn, would produce through gathering evidence and consulting with the community). She would then use this information to help her write the plan, as Andrea explained to the NPG in her first meeting with them in March 2015, with phrases such as: "We're trying to help you with the process so that you know what you can and can't do. ... We will find out what's feasible, what's technically possible"; "You'll provide the evidence to start with, we'll work out what's out there already, what else we need. It's all got to be based on real evidence"; and "What we do today will enable me to make a skeleton draft plan ... we want to find out exactly what you want for Oakley and what that means in practice for writing policies."

This first workshop was introduced, and referred to throughout and afterwards by all parties, as 'training', indicating a hierarchical relationship of expertise between consultant and NPG. Her ability to command and define what is "real evidence" and what is "technically possible" indicates her ability to define reality and possibility for the NPG. But her possibilities and realities are also defined by the material networks in which she finds herself, such as plans that have already passed examination, examiners' reports, guidance documents and the texts of court judgments, and the specificity of available grant funding.

Andrea repeatedly insisted that developing the plan would be an iterative process, with the NPG helping to shape each iteration of draft policy to ensure that it did what they wanted it to, and she frequently asserted that decision making and ownership rested with the NPG, for example: "What we think is immaterial, it's what you think that's material. Our job is to take your recommendations, once you've got steering group agreement and the community behind you" (March 2015); "I won't judge what you want, it's your community, it's your plan, what you do is entirely up to you" (May 2015).

However, as the expert figure, Andrea controlled the process in three important dimensions, performed unquestioningly by both her and the NPG. First, she controlled the individual meetings at which she was present. When she was present, she ran the sessions more like a team leader or a schoolteacher than a facilitator. She directed specific questions to the NPG, formed them into subgroups, allocated tasks to them, took reports back from them, praised and encouraged them, and set them further tasks. The atmosphere produced was more of a manager directing her team than a dialogue between equal partners, with efficiency rather than democracy as a guiding principle, as my fieldnotes from March 2015 record:

FIELDNOTES
Oakley NPG meeting
March 2015

[Andrea] takes control, runs through the agenda on an 'if you want a policy for x, you'll have to do y, by z time' basis. ... Asks for volunteers to develop the vision, to be brought back to whole NPG. Checks they're happy they know what they need to do, that the rest of the group are happy with that. Stresses the need for a vision before they can move on to objectives. She's setting the discrete tasks – 'this is what you have to do'. Relationship seems to have shifted somewhat, she's not facilitating, she's managing, coordinating.

The NPG were able to 'push back' against this to an extent. For example, in February 2015 Stephanie encouraged the group to depart from the questions that Andrea had asked them to address and instead follow their own instincts about what was important, saying "It's our local understanding of what the issues are that Andrea doesn't know about; it's our local knowledge that needs to be put in as well as the questions that Andrea is asking." But overall, the pattern of 'steering the steering group' remained a prominent feature, accepted by NPG and consultant alike as the natural order of things.

Second, Andrea controlled the overall process, like a producer recording a music track. Everything that the NPG did – in their extensive work between, as well as in meetings – was geared towards satisfying the requests that Andrea had made of them. Each of the subgroups (covering their allocated policy areas of housing, economy, environment, transport, health and wellbeing, and vision and objectives), were delivering their own partitioned pieces of work – as if laying down their individual tracks for drums, guitar, bass, vocals – but only Andrea had in mind (shaped by the inscriptions of previous plans and templates) what the final piece would look like, how these different inputs would combine. This eventually led to a feeling among the NPG that they lacked direction and control. John captured their disquiet in an NPG meeting in September 2015: "What's been happening is, in a sense we've been driven by the consultants and what they've required from us to meet their if you like almost a technical specification and we've really thrown ourselves over the last two or three months into that to meet the consultants' needs." And, as Stephanie amplified during an NPG meeting in October 2015:

'The thing that's partially holding us back now is that Andrea herself has not got a clear idea of what the gaps are, which is very annoying, actually, because we can't work on it until we know, and I think we've got too much of some stuff and not enough of another ... so we'll wait and see what she says.' (Stephanie, Oakley NPG meeting, October 2015)

And this leads to the third, and perhaps most crucial, dimension of control. Andrea was in control of *actually writing the plan*, of performing the alchemy that would bring together vision and objectives with evidence and transform them into policy. There was a strong sense throughout process that the NPG were providing Andrea with raw materials that she would then convert into policies. This crucial aspect of plan production was taken for granted as being outside the competence of the NPG, and solely within the purview of the expert. This was illustrated in an NPG meeting in September 2015, while they were preparing for a community event in December. At one point, Julia asked "Will we have something from Andrea that we're able to present?"; later Andrew commented that it was hard to make detailed plans for the event "until we know if she's produced anything we can consult on". And in October 2015, Stephanie related that: "What Andrea said was that … if we wanted to protect the landscapes, we needed to be able to say why the landscapes needed protecting and which ones and so on, and then she would try and find a policy that matched what we wanted to do."

This last quote highlights the material agency of inscriptions in shaping the actions of professionals and NPGs alike. Andrea relied heavily on the embodied expertise of inscriptions,[3] her approach often being to "find a policy that matched what we wanted to do" rather than to develop one based on the unique circumstances of the locality as experienced.

Once the consultants had produced draft policies, they did bring them back to the NPGs on several occasions for comment, to check whether they said what the NPGs thought they should to achieve their objectives. But their means of doing this was similar to some of the consultation practices of LPAs about which communities are very critical. For example, the NPG were initially asked to make comments just at a very high level, on the broad principles of what the policies were trying to achieve. In April 2016, on Andrea's instructions, Stephanie repeatedly asked the group to focus on this level: "So, now this is, broadly agree the outline plan, broadly agree. … I don't want us to get caught up on the minor corrections, it's the broader agreement to begin with." Then, months later, they were asked to comment on very specific details – such as the accuracy of descriptions, typos and formatting. They rarely had the opportunity to make 'mid-range' comments, below the level of 'broad principles' but above presentational detail.

The NPG took it for granted that this was how the process of producing a neighbourhood plan would unfold, as the expert–lay relation was continuously reproduced through the material encounters of meetings, draft texts and accumulating evidence. It was not necessarily a source of dissatisfaction for them, and they never resisted or questioned it as an overall approach. At times they did chafe at it, for example, Robert described Andrea's emailed instructions as "the thou-shalt job from down south" in October 2015, and they did have critical discussions among themselves, although they never confronted her directly. But these discussions were about the quality of specific pieces of work, not about the structures of expertise or arrangements of power relations. Indeed, they sometimes felt that these arrangements needed tightening rather than reconfiguring. For example, again in October 2015, the NPG were unable to identify how the policies suggested by Andrea mapped on to their objectives and the evidence they had provided her with (Sarah summed it up by saying "I'm just baffled by her document, frankly!"). This meant that they were unable to assess whether her policies would achieve what they had said they wanted, and what gaps may exist in the supporting evidence for each. In response, John suggested that:

'What we need from her is a list of tasks that we've still to do. A clear list that we can see so we can work our way through it and tick it off, like a bullet-pointed list that she's extracted out of the plan, and said, "Right, can you get on and do that?" And then it's clear where we're going, because the problem was, after the last visit, I mean, it was alright when she was there, but when she went, I completely lost in my head what it was that she wanted us to do. So, I think she's going to have to be much more specific in her requests of us really.' (John, Oakley NPG meeting, October 2015)

The unfolding reality of neighbourhood planning in Oakley performed power, expertise and agency in particular ways that sedimented out through its practices and the materials and inscriptions that were relied on. Andrea was enacted from the outset as being in possession of specialised, expert knowledge, and therefore able to frame the plan, what the NPG could hope to achieve, and how they could do it. This defined the conditions of possibility for the entire enterprise. These framings were maintained and reinforced throughout the process, by allocating individual tasks and making specific requests that would contribute to Andrea's expert vision of the completed plan, on the basis of privileged knowledge of what the independent examiner would accept or find 'reasonable' (as discussed further in the previous chapter). Andrea (along with her colleagues) wrote the actual policies and supporting text, as they were enacted as being in possession of a specific skill set, being able to translate the NPG's intentions and evidence into the required expert language, known colloquially as 'planning speak'. And once those policies were drafted, only very limited amendments were permitted to be made to them.

As time went on, members of the NPG began to express a palpable sense of disappointment about outcomes and a disconnect between the work that they had done and the emerging plan. In a meeting with specialist planning consultants in December 2015 (arranged by Andrea), the three members of the NPG present all expressed discontent: "We've worked solidly on evidence until it comes out of our ears, but we don't know if it's the right evidence" (Mary); "We've had five versions of the main document now, we've tried to match up the emerging policies with the evidence we've collected and the things we want to get out of it, but it's been really hard" (Stephanie); "We haven't really had time to discuss the policies, but they're very general, I think that as far as we're concerned they're a bit feeble, a bit lacking" (Jane).

By the end of May 2016, there was a sense that the group could barely reconcile their almost-finalised plan with their original intentions, or even recognise its depiction of their town, combined with feelings of impotence and helplessness, as voiced by various group members throughout that month: "We started with a list of ideas about what people wanted, and they've been knocked out one by one" (Stephanie); "I just can't see anything of us in there, it's just like a document from the council, it doesn't feel like Oakley" (Jane); "It doesn't sound like our voice" (Sarah); "We've done all that work, and it counts for nothing" (John).

The imaginary of neighbourhood planning which framed these actions and reactions enacted power in actors that could mobilise expertise through their association with specific techniques, inscriptions and professional qualifications. This imaginary holds together the material present and its possible futures in specific relations. It clearly illustrates the pattern referred to earlier: the government provides a grant for NPGs to hire specialists for technical or particularly difficult tasks, which reproduces the expert–lay divide. NPGs, performed again as being in deficit, contract consultants for tasks that appear to them to be particularly difficult for those defined again as non-experts (in particular plan writing and 'identify[ing] the "policy space" that the plan may choose to occupy and ... how to go about examining ... different ways in which it could be occupied' [Bradley and Brownill, 2017b: 123]). This is, of course, perfectly valid and there are indeed things that amateur NPGs will require professional and specialist assistance with. Consultants, however, aware of the limited resources available, tend to adhere to a calculative regime (Parker et al, 2017a), and tailor and limit their interactions with NPGs to that parameter, often relying on the embodied expertise of inscriptions and devices (such as already-approved plans, model forms of policy wording, examiners' reports, tried-and-tested surveys and assessment templates). As the experts, consultants frame the conditions of possibility for NPGs by defining what can and cannot be included in the plan and how it will be structured. This then shapes the work that NPGs do by providing a script to follow and rescripting their aspirations 'often to the detriment of community desires and legibility' (Parker et al, 2015: 530). As Gaventa and Cornwall (2006: 122) observe in relation to democratic participation in knowledge production more generally, '[t]hrough access to knowledge and participation in its production, use and dissemination, actors can affect the boundaries and indeed the conceptualisation of the possible.

In some situations, the asymmetrical control of knowledge productions of "others" can severely limit the possibilities, which can be either imagined or acted upon'.

In Wroston, similar dynamics operated in the early stages of the process, which defined Scott, their consultant, in a central role. Scott drove the process along, coordinating the action, taking lead responsibility for the work that was considered most important and technical (as discussed in Chapter 5) and recommending a shape for the plan, a structure which the group could populate with their own content. It was notable that, in the first few months, meetings at which Scott was not present were concluded much faster – without his input there was often little business to discuss, a point which the group frequently joked about. Scott would sometimes deal directly with the LPA – for example, in February 2015, when discussing further potential amendments to their housing needs survey, Anne pointed out that "if Scott's agreed his draft with the LPA then it's pretty much a done deal". The specific arrangement of relations between key actors enacted them in specific ways: while the NPG were notionally in control, in practice decisions over form and content (in this case, with respect to what they then considered their key evidence-gathering device) could be taken elsewhere.

However, Scott took a different approach to Andrea, attempting to construct a different neighbourhood planning process. While Oakley NPG were constrained in their scope for action by assumptions about what was achievable and what the future examiner would find 'reasonable', Scott urged his NPG to push for what they wanted, to test the boundaries of the possible: for example, at a day-long workshop in December 2015 I noted that 'Scott suggests early on, and repeats several times, that the group, if they want to do or say something, should do so and "make the council say no, put the onus on them to show why you can't. Otherwise you're self-policing"'.

Agency is enacted in experts, and expertise is enacted in and distributed through specific human and non-human 'actors' (such as surveys and funding). The Wroston NPG, by virtue of the legitimacy enacted through their multiple identities, is here performed as capable of challenging established policy and practice – which, as shown earlier in this chapter, was in some cases possible. The imaginary enacted in Wroston appeared to have more expansive boundaries than that of Oakley – but in both cases, while the NPGs became active participants in the enactment of these imaginaries, they were originally defined by the actors in the specific expert role of NPG consultants. Any imaginary is a form of material control, both enabling and limiting the potential to act. Like Andrea and Oakley NPG, Scott and Wroston NPG relied heavily on the 'safe space' provided by inscriptions embodying expertise for a range of tasks: for structuring their work on the plan (from September 2015 they start to plan their work around a document that Scott had adapted from a template in the 'Neighbourhood Plans

Roadmap', one of the key technologies of participation); for developing policy (as described later in this section); and for producing evidence (as discussed in Chapter 5). Despite Scott's encouragement to be experimental, the wider set of relations in which the NPG were embedded tended towards reproducing already existing modes of ordering and instantiations of expertise. Despite the consultants' proximate role in defining the imaginary of neighbourhood planning and the NPGs' relative roles and agencies, these are already (constantly) being produced in wider circulations of expertise in the shape of these inscriptions and devices.

In May 2015, while the Wroston NPG were waiting to hear the results of the application for their next tranche of funding from the government, Rebecca asked what they'd do if the funding didn't come through. Simon replied, "Having come to rely on Scott and Andy to hold our hands through it all, I'd feel a bit daunted by that", indicating their reliance on external expertise. 'The community' felt unable to undertake neighbourhood planning without expert support and guidance, which inevitably shapes what it is that 'the community' can and will say and how they go about it. Without Scott's involvement, there was a hiatus in activity.

They trusted in his expertise and ability to do what is best for them, to provide a structure for them to work within, to frame their efforts. I noted in March 2015 that:

FIELDNOTES
Wroston NPG meeting
March 2015

Scott, as part of next tranche of funding, suggests considering a character assessment – formalising as evidence the kinds of things they've been saying. ... Scott also talks them through a series of things they may need to do for the next phase, including screening for SEA [strategic environmental assessment] & HRA [habitats regulations assessment], site surveys and ecological site surveys if allocating. Simon suggests and the group agrees that Scott writes up 'his own job description' for the next funding application, which they can then submit – i.e. he manages the process totally, he sets out what needs to be done, how to do it, and how long it will take. The group are interested in the content and the intention; they want the complicated, 'experty' parts of the process taken off their plates.

As in Oakley, the NPG did not have a concrete imaginary of the eventual plan, a clear idea of what it would look like, for most of the process. In a discussion about the shape of the plan in December 2015, Simon (who, along with Ray, had the firmest grip on the process) said: "I haven't got a clear picture of the plan we're going to write ... we have these discussions saying we'll cover this and that, but I'm not really clear about what that means." This initiated a long discussion about how the plan would be developed, revolving around two opposing views – whether it should closely mirror the local plan (advocated by Ray), or be "structured by the things you care about" (advocated by Scott). These conflicting views resulted in the development of two different 'skeletons' on which the NPG and Scott began to hang the evidential and policy substance of the plan, which caused some ongoing confusion and conflict. The plan was increasingly seen as having a life and an agency of its own, of exceeding their grasp and control. Echoing the situation in Oakley, as I noted in an overview of a Wroston NPG meeting in September 2015:

FIELDNOTES
Wroston NPG meeting
September 2015

They have a sense that they have taken their eyes off the prize, that lots of analysis and evidence gathering work has been done but that they don't really know what to do with this, and don't see how it will lead to a plan that will do what they want. They repeat several times that what should have been a small, focused project aimed at restricting housing growth to an organic rate to meet local needs has grown into 'a monster', with a much wider remit and scope than they wanted, something they don't really feel that they can, or want to, handle.

However, unlike in Oakley, Scott was very reluctant to write the actual plan policies, preferring to deploy his expertise in other ways – such as producing what he and the NPG conceived of as the most important evidence. The NPG were also reluctant to take on writing policies and tried hard to convince him otherwise. In the end, NPG member Ray took on writing the vast majority of the plan, with regular, if limited, feedback from the rest of the group. However, this process also illustrated the central role that professional expertise continued to play at the heart of neighbourhood planning. First, Ray was a retired planning inspector, and was therefore able to draw on his specialised knowledge and experience from the planning system generally – even though neighbourhood planning operates to unique standards and criteria. Second, he drew very heavily on the expertise embodied in an inscription: a draft development plan that the LPA were producing for an Area of Outstanding Natural Beauty (AONB) elsewhere in the district. Wroston is also in an AONB, and it had been a cause of considerable discontent that this other AONB received substantially different (and in the NPG's eyes, preferential) treatment compared to their own in relation to planning. Mirroring this draft document fulfilled several functions for the

NPG: it promised their sought-after equivalence of treatment between the two places; it saved them from the burdensome and difficult tasks of deciding which policy areas they need to cover and gave them some guidance on how to phrase policies; and it provided them with institutional legitimacy in the form of the expertise embodied and embedded in that draft plan.

The NPG did however continue to rely on Scott to 'expert-proof' their plan before they submitted it for examination: he agreed to check through the plan once it was written; check that they had, in his view, adequate evidence in place to support it; and, crucially, write their 'basic conditions statement'. This is a document that sets out how a plan conforms to the four basic conditions that define its baseline conditions of possibility, and this conformity is what the independent examination is intended to test. But as Andrea admitted, "The basic conditions statement is terribly technical, you know, even I don't understand it when it's done" (November 2015). The key inscription that will demonstrate the plan's legitimacy is represented as being beyond the grasp of the people who are ostensibly being given the power to produce the plan – and even beyond some of the experts who are accredited with being able to assist them.

There is considerable openness and scope for interpretation around what constitutes, what is required of, and what is possible for a neighbourhood plan (Parker et al, 2016). But in many cases, rather than leading to experimentation and creativity, to testing the boundaries of possibility, this openness has driven participants to very conservative positions, to a strategy of 'safety first' in an uncertain new arena. This is marked by an extensive reliance on inscriptions such as plans that have already got through the process as templates and standards (Parker et al, 2017a). These inscriptions embody acknowledged expertise and enable that expertise to travel and 'reach in' to new sites from remote locations in space and time. Where NPGs may be inclined to try to develop ambitious and far-reaching policies in order to enact their hopes and intentions, the main concern of many consultants is often to get the plan through examination – this being the mark of success for them (Parker et al, 2015: 530–531). As shown in Wroston, even where consultants encourage a more experimental approach, this can also be an overriding consideration for the NPGs themselves.

The reliance of consultants and NPGs on the embodied expertise of inscriptions and devices indicates the material agency of these artefacts and the extent to which they are embedded in and defined by a web of relations. The actions of NPGs and consultants are driven not simply by their own interests, but by, for example, the specificity of the availability and documented uses of government funding. They are shaped by inscriptions that have emerged from the earliest experiences of neighbourhood planning and by the technologies of participation that have shown themselves 'able to travel' between neighbourhoods (Latour, 1995). These materials close down the experimental possibilities of neighbourhood planning, as 'what has been done' – embodied in these inscriptions – morphs, not as a matter of necessity but with considerable frequency, into 'what can be done'.

A contingent and fairly narrow set of inscriptions (such as a few early plans and their examination reports; specific technologies of participation such as survey templates and the Roadmap; other development plan documents) rapidly come to sediment down into the horizons of possibility for resource-constrained consultants tasked with scoping out what a plan can contain, how it should be expressed and how it can be justified. Existing inscriptions act less like a resource pool to draw on to avoid having to reinvent the wheel, than as a rulebook to be followed. Rather than providing a baseline to build upwards and outwards from, they are often treated as parameters that constrain action and options. The conditions of possibility for the NPGs are thus limited, not by what legislation and policy enable them to do, but rather by the path dependencies marked out by material associations such as resource constraints, inscribed precedents, technologies of participation, and reproduced hierarchical relations of expertise (David, 1985; Urry, 2004). Artefacts and procedures become sedimented into ongoing practices and circumscribe the field of possibility into the future, 'locking in' particular arrangements and relations (Arthur, 1994). These configurations markedly constrain the scope of the NPGs – and their consultants, for that matter – to be creative, experimental and to push the boundaries of what neighbourhood planning can achieve. However, once we start to attend to the practices and processes through which neighbourhood planning is stabilised and simplified, we can begin to understand how they can be recomplexified, destabilised and opened back out again (Law and Mol, 2002).

The right letters

Over time, Scott's involvement with Wroston decreased, primarily due to the considerable time the NPG spent on assessing sites around the village for their suitability for housing. Their main interest was in two large sites that enclosed the village on the north and east sides. These sites featured in the LPA's Strategic Housing Land Availability Assessment and the potential for large-scale building on them (increasing the population of the village up to threefold) had triggered the neighbourhood plan process. The other key site of controversy was the farm that the NPG wanted to help relocate in order to provide a housing site in the centre of the village, but they also investigated 13 other sites in and around the village.

The edges of the village facing both of the large sites were indented and 'organic' (that is, not a flat wall of built development in a straight line). The site to the east of the village was made up of pastured fields, divided by hedgerows and fences, that sloped gently down from the edge of the village towards the river, faced by a woodland on a steep slope (clough) rising up from the opposite riverbank. There were unobstructed views out of the playing field in the middle of the village into this site and to the countryside beyond, connecting the heart of the village (Main Street) to its rural setting. The site was important in defining the village setting as nestling within the landscape, and the unique profile of the clough was a defining landscape feature seen from many places within and around the village. A well-used footpath ran parallel to the river. The site to the north was marked by a rare intact medieval strip field pattern, divided by hedgerows and dry-stone walls. It also sloped gently away from the village, providing open views out to a nearby castle and a more distant wooded ridge. Historic green lanes throughout the site connected with footpaths and tracks to the north and west.

The NPG, with wide support from the neighbourhood, felt that these sites played an important role in giving the village its sense of place, its particular feel, by framing Wroston and giving physical and visual access to the countryside. Their experience of these places was visceral and embodied, constituted by all the senses of sight, smell, sound, touch, taste and beyond, infused by memory and the kinaesthetic connection of walking in and through an environment (Ingold and Vergunst, 2008), of being surrounded by living greens, birdsong, river chatter, spring flowers, a warm breeze on a hot day or the taste of rain coming in from the fells.

Initially, the NPG took on the task of assessing these sites for suitability for development themselves. They used template forms that had been used by the consultants who had conducted site assessments for the development plan in the other AONB in the LPA area. This partially mobilised the institutional legitimacy and embedded expertise of the forms, in an attempt to translate their embodied knowledge into a form that was legible as evidence. However, Tony, their main contact at the LPA, strongly and repeatedly advised them that if they wanted to challenge the findings of the consultants who had assessed the sites for the local plan and had declared both large sites to be developable, they would need a professional assessment carried out by a certified expert.[4] The NPG therefore had to carefully weigh up on what kind of expertise they could best spend their limited funds. As previously described, with access to the embedded expertise of the draft AONB development plan to help with policy writing, they decided that their greatest need was for expert-produced evidence of landscape and visual impact of potential development. However, without Scott's involvement, progress on the plan substantially stalled for many months while the issue of site assessment dominated.

The landscape assessments produced by the LPA's consultants appeared technically robust at first, but on closer inspection by the NPG lacked qualitative depth. The consultants had used template landscape character assessment forms, which were more landscape-specific than the general site assessment forms that the NPG had originally used, which covered a range of factors. The landscape survey templates had predefined categories arranged in a set of matrices to identify the most significant characteristics of the landscape. A first matrix listed key landscape elements such as topography, vegetation cover, built form, hydrology, and so on. Each of these broad headings had a set of predefined categories that could be selected (for example, under topography the surveyor could choose from categories such as flat, low lying, gently rolling, crag, and so on). A second matrix provided a similar tickbox template for visual characteristics including pattern, scale, texture, colour, complexity, unity, remoteness, enclosure and form. Each characteristic had four potential options to choose from, for example, pattern could be defined as dominant, strong, broken or weak, and scale as intimate, small, medium or large. A third matrix required key site qualities to be assessed with reference to tranquillity, landscape condition/quality, settlement character, history and access. This matrix-led template gave the air of a scientific approach, but as revealed by the NPG's analysis, it artificially constrained the characterisation of the sites and led to inadequate and inaccurate descriptions. The effort to mechanically render landscape objectively knowable as an abstract summation of a sequence of pre-given categories removed any traces of meaningfulness from the description, erasing the sense of place which was central to the care and concern for these sites and their place in the neighbourhood. By attempting to render the landscape in objectively factual terms, they were unable to represent the landscape as experienced, and therefore the ways in which it mattered.

The NPG were very critical of the absence of a clear chain of reasoning from the 'objective' findings on the character of the landscape generated through the consultants' completed templates, to their conclusions. Ray described them in December 2015 as "incoherent. ... It looks like a cut and paste job, something knocked up in three minutes". They were also critical of the photos used to illustrate the assessments, as not being taken from the most appropriate spots or picking up on the most important features. Barbara critiqued the findings themselves in detail in late 2016, highlighting relevant features that the consultants had missed, misinterpreted or described inaccurately (such as footpaths, views, slopes, the presence of plant and animal species, and visual connections with other places).

These were places that the NPG knew intimately, in detail, at all times of the day and seasons of the year, in all weathers and lights and as they changed over time. They were key parts of their stories of living in Wroston, of what it meant to them to live in Wroston, as settings for experiences but also as lively, changing actors in themselves. The opinion of the NPG was that the consultants' assessments had been based on a single, brief visit to the sites and on inscriptions borrowed from elsewhere (such as higher-level landscape assessments, that did not go into fine-grained detail at this micro level). The superficial tickbox methodology of the consultants contrasted sharply with the NPG's in-depth knowledge of and engagement with the sites, and their conclusions were likewise different. Nevertheless, it was taken for granted by both the NPG and the LPA that only a qualified professional could produce acceptable evidence on the matter, echoing Raco et al's conclusion that '[l]ay criticism of expert-led proposals is dismissed as a byproduct of subjective vested interests and/or ignorance and mis-understanding of what it is that experts are seeking to do' (2016: 8). As I noted at a day-long workshop of the NPG in December 2015, where considerable time was spent discussing how to go about site assessment:

FIELDNOTES

Wroston NPG workshop

December 2015

The group agreed with Elliot on the need for 'proper evidence to properly challenge the council', and that only a properly qualified person 'with the right letters after their name' could produce this. Simon added that 'I'm sure we could all do it with the matrix they used, but it would have no strength'.

The NPG eventually commissioned an independent landscape architect from Cambridge, who had previously done work commissioned by their AONB, to carry out the assessments. They briefed her in detail about the work that needed doing, their critiques of the flaws in the original assessment, the background to the project and the context of the sites in relation to Wroston and the wider landscape, along with important viewpoints, approaches and travel lines. This new expert spent a whole day undertaking fieldwork, in contrast to the apparently hurried visit of the LPA's consultants. She walked around (and where possible through) all of the sites that the NPG had identified as having potential for development, not just the two large sites. She also spent time walking around and through the village and its surroundings, building up a picture of the area as a whole and making use of the NPG's advice.

She located her assessments of the sites within a broader appraisal of the area as a whole, which she divided into discrete character areas, while also recognising the interplay between these areas. As well as being deeply informed by the NPG's spoken and written information, her material practice of fieldwork also more closely resembled their modes of engagement with place. She finalised her report in March 2017, after giving the NPG the opportunity to comment on a draft report. The final report reflected some, but not all of those comments, indicating that tensions remained between their ways of knowing. This tension had however been productive, and working their ways of knowing together had generated new representations of the world that enriched both lay and expert perspectives and generated new effects (Verran, 2001; Tsing, 2005). It was, however, still an expert-led process that benefited from extensive lay input, rather than a genuinely coproduced process or output.

The final report provided a stark contrast to the assessment of the LPA's consultants, which it directly critiqued, as well as developing a much more in-depth and nuanced picture of the individual sites and their relationship to Wroston and its setting. It relied on richly textured qualitative description rather than the pre-given categories of a matrix. Its methodology and findings differed greatly from the previous assessment, and clearly incorporated elements of the NPG's embodied and intimate knowledge of the place. Its conclusions and recommendations about the suitability of sites for development were also very different.

Despite the production of new evidence by a qualified expert, the LPA continued to insist that their consultants' assessments were authoritative and therefore continued to object to the NPG ruling out building on either of the large greenfield sites, and to proposing building on the brownfield site in the centre of the village. However, at examination, the examiner accepted the NPG's evidence as authoritative and approved the plan to be taken forward to a referendum in spite of the LPA's formal objections. The worked-together expert and lay knowledges that constituted the NPG's assessment were therefore able to 'travel' – to have effects in the kind of setting in which an LPA would usually expect to have their evidence and conclusions given greater weight than those of the community.

However, the NPG had struggled for some time to find a suitable expert willing to take the commission. They were turned down by several who freely admitted that they did not want to be associated with an NPG opposing an LPA, as they feared that would damage their reputation and future commercial prospects. In the relational terms I am using here, that would mean that the networks that constituted them would be destabilised. This again illustrates how the practice of neighbourhood planning does not live up to the promise of delivering power to neighbourhoods. In relational terms, the reconfiguration of relations generated through neighbourhood planning does not necessarily enact power in the neighbourhood: without alignment with suitable experts, they remain powerless.

It also demonstrates how the configurations of expertise and agency extend into other material dimensions beyond the coupling between the ability to produce credible knowledge and the power to act. Experts are also humans who need to make a living, and their capacity to make a living interfaces with their capacity to produce credible knowledge in complex ways. Experts' views may also differ dramatically. The results of assessments are not truths out there waiting to be discovered, but are constructed through the materials, devices and discourses that are enrolled in the process. And crucial to this construction is the rigorously enforced boundary between the qualified expert who can legitimately make findings and draw conclusions, and the lay community who cannot: enacted as being trapped in 'irrationality and archaism ... muddled natives caught up in strange beliefs or representations of the world' (Callon et al, 2009: 93). The challenge for better planning is working out how different kinds of knowledge and ways of knowing can be worked together better without such automatic privileging and marginalising, while acknowledging that all forms of knowledge production, by paid professionals as much as community groups, are also embedded in wider networks that will shape and influence the knowledge produced.

The long reach of the local authority

As discussed at the start of this chapter, in both of these cases the LPAs had, in some ways at least, recognised the NPGs as belonging to the 'charmed circle' of experts. Their very presence at the table appeared to give them license to present knowledge claims and arguments that would be listened to and recognised as coming from the 'right' side of the expert–lay divide. The neighbourhood plan was acknowledged in these instances as being the NPG's territory, in which they can exercise the agency conferred by expertise – the right to decide what the policies will be and how they will be justified. But despite this recognition of a boundary between the territories of the LPA and the NPG (Bradley, 2015), the LPA still reaches into neighbourhood planning spaces as an expert into a lay community. Quite apart from the 'basic condition' requirement that neighbourhood plan policies must be in general conformity with the LPA's strategic local plan policies, the influence of the LPA permeates the practices of neighbourhood planning in several important ways (Parker et al, 2017a).

They have formal roles from the start to the end of the process of producing a neighbourhood plan: designating (or rejecting) the proposed neighbourhood plan area, and the Neighbourhood Forum in unparished areas; assessing whether submitted draft plans meet the legal requirements to go forward to examination; organising the examination and associated formal consultation (including appointing an examiner, in agreement with the qualifying body); making any changes to the plan recommended by the examiner; organising the referendum; and, eventually, formally adopting the plan. All of these stages can and have produced conflict and contestation in a number of places and can directly or indirectly hinder or prevent the development of a plan. While consultants play a major role in defining the conditions of possibility for NPGs, in terms of shaping their imaginary of the enterprise of neighbourhood planning, the LPAs define those conditions in much more directly material ways, starting with the ability to define the boundaries that will determine how 'the neighbourhood' is constituted.

Alongside these formal roles, framed by their somewhat vague 'duty to support', LPAs also engage with NPGs to a greater or lesser extent as possessors of specialised knowledge, skills or resources. In both of my case studies, the LPA conducted a screening assessment on the emerging plans to see if they required Strategic Environmental Assessment. They provided ongoing advice on what, in their expert opinion, the plans and their evidence bases might need to make them sufficiently robust to pass examination. They provided maps that could meet the NPGs' very specific requirements, which became some of the most significant materials in ordering the planning process and the engagement between social community and material neighbourhood. They played the role of 'critical friends' – but friends who occupy the upper part of the value-hierarchical dualism of expert and lay, and whose advice and critique therefore acquires more pressing force. In Wroston, this critical advice led the NPG to spend a sizable chunk of their limited funds on a landscape professional to produce evidence that was more commensurable with their lived experience. However, they continued to resist the pressure from the LPA to change their policies, and through aligning their hired-in human expertise with other material 'allies' (such as the LPA's development plan for the other AONB in its area and the tried-and-tested housing needs survey), they were able to successfully take those policies through examination.

Perhaps the LPA's most important role in relation to neighbourhood plans begins after the plan is adopted: they are key end-users of the plans. Neighbourhood plans can shape decisions, but those decisions are still made, in the first instance, by the LPA. Decisions may also be taken at an even greater literal and figurative distance from the communities who produced the plans, as developers can appeal against LPA decisions, which are then decided by planning inspectors or by the Secretary of State, and the Secretary of State can also call in or recover cases to decide him/herself. It is commonly accepted that different policies in a development plan will be, to varying degrees, in tension with each other, and that it is for the discretion of the decisionmaker to decide how much weight to give such competing policies. And even the most clearly expressed and finely crafted planning policies are almost always open to a degree of interpretation.

So while the neighbourhood now has the power to produce a plan (albeit a rather limited and constrained power), the power to interpret that plan's meaning and its relation to the local plan and to other material considerations remains with the experts and decisionmakers in the LPA, the planning inspectorate and the relevant government department. This ensures that the expert/lay, citizen/decisionmaker 'double divide' continues to be performed. The actors' relations are reconfigured, to an extent, as far as the practice of plan-making is concerned, but they remain undisturbed with regard to decision taking. Burns and Yuille (2018), in an analysis of a large sample of appeal decisions involving neighbourhood plans, show that in very many cases other policy considerations are able to 'trump' neighbourhood plans, leading to decisions which conflict with those plans.

Beyond neighbourhood planning

Neighbourhood planners were, rhetorically at least, intended to be empowered to make decisions for themselves, with professional expertise firmly consigned to a supporting role in a process led by the neighbourhood itself. However, I have shown in this chapter that professional expertise and authority does not just permeate the assemblage of neighbourhood planning, but can often in effect displace neighbourhood planners from their notional place at the centre of that assemblage. And, in their different ways, similar processes of reliance upon, and displacement by, external expertise and authority can be seen in the other cases of participatory democracy that we have been considering.

Environmental justice

Environmental justice movements gain a crucial element of legitimacy from the production of knowledge about local environmental conditions. But as knowledge claims are, in effect, claims to power and authority, the boundary of what counts as knowledge – which claims should be respected and which should be discounted or considered inferior – are strongly contested (Gieryn, 1983, 1999). The results of citizen science are sometimes seen as 'just good enough' (Gabrys et al, 2016), but whether this is the case is also often disputed. Even where activists can make claims to expertise and rigour, for example, through the involvement or provision of training by academics or non-governmental organisations (NGOs), or by using technologies that are recognised as reliable by government agencies, they can be dismissed as 'not expert enough' or not fitting into conventional scientific frameworks. Their central concerns and questions, standards of proof, and insistence on the importance of synergistic effects and cumulative impacts all often depart from mainstream scientific practice, leaving them open to challenge (Allen, 2003; Corburn, 2005; Bryant, 2011).

As an example, fenceline communities (located next to refineries, chemical plants and similar potential sources of pollution) are often concerned about periodic episodes of high levels of pollution released during accidents, fires and other unplanned discharges. The exceptionally high levels of chemicals present in the air at such times are often measured by Bucket Brigades using low-cost, DIY equipment to capture air samples during peak pollution incidents, and which are then analysed in accredited laboratories. This captures scientific data that is not gathered by the industrial facilities or regulatory agencies. However, it is also data that does not fit into official frameworks for assessing either chronic or acute exposure. Corporate and regulatory experts can therefore attempt to dismiss them as irrelevant to 'scientific' monitoring of air quality and health impacts (Ottinger, 2009). Because standard scientific frameworks often do not align well with community concerns about risk and environmental hazards, the knowledge produced to investigate those concerns is open to critique as being 'unscientific'.

In hearings, inquiries and other public forums, technical experts are automatically afforded a privileged role, as are their claims and the methods which support them, while participants who are not familiar with the specific conventions and jargon of such proceedings are marginalised (Wynne, 1982; Cole and Foster, 2001). The claims of certified experts are often accepted as fact (or at least as 'good enough'), regardless of the scientific uncertainties and contingencies behind their often 'black-boxed' pronouncements (Walker, 2012). Those classed as non-experts, by contrast, may have their status undermined and their knowledge discredited by means of a variety of more or less subtle demonstrations of disrespect expressed through intersecting discourses of exclusion linked to race, class, gender, geography and even religious affiliation (Kurtz, 2007). This can vary from variations in modes of address, stressing participants' lack of formal qualifications (Schlosberg, 2007), through to blatant insults, such as Hilda Kurtz's reports of government officials publicly referring to members of an environmental justice group in Louisiana as 'hysterical housewives' (2007: 419).

Contributions and questions raised by non-experts, regardless of their pertinence, can be dismissed as irrelevant to the technical questions at hand (Ottinger, 2013). As Sally Eden summarises, 'environmental publics are constructed not as knowing but as unknowing, as poorly informed or even misinformed' (Eden, 2017: 23). This replicates the deficit model, whereby people who are not certified as experts are assumed to have a deficit of correct information, which can be remedied by experts providing correct information, regardless of the relevant (but non-certified) skills, experience and knowledge they may possess (Wynne, 1996). Even where environmental justice advocates or policies are embedded into regulatory agencies and other authorities, they often remain marginalised as a 'third party', with officials resisting, undermining and disparaging their integration into the mainstream of how business is done (Shilling et al, 2009; Harrison, 2019). There is considerable evidence that this displacement or sidelining of environmental justice priorities within environmental protection and regulation agencies is in some cases a result of deliberate co-option by counter-movement actors (Holifield, 2012; Lievanos, 2012). However, it can also be understood as a reflection of different understandings of those priorities between activists and agency staff, and between different members of agency staff, in which interpretations that preserve the status quo tend to push out more radical versions (Harrison, 2016, 2017).

Environmental justice claims can also often be displaced by the attempted capture of regulatory systems and processes by powerful corporate interests. One of many examples provided by Faber (2008) is of an influential study which concluded that the chemical compound hexavalent chromium did not cause high cancer rates. It was later retracted when it was revealed that it had been produced by consultants for the Pacific Gas and Electric Company, which was engaged in a legal battle over accusations about the health impacts of its hexavalent chromium contamination in California. More generally, the resources available to high-polluting corporate interests to employ consultants, scientists and lawyers, the nub of whose role is often to focus disputes on purely technical matters, and to assert the inability of non-certified experts to speak on technical matters (alongside other manipulative techniques to marginalise community claims), can also lead to displacement effects and the sidelining of environmental justice activists (Ottinger, 2013).

However, environmental justice movements have also made productive partnerships with professionals within conventional establishments of expertise in epidemiology, public health and environmental science, that have resulted in successful outcomes for environmental justice advocates and which have laid the foundations for future partnerships to learn from (Wilson et al, 2007, 2018). It has also been argued that these partnerships have started to have displacement effects in the other direction, reassembling relations between scientific institutions, individuals and practices. Once-closed debates have been opened around issues such as incorporating human diversity and differential vulnerability into risk assessments, communicating research outcomes and setting standards of proof, and addressing issues such as justice, sustainability and health 'upstream' (Ottinger and Cohen, 2012). And as well as providing evidence and advocacy for affected communities, there are a growing number of scientist-activists that are playing significant roles in the environmental justice movement alongside and in partnership with grassroots activists, supporting rather than undermining their central position (Frickel, 2004).

Community organising

In previous chapters I have described the potential for community organising in informal settlements to develop 'insurgent' knowledges and forms of citizenship and democratic participation. And certainly, participation and inclusivity in decision making can empower and build capacities in these communities, enabling cocreation of knowledge which draws on a diversity of knowledge systems in ways which enable the voices of marginalised people to be better heard and trusted (Ziervogel et al, 2021). However, this kind of knowledge and citizenship remains 'insurgent' – that is, the communities who have the potential to produce and enact it remain largely marginalised, subjugated, and on the periphery of the imaginaries and knowledge systems of the modern state, economy and society (Scott, 1998). Even where such communities are invited to participate in decision making about their social and material futures, they are often displaced or decentred by the dominant knowledge/power structures and the association of agency and legitimate knowledge with certified expertise. Such processes thus run the risk of entrenching existing inequalities and relationships rather than delivering the transformative change that they espouse (Archer and Dodman, 2015).

Knowledge production and dissemination in upgrading and development projects in informal settlements in the global South have a long history of being guided by Northern/Western experts and imaginaries of expertise. This has resulted in the legitimisation of a narrow range of professionals, agencies and institutions able to produce and determine what counts as meaningful knowledge (Bradlow, 2015). This can lead to clashes in the very definitions of success for such projects, when the rationales and imaginaries of such legitimised experts conflict with the lived realities of their 'target populations'. The methods of translation that make the worlds of informal settlements legible to planners, funders and bureaucrats often result in an analysis which 'bears amazingly little relation to the lived reality of slum dwellers' (Koster and Nuijten, 2012: 177).

While such projects may in some cases hold much promise and attraction to marginalised urban poor communities, if (as is often the case) they are implemented as technical exercises to improve physical infrastructure, they fail to engage with, much less transform, the socio-political marginalisation of the poor (Scott, 1998). The multiple dimensions of need and knowledge of poor communities are engaged with through invited participatory spaces, but are all too often reduced to a singular manageable dimension that presents itself as a 'do-able problem' in an expert-led framework (Hoppe, 2010). Such technicalised solutions to complex socio-technical problems can even result in increased inequalities: the failure to take account of all the relevant factors in the sociomaterial assemblage can result in the most vulnerable communities or community members not experiencing any benefit or even being negatively impacted (Seeliger and Turok, 2014). And this technocratic approach – particularly when projects are not carried through in a participatory way – can fuel long-standing feelings of resentment and mistrust on all sides which become more intractable than ever and make future cooperation and coproduction even more difficult (Peirson and Ziervogel, 2021).

As in other sites of participatory democracy, processes that involve grassroots social movements alongside others are, of course, vulnerable to capture by more powerful or well-resourced actors among the population. Caldeira and Holston describe the participatory development of urban policy in Brazil, which 'engage[s] citizens of all classes, and express[es] a degree of democratic inventiveness rarely found in the formulation of public policy anywhere' (Caldeira and Holston, 2015: 2001). However, despite its explicit intention to counter entrenched social inequalities, they found that while urban poor social movements have become involved in these formal processes, they have been subject to displacement – their knowledges and contributions sidelined – by more affluent citizens, professionals and corporate interests who are better able to enact the kind of expert identities with which the process is equipped to engage, or employ others to do so.

Displacement of knowledge based on lived experience can also occur through the internalisation of identities and imaginaries enacted for informal settlement communities by others. In self-governed research into the multidimensional aspects and causes of poverty carried out by the poor, for the poor and with the poor in informal settlements across six countries (briefly described in Chapter 5), one national team included 'laziness' as a reason for why people were poor. This was highly contentious, with other delegates insisting that this was an external framing of their identity that decentred both them and the structural problems that they were attempting to evidence:

> I don't agree with this word lazy. That is not our word. That is the word the authorities use when they look down on us and call us lazy and incapable of being helped. That's their excuse for giving no support to the poor. The poor are not lazy! Hopelessness is not the same as laziness. (Boonyabancha and Kerr, 2015: 648)

Informal settlements are also highly politicised contexts, and engagement with political parties – and even becoming embedded in the machinery of government – can provide social movements with opportunities for greater engagement with decisionmakers. However, it can also result in the decentring of their priorities in favour of political assessments of electoral needs, resulting in a difficult balancing act between autonomy, influence and co-option (Earle, 2013). More straightforwardly, it can also result in relations of clientelism, in which (often inadequate or inequitable) benefits or services are provide to poor communities in return for political support, which actively discourages genuine socio-political change and community empowerment (Deuskar, 2019). Paradoxically, perhaps, it is the distance from government and official forms of knowledge production and presentation, and its association with self-help in the absence of state support, that imbues insurgent knowledge and citizenship with much of its power. Invited spaces often have the effect of marginalising the voices of those they ostensibly intend to empower (Cornwall and Coelho, 2007). However, in order to influence change, communities have to engage with states and other powerful actors, suggesting a need for a complex iteration of action between invited and invented spaces to develop new relations, enact new identities, and avoid dominant structures of knowledge and power being reproduced and reimposed.

Participatory rural development

Like neighbourhood planning, participatory rural development is an 'invited space', in which the state (or other external actors, including donor agencies, development organisations and NGOs) deliberately seek to mobilise the knowledge, values and experiences of local communities in shaping their own futures. Like neighbourhood planning, this is a conscious reaction against a previous situation in which affected communities were peripheral to decisions made by others, an attempt to transfer a measure of power from the centre to the periphery. Like neighbourhood planning, there is certainly evidence of community development approaches generating positive effects for (at least some members of) the communities where they are practised, and many authors and practitioners believe that they 'retain valuable scope to speak to people's real concerns, perhaps even cultivating prefigurative relations where ideals of justice and equality are lived out in the here and now' (Meade et al, 2016b: 6). But also like neighbourhood planning, these new community-based centres of power are also subject to displacement and decentring by other actors, knowledges and expertise.

First, the professional, external community development worker retains a central role in the process. Early versions of this role were primarily extractive and analytic – using specialised techniques to gain information and insights from local people about local conditions, and then using them to inform their expert judgement about the most productive and appropriate local social and economic development approaches. This role was deliberately shifted over time to being more of a catalyst, convenor and facilitator, working as a partner with local people to provide them with the tools and techniques needed to enable them to define their own problems, conduct their own investigations, and develop their own solutions (Chambers, 1997). This shift from community participation in outsiders' projects to community ownership of their own plans and projects can be seen as analogous to the shift in English land use planning from community engagement in local planning to community development of neighbourhood plans.

In this analogy, the community development worker role shifts from resembling that of the expert local authority planner consulting with the community, to the expert consultant hired by an NPG to help them deliver their own plan (although of course development workers are not hired by rural poor communities but introduced to them by external actors). In reality, like many NPG consultants, development workers' roles often shift and blur between leadership and facilitation (Kenny, 2016). And as with the examples detailed earlier in this chapter, this means that while the community development worker's role is to empower, they are also in effect establishing the conditions of possibility for the communities that they work with (Kothari, 2005). While the development worker provides the community with the tools to ask and answer their own questions, the framings and imaginaries within which they locate and present these tools make some types of question not just more answerable, but also more askable (Craig and Porter, 1997).

This act of framing is not in itself to be criticised – framing is inevitable and essential to sensemaking (Brugnach and Ingram, 2012). But it does entail a decentring of the community by the very actor whose role is to enact them as a new centre of agency. The act of facilitating a process to bring the peripheral, the 'done to', into the centre, of 'putting the last first', simultaneously reproduces the power and status of the professional, the expert (Williams, 2004). And while this central role can be performed with positive results, it can also serve to reproduce and entrench the very colonial, inegalitarian framings that it is intended to upend (Escobar, 1995; Kapoor, 2005).

But development workers are likewise already implicated in, empowered and constrained by, the framings and imaginaries that permeate the worlds that they are a part of. While the meaning of the word 'development' has always been to an extent multivalent and ambiguous, it is nevertheless in terms of development that this mode of participation is framed. Participatory development projects have to be intelligible to the agencies that sponsor them, and function in terms of their particular objectives and understandings of 'development' (Mohan, 2001; Mansuri et al, 2013). This constrains the agency of local actors to articulate and interpret their knowledge, values and experience in their own terms. It is argued that that this tends to reduce the problems (and therefore potential solutions) of participating communities to technical ones, depoliticising relations within communities and between communities and other actors (such as states and donor agencies), simultaneously concealing and naturalising a range of social inequalities (Ferguson, 1990; Cooke and Kothari, 2001). The discourse and practice of participation and empowerment is decentred by the discourse and practice of development, with agency enacted in remote authorities through participatory arrangements, as local people are empowered to make some kinds of choices but not others.

The effect of this is very often that 'decentralization is used to tighten central control and increase incentives for upward accountability rather than to increase local discretion' (Mansuri et al, 2013: 6). Such upward accountability (that is, accountability to sponsor agencies [states, donors or NGOs] rather than 'downward accountability' to local communities) requires the establishment of regimes of monitoring and quantification. These enact agency in certified professionals through modernist and managerialist imaginaries (Shaw, 2011) and create 'calculable spaces that can be made governable through experts and expertise' (Mueller-Hirth, 2012: 656). The local knowledge and experience of community members is thus displaced by the calculative, abstract rationality of the expert, as framed by a modernist imaginary, invoked to enact the power of remote authorities.

These decentring effects are amplified by the 'corporatisation' of both states and development practices, both through 'philanthrocapitalism' (in which corporations directly invest in development projects) and the widespread importation of market and corporate norms, conventions and standards into social and democratic spheres through processes of neoliberalisation (Edwards, 2008). Indeed, at least partly because of the decentring effects of the continued dominance of external forms of expertise and regulation of what counts as knowledge and whose knowledge counts, in some cases a more activist-led model of community organising is emerging, an invented space in distinction from the invited space of participatory development (Jha, 2016).

Conclusion

Despite the rhetoric of community empowerment and letting local people rather than experts and insiders 'do' planning, the figure of the expert retains a central position within neighbourhood planning: 'citizens achieved the status of (lay) planners but their successful incorporation in the profession reinforced the universality of abstract rationality and underlined the exclusion of other spatial cultures' (Bradley, 2018: 31). Similar processes can be observed across the other instances of participatory democracy discussed.

This is in no way intended as a critique of expertise or of experts. There is of course technical work to be done in all of these arenas that non-experts will not have the skills or experience for. Returning to focus on neighbourhood planning, there are challenges that NPGs will not feel able to tackle alone; there is specialised knowledge that is essential for informing the actions and decisions of NPGs, and contextual and processual knowledge that would be costly and time-consuming for them to rediscover themselves with each new plan. However, the rhetoric of community empowerment conceals the continued valorisation of the expert position at the expense of community actors. The 'charmed circle' of expertise is conditionally widened to partially include NPGs, but this simultaneously reproduces problematic expert–lay relations and the expert–agency coupling. This coupling of expertise and agency, and the subsequent decentring of community actors, is also reflected across the other cases.

Where the neighbourhood planning literature engages with the role of experts, it is often to discuss the privatisation and marketisation of planning, in terms of a shift of power and resources from the public to the private sector, rather than addressing the ways that power relations unfold between communities, NPGs and the experts that both serve and shape them (Lord and Tewdwr-Jones, 2014; Bailey and Pill, 2015; Lord et al 2017). There are however some notable exceptions, such as Parker et al (2015, 2017a), which discuss the constraining and rescripting of community desires into more conservative forms through the interests and commitments of experts and other pressures. There is more extensive discussion of the relations between external experts and community actors in the literature on the other cases of participatory democracy that this book touches on, particularly on environmental justice and participatory rural development, and experiences in those arenas could usefully inform and sensitise analysis and development of neighbourhood planning practices.

Experts play integral and multiple roles in the practices of neighbourhood planning, but these are not made highly visible. The discourse of government, neighbourhood planning support agencies and the specialists themselves all emphasise the devolution of power and the ability of communities to populate plans with the issues that concern them, rhetorically reinforcing the 'community-led' nature of neighbourhood planning. The plans themselves, publicity around them, national policy and guidance all tend to refer to experts in vague and general ways (if at all) as being in supporting roles. Their active and central involvement is literally written out of the inscriptions that are the outputs of the process. Little attention is paid to how experts' relations with NPGs produce specific enactments of neighbourhood planning, order processes in particular ways, and translate material relations into inscriptions in contingent ways that tend to be enacted as necessary.

Even less attention is paid to the agency – the capacity to have effects – of inscriptions such as templates, examiners' reports and adopted plans, which order the imaginaries and actions of experts and NPGs alike. These are rather presented as neutral means of facilitating the achievement of the NPGs' intentions, not as agents which actively shape NPGs actions and outcomes.[5] These networks of human and non-human 'actors' constitute the realities in which NPGs operate, and which they subsequently reproduce through their own enactments. The tendency to devalue local and non-accredited actors, and the use of artefacts, embodied expertise and institutional legitimacy to close down contestation or experimentation, reflects Rydin et al's findings (2018) at the other scalar 'end' of the planning system, in inquiries into Nationally Significant Infrastructure Projects. But while this kind of technoscientific closure might be expected in such a large-scale, highly formalised arena, its 'bleeding' into the arena of neighbourhood planning is perhaps more surprising.

The contingent realities of the neighbourhood planning process constrain (as well as enable) the actions of the NPGs, ordering their imaginaries in specific ways, sometimes to the extent of pushing them into conservative, risk-averse positions that do not necessarily serve their interests well or reflect the individuality of their particular situation, and which reinforce their reliance on the figure of 'the expert'. The NPGs in these case studies often showed a healthy scepticism towards 'purified' expert knowledge, but nevertheless recognised its power and status. They were very much aware of their own framing as 'not-expert-enough'. They were aware of the partial and situated nature of their experiential knowledge, and attempted to purify it into the universal, abstract knowledge of expertise. However, they were also aware of the partial and situated nature of the knowledge of expertise, not least because they saw its faults and its flaws in its failures to connect with and represent their experiences of place.

The simplifications made by experts in order to translate a messy and complex intersection of social and material relations into a manageable, representable neighbourhood are not the only simplifications that could be made (Law, 2004). They may not be those that the NPG would have chosen, and others would be possible within the legal and policy framework of neighbourhood planning. The reliance on templates and other inscriptions to produce evidence and plans can result in standardised policies and a somewhat 'identikit' quality that appears markedly at odds with the stated intention of neighbourhood planning to be very locally specific, to draw out the special distinctiveness of particular places, and to do so using the deep and detailed knowledge and care that only local residents can bring. Both NPGs I worked with expressed concern about their consultants' lack of local knowledge and their related tendency to 'find' policy solutions from elsewhere (although the NPGs also used inscriptions as templates and guides in their own work). The results of these processes were epitomised by Oakley NPG chair Stephanie in March 2017, when she reflected on the shrinking of the plan from their original ambitions to "the smallest shreds of what we'd wanted to do", and NPG member Martin saying in May 2017 that "it just doesn't sound like us, I can't see Oakley in there when I read it". And as Stephanie commented the following month "We have tensions pulling in two opposite directions, Andrea keeps saying to make it simple, and we're saying, 'make it good!'". The path dependencies that have become sedimented down – but which are not required by policy or legislation – made it very difficult to "make it good" from the NPG's perspective.

Beneath the veneer of coproduction is a deep, intransigent and automatic privileging of expertise and associated ways of knowing. The practices of neighbourhood planning reproduce this at the figurative level, while simultaneously reconfiguring the specific actors that can enact the expert role. Parallel reproductions and reconfigurations can be recognised in the experiences of environmental justice movements, community organising and participatory rural development. In all these cases, while in certain circumstances community actors are recognised as being a new centre of expertise in their own right, in other ways they are decentred and relegated once again to the lay side of the divide. This acts to suppress the expression of certain types of knowledge and value that are considered to be on the wrong side of the line that divides 'nature, facts, objectivity, reason and policy from ... culture, values, subjectivity, emotion and politics' (Jasanoff, 2004b: 3). It closes down potentially open spaces through the obduracy of taken-for-granted assumptions that valorise the impossible 'singular definitively prescriptive "sound scientific", "evidence-based" "rational choice"', which excludes other ways of knowing and valuing from decision making (Stirling, 2014: 88).

This limits the potential for 'understanding what the social world means for the people who live in it' (Davoudi, 2015: 320). However, in each of the cases considered here, I have also highlighted the potential for doing things differently and that there exist the seeds of more transformative practices. In neighbourhood planning, it matters that, while the expert– agency coupling is reproduced, the NPG-as-experts sit in a different relation to their neighbourhoods than the experts they have partially displaced, in an identity-multiple that necessarily incorporates relations other than expertise. These relations, even if their visibility is marginalised in formal inscriptions, nevertheless persist and continue to frame the actions and understandings of the NPGs. The shifting of relations and identities as these multiple displacements take place close down some possibilities, but also open up other possibilities for intervention and different outcomes. It also matters that even within this expert-dominated framework, other ways of working knowledges together do sometimes emerge (Watson-Verran and Turnbull, 1995).

7

Care and concern

'If it's supposed to be a new way of planning, it's for the planners
to learn to speak like us, not the other way around. We get sucked
into their world, they do and say things like this because it's what
they're used to, and then we just go along with it because they
know that they know what they're doing, even if they don't, if
you see what I mean, because they're the experts.'

Martin (Oakley neighbourhood planning
group [NPG] member, May 2017)

Introduction

This chapter addresses some of the neglected things in neighbourhood
planning: the affective, relational, experiential knowledges that previous
chapters have shown often get excluded.

As the opening quotation from Oakley NPG member Martin articulates
very eloquently, the NPGs felt that rather than neighbourhood planning
leading to planners (and the planning system) engaging better with their world
of lived experience, it instead drew them, the neighbourhood planners, into
a situation in which they had to adopt the language, norms and conventions
of a professional community of practice. And within this community, they
often felt that they had to defer to the practices of the professionals, even
when this conflicted with or excluded their understandings of situations,
simply because of their accredited status: "they know that they know what
they're doing, even if they don't".

The chapter begins by describing some of the attempts that the NPGs
made to engage with experiential knowledge and care for place, and the
difficulties they encountered in articulating, capturing and translating them
into evidence. I suggest that if a process that is intended to be driven by the
community's knowledge of and care for place struggles to engage directly
with those matters, then some change of approach is needed. I then draw
on the concepts of matters of concern (Latour, 2004b) and matters of care
(Puig de la Bellacasa, 2017) to develop a theoretical reflection on what such a
change of approach might involve. I propose operationalising these concepts
in the production and evaluation of evidence for neighbourhood planning.
This would support an imaginary in which the diversity of things that matter
to NPGs and the neighbourhoods they speak for can be taken seriously and

be capable of becoming 'weighty' evidence. It would also enable a more faithful rendering of the things that are made to matter as 'facts' (Latour, 1993), and would help avoid prematurely closing down which issues and sources of knowledge are included (Stirling, 2008), by acknowledging the partiality and situatedness of all knowledge claims. I briefly review narrative and other approaches that have attempted to integrate excluded knowledges into planning and related spheres, but which remain marginal. I suggest that neighbourhood planning, despite the foreclosures indicated in these chapters, remains an arena in which such a 'modest' form of planning could take place (Haraway, 1997).

Lost in translation

'Felt in the bones'

The NPGs produced representations that conform with the planning imaginary of abstract space, but which are nevertheless shaped by meaningful relations with experienced place. This enables them to make material differences (see Chapter 6, and also Bradley and Sparling, 2016; Bailey, 2017; Bradley, 2017b; Brownill and Bradley, 2017; Vigar et al, 2017). However, it is also somewhat misrepresentative. It is not transparent. It does not allow 'othered' knowledges and ways of knowing to be opened to examination: analysed, interpreted and worked together with dominant ways of knowing. The automatic privileging of the language and logics of abstract space also prevents an adequate interrogation of claims couched in those terms, by black-boxing their complex situatedness and partiality. The way that evidence is figured therefore risks replicating the situation common across the rest of the planning system, in which 'planners end up thinking with only part of their mind about part of what matters to people, part of why they act as they do, and part of what would move them to act' and where '[t]he resulting partial understanding is undermined by the resulting misunderstanding' that this represents a complete picture (Baum, 2015: 513). It performs certain versions of neighbourhood (and of neighbourhood planners) at the expense of others.

As previously indicated, NPG members and other residents had a deep sense of what made their neighbourhoods valued. However, articulating this sense was an entirely different matter. As Tuan (1975: 165) concluded, the experience of and relationship with place is 'felt in the bones', and for Metzger,

> places exist in registers of intensities that are wickedly challenging to grasp or enumerate, to put into words or agree upon a definition of, to map or sketch exhaustively – at least without committing a serious fallacy of unwarranted reduction. Place-phenomena nevertheless

appear to be crucial to be aware of in any endeavour to understand the complex entanglements of social realities. (Metzger, 2014b: 90)

The kind of experiential engagements that people have with place – crucial components of sense of place and how we know and value our surroundings – are often tacit, felt, affective and/or corporeal, and hard to articulate. The difficulties in expressing them are magnified in a knowledge tradition and practice that tends to marginalise such ways of knowing as a matter of course. They are not considered to be evidence, or material considerations – not the kind of thing that planning can be about. As such, the processes of knowledge production and decision making are implicitly designed in such a way as to exclude them. However, as Despret puts it, 'to "de-passion" knowledge does not give us a more objective world, it just gives us a world "without us". ... And as long as this world appears as a world "we don't care for", it also becomes an impoverished world ... a poorly articulated (and poorly articulating) world' (Despret, 2004: 131). Because these things are also quintessentially what planning *is* about: how people and place relate to each other. They are what motivate people to engage with neighbourhood planning. And while they tend not to be presented as evidence or made explicit in plans, to an extent they are able to penetrate and shape policies.

Both NPGs were conscious that their evidence did not adequately represent their (or their neighbours) lived experience of place, or what made their neighbourhood special, and they repeatedly referred to this. While recognising a need to articulate this sense of place and emplacement, formulating and presenting this kind of knowledge-value hybrid as an acceptable material form of evidence was extremely challenging, lacking any clearly defined process or outcome. It was also something that was repeatedly deprioritised by both groups in favour of gathering 'hard facts' through technical work. Although both NPGs repeatedly agreed that it should not be difficult, because "We've got it all in our heads, the only thing is getting it down on paper" (Simon, Wroston NPG Chair, December 2015), in practice, weaving together these disparate sources of knowledge and value into an acceptable material form was overwhelming. Unable to find ways to foreground these matters that would do justice to their significance to the NPGs and their neighbourhoods, they tended to be marginalised, translated into forms and frameworks that were deemed appropriate, but which were unable to capture the richness and texture of experiential knowledge (although see Chapter 6 for an example of a relatively successful translation which worked together the lived experience of the NPG with the professional expertise of a landscape architect). The material relations and knowledge practices associated with the NPGs' identity 'in' the community were suppressed in formal inscriptions and discourse, and the experiential entanglements of other neighbourhood residents were purified through the knowledge practices associated with their identity 'of' the neighbourhood.

Travelling from experience to evidence?

Both NPGs engaged with experiential knowledges in a variety of ways throughout the development of their plans. For some weeks before and during my first few weeks with them, NPG member Susan had been consulting with various community groups in Wroston on the initial lists of assets and issues that the NPG had drawn up. She emphasised the importance of face-to-face discussion with people, and the ability to talk around the meanings of questions, answers and their referents. She reported that the response from one group was much less informative than from others because she hadn't been present for their discussion – she gave a short presentation and left them some forms to fill in. On collecting the forms, she said that "I looked at it and thought, that's not what I meant by asking that question" (April 2015). However, these contested and meaning-full discussions and interpretations were not recorded, only a truncated summary of conclusions. Susan had also run a discussion group with some of the village's older children and teenagers (15–19 years old), who had produced mindmap diagrams about the assets, issues and development potential of the village rather than completing forms. Likewise, these were not taken forwards as evidence in their own right but left vaguely to somehow inform the thinking of the NPGs. They were treated more like points of data to be abstracted and aggregated, rather than points of departure to be opened up and explored.

The first Wroston consultation event in July 2015 displayed these mindmaps as part of a set of displays featuring information and images about the neighbourhood plan process, the results of community surveys and other consultation so far, the village's history and heritage, collages from children at the local school, a proposed vision and objectives, and next steps. The event offered formal feedback channels (a form with structured questions, a map to identify [with different coloured sticky labels] suitable locations for development and features to protect or take action about, and sticky labels to comment on the vision and objectives). But as well as the displays and the formal feedback channels, I noted that:

FIELDNOTES
Wroston consultation event
July 2015

there was no formal consultation face-to-face, but visitors talked amongst themselves and to steering group members in a fluid and unstructured manner, asking questions and making comments. This could be thought of in terms of a shared space to co-construct Wroston and its meanings.

Visitors' attention was focused on Wroston and the parish in a way in which they were not accustomed to; it provided the space to think about and to shape what the village meant, how it was, how it is and how it might be. Informal commentaries and unforced social interaction made for a much less structured, formalised and constrained means of gathering/co-constructing knowledge with the community than the largely quantitative surveys. People clearly felt able to express themselves freely and fluently; there were no epistemological divisions, no us and them, no (obvious) filters on expression. However, likewise none of this was formally captured.

This extract illustrates how the lived, affective experience of place both shaped and was excluded from the process of developing the plan. As an open, informal event there were no restrictions on what could be discussed, what issues could be raised, what ideas could be put forward. The NPG were able to learn directly from people, and indeed the very fact that they were able to engage in conversations naturalistically, like neighbours rather than experts conducting consultation, enabled a more open and natural expression of knowledge, cares and concerns.[1] The displays triggered memories, the (re)telling of stories, the discovery of common interests and practices, a sense of curiosity and engagement between attendees and NPG members. These would all shape the approaches and decisions of the NPG, who were keenly aware of the need for wide community support. But the lack of any mechanism to record these conversations meant that much of this was formally 'lost': the inscriptions that formally reported the results of the event were the limited responses to the structured feedback questions and the stickers on the map and the vision and objectives. These represented the tiniest fraction of the interactions over the course of the event. While the event did act to open up issues for relatively unrestricted discussion, the methods of recording it constrained both the content and form of what could be presented as evidence. The specific processes of knowledge production determined the knowledge that could be (officially) produced and the forms it could take. But at the same time knowledges were unofficially mobilised and produced in the interactions occasioned by the event and the material specificity of its format, but they remained immaterial, their influence present but untraceable in the inscriptions supporting the plan.

Collages made by pupils from the local primary school featured prominently in the displays, made up of their own drawings, creative writing, descriptions of things that were important to them about Wroston, ideas about what would make things better and what might spoil it, and photos of valued locations and features. But again, although they sparked significant discussion, it was not clear what contribution these made to shaping the plan or how, or the pathway between evidence and policy. They were referred to in the documents submitted to the independent examiner, as one item among 41 listed in a consultation chart, which was itself one appendix among four to the consultation statement required to show that the NPG had met its legal obligation to consult widely on the plan. But they featured much more prominently than this at this consultation event, and were displayed on the walls of the room in the village hall where the NPG met for many months afterwards. The material form of the collages produced by the children folded in far more meaning, substance and affect than their truncated representation in the consultation chart. For me, they became ghostly reminders of the experiential knowledges that were lost in translation through the extensive processes of consultation and evidence production, 'the plural worlds and multiple stories of irreducible inhabitants whose lives are characterized by relations, expectations, feelings, reminiscences, bodies, voices and histories, all layered into living urbanities' (Sandercock and Attili, 2010: xix).

In August 2016, Simon emphasised that as well as their technical work, "then there's all the softer stuff, we need a lot more information, the context, that's really important, to get a flavour of what the village feels like". At the time, Barbara was trying to develop a project for heritage lottery funding about "the heritage and the feel of the village" that would involve talking to schoolchildren and adult residents to get information from them about their favourite landscapes, their favourite views of, and out of, the village, building on the work that Susan had done in talking to community groups at the start of the neighbourhood plan process. She suggested that "it could be really quite powerful ... you get people saying, 'we live here, and this is valuable ... this is important to us, whatever it is' ... so you can add a formal layer to your maps, where people are saying 'this is what we value'".

However, the NPG as a whole, while agreeing that this would be a good thing to do, and might provide a representation of the village that would be more recognisable to residents than the evidence that they had gathered, decided that it was not a priority for them: they did not count it as real, weighty evidence, because they did not think that the examiner would treat it that way. Neither the form nor the content matched their understanding of the kind of expert knowledge that could endow them with agency.

Difficult articulations

Similar discussions and processes took place in Oakley NPG. Even when some attention was given to voicing these experiential aspects of place knowledge, part of the difficulty of capturing it was that it appeared to require articulating something that was in some sense obvious, but which was nevertheless very hard to express in the dominant language of planning. Oakley's consultants had asked the NPG to distil a sense of place of the town for them into a few sentences, because "We need a very clear understanding of what you mean by that [sense of place] ... what is that really important bit? … [W]e need to know for ourselves" so that "I can then relate that to all the policies" (Andrea, Oakley consultant, June 2015). In response, the NPG kept a standing item on their fortnightly agenda throughout summer 2015 to spend at least some time each meeting trying to define the character of Oakley and what made it special. The difficulty in expressing something so seemingly evident clearly made people feel uncomfortable and disconcerted, and exposed real differences among the NPG about what it was that they were trying to express, as well as how to express it. In July 2015, when the NPG were discussing some draft statements drawn up by Katie, the town clerk, based on ideas from the previous meeting, my fieldnotes recorded that:

FIELDNOTES
Oakley NPG meeting
July 2015

The discussion is very heated. The usual polite, respectful turn-taking breaks down almost entirely, with people chipping in dis/agreements from all sides, and side conversations starting up around the table. 'Genteel' is the first suggested characterisation under attack: it's nothing like that, someone hates the word, it's so old-fashioned, it's a lively town, it's not, there's a lot going on, there's nothing to do. Some people never venture into town … other words are suggested, and equally torn apart.

The debate aroused participants' passions, indicating different affective relations with place, as well as the difficulty of trying to meaningfully express affective relations in a few short sentences. The way that the exercise was framed pushed the NPG into trying to close down the meanings and sense of place of Oakley, to condense and capture them in "a few sentences", rather than to first open them up and explore their diversity and potential synergies and conflicts. It implied that such a sense of place could be effectively articulated through the material form of a few typed sentences.

In August 2015, Katie asked the NPG to think about what made people want to live there – why they, in particular, had chosen to live there. However, despite their evidently strong affective relations with the place, their responses did not really engage these. An initial lack of responses and some awkward mumbles became more animated once John volunteered that he had asked a visiting friend what he thought was special about Oakley, and the group then quickly settled into discussing why tourists and others chose to visit. They couched their comments in terms of instrumentally rational choices (such as "It's a logical location" [Henry], "Oakley's a good base to explore from" [Andrew]), eluding and sidestepping affective relations with place and their own narratives of living, or choosing to live, there. These kinds of answers fitted better into their imaginary of what kind of knowledge can count in the rationalities of neighbourhood planning, and planning more broadly.

Later in the process, similar issues arose when the NPG tackled a narrower, but related, challenge of describing what was special about certain views that they wanted to protect. For the NPG, certain things appeared to be so obvious that they did not require saying, but were also very difficult to articulate when they were required to be said.[2] Trying to lead her struggling NPG to explain the value of these views for their consultant in May 2016, Oakley NPG's Chair, Stephanie, emphasised for them to "bear in mind she doesn't know the town, and she's writing it for somebody who doesn't know the town, so don't be defensive towards me, make it work. ... Think of explaining it to somebody who doesn't know this place".

However, it proved exceptionally difficult to capture this sense for someone who did not have any significant direct experience. Oakley NPG showed a very reflexive awareness of this tension between experience and representation – between the different modes of attention that the epistemologies of space and place rely on and reproduce (Gill et al, 2017) – and the barriers and flaws that they felt were imposed on the translations made from one to the other. In March 2017, reflecting on the process to date, Stephanie commented that after their initial period of intensive evidence gathering they had been told by their consultants that "all the things that people have told you have nothing to do with planning policy". This was something of an exaggeration, but clearly demonstrated the difficulties they experienced in representing people's concerns in terms that mattered within their neighbourhood planning imaginary.

This approach resulted in many of the issues raised by the public and researched and debated by the NPG being omitted from the plan and the final evidence base. However, these issues were thoroughly imbricated with spatial planning and placemaking (such as traffic and parking, public transport and active travel, the specifics of retail and employment development, the future of a derelict public building). Although they were not amenable to complete solutions through planning policy alone, planning policies could have partially addressed many of these issues, and the knowledge produced by the NPG about them could both have provided useful context and support to policies, and helped to shape the wider placemaking role of the plan. Stephanie went on to critique the processes of translation that they were forced to go through: "You've got to use their language, and it's not neutral, it's there to do certain things, and it's supposed to be objective but it's not. It does things, it makes you think in certain ways."

Neighbourhood planning appears here as an attempt to work together the rationalities of planning expertise with the cares and concerns of community, albeit one in which the rationalities of expertise often colonise the newly opened experimental space. In both NPGs a gap arose in discussions about what they knew and valued about the place and what they wanted to achieve in relation to it on the one hand, and how they could justify their proposals – that is, the matters and material forms they believed could achieve leverage – on the other. Conversations about these two distinct issues often conflated them and slid from the more relational one to the more detached one: from 'what do we know' and 'what do we feel' to 'what will we put on paper'. But despite this fluidity, these issues were also at times identified as quite separate in the conversations and perceptions of the NPGs, as epitomised by NPG member Laura in a discussion about how to present a description of the way they envisaged the future role of Wroston and its particular qualities: "I suppose it depends which plays better ... which would be more credibly received by the planners" (September 2015). Their evidence did not represent what mattered to them about their neighbourhoods; it represented what they believed would carry weight in a specific evaluative framework. This translation was not a representation of their cares, concerns and knowledge, but was nevertheless a carrier of them. It manifested care for achieving credibility in the eyes of planners, rather than care for authentically representing the neighbourhood of experience. However, these arrangements are precarious because that which is cared for – the neighbourhood of experience – remains un(der)-represented (Yuille, 2021). The object of care is therefore particularly vulnerable to (mis)interpretation of policy, future changes in policy and so on as it is made present only by proxy. Distancing decision making from the rich, textured, lived experience of people's life-worlds distances it from reality (Holland, 1997). In the remainder of this chapter I speculate about how things might be otherwise, through a discussion of conceptual and practical frameworks that might enable the cares, concerns and knowledges of the neighbourhood to be mobilised more directly as evidence.

Matters of care and concern

Interpreting the deficit

The previous section has explored several instances where NPGs have attempted to grapple with experiential knowledge of place and, in one way or another, substantial elements of this have been 'lost in translation' – have failed to make the journey from experience to evidence. This is not intended as criticism of the NPGs, but as an indication of the difficulties of making these articulations within the dominant imaginary of neighbourhood planning. It further develops a theme opened up in previous chapters: that a process which is ostensibly about letting communities plan for the places that they know and care about, in practice struggles to recognise or represent the ways in which people know and care. Conventionally, this situation might be explained in one of two ways:

1. What might be called a 'community-deficit' interpretation. This relates to the public deficit model often found in the field of public understanding of science, and frequently mentioned earlier (Wynne, 1991, 2007). Under this interpretation, the community simply don't know enough about planning, or lack the relevant skills to 'properly' frame their knowledge, concerns and cares. In which case, they must either be educated (including self-education) so that they are able to respond in suitable ways, or their responses must be translated by a suitably knowledgeable and skilled expert. In these ways, their views can be presented in terms and material forms that are commensurable with the conventions and norms of relevant policy frameworks and can be given weight and withstand challenge. This appears to be the broad position of many planning scholars (Parker et al, 2016; Lord et al, 2017; Salter, 2017), and as previous chapters suggest, is the position broadly enacted by the NPGs themselves.

2. What might be called a 'policy-deficit' interpretation. Under this interpretation, the planning policy framework itself is not able to perform the functions that it is intended for. It is unable to hear, capture or engage with many of the cares and concerns of communities as experienced or expressed: things that matter to them. It is unable to deal with these (situated, concrete, meaningful, relational) matters of care and concern, and instead insists that they are reconstructed as (detached, abstract, context-free, objective) matters of fact (Latour, 2004b). Under this reading, the policy itself would need radical change.

But what if, instead of this rather rigid and reductionist understanding of the communities and policies of neighbourhood planning, we thought of both policy and communities as being enacted together through the concrete practices performed in different locations (Law and Singleton, 2014)? If we thought not about many local implementations of a singular national neighbourhood planning policy, but about many local enactments which together come to define the meaning of national policy? Because the meaning of policy lies not just in the intentions of its authors, or the words on a page, but in its concrete interpretations and enactments by a diverse range of policy actors (Yanow, 2000). This approach enables us to take seriously both the injunction of policy to base neighbourhood plans on a robust evidence base, and also the insistence that multiple and diverse ways of knowing the neighbourhood can meaningfully contribute to that evidence base. And from this perspective, we do not have to either dismiss the communities of neighbourhood planning as not expert enough, or the policy framework as not inclusive enough, but look instead to the concrete practices by which knowledge and (local) policies are produced.

From this perspective, the issues at stake in neighbourhood planning, far from being simple, singular, one-dimensional 'facts', are better understood as 'gatherings' which bring together diverse sociomaterial strands into a knot of interest (Latour, 2004b: 233). Questions about whether a Local Green Space should be protected and why, for example, gather together the physical characteristics of the space itself (its constituent flora, fauna, topography, geology, hydrology and so on), its social and material relations to its surroundings, how and why it is used and by whom, various experiences of its use, and its history, along with representations of all these features and the methods and materials used to make those representations. How people feel about it, the lived experience of place, matters: it must be 'demonstrably special to a local community and [hold] a particular local significance' (DCLG, 2012a: 18). However, as I show in Chapter 5, even issues like this, recognised as knowledge-value hybrids, can be reduced to numerical indicators under the pressure of the dominant planning imaginary to represent issues in the objectifying registers of quantification.

I have also shown that this reductive tendency is even stronger for other 'gatherings' that are presented as being matters of fact: closed, inert, naturalised as what they 'objectively' are in the categories of abstract space – such as 'objective' assessments of housing need. Precisely what the facts are can be contested during the process of assembling them, but what people feel about them does not matter. However, under closer analysis, such matters of fact can be seen as 'only very partial and, I would argue, very polemical, very political renderings of matters of concern' (Latour, 2004b: 232). When the processes of making matters of fact are traced back and the means by which their sociomaterial dependencies are erased are attended to, they are also revealed as partial, situated, in the process of being done, and intimately connected to 'subjective' states and value-laden assumptions and choices (Latour, 2004a).

This is not to suggest that planning should not be based on evidence. It is to suggest that the objective facts of abstract space and the subjective experiences of lived place are both 'gatherings', both matters of care and concern. It is to suggest that the line between them, far from being given and self-evident, is fluid and constantly in the making. As Latour (2004b: 231) insists, the intention of critique of this kind 'was never to get away from facts but closer to them, not fighting empiricism but, on the contrary, renewing empiricism'. Empiricism is, quite literally, learning from experience. Planning needs a way to engage with the experience of place which makes people care for it and want to actively take part in shaping its future. It is an aim of planning policy to engage with the cares, concerns and knowledges of the community, and it is the aim of neighbourhood planning that it should be *led* by those cares, concerns and knowledges. If they are unable to be expressed directly in the current policy framework, the practices which enact that framework need to change. Opening the practices of neighbourhood planning to a more 'generous' approach to evidence (Law, 2004) could enable its practitioners to engage better with both the meaningful experiences of lived place and the black-boxed technical facts of abstract space.

Neighbourhoods of care and concern

As described in Chapter 3, for Latour, viewing the world as 'matters of concern' means acknowledging the necessary situatedness and incompleteness of all knowledge; recognising the complex material and social relations that enable and constitute that knowledge; and rejecting the notion that objects (of knowledge 'in here' or as material objects 'out there') are autonomously 'given' as they are, rather understanding them as constantly in a process of 'being done'. Matters of fact are carved out of matters of concern, but the contingent cuts that make them are made invisible, thereby naturalising the matter of fact as the thing in itself, and concealing the work that necessarily holds it in place.

For neighbourhood planners, viewing the world as 'matters of concern' would mean producing evidence that engaged directly with lived experiences and the things that people care about, without having to reframe them: exploring and articulating the relationships between communities, individuals, practices and places. In other words, taking place-based knowledge and values seriously as key factors which matter in their own right (Perkins and Manzo, 2006). It would also acknowledge the 'controversies concerning the correct definition of the identity, boundaries, components and important values related to a specific place' (Metzger, 2014b: 100) that they bring – recognising that there are many valid experiences of place.

'Matters of concern' are clearly not the same things in these descriptions. However, for both Latour and participants in neighbourhood planning, matters of concern have much in common. They are relational, produced in the interactions between people and place. They are knowledge–value hybrids, neither wholly objective nor wholly subjective. They are necessarily partial. They are concrete and situated, and get obscured or occluded by the abstractions of matters of fact and by practices which insist upon matters of fact. They can be better understood through a recognition that the technical and the political, facts and values, are inseparably bound up. If the world is understood in terms of matters of concern in Latour's sense – if *all* evidence is recognised as partial, situated, open-ended and in the process of 'being done', rather than black-boxed as unmediated, indisputable matters of fact – then the matters of concern of the neighbourhood planners become easier to recognise as tangible, real and worthy of attention.

In Maria Puig de la Bellacasa's terms, these issues can also be described as matters of care (2011). Her approach embraces Latour's explanation of matters of fact as necessarily partial, incomplete and open-ended renderings of complex gatherings of social and material elements, as 'impure' knowledge-value hybrids. In addition, it brings a focus on the centrality of care and caring relations: to how, in practice, we can live in the world. She specifically draws attention to the various, sometimes contradictory, ways that care is both entwined with and held apart from knowledge. I have shown how this occurs through the processes of neighbourhood planning, and in critically analysing this, I hope to suggest ways forward that can account for and even embrace that entwining.

The inability of the practices of neighbourhood planning to formally recognise material and affective relations of care suggests an immanent critique of those practices. My analysis of those practices is intended to foster new caring relations, in two dimensions. First, in terms of improving communities' abilities to materially care for the neighbourhood through shaping its trajectories of development and change. And second, in terms of fostering care *for* that care: recognising those caring relations and the experiential knowledge they grow out of as meaningful and valuable, and finding ways to mobilise them so that they can have effects. Place as experienced and care for place are both things that have often been neglected by English planning practices. Understanding both matters presented as fact, and matters dismissed as 'not-fact', as matters of care can generate care for neglected things by 'counting in participants and issues who have not managed or are not likely to succeed in articulating their concerns, or whose modes of articulation indicate a politics that is "imperceptible" within prevalent ways of understanding' (Puig de la Bellacasa, 2011: 94–95).

Treating issues as matters of care also suggests *how* care might be mobilised. Through a re-reading of Haraway's works on situated knowledges, Puig de la Bellacasa identifies three practices – '*thinking-with*', '*dissenting-within*' and '*thinking-for*' – that might unfold in knowledge practices in which care is embraced (2012). '*Thinking-with*' pushes back against the individualisation and atomisation of thought and knowledge. It requires recognising the multiple human and non-human elements that constitute our knowledge practices. It insists on always seeing knowledge and knowing as multiply (and maybe contradictorily) in-relation-to and in the making, never detached, pure or final. '*Dissenting-within*' recognises that knowledge making based on care is not free from conflict, and that there will necessarily be multiple, possibly contradictory layers to the cares, relationships and knowledge thus produced. As described in Chapter 3, when producing knowledge we make cuts in the world – we define and isolate objects of study that are necessarily entangled in a hinterland of other relations that extend out beyond 'themselves', and which could be defined and isolated differently. Thinking with care requires us to consider how these cuts foster particular relations and the effects they might produce, rather than assuming that they somehow remove objects from relations of power and care. And it requires an awareness of the efforts necessary to cultivate collective and accountable knowledge production without ignoring or denying dissent or difference. '*Thinking-for*' describes the production of knowledge that creates relations between ways of knowing that have previously been disconnected, and especially in which one has been marginalised. It builds on alternative visions of the world, especially those arising from everyday experiences and relations, that are ignored or suppressed by official, conventional or established ways of knowing. And it also requires a reflexive acknowledgement of how the producers of knowledge are implicated and positioned in the world, especially in relation to those they claim to represent. In what follows I outline what the operationalisation of these practices might entail specifically within the practice of neighbourhood planning.

'*Thinking-with*' the sociomaterial assemblages that generate neighbourhood issues as matters of care would require resisting the reductionism that would translate those issues into abstract, black-boxed facts. It would acknowledge the ecologies of social and material participation – the everyday experience of emplaced living – that enabled these issues to arise in the first place, and which maintain them as live things (Chilvers and Kearnes, 2016). Neighbourhood planning and its evidence base would become less isolated, less 'pure', and more explicitly connected into the everyday practices and interactions of neighbourhood, drawing more heavily and more directly on the informal and mobilising the lived experiences of relations with place (Bødker et al, 2017).

'*Dissenting-within*' the practices of neighbourhood planning would require NPGs to acknowledge the different ways that they are implicated in the world. This would involve a reflexive recognition of the three disparate identities that they must perform – and both hold together and hold apart – and of the different ways of knowing and types of knowledge associated with each. This would mean recognising the tensions between the different ways of knowing place enacted in each identity, but also the value of each. This may help them to retain a balance between these identities and relations that resists the suppression or dominance of any one of them, enabling the knowledges produced by each to be articulated and opened up to critical appraisal. It would also require a relationship with the wider community that was open to dissent as well as consensus, contestation as well as collaboration, and processes for engaging with different types of relation.

'*Thinking-for*' the neighbourhood would require drawing explicitly on all three sources of knowledge and authority, enabling representations and decisions to be made that more adequately reflect the lived, experiential knowledges of the community in all of their diversity. Recognising the 'dark side' of care (in that care for some objects must imply neglect or lack of care for others), it would also require reflexively engaging with and responding to the implications of these practices. Who, and what, is not being heard or spoken for within the object of care (the neighbourhood)? Who, and what, will this affect beyond the neighbourhood, and how?

Opening up and closing down

Neighbourhood planning is a process that necessarily involves both appraisal and decision making, participation and analysis, and opening up and closing down of issues (Stirling, 2008). However, as I have shown, as practised in the locations of study it has tended to quickly shift from favouring participatory to analytic styles, and closing down issues over opening up their full complexity from a range of different ways of knowing. Clearly, the earlier part of the neighbourhood planning process should be focused on opening up as NPGs work with their communities to explore the issues which the plan can and should engage with, and the later parts on closing down, as neighbourhood priorities are clarified and refined within the scope of the policy framework. However, much of the work of 'opening up' was prematurely or unnecessarily 'closed down' by the reproduction of boundaries between expert and lay knowledges and ways of knowing, between quantifiable facts and qualitative values, and the automatic privileging or denigrating of the categories on either side.

Matters such as housing need are purified into matters of fact, stabilising them and endowing them with agency. Matters such as experience of place are purified out of the realm of what can count as reliable evidence or reduced to impoverished material forms that sap their agency. These practices reinforce the rigid boundaries between knowledge of lived place and abstract space, between lay and expert, even while the rhetoric around neighbourhood planning promised to bridge these gaps. However, both ways of knowing are integral to the purpose of planning. Both are enacted, partial, situated, contingent knowledge-value hybrids. But one is represented as such and thereby denied the status of evidence, closing down the range and type of issues that can be considered. The other is purified to conceal this hybridity in order to be admitted as factual evidence, thereby also closing down opportunities for contestation even within this narrowed band of available issues.

These boundaries and categories are both performed (that is, constantly being done, not fixed or given but 'a collective accomplishment which endures only in its continuing reiteration' [Freeman, 2017: 195]) and performative (through enacting them, identities and possibilities for being in the world are brought into being and/or suppressed). Only that which is made visible is capable of being cared for through policy – and that which is erased or concealed is liable to be harmed as a consequence (Gill et al, 2017). These case studies have provided numerous instances of the reproduction of these boundaries and categories and the marginalisation of affective relations with place and the knowledge of lived experience.

Treating knowledge claims as matters of care and concern may enable the epistemologies of place and space to be worked together differently, providing more diverse ways to both open issues up for attention and reflection and, later, to close them down for decision making. One example arising from these case studies was the Wroston Landscape Character Appraisal (discussed in Chapter 6), which was conducted by an expert but was richly informed by the collaboration of the NPG, and successfully included rather than excluded experiential knowledge. This is one concrete indication (and see also Bradley, 2018) that neighbourhood planning practices may be able to gather different knowledge practices together in ways that can 'work together and in relation to each other without trying to reduce them to the same thing … allowing the two sets of practices to go on better in difference' (Freeman, 2017: 199). It is often in such tensions between practices and epistemologies – ways of doing and knowing – that new and productive ways of 'going-on' can arise, working expert and lay knowledges together differently, without automatically privileging one over the other or insisting that one is framed or described in the terms and logics of another (Haraway, 1991; Verran, 2001; Tsing, 2005).

Implications and applications

As indicated in Chapter 6, neighbourhood planning is making a difference. But, as shown earlier in this chapter and previously, this difference is not transparently based on the experiential knowledge of and care for place that (partly) underpins NPGs' legitimacy to act. Their objects of knowledge and care are not being represented: they are largely being silenced at the same time as they are being planned for by proxy through the objects of abstract space. Many attempts have been made by researchers and practitioners to find methods through which other ways of knowing, valuing and caring can be incorporated into decision making in planning and associated arenas: creative approaches that generate 'a radical potential for planning' to enable more open and generous ways of developing evidence and policy (Metzger, 2011: 213). Some of these have been advocated for and even practised to some extent for many years; some are new or are new evolutions of older techniques, but few have entered the mainstream of English local or neighbourhood planning practice. I sketch out some of these here as potential practical mechanisms through which the foregoing theoretical arguments could be applied.

Manuel and Vigar explore the use of participatory film making to enhance the neighbourhood planning process, in an attempt to develop 'alternative ways of representing planning issues and producing plans that more accurately represent citizen concerns' (Manuel and Vigar, 2021: 1559). They conclude that creative approaches like this can be successful at eliciting issues and knowledges that would often be obscured in conventional planning processes, including participatory ones. They can also highlight absences in the knowledge base, especially around such experiential knowledges, prompting understanding of the need for wider participation, and provoke more extensive deliberation by providing spaces and stimulation for reflection and debate. They can thus open up the process of neighbourhood planning to a deeper, more inclusive set of narratives that capture emotional responses to place and the lived experience of interacting with it.

Several projects associated with the Arts and Humanities Research Council's Connected Communities programme have explored issues around articulating place and human–environment relations.[3] The Localism, Narrative and Myth project used arts-based interventions to interrogate academic and narrative interpretations of 'the local', to draw out plural understandings of place that could inform new hyper-local forms of governance (Layard et al, 2013b). The Stories of Change project (Smith et al, 2016) recognised that many people feel put off by the way that environmental issues are talked about, and find it difficult to respond in kind. It used narratives and storytelling to encourage more imaginative approaches to energy choices, making a space to work through the tensions that arise between the wide acceptance that action is necessary, and the disputes generated by individual planning proposals. Creative Participation in Place-making (Layard et al, 2013a) found that for community participants, placemaking is broader and more material than conventionally conceived planning practices. Communities can be more effectively and creatively involved if their engagement extends from 'merely' planning the built environment to include the 'felt environment' (Layard et al, 2013a: 1), that is, the rich and textured neighbourhood that they experience, as distinct from the reduced and flattened materiality of abstract space.

The Loweswater Care Project is an example of participatory environmental governance that directly tackles many of the issues raised in this book. It was developed as part of an interdisciplinary project to bring together local residents, farmers, scientists, researchers, institutional representatives and others as equals to work on the complex challenges posed by blue-green algae in Loweswater, a lake in Cumbria. It explicitly set out to avoid the common problem in participatory processes of focusing too quickly on 'closing down' and moving to solutions without first 'opening up' and appreciating the full range of complexities of a problem, as understood through different knowledge practices. It also sought to challenge the idea that such problems could be resolved through the application of scientific and technical methods alone by 'un-black-boxing' those methods and their objects (Tsouvalis and Waterton, 2012). It did this by applying the principles, agreed by its members, that there is not a single 'right' way of understanding the problem; that all knowledge and expertise needs to be debated; that uncertainties in knowledge need highlighting and accepting; and that doubt and questioning needs to be extended to all representations, including scientific ones (Waterton et al, 2015). In this way it reframed both 'matters of fact' and knowledges that would typically be excluded as insufficiently factual as matters of concern and care that could be built upon (Tsouvalis, 2016).

Community mapping is a participatory way of building up a picture of what it is like to live in a place, and what the future of that place might look like, which may or may not involve actual spatial maps (Perkins, 2007). Conventionally this tends to focus on identifying the assets and opportunities of a place – and processes like this will be used in the preparation of most neighbourhood plans. However, they can also be adapted specifically to focus on or engage with lived experience, for example, with story mapping techniques that are better able to capture everyday place meanings and values (Saija et al, 2017; Lung-Amam and Dawkins, 2020). This can be particularly effective when combined with the use of visual media such as different kinds of maps, images, photos and videos – approaches that are visual and easy to relate to, and which 'cut through communication difficulties to reveal feelings and ideas which otherwise might be hard to express' (Preston City Council, 2018: 4). They can also engage forms of mapping which depart from cartographic accuracy to enable greater freedom of expression, enabling participants to generate their own cartographic space which can tell powerful stories about the values attributed to and engagements with place, for example, through emphasising or omitting particular features or stretching or compressing distances (Catney et al, 2019).

One of the UK government's intentions for planning reform in the early 2020s was to make greater use of digital technologies in neighbourhood planning. This has significant potential for opening up new methods for representing and engaging with experiential knowledges, bringing qualitative, narrative and meaningful inputs into dialogue with spatial and quantitative evidence. However, these must be seen as a supplement to more traditional means of democratic engagement and used with awareness of the potential for generating new forms of digital exclusion. Kelly Duggan, for example, charts the use of a digitally aided 'collaborative envisioning framework' aimed specifically at involving disengaged young people in generating a shared vision for a neighbourhood plan (Duggan, 2017). She concludes that such digital tools offer real potential to deepen and widen often inadequate methods for engaging communities with neighbourhood planning and to support more creative and generative approaches. However, she also notes that digital tools to engage younger people may simultaneously exclude older, poorer or other social groups.

Mobile and Geographic Information System (GIS) technologies offer particularly fertile ground for engaging experiential knowledges. Public participatory GIS mapping uses digital technologies to develop the principles of community mapping. It offers a variety of means to attach people's experience of place and responses to specific features and locations to spatial representations of place (Mukherjee, 2015). It combines GIS mapping with the tools and principles of Participatory Action and Learning, developed from the experience of Participatory Rural Appraisal (Rambaldi et al, 2006). This enables maps to become part of the narratives of place and to represent combinations of narratives in spatial form, drawing on 'the wisdom of crowds' to articulate spatially explicit experiential knowledges (Brown, 2015). They can become interactive tools for bringing together different knowledges for discussion, analysis and informing decisions. While no longer a particularly new technology or approach, its use in community-led action such as neighbourhood planning is limited and, especially if specifically oriented to articulating knowledges and engagements that are often marginalised in planning, holds significant promise for enabling those knowledges to be heard (Radil and Anderson, 2019). Used with care, and in combination with other methods of participatory evidence production, it can be highly effective at producing and presenting high quality and versatile knowledge from a wide range of people and perspectives (Kahila-Tani et al, 2019).

Exemplifying the use of such techniques, Jones et al (2013, 2015) led a pilot project in which residents walked around the neighbourhood with borrowed smartphones, recording audio clips, taking photographs and adding comments, all of which were mapped using GPS and uploaded to a central community map. The explicit intention was to inform neighbourhood plan-making with experiential knowledge of the 'felt environment' as well as spatial knowledge of the built environment. Similarly, Pánek and Pászto (2020) chart the use of an online, map-based crowdsourcing tool used to collect and visualise the emotional and subjective relational responses of people to place in four neighbourhood development case studies in the Czech Republic. And Insole and Piccini (2013) describe a project in which participants could add their own media (photos, videos and so on) and metadata to the Local Planning Authority's planning website in order to inform decisions about planning at the neighbourhood scale. The intention was to include and validate informal and domestically produced visual information as evidence that could influence formal planning processes.

Commonplace is one example of a community mapping tool that has been used in 20 neighbourhood plans (Janner-Klausner, 2022). It enables people to provide freeform or multiple-choice comments through a variety of devices on any aspects of the neighbourhood, identifying features, issues, felt responses to them, potential solutions and any other information on a shared online community map. Comments are visible to others, enabling sharing of experience and interaction, and it is also connected to social media platforms to enable wider, direct sharing of experience and wider engagement. Similarly, Maptionnaire provides online map-based surveys which can include options for participants to interact in a variety of ways, for example, drawing their everyday routes through the neighbourhood and highlighting the most and least pleasant aspects and why (Eurocities, 2018). Tools like these can embed evidence gathering into the everyday narratives of lived experience (and vice versa) and present the knowledge generated in spatially explicit formats.

These are just a few examples of approaches that attempt to take seriously ways of knowing lived place that planning typically struggles to engage with, by finding alternative ways to articulate and represent them. They are not, of course, silver bullets or panaceas – decisions must still be made on the basis of the evidence thus produced, and finding ways to incorporate more diverse experiential knowledge into the evidence base is at least as likely to lead to more conflict as to greater consensus. Genuinely pluralising the knowledges considered in evidence does not make for easier plan-making – but is essential to fulfil the claims made for the empowering nature of neighbourhood planning and other participatory projects, by foregrounding for debate and contestation the issues that matter to people but which are so often excluded from meaningful consideration.

Such approaches can be understood as attempts to develop 'alternative material, social and literary technologies' (Wylie et al, 2014: 121) that might resist the dominance of the material, social and literary technologies upon which the culture of scientism has been built (Shapin and Schaffer, 1985) – and which the culture of planning reproduces in adapted forms. These alternative technologies attempt to represent what David Strong (1994) described as 'disclosive discourse': the language of engagement, standing in sharp contrast to the abstractions of detachment. Disclosive discourse (verbal or nonverbal) expresses precisely that which cannot be captured by abstract discourse, which cannot by its very nature be measured or quantified. It articulates situated knowledge deriving from lived experience and particular relationships to particular entities and places. It is of its essence not an abstraction from the world, but demonstrative of engagement with the world, orienting its audience in the world to make them present and engaged rather than absent and detached. These alternative technologies thus unsettle the boundaries between expert and lay, providing legitimacy to sources and types of knowledge that would otherwise tend to be marginalised.

Narrative approaches in particular have been posited for three decades as offering material, social and literary technologies that can better engage excluded knowledges in planning (see, for example, Fischer and Forester, 1993; Sandercock, 2003). Storytelling has been proposed as both a model of planning (how it is done) and a model for planning (how it could and should be done), providing potentially 'powerful tools of a democratic, progressive planning practice' (van Hulst, 2012: 304; see also Throgmorton, 1996, 2003). Planning as storytelling is conceived of as a way of destabilising dominant planning discourses, opening cracks in the structure that will allow other ways of knowing place to be asserted, a 'useful way to get to these visceral perspectives' (Bulkens et al, 2015: 2324). And as Manuel et al note, '[p]olicy documents, in themselves, tell their own stories but they are often not representative of the communities they are referring to' (Manuel et al, 2017: 1698).

Weaving the knowledge practices of abstract space and of lived place explicitly into stories, forms through which they gain and convey meaning, is one way of operationalising them as matters of care. Situating knowledge claims within narratives that give them meaning can bring together different knowledge practices in productive tension. The issues that planning addresses are 'wicked problems' (Rittel and Webber, 1973) which by definition can't be solved purely by processes of expert calculation, and so experiential knowledge given meaning through narrative situating can help decisionmakers navigate their complex terrain (Thiele and Young, 2016). This happens already – inevitably – but is often obscured in accounts of decision making, and should be both more fully recognised and explicitly developed. As Singleton and Mee observe in the parallel arena of healthcare, 'stories offer the potential for reflexivity at a deep and nuanced level. … Patient stories tend to narrativize patient experience in ways that differ from dominant professional and policy narratives' (2017: 132). Stories can reveal materials, affects, relations and practices that are silenced by conventional planning practices, but which are acknowledged as important in planning discourse in terms of wellbeing, quality of life and sense of place.

As well as enabling better care to be taken of planning's neglected things, narrative approaches can also help to understand matters often presented as 'transparent, unmediated, indisputable facts' as matters of care (Manuel et al, 2017: 1699). The tropes of objectivity, quantification and calculation that dominate the practices of planning are themselves embedded in specific stories about how the world is and how we can know it, and in turn they embed those stories further. Their telling as being able to reveal the world 'as it really is' prevents the telling of other stories. If these 'unmediated facts' were seen instead as integral parts of ongoing narratives, they could gain a richer and more textured meaning, rather than being understood as atomistic points that are isolated from meaningful connection to wider stories (for example, housing requirements could be seen in the context of past, present and future patterns and changes in neighbourhood life). By opening the black boxes of evidence production (as, for example, Wroston NPG did in relation to the Lcoal Planning Authority's landscape character assessment) stories can also be told about how points of data were produced and how the processes of production relate to outputs and conclusions – and about how alternative modes of production, with greater responsiveness to the concrete characteristics of particular places, could produce richer information.

Stories in and of themselves are not, of course, any more reliable than abstract numbers. No matter how detailed or laden with meaning, they will never be complete, and 'we still need to question the truth of our own and others' stories. We need to be attentive to how power shapes which stories get told, get heard, carry weight' (Sandercock, 2003: 12). Like any other knowledge practice, they are partial, situated and connected to vast hinterlands of associated performances (Law, 2004). They are, necessarily, simplifications (Law and Mol, 2002). But thinking through stories – through knowledge given meaning by being situated in a narrative flow – can help actors to negotiate and decide which simplifications might be most appropriate in this particular setting, which features and relations are most significant, which ways of knowing are most useful, and how different knowledges might be juxtaposed or interlaced. Stories organise our attention in ways that can reveal meaning and connections, in contrast to planning practices that bulldoze participants into making the simplifications demanded by instrumental scientistic rationalities. Framing a neighbourhood plan as guiding the most appropriate continuation of an already-unfolding narrative could give context and meaning to both 'hard' and 'soft' forms of evidence and enable them to be combined and worked together more productively.

Adopting a more open approach to evidence, especially through a narrative approach, would also enable better connections to be made between land use policies and wider issues and actions. Many neighbourhood plans relegate issues raised by the community and developed by the NPG, but which are not considered to be solely amenable to spatial planning policies, to a 'community aspirations' or 'community projects' appendix. This isolates them from the main substance of the plan rather than representing them in ways that would situate both them and the plan's statutory planning policies in an ongoing, locally specific, meaningful, engaged narrative about the development and change of the neighbourhood. This draws yet another hard boundary, between those issues that are amenable to land use planning and those that are not. When the Oakley consultants proposed doing this, NPG member John complained that "We mustn't lose that it's Oakley neighbourhood plan, not just a general one with Oakley in mind, it's these references to local things that make it unique" (June 2017).[4]

In practice, of course, these land use planning and non-land use planning issues do not exist in isolation, as recognised by national governance reforms of the early 2000s which aimed to integrate land use planning with other placemaking policy areas, enabling better spatial sensitisation of wider development narratives (Lambert, 2006). Neighbourhood plans that built in the interconnections between land use policy and other modes of relating to and acting in and on place rather than trying to artificially separate them would be better able to make visible matters of care and concern. Making explicit the connections between statutory policies and other actions and orientations could provide greater clarity and deeper understanding for decisionmakers, help community, the development industry and other actors see how it all connects, and retain in view some of the liveliness of the issues at stake.

Exeter St James' neighbourhood plan provides one early example of strongly making these connections (before the practice of separating non-land use policies, projects and actions into a separate appendix became sedimented down as common practice). The section entitled 'Delivering the Plan' starts with a set of projects that 'will be the focus of community action to implement the Plan' (Exeter St James Forum, 2013: 14), outlining actions that the neighbourhood will take (such as enhancing public community spaces and developing partnerships with other agencies to tackle planning-related problems), which is followed by the land use policies. As well as acting as a focus to mobilise and stabilise the resources and relations that were brought into new alignments through the neighbourhood planning process, these projects provide context and meaning for the statutory policies by setting out the neighbourhood's intentions and active plans for the areas and features the planning policies refer to. Imbricating planning policies and community projects, while clearly distinguishing their statutory status, would also contribute to keeping the neighbourhood plan a live document, a technology of ongoing engagement in the narrative of place as lived and experienced, rather than a one-off event. It would thus help to generate and perpetuate the active material doing of care for neighbourhood that 'is essential to producing liveable worlds and yet is undervalued and has been consistently seen as secondary and supportive to technical expertise' (Singleton and Mee, 2017: 146, endnote 11).

So matters of care and concern, the knots of interest made up of sociomaterial assemblages and their multiple relations and representations, may be better described in stories that are recognised as stories than by the automatic de/privileging processes embodied in the concealed yet continuous enactment of boundaries which divide the world into oppositional categories such as fact/value and reason/emotion. Most obviously, stories can better capture the dimensions of meaning that are marginalised by these processes. They can also incorporate and give context and meaning to those necessary technical elements of evidence, without reproducing the stories that perform them as transcendent and beyond the realms of culture and value. Neighbourhood plans, are, after all, a form of performative storytelling (Throgmorton, 2003). They tell stories about what a place is like now, how it got to be here, and how it could and should change in future to most appropriately continue that story (Rawles and Holland, 1996). Producing and presenting evidence framed in this narrative vein makes space for the everyday narratives of neighbourhood life to be woven together, alongside technical information, into compelling representations of what it is like to be in and part of a place, and what that might mean for how it should change. And more profoundly, it would tell different stories about what it is like to be in the world and what we can meaningfully know about it.

Situating both facts accepted as evidence and experiential knowledge rejected as not-factual-enough, and also the processes of making facts and evidence in and as narratives opens up all knowledge claims to critical engagement (Haraway, 1989). This may sound to some like a Trumpian post-truth dystopia, but enacted in the spirit of Latour's intention 'never to get away from facts but closer to them' (2004b: 231) and Haraway's 'no-nonsense commitment to faithful accounts of a "real" world' (1991: 187), it offers quite the reverse: a method through which to gain a deeper and more critical understanding of all knowledge claims, the meanings that they carry and which carry them, the processes of their production and the principles and commitments that underpin them. Working different knowledges together should improve rather than detract from the robustness of plans. 'Critical judgment will always be necessary in deciding what weight to give to different stories, as well as what stories are appropriate in what circumstances. The telling of stories is nothing less than a profoundly political act' (Sandercock, 2003: 27). But at present, it is very hard, if not impossible, to bring that critical judgement to bear, as one set of stories has managed to tell itself as 'mere description, or pure facts' (Sandercock, 2003: 21), with the effect that other stories are marginalised or silenced – which is also a profoundly political act.

Practicalities and possibilities

It is not of course for NPGs or the professionals supporting them to undertake a Science and Technology Studies-style deconstruction and reconstruction of the technical evidence base. But an understanding of the contingencies and uncertainties, the subjective assumptions and value judgements embedded in even the 'hardest' of evidence, may help alleviate concerns about the 'softness' of experiential evidence, and build confidence in the capacity and role of such evidence in working alongside technical data to convey a more complete picture of place. It may help in adapting and developing practices that enable experiential knowledges and cares to be articulated, rather than suppressed by ways of thinking and knowing (and ways of thinking about knowing) that reproduce conservative understandings of locality in the terms of abstract space. However, any such changes would require support from a progressive state and a strong and properly resourced (and somewhat reoriented) planning profession, rather than the environment of neoliberalism, austerity and hostility to planners in which the Localism Act 2011 was launched (Lord et al, 2017).

In some ways, this approach seems to suggest profound change. Opening up all knowledge claims in planning to analysis as matters of care and concern, rather than elevating them to matters of fact or reducing them to matters of opinion, would indeed change the face of the planning system. But more modest changes in practice within the existing policy framework could make a significant difference to the capacity for experiential knowledge to be engaged and have effects. As suggested in this chapter, there are a wealth of established and emerging practices which can be oriented towards enabling communities to articulate and analyse experiential knowledge. Experimental practices such as those mentioned earlier, conducted specifically for research purposes and found to be effective, but without clear mechanisms to connect research to changes in practice, training or funding, have tended to remain at best fringe activities, and could be developed and mainstreamed. In fact, what I am suggesting here is in some ways no more radical than advocating that we act on a significant body of research stretching back more than two decades. There is also much that could be learned from other arenas of participatory democracy, practices that could be adapted to the specific needs and enactments of neighbourhood planning, in light both of its specific situatedness and of critique of those other forms. Many of the practices mentioned earlier have their roots, at a greater or lesser distance, in participatory development practices such as Participatory Rural Appraisal/Participatory Learning and Action. Perhaps something could also be learned from the development of insurgent knowledges, when communities build their knowledge bases at a distance from officialdom, rather than attempting to imitate its modes? Or from the ways in which environmental justice movements balance the presentation of technologically mediated data with personal testimony?

This speaks to one significant challenge to implementing any changes to how planning is done: the knowledge and skills needed to do planning differently. As emphasised previously, neighbourhood planning suffers from a strong strain of conservativism, deriving partly from the imaginaries of knowledge in which planning is embedded, but also from the tendency of consultants and planning officers to, perfectly reasonably, stick to what they know. This then reproduces practices that reproduce those imaginaries and unintentionally stifle innovation, creativity and communities' ability to articulate the things that matter to them in ways that matter. And to shift from this dynamic would require significant skills development across the private, public and third sectors. While acknowledging of course that there are already planners practising across sectors that are highly innovative, creative and community-oriented, the skills needed to navigate the (potentially productive) tensions between the constraints and possibilities of policy and legislation, the threat of appeals and legal challenges, the assumptions and routines of wider planning practice, and the attachments, ambitions and experiences of communities are, broadly speaking, at best under-developed.

This is a matter of collective practices, norms, conventions, assumptions and expectations. It is not just about individual change (although that is also possible) but cultural change. And this in turn would require a steer from government to all the actors of neighbourhood planning – most prominently NPGs and their neighbourhoods, planning officers, consultants, support agencies and examiners – that they expect their rhetoric about the value of local residents' knowledge of and care for place to be enacted on the ground in the actual practices of neighbourhood planning. Such a steer, at the time of writing, may yet arise from the reforms of the early 2020s. Neighbourhood planning is starting to be framed as one form of 'levelling up from the bottom up', promoting improvements in pride of place and perceived wellbeing, two of the UK government's 12 'levelling up' missions, which have become the key policy context in which planning reform is situated (HM Government, 2022). This framing could be highly conducive to a renewed emphasis on experiential knowledge, place narratives and the felt environment. However, the shift to the levelling up focus is still evolving and exactly what role neighbourhood planning will play in this agenda, and whether any changes are made to the guidance and support available as a result, remains uncertain. Nevertheless, individual professionals, working with individual NPGs, can also make a difference and can start the cultural sands shifting.

If one difficulty with embracing a more creative and experimental approach is a lack of capacity in the professional sectors that support NPGs, another is a lack of capacity within actual and incipient NPGs themselves. Producing neighbourhood plans is burdensome and time-consuming, and there is a significant risk that the kinds of processes outlined in this chapter, by enabling more open-ended and ongoing participation throughout the neighbourhood, by encouraging plural forms of participation and evidence production, could increase the amount of time required and the work to be done. Technology could play a labour-saving role in gathering, marshalling and presenting such forms of evidence, and time and effort could be saved by making plan development more efficient, with greater clarity about how the process functions as a whole and draws on different sources of knowledge and value. However, an approach which adds significantly to the load borne by the volunteers at the heart of neighbourhood planning is likely to be unsustainable, especially when a key imperative is to extend its use to more urban and deprived communities where there is often less existing available social infrastructure and capacity.

There are also other challenges to developing forms of neighbourhood planning that are more able to engage with a plurality of knowledges and values. While a range of narrative, participatory mapping, visual, arts-based and other creative techniques can help to open up what counts as evidence and how different kinds of knowledge can be articulated, captured and presented, this is only one part of the process. Neighbourhood planning does need to get better at engaging with experiential knowledges, with matters of care and concern, and not prematurely closing down the issues and agendas that they signal. But at some point closing down is necessary: decisions must be made. As noted earlier, paying more attention to plural knowledges is at least as likely to lead to greater contestation as greater consensus. Resolving these issues – not solving differences, but allowing decisions to be made in a way in which all claims can be articulated, heard and considered – is likely to require both agonistic and deliberative approaches (Bond, 2011; Inch, 2015). Again, the skills for working through these processes, within communities and the professionals who support them, are in need of much development.

A further challenge concerns contingent norms around the material forms of evidence that are conventionally recognised in traditional planning. A key point to be reiterated here is that 'unconventional' forms of evidence cannot replace technical evidence, but can and should complement it. There is literally no other way to convey the richness and texture of lived place – without which the full implications of planning decisions cannot be understood – than to augment the conventional evidence bases which have for so long failed to capture it. The courts continue to uphold the acceptability of a plurality of evidence, even where at first glance they may seem to constrain it. For example, the Henfield neighbourhood plan was quashed by the courts on the basis of inadequate evidence, but as a partner at the law firm which brought the challenge explained, 'This case has not said that only professionals' technical evidence can meet the required standards needed to underpin a neighbourhood plan; simply that plans cannot be run according entirely to a local agenda that has no evidential basis' (Donnelly, 2016). There is room in neighbourhood planning for many kinds and many combinations of evidence. To draw an analogy, the nationwide network of Poverty Truth Commissions rely heavily on the power of first-hand testimony to illuminate and illustrate structural issues with a force and depth that cannot be conveyed by facts and figures alone. These narratives allow commissioners, including both local community members with direct experience of struggling against poverty and civic leaders, to 'listen deeply with our hearts and our heads rather than rushing to fix problems', enabling these lived, experiential realities to shape the agenda through their compelling articulation of important issues (Poverty Truth Network, 2022). Likewise, the lived reality of place comes closer to being grasped through stories, film, images and other creative approaches, whether spatially embedded through maps or other methods.

Pluralising the knowledge bases of neighbourhood planning, resisting reductionism, countering conservatism and engaging with matters of care and concern will not be easy, or straightforward, or happen overnight. It is not without risk, or challenge. But it does speak to the ethos, supposedly at the heart of the initiative, of letting the people who know and care about a place plan for it. It is necessary to enable those knowledges and cares to set agendas and shape decisions, working alongside more technical data and strategic considerations. There is arguably more scope to achieve this in neighbourhood planning than elsewhere in the planning system, constrained as it is in a 'safe space' within the strategic policies of local plans, meaning that debate over many 'technical' issues (for example, about housing need) have often already been resolved, albeit as contingent value-driven decisions rather than matters of fact. And, as mentioned in the previous chapter, it resonates with the heart-felt cry of Oakley NPG Chair Stephanie in June 2017 in relation to the reductionist, conservative approaches imposed by their consultants, saying "We have tensions pulling in two opposite directions, Andrea keeps saying to make it simple, and we're saying, 'make it good!'". Making it 'good' would require a more adequate articulation of experiential knowledges of place, and of policy that responded to those knowledges. It would require a more equitable combination of the knowledges associated with each of the NPG's identities, to produce a plan that is both robust and resistant to challenge but also better captures community experience of place and which can shape the future of place accordingly.

Conclusion

Tim Cresswell describes the difference between thinking in terms of abstract space and lived place as follows:

> When we look at the world as a world of places, we see different things. We see attachments and connections between people and place. We see worlds of meaning and experience. Sometimes this way of seeing can seem to be an act of resistance against a rationalization of the world that focuses more on space than place. To think of an area of the world as a rich and complicated interplay of people and the environment – as a place – is to free us from thinking of it as facts and figures. (Cresswell, 2015: 18)

Of course, in neighbourhood planning we cannot be free from thinking of locality in terms of facts and figures. These are very clearly a requirement of public examination, of rigour and robustness, of defensibility. The argument I am making here is much more modest – that we must not *only* think of neighbourhood in terms of facts and figures. That if we do, then communities will inevitably be disappointed and disenchanted with what neighbourhood planning can achieve. And I also argue that it is possible, albeit challenging, to achieve this within existing regulations and policy.

A key tension in planning in general, and neighbourhood planning in particular, is how processes and policies that are dominated by the language and logics of abstract space can better reflect and engage with the cares and concerns of lived place: how policy can be made to do care better (Gill et al, 2017). I have shown that care for place, and the reasons why people care for place, are difficult to capture, codify and quantify. But this doesn't make them any less central to the purpose of planning – indeed, an account of planning realities that omits affective and experiential knowledge is an inadequate account – 'we cannot grasp the full complexity of the phenomenon of place if we disqualify a priori its crucial subjective side from the analysis' (Metzger, 2014b: 102). This points to a need for new approaches to enable and legitimise articulations of such knowledge. Indeed, there is arguably a need to be especially attentive to such marginalised things and vulnerable viewpoints precisely because they are more likely to be neglected (Stirling, 2015; Puig de la Bellacasa, 2017). Attending to these neglected things can show how policies that are intended to protect and nurture can harbour relations of harm (Gill et al, 2017) – such as when 'dry as dust' planning policies (Sandercock, 2003: 21) that are stripped of their referential meaning, colour and texture are interpreted by decisionmakers in ways that directly conflict with the intentions of their authors (Burns and Yuille, 2018: 57–58).

In this chapter I have suggested that treating planning matters as matters of care and concern, and operationalising these concepts through narrative and other creative approaches, might allow an approach to knowing, planning and evidencing that is at once more modest and more expansive. This would enact NPGs more like Donna Haraway's modest witness (1997) than the modest witness of the Enlightenment ideal: that is, implicated in the world, with partial knowledge deriving from multiple relations with multiple sources and ways of knowing, rather than self-invisible, detached and remote, in possession of objective facts that have lost their meaning through the process of objectification.

All knowledge claims are most certainly not equal, but the practices through which the boundaries between facts and values, evidence and policy, reason and emotion, expert and layperson, are constructed and reproduced prevent an adequate analysis of claims that end up on either side of those boundaries. I am arguing for an approach that would enable greater weight to be given to claims that end up on the 'wrong' side of this boundary. I suggest that this could be assisted not just through the enactment of a more diverse set of knowledge-making practices, but also through an understanding of objects that end up on both sides of the boundary as fundamentally entangled – through an understanding that the boundary itself is an artefact, a story told about how things are in the world. Such an approach would absolutely not seek to do without or ignore the technical facts and modes of inquiry which currently drive planning, but rather to shed light on their particular situatedness and bring them into more open conversation with other situated ways of knowing. It would conceptualise planning as a practice of knowing, with knowledge understood as something that planners, citizens and citizen planners *do*, rather than something that they *have* (Davoudi, 2015). It is not a silver bullet for the problems of hyper-local planning, but rather a way of 'staying with the trouble' (Haraway, 2016): of acknowledging the difficulties and contradictions inherent in the project of neighbourhood planning, including the NPGs' implication in the world in contradictory ways, and of foregrounding and working with these contradictions instead of silencing them.

8

Conclusion: Neighbourhood planning and beyond

We ignore at our peril the anger and disaffection felt by so many communities at the failure of current planning policies and procedures to listen to their concerns and respond to their needs. Restoring public confidence in the planning system is one of our generation's greatest challenges.

Raynsford (2018)

In this chapter I summarise the arguments made in the previous chapters, and then go on to discuss some of the practical and theoretical implications of those arguments.

Cat's cradle: weaving the threads together

Planning is supposed to be an inclusive arena that engages a wide range of stakeholders, knowledges and ways of knowing. Yet it has consistently been perceived by communities as exclusionary and inaccessible. The decades of reforms intended to address this problem are, on the whole, perceived to have failed, as demonstrated by each successive set of reforms intended to yet again promote inclusivity in the face of a system that militates against it, and as the opening quotation from Nick Raynsford bears witness to. Raynsford was a former housing and planning minister, commissioned to conduct an independent, root-and-branch review of the English planning system on behalf of the Town and Country Planning Association, which reported in 2018 (Raynsford et al, 2018). This quotation was taken from his remarks on launching the findings of his report, and highlights the ever-more urgent need to address this issue.

The challenge highlighted by Raynsford remains so intractable at least partly because the knowledge and ways of knowing that citizens bring to planning, in particular their cares and concerns based on lived experience, are not able to be meaningfully heard in planning institutions. They tend to be expressed by citizens and understood by planners as knowledge-value hybrids that emerge from the phenomenological experience of 'emplacement' – of lived and practical entangled engagement in and with place. In contrast, through all its reforms the planning system has only been able to 'hear' matters couched in terms of abstract space and objective fact (or, at the very least, exponentially more weight and value are attributed to claims made in these terms). For these cares and concerns to have effects, they must be translated into matters that are compatible with the norms and conventions of the system. These translations often betray as much – if not more – than they convey, by preventing important elements from travelling from experience to evidence.

A central element of the rhetorical construction of neighbourhood planning by government and its support agencies was that it would widen and pluralise the ways of knowing available to evidence production and policy development. Due to its characteristic features, relating to its scale, its emphases on community leadership and involvement and on experiential knowledge and care, and its legal and policy parameters, this seemed to be a plausible claim. In particular, it appeared likely to enable the articulation and translation into evidence and policy of some of the affective and embodied knowledges and values that had previously tended to be ignored, silenced or otherwise made invisible within the planning system. It appeared to offer the potential to assemble the neighbourhood differently.

The chapters of this book have described a series of processes through which neighbourhood planning groups (NPGs) self-censored and self-regulated to try, broadly speaking, to reproduce the ways of knowing and valuing that are dominant within the planning system, but external to the neighbourhood planning regime. To establish themselves as legitimate spokespersons for the neighbourhood, NPGs enacted three distinct identities, each with its own distinctive material-semiotic relations with the neighbourhood – distinctive ways of interacting with, experiencing, knowing and representing it. These identities were, respectively:

- *in* the neighbourhood – wholly immersed in the neighbourhood as embodied synecdoche (the part standing in for the whole);
- *of* the neighbourhood – distinct from but connected to the neighbourhood as reflexive mediator; and
- *beyond* the neighbourhood – detached from the neighbourhood as remote expert.

Each of these identities enacts the communities, issues and places of neighbourhood planning in different ways: each assembles the neighbourhood differently, revealing and concealing different worlds. Each stands in a different relation to the world and engages with it through different practices, producing different types of knowledge as a consequence. The NPGs had to hold these identities together in order to perform all the necessary elements of legitimacy. But they also had to hold them apart to insulate them from the conflicts inherent among them. In particular, the detached expert identity which produced epistemic authority, whose knowledge was privileged, had to remain untainted in a planning imaginary where emotive, relational knowledge of place as experienced is marginalised, implicitly without worth. While the successful performance of each identity was necessary, the knowledges produced by each were not equally valued. The effect was that the NPGs produced representations of abstract space and silenced those of lived place: they represented (and enacted) the neighbourhood in certain ways, and not in others. Only those versions of the neighbourhood that were made visible could be directly planned for.

While the NPGs were able to have material effects, this did not fulfil the radical promise of neighbourhood planning. Where the discourse of neighbourhood planning appeared to invite openness, experimentality and plurality, to represent more and different spatial imaginaries, its practices led to foreclosure, conservatism and narrowness. Where it seemed to call for the embedded voices of direct lived experience, instead it produced purified inscriptions mediated by technologies. Affective relations with place were clearly strong drivers for people to engage with the process, but they were difficult to articulate and to translate into material forms of evidence that were considered appropriate within this framework of knowledge practices. They were therefore marginalised or entirely written out of the record, driven out by tropic figurations of evidence and expertise.

Knowledge arising from the NPGs' identity 'in' the neighbourhood was suppressed in the production of evidence. Knowledge arising from the wider community's entangledness with neighbourhood was purified by technologies of participation through the NPGs' specific performances 'of' the neighbourhood. The category of the expert and the expert–agency coupling were reproduced, with the NPGs enacting a new centre of expertise – albeit a rather precarious one, both reliant on established expertise to stabilise their position, but also subject to unsettling and displacement by that expertise. Ways of knowing and doing established elsewhere in the planning system and imported into the practice of neighbourhood planning proved obdurate, resisting destabilisation even through a process that was (at least notionally) intended to unsettle them by enabling the pluralisation of effective knowledges and knowledge practices. Stabilised categories, institutions, power relations and norms were reasserted alongside stabilised forms of knowledge that could be accepted as valid, highlighting the difficulty, in a co-produced world, of doing or knowing in new ways.

Notwithstanding this, positive differences were achieved in the neighbourhoods. A new spokesperson (the NPG) was created for a new instantiation of community (the neighbourhood), whose presence and actions rearranged the relations of local planning, realigning the flows and knots of power. The status and position of 'the community' in relation to the local authority, developers and landowners (and indeed to the planning system itself) was fundamentally changed – at least in its instantiation as a neighbourhood represented by an NPG. Statutory plans were produced that contained policies that would not have existed otherwise, changing the parameters for how and for whom development would take place in these localities. Different sites were allocated for and protected from development than otherwise would have been. The NPGs influenced policy development beyond their own plans in ways that would not previously have been possible. In the act of foreclosing certain possibilities (of producing a plan and evidence that foregrounded experiential knowledge and felt connection with place), other possibilities were opened up (of producing a plan and an institution that could have effects in the expert-dominated regime of planning).

The sociomaterial assemblages that jointly produced the realities in which the NPGs operated – constituted by consultants and Local Planning Authority (LPA) officers; templates, surveys and other technologies of participation; published plans and examiners' reports; local people and places; imaginaries both general and specific (from the figure of modern knowledge to the figure of the examiner), and much else besides – reproduced framings, practices and meanings from outside of neighbourhood planning which constrained the ability of NPGs (and the neighbourhoods for which they spoke) to enact 'neighbourhood' in relational, place-based terms. But these assemblages were enabling as well. They enacted the NPGs as having the authority to act by enabling their performance as 'beyond' the neighbourhood and the purification of the knowledge arising from the NPGs' identity as mediator. The NPGs became recognised as the bearers of expertise, and therefore of legitimate agency. Despite a succession of unexpected challenges and disappointments, neither of the NPGs that I worked with had the slightest doubt that real differences were made because of their work in developing their plans. Both were, in the end, proud of their achievements.

Furthermore, despite their elimination from the formal inscriptions of neighbourhood planning, the cares and concerns of neighbourhood got woven into its outputs and outcomes anyway. The experience of place, with its inextricably emotive components, inflected the representations of abstract space that ended up inscribed in policy by framing the questions asked, the orientations taken, the methods used, the choices made. The sterile language of planning policy was steered by the affective forces that were rendered invisible, but not eliminated, by the translations of neighbourhood planning. While NPGs are constituted as lay-experts and it is through this constitution that much of their power arises, this aspect of identity cannot exist as a legitimate NPG on its own. Even if it is this identity that is enabled to exercise agency through relations with other social and material actors which would usually (intentionally or otherwise) silence the experience of community, this identity depends on the other two. The enactment of NPG as expert relies upon the enactment of NPG as affectively embedded and

NPG as consultative and mediating to fulfil the full range of conditions of an NPG. It is only the holding-together of these conflicting identities that provides a platform for the lay-expert to exercise agency. NPGs can therefore be thought of as a node where the rich and varied sociomaterial experience of neighbourhood is brought together with information from formal consultation and with the measurements and categorisations of abstract space. So, it is significant that it is NPGs themselves who are producing these representations of place as space, rather than experts who are socially and spatially remote from the lived experience of neighbourhood. The situated knowledge practices of their identities 'in' and 'of' the neighbourhood, essential to establishing their situated legitimacy, influence the actions and representations of their identities as experts 'beyond' the neighbourhood. However, the neighbourhood as experienced, as an (almost) invisible object of policy and care, represented only by proxy, is highly vulnerable to interpretations and future changes in policy which do not and cannot engage with the underlying sub-text of the policy as written.

Neighbourhood planning does expand local participation in planning, but the knowledges and values – and ways of knowing and valuing – that have traditionally been excluded from the planning system are again marginalised by the importation and adaptation of meanings, norms and practices from elsewhere in the system. The practices of neighbourhood planning often result in the exclusion from explicit visibility of the very kinds of knowledge and value that it promised to take seriously. However, because of the central role of the NPG, and because the NPG is necessarily constituted in a variety of different knowledge-relations to the neighbourhood, knowledges and values that are largely made invisible in the inscriptions of neighbourhood planning are nevertheless carried by them and able to permeate the eventual plan policies. In some cases, ways of working knowledges together in new ways have been found.

While representations and logics of abstract space tended to crowd out and suppress those of lived place in most of the formal inscriptions across both sites, the development, output and outcome of the Wroston Landscape Character Appraisal provides an example of 'expert' and 'lay' ways of knowing being worked together effectively. The NPG disagreed with the conclusions of the original assessments from the LPA's consultants. They felt that the mechanistic methodology had failed to capture key elements of the sites and to respond adequately to their internal characteristics and their relation to the village and the wider landscape. The LPA had insisted that if the NPG wanted to contest the assessment's results (in order to draw different conclusions and to allocate different sites for development), they would need an alternative assessment by a qualified expert. The NPG engaged such an expert, who they briefed thoroughly on their concerns about the previous assessment, highlighting the factors that had been missed or captured inadequately. They directed her to relevant locations and viewpoints, helping her to understand the sites to be assessed in the holistic context which they experienced them. Her methodology – of walking around and through Wroston and its setting as well as in and around the sites, taking time and space to understand the sites as integral parts of a wider lived landscape – also reflected more closely the ways in which the sites were experienced by the neighbourhood. Informed by this material practice and the detailed input from the NPG (who were not at this point attempting to produce evidence themselves, and who were therefore less limited by the constraints that producing evidence places on the expression of affective, relational knowledge), she produced an assessment which was able to take account of much that the original assessment had neglected, and which therefore drew different conclusions as to the suitability of specific sites to be allocated for development.

I have also speculated about the possibility for the practices of neighbourhood planning to come closer to their rhetorical claims, by understanding planning matters as matters of care and concern. This would entail a more 'generous' approach to evidence, understanding affective, experiential, 'lay' knowledges, and abstract, quantified 'expert' ones alike as incomplete sociomaterial assemblages that are in the process of being done. While this approach is often taken by Science and Technology Studies (STS) scholars researching knowledge production and mobilisation, it remains extremely rare as an approach in actual decision-making situations. I have drawn attention to some attempts to include excluded knowledges in planning-related decision making that in various ways seek to undo the binary oppositions between different knowledge categories, and to enable inclusion of excluded knowledges. I have suggested that, within the current legislative and policy framework of neighbourhood planning, adopting a more explicitly narrative approach to evidence production might offer a fruitful way forward to better work together different knowledges and ways of knowing, as it is through such narrative frameworks that evidence gains and conveys meaning. I have also suggested that a narrative approach could better integrate land use planning issues with other issues, as they are experienced in practice by communities, which could increase participation in neighbourhood planning, help to ensure that a made plan remains a live document that continues to engage, mobilise and generate the care that initiated it, and provide a springboard to wider local governance and participatory opportunities.

Neighbourhood planning is one very specific form of participatory democracy. Throughout the book I have also discussed three very different instances of participatory democratic interventions, with widely differing characteristics in terms of their participants, situations, locations, methods, issues and consequences. In their different ways, each of these also represent attempts to assemble places and people differently – foregrounding matters that had not previously been attended to, telling different stories about themselves and the places where they live, in order to shape the direction of their future narratives. While participatory rural development, like neighbourhood planning, starts out as an externally initiated, invited space, and community organising and environmental justice movements start out as invented spaces of resistance, each can, in some instances, slip between these categories, as the invited spaces of collaboration and invented spaces of resistance offer different opportunities and constraints for reassembling neighbourhoods and how we know them. Despite their profound differences, similarities can be identified in the processes by which they achieve legitimacy and achieve effects – and also by which they experience constraints and limitations.

In different ways borne out of their own particular situations, groups of citizens involved across these examples also performed synecdochical, mediating and expert identities, each of which positions them in fundamentally different relations to the assemblages which they seek to represent. The different relations that each identity has with the world and different ways in which they enact and assemble people, place and issues are similarly drawn upon to enact their legitimacy as claim-makers, to legitimise the claims that they make. Performing a combination of these identities enables each of these groups to act in some way as spokespeople for a neighbourhood or a community, an intermediary between citizens and the state. However, the ways in which those identities are assembled – in which the groups' different relations with the world are performed – varies widely depending on the particular constraints and possibilities facing them. Their specific situatedness determines the knowledges they are able to articulate, and therefore the versions of reality that they are able to construct and contest.

In their different ways, these different modes of assembling community and locality also enable effects to be made. Communities affected by industrial pollution can be relocated, compensated, or have the sources or effects of pollution mitigated. The material infrastructures of informal urban settlements and rural communities and the wellbeing of their inhabitants can be improved, alongside the rights of those inhabitants to shape those improvements. Material effects have been achieved by each of these varied types of participatory democratic intervention. But they are also subject to constraints that arise from the performance of the same identities that enable them to have effects. They are subject to displacement by external experts and notions of expertise, and by existing relations of power and authority. They are constrained by norms and conventions about what counts as knowledge, and whose knowledge counts. Each of these examples suggests different patterns in which relational identities can be performed and combined: ways in which they can be enacted in different arrangements. These different arrangements of identities and associated knowledge practices offer different ways of assembling places, people and issues, and thus allow different worlds to be made visible and acted upon. Recognition of the different kinds of relation with and knowledge of the world that are produced by the enactment of each different identity, and of the different worlds that are assembled by combining these relations and knowledges in different ways, offers the potential to rethink and rework the imaginaries which frame those constraints and displacements.

Remaking participation?

The turn to participation has, over several decades, seen many attempts to find ways to empower citizens to have more influence over decisions that affect them. The remote establishments and specialist expertise in which power has been regarded as residing have, over this time, increasingly struggled to retain authority and credibility in the face of increasingly visible uncertainties, inequalities and complexities (Chilvers and Kearnes, 2016). These attempts have taken the form of both 'invited' spaces, driven by institutions such as governments, corporations and agencies seeking user or citizen involvement in their processes, and 'invented' spaces, driven by the people (and their allies) who find themselves excluded from and disadvantaged by those processes. The frequent reforms of the English planning system – most recently the introduction of neighbourhood planning – represent just one (or rather, one series) of such interventions, bounded and characterised by its own set of particularly situated features. Throughout these chapters I have also drawn attention to a set of other attempts at democratising decision making, diverse in their locations, origins, driving forces, participants, issues, cultural and historical situatedness, and implications.

Negotiating between critique and celebration

'Standard' models of participation and accounts of efforts to democratise decision making across a wide range of fields and subjects tend to call for more citizen and community participation in decision making to shift balances of power. Such participation is often understood as a matter of degree, from information giving, through consultation, to coproduction and community control. Starting with Sherry Arnstein (1969), this understanding of participatory democracy has given rise to conceptual 'ladders' of participation, with higher rungs on the ladder equalling greater citizen empowerment. Such conceptual frameworks remain a touchstone for policy makers and practitioners seeking to advocate for and promote participatory democratisation of decision making, and, albeit with modifications and complexifications, for researchers seeking to explain the mechanisms and relative success or failure of such interventions (Wilcox, 1994; Tritter and McCallum, 2006; Ianniello et al, 2019). A corollary of this is that more participation is seen as equalling better participation and more democratic outcomes, or at least processes. If communities or citizens are engaged, but still not empowered, it can be explained as reflecting a failure to progress up the rungs of a conceptual participatory ladder. More participation, and more control over decision making, is considered more empowering. Participation at these 'higher' levels is considered to be transformative for the citizens and communities involved, shifting them from relatively powerless objects who are 'done to', to empowered subjects with the agency to shape their own futures.

Set against this view of the transformative potential of participation are a set of critiques that can broadly be described as 'post-political' (Cooke and Kothari, 2001; Mouffe, 2005; Wilson and Swyngedouw, 2014). These critiques argue that participation, far from having transformative effects for the citizens and communities involved, only empowers them to make decisions within a narrow band of parameters that have been predetermined by external agencies (such as governments and corporations). Participation is thus argued as acting instrumentally to legitimise decisions effectively made elsewhere, rather than to enable citizens or communities to genuinely take greater control over their lives or environments. In the guise of shifting power downwards and outwards, it rather reinforces existing social identities and power relations while also concealing that reinforcement. The assumptions and framings built into participatory processes regulate the kinds of knowledge, values and experience that can be contributed, thus effectively limiting any hypothetical aim to pluralise the inputs to decision making. On this interpretation, participation is both manipulative and potentially harmful to those who take part. These critiques of course largely refer to institutionalised or 'invited' participatory practices, but many instances of participatory democracy involve an iterative movement between 'invited' and 'invented' spaces – and engagement with institutional participatory settings can sometimes be seen as a mark of progress or success for 'outsider' movements (Bua and Bussu, 2020).

The STS-inspired analysis in this book attempts to show how these two opposing analytical poles, while both useful and generative for informing policy, practice and research, can only offer partial and incomplete accounts of participatory practices. While focusing strongly on the case of neighbourhood planning, it has also shown, albeit at a fairly superficial level, how the concepts I have used to explore the practices of neighbourhood planning, and which I have further developed through that exploration, can also be used to inform and sensitise readings of other instances of participatory democracy. It offers a reading of the citizens, communities, places, issues and processes that are involved in these practices that contrasts with the two analytical poles outlined earlier. In doing so, it contributes to the movement in STS and related disciplines that seeks to develop alternative understandings of participatory democracy, and thus to open up possibilities for doing participation in ways that are more reflexive, accountable, transparent and responsive (exemplified by, for example, Lezaun and Soneryd, 2007; Felt and Fochler, 2010; Horst and Irwin, 2010; Marres, 2012; Waterton et al, 2015; Irwin, 2016; Soneryd, 2016; Voß and Amelung, 2016; Lezaun et al, 2017; Metzger et al, 2017; Braun and Könninger, 2018; Chilvers and Kearnes, 2020; and perhaps most fully developed in Chilvers and Kearnes' edited volume *Remaking Participation: Science, Environment and Emerging Publics* [2016]).

This movement seeks to reframe participatory practices away from the idea of discrete, more or less effective transfers of powers between pre-given individuals or aggregates of individuals, and pre-given institutions such as states, in relation to pre-given issues or problems. It focuses instead on the ways in which participation – in invited or invented spaces – actively assembles collective identities through collective practices, bringing into being particular instantiations of community. Crucially, these collectives are considered as relational – they do not exist in isolation, in and of themselves, but in particular relations to the social and material worlds in which they are embedded. And they are more than human – they are constituted not just by the individual humans that standard accounts of participation would say make them up, but by the relations between those humans and the social and material elements – the places, objects, infrastructures, institutions, policies, technologies and so on – which contribute to defining who and what they are. These collective identities imply particular ways of being in the world, of knowing and valuing the world, and of how those knowledges and values can be articulated and mobilised. They are co-produced – their characteristics emerge as an effect of the issues and worlds with which they engage, and the ways in which they engage with them (Jasanoff, 2004b). A collective that is brought into being through developing a neighbourhood plan, for example, may have very different characteristics and relations with their world than one brought into being through an environmental protest movement.

Those issues and worlds also simultaneously take on particular concrete characteristics as an effect of the collective identities which are thus produced and the relations between them. The specific participatory encounters through which these processes of co-production occur are also themselves co-produced, enacted in specific ways by the development of specific relations between emergent identities and issues. And while these enactments are to a considerable degree path-dependent, shaped by previous enactments and dominant imaginaries, the very fact that they are always in the process of being enacted, always dynamic, fluid and in the making, means that there is always the possibility for things to be done differently, for identities and issues and the relations between them to emerge differently. Furthermore, these acts of participation – such as developing a neighbourhood plan, taking part in a protest or campaign, or organising a mutual support group – are not isolated from the rest of people's lives, but are connected into multiple other engagements with the issues at stake in everyday life (Chilvers and Kearnes, 2016; Braun and Könninger, 2018). This movement thus seeks not to *resolve* the tensions between advocacy for the transformative potential of participatory democratic practices and critique of their harmful effects, but to *dissolve* and move beyond this tension by reconceiving how we understand those practices, how they function, and their implications for their subjects (the people involved) and objects (the issues at stake). It does not replace a discussion of power, but rather shines a light on some of the ways in which power is *done*.

This book engages with this movement by describing and analysing some of the ways in which these processes of 'doing' power take place, and the effects that they have, offering new ways of understanding the participatory encounter. By making these processes visible and paying attention to them, it opens up possibilities for understanding the practices of participatory democracy differently, and thus for doing them differently. It offers an additional way between what Metzger caricatures as the poles of being merely 'a useful idiot for the powers that be' and 'self-righteous zealotry or cynical nihilism' (Metzger, 2014a: 1001), between echoing official enthusiasm for a type of practice that has often wholly or partially failed, and rejecting any possibility that those practices could be of genuine benefit to participants and their wider communities.

Multiplicity, visibility, possibility

The detailed exploration of the ways in which NPGs achieve legitimacy through the performance of three distinct identities, in particular through the production and presentation of evidence, clearly demonstrates the emergence of collective subjectivities through participatory practices. It also demonstrates the multiplicity of these collective identities. It is not the case that they are 'really' one or the other. Despite the clear tensions and sometimes outright contradictions between them (as illustrated by Table 4.1), in enacting these identities they become each of them. And they, and the worlds associated with them, are in a continual process of becoming, always in the making, always being enacted. The collectives are assembled in multiple ways through multiple different relations with the world (Mol, 2002). Each of these identities emerges as an effect of the issues and worlds which have called them into being and the ways in which they engage with them (Marres, 2012). Each identity is defined by a particular way of being in the world, of relating to the social and material worlds which constitute it. Each is, fundamentally, defined by its relation to the sociomaterial neighbourhood from which it emerges, and which in turn it defines and constitutes.

In turn, the enactment of each identity makes a particular version of the world visible, makes it capable of being attended to and engaged with in certain ways and not others. The participatory practice thus brings into being identities, issues and worlds. I have proposed that in the absence of the formal authority provided by democratic elections, NPGs need to enact each of these identities to establish their legitimacy – and consequently bring each of the associated worlds and issues to attention in particular ways. However, I have also shown that these identities and their associated worlds are not performed equally – that the processes through which they are enacted show a tendency to support the dominance of some versions of reality and the marginalisation of others. While all are necessary to enact, those enactments emerge unequally. And the disproportionate attention paid to the expert identity and its accompanying world result in the exclusion of matters that matter to the emergent collectives, and that are, or should be, at the heart of planning – the relation between people and place, the lived experience of place.

It is widely recognised (in theory, if not always in practice) that communities or publics are internally diverse, and that to understand community or public knowledge, efforts must be made to ensure that a wide range of diverse voices are heard. But what this analysis shows is that even in relatively homogeneous communities, the *ways* in which voices are heard are also crucial. Communities are multiple as well as diverse. Participatory practices need to find ways to enable not just a diversity of voices to be heard, but a diversity of types of knowledge and ways of knowing. It is not all that empowering to enable a wide range of voices to be heard if they can only be heard in one register, if the losses in translating their contributions into the kind of voice that can be heard are too great.

NPGs might conventionally be considered as being towards the upper reaches of conceptual ladders of participation, given their power to make their own statutory planning policies. But attention to processes of framing, of the reinforcement or marginalisation of different social and spatial imaginaries, of the enactment or repression of different collective identities, can provide more nuanced insights not only into how power relations may be reproduced, but also into how they might be – and are being – done differently. It reveals the precarity and fragility of such empowerment, but also its potential. Likewise, the patterns of displacement and decentring by external authorities and expertise, rather than simply indicating post-political instrumentalisation of these communities to legitimise the implementation of external agendas, suggests a need for closer attention to the practices by which they and their worlds are enacted. Understanding the multiplicity as well as the diversity of people, places and issues, and the relations between different collective identities and external actors, opens new possibilities for understanding how power is 'done' in these situations. Making these processes visible, paying attention to them, is the first step towards practical interventions that might enable them to be done differently, in ways that are more responsive to the multiplicity of community knowledges and values, and more accountable to their aspirations.

This matters because it gives us a new way to understand both the relatively rare explicit failures of neighbourhood planning – failures to pass technical examination, or to secure votes in a referendum – and also the 'alienation of neighbourhood planning' (Bradley, 2018: 29), the more subtle, more common failure for plans to represent the worlds which matter to people. It gives us a way to understand how things have been – and could be – done differently within the practices of neighbourhood planning, and the potential both to reframe those practices within existing policy constraints, and to reframe policy to encourage more reflexive practices. It also highlights the intense efforts involved in such practices, alongside their potential, their fragility and their fallibility.

Implications and ontological politics

This has both practical and theoretical implications. On a practical level, in relation to neighbourhood planning itself as a distinct form of participatory democracy, it provides a tool for government, NPGs, planning officers, consultants and other actors to consider how to embark on the process of developing a plan and its evidence base. It provides a framework to proactively plan to pluralise the knowledges and relations with place that will be sought out, captured and worked together, which recognises the incommensurability of different types of knowledge but respects those differences, rather than insisting on collapsing one into another, or automatically relegating some and privileging others. And it also provides a framework for monitoring the progress of plan development, for identifying if and how, often unintentionally, reductions and simplifications that confound the intentions and aspirations of NPGs and their neighbourhoods are taking place. And by providing such a framework, it offers the potential to reflexively and deliberately assemble the neighbourhood in a different way, attending to and strengthening important relations that are at risk of being otherwise neglected. It offers a new lens through which to do care for neighbourhood.

While this theorisation arises directly through the application of STS-inspired methods of investigation to the particular case of neighbourhood planning, I have also suggested that it could be used as a sensitising concept in other situations of practice and research (Blumer, 1954). I have gestured towards ways in which other, radically different, sites of participatory democracy could be interpreted through this lens. These readings are also, of course, partial and incomplete, but they offer a novel way of analysing how legitimacy is achieved by intermediaries between citizens and states (and other institutions).[1] Analysis of this kind will have implications for how we understand the subjects and objects of these different sites, and their relations with each other and the worlds in which they act. They will not apply in all situations, and will apply partially, and differently, and tangentially in others – but these variations in themselves provide a new way of thinking through the similarities and differences of diverse situations, and what may or may not be learned from one to the other, which ideas may or may not be made able to travel between sites. They are far from universal generalisations, but they enable us to ask new sets of questions and suggest new possibilities for how both researchers and practitioners might attend to, analyse and intervene in participatory practices, and better understand and shape the political openings and closures that result (Mol, 2010).

All of this helps us to understand – or at least provides one way of understanding – the crucial issue of how ontological politics is done, and through that understanding, how it could be done differently. Worlds, issues and identities are enacted together through participatory practices (Chilvers and Kearnes, 2016). The characteristics of the world that are available to be engaged with – what is foregrounded and backgrounded, what is made relevant and important, where the object of interest begins and ends both spatially and conceptually – are framed and shaped by these processes. And so too are the characteristics of the participating citizens or communities – what knowledges, values and experiences are relevant and important, how they can be articulated, and what kinds of participation are legitimate. These processes frame both the material ontology of the world (what is out there to be engaged with) and also the political ontology of participants (how that engagement might legitimately be conducted).

Publics that are framed as having certain characteristics and certain forms of agency will be able to act only in certain ways, and only on certain versions of reality. So in the example of neighbourhood planning, the political possibilities of the NPG, and therefore of the neighbourhood it represents, are determined by the way in which their roles as embedded embodiment of neighbourhood, as engaged mediator for neighbourhood, and detached analyst of neighbourhood are combined in their representations in evidence and policy. And those representations, those enactments of neighbourhood, simultaneously determine the material ontology of the neighbourhood that is available to be planned for in policy.

Every different instance of participatory democracy has its own situated boundaries, constraints and possibilities, and the ontological politics of each instance will unfold differently according to these. Different worlds and different publics, with different features and different capabilities, will be brought into being through different practices in different situations. Looking through this lens, of the enactment of multiple relational identities between intermediaries and publics, gives us a way to explore how this happens in different situations. This approach offers a way to reframe the material and political ontologies that are being produced by reasserting the relevance and importance of neglected identities and the versions of reality and ways of knowing associated with them. By providing a new interpretation of the diverse boundaries and constraints in a given situation, it enables a reflexive response to them, opening up new possibilities for working productively with them and pushing at the cracks which always exist in those boundaries. Because even in cases where they seem utterly immovable, boundaries and constraints are also always in the process of enactment, always already and still in the making. Taking a different approach to understanding their flexibilities and obduracies may help to understand why they are obdurate in particular ways, and, again, how that might be changed.

In this analysis it is the knowledge practices of the collectives themselves that produce different ontologies. And while those practices are constrained by the wider assemblages and imaginaries that they find themselves a part of, they also offer the potential for making these practices (and thus ontologies) more flexible, relatable and combinable in different ways. It may not be the case that a particular collective in a specific situation performs all or any of these particular identities. But multiple identities will be enacted – by collectives themselves, or by others that engage with them in some way. And if different relational identities entail different capabilities, different ways of knowing and engaging the world (and, indeed, different worlds!), then it is better to be aware of the possibilities and openings that different enactments entail, as well as their constraints and closures. Reflexive engagement with the enactment of identities will enable, at least to an extent, a more deliberate management of the ways in which those identities are enacted, rather than being impelled into performed particular identities in particular ways, with their associated constraints and limitations. This approach therefore gives practitioners a way of thinking about their representations of themselves, their knowledge, their places and their issues, and the effects that those representations might have.

In addition, where these particular identities are drawn upon to perform legitimacy, the need to enact all of them ensures that there will always be space for resistance against existing power relations, and therefore the possibility of disruption of those relations. It is significant that the collectives, in their multiplicity, are constituted by enactments of each of the three identities, *in*, *of* and *beyond* their neighbourhoods and communities. This is significant because, even while the identity *beyond* the neighbourhood and the associated ways of knowing and representing the world came to dominate in the cases explored here, the necessary presence, albeit suppressed, of the other identities keeps alive other ways of knowing and engaging with the world. The multiplicity of the collectives may result in 'proxy ontologies', with collectives planning for versions of place or issue that have not been made visible in evidence, but which nevertheless continue to matter to them and their communities. The matters that matter to one identity are reframed and represented as matters that can matter in the knowledge practices of another. This enables care to permeate participatory practices such as neighbourhood planning, even while it is often explicitly written out of the evidence base. However, this makes the presence of care even more fragile and precarious, vulnerable to displacement or exclusion in decisions or further iterations, as the object of care has not been made visible and therefore cannot be engaged with directly.

In the previous chapter I reviewed a range of attempts that have been made – and that could be applied much more widely – to engage more directly with such suppressed matters of care. Placed in the framework suggested here, these – and many other techniques besides – may provide routes to rebalancing the ways in which identities and their attendant worlds are combined in participatory practices, to opening up possibilities for enabling more plural and diverse knowledges to have effect.

However, especially in invited, institutional participatory settings, not all worlds are open for interpretation. In neighbourhood planning, for example, national policies provide some specific constraints. To give just one example, neighbourhood plans are constrained by a figure for 'objectively assessed housing need' – the number of houses that need to be provided within the area over the plan period – which, for all intents and purposes, must be treated by NPGs as a fact. But understanding it not as a fact, but as a highly contingent, selectively framed, value-laden judgement does not prevent its acceptance as a parameter if it is accepted that all facts are highly contingent, selectively framed, value-laden judgements. And understanding it in this way does perhaps enable us to think more widely about what else might be considered evidence, considered as relevant and important, especially within the 'safe space' generated by such parameters. It may make it easier to resist the matters that matter to one identity being squeezed out by the matters that matter to another. Citizens don't accept as objective truths those versions of reality that exclude their experiential knowledge. But working from a framework where all truths are partial and situated – albeit in some cases framed by practical parameters within which participation can take place – may help to pluralise social and spatial imaginaries to enable the experiential knowledges conventionally conceived of as 'less-than-factual' to be articulated, captured and understood as, at least, illustrative of structural concerns.

Emergent realities

The performance of subjects and objects, of identities and worlds, the framing and shaping of the people, places and issues of participatory democracy, are inevitable. Publics and public meanings are endlessly emergent. Participatory processes are 'machineries for making publics' and the worlds associated with them (Felt and Fochler, 2010), 'exercises in imagining their publics, and attempting to bring into material being the kinds of public they desire' (Wynne, 2016). The public 'is never immediately given but inevitably the outcome of processes of naming and framing, staging, selection and priority setting, attribution, interpellation, categorisation and classification' (Braun and Schultz, 2010: 406). There is no 'residual reality' beyond enactment (Chilvers and Kearnes, 2016). As researchers and practitioners, we need to acknowledge this, and be reflexive and care-full about the kinds of publics, worlds and issues which we contribute to enacting, taking some responsibility for those enactments. And in doing so we might also help to reveal some of the conditions for doing participation better, based on greater reflexivity about the ways in which these co-productions occur in particular situations. I hope that the characterisations of people, place and process that I have presented here can play some modest part in moving both research and practice in this direction.

I need to emphasise, again, that these are not totalising generalisations, but one set of tools in a vast toolbox. There are many ways of understanding and interpreting the production of publics (or citizens, or communities) through the practices of participatory democracy, and the simultaneous production of the worlds in which they exist and the issues with which they engage. All I suggest is that this particular approach may be of use, in some cases, in analysing the production of intermediaries between citizens and states (and similar situations), and understanding how their possibilities for action might be opened up or closed down.

This approach provides a framework for understanding and doing things differently, for reflexively engaging with participatory practices in ways that deliberately seek to unsettle the reinforcement and marginalisation of different identities and their associated worlds, and thus the material and political ontologies that are made available through those practices. The intention would not be to displace the centrality of evidence, but to pluralise and widen it so that more of the multiple worlds that constitute any one neighbourhood (or any other site or issue of participatory democracy) can be engaged with and be worked with alongside each other. However, it also highlights that doing things differently is not easy, that it requires not just new understandings and interpretations of the subjects and objects of participatory practices, but huge effort and resistance against the hegemony of dominant imaginaries to assemble things differently. While the subjects and objects of participatory democracy are always in the making, always in the process of being enacted, any one instance is embedded in a hinterland of enactments that provide it with context and meaning. In the example of neighbourhood planning, the reproduction of dominant norms, assumptions, practices and conventions through the everyday practices of planners, examiners, consultants and NPGs themselves restrict the possibilities for change and doing things differently. New forms of agency are possible, but we are already embedded in multiple flows of social and material relations, and swimming against the current is hard. However, recognising the potential for new possibilities through new ways of understanding participatory democracy is an important step towards more open, responsive, accountable and democratic futures.

Conclusion

A future in which diverse forms of participatory democracy do not continue to multiply, and do not continue to be the subject of acclaim, critique and controversy, is almost inconceivable. Participatory practices have become embedded in the assemblages of national and local states, governmental agencies, private corporations, non-governmental organisations, social movements, unions and more (Bherer et al, 2016b). An entire industry of participation professionals has emerged, simultaneously proliferating and standardising actual enactments of participatory practices. And even if the still-accelerating trend of institutionalised participation in invited spaces were to slow or even reverse, invented spaces of resistance will remain, and likely expand further in response. Research on the dynamics and workings of this diverse phenomenon will therefore remain of central importance to understanding the relations between citizens and communities, on the one hand, and states, corporations, and other institutions on the other, and the inequalities, injustices and power relations that emerge between them.

Neighbourhood planning, as one specific enactment of this trend, also looks set to remain a prominent element of the English planning system. Despite the UK government's retreat from the radical reforms set out in the 2020 *Planning for the Future* White Paper (MHCLG, 2020), changes to the system and to national policy are still due to be enacted, with considerable uncertainty over exactly what these will consist of. Ministers have insisted that 'the government are committed to putting communities at the very heart of our planning system, with neighbourhood plans playing a crucial role' (Hansard, 2022a), emphasising 'the important role that neighbourhood plans will continue to play in the planning system' and their desire to 'strengthen the role of neighbourhood plans in decision making' (Hansard, 2022b). They have also trailed an intention to introduce 'neighbourhood priorities statements'. These are a simplified form of neighbourhood planning, by which neighbourhoods can officially articulate their priorities and which LPAs will be obliged to take into account when preparing their local plans. They are intended to make neighbourhood planning more accessible, and to either stand on their own or to lead on to the future development of full neighbourhood plans. Either way, the intention to make them simpler, less formal and more accessible – therefore increasing their conceptual distance from the practices and imaginaries of the planning system – may open up new possibilities for the articulation of knowledges and experiences that continue to be excluded.

The *Levelling Up* White Paper also promised to launch 'a *review of neighbourhood governance* in England, looking at how to make it easier for local people and community groups to come together, set local priorities and shape the future of their neighbourhoods' (HM Government, 2022: 215, emphasis in original). This may, possibly, make it easier to connect the dots between those matters that are strictly the subject of land use planning policy, and the wider elements of placemaking that ordinary citizens intuitively grasp as being closely interconnected, but which the conventions of the system continue to artificially force apart. However, as even senior members of the government's own backbenches have described the new proposals as a 'power-grab by the centre' (Villiers, 2022), quite the opposite of the government's own claims to be pushing power downwards and outwards, the meanings and enactments of participatory democracy in the planning system look likely to remain hotly contested as well.

And it is perhaps precisely for that reason – that the same policy can be claimed as empowering communities by one 'side', and as disempowering them and subjecting them to the will of external agencies by another – that makes the careful and detailed exploration of actually-emerging instances of participation so important. I am of course not denying that there are power struggles between, say, local and national, state and community, corporation and citizen. What I am saying is that much of that power struggle happens behind the scenes, in the ongoing enactment of assemblages and practices that determine the territory on which more visible struggles get played out.

Simplifications of the complexity of the world are always necessary in any representations of it. But there is never only one simplification that could be made. And which simplifications and translations are made, what is foregrounded and backgrounded, attended to or ignored, identified as relevant or insignificant – which versions of reality are made visible and brought to presence – shape the possibilities for action of all actors in that world. Likewise, the definition, explicitly or implicitly, of what kind of citizens can legitimately participate in its governance, and how they may do that, both opens some possibilities for action and closes others. Or, as Donna Haraway puts it, 'who and what are in the world is precisely what is at stake' (Haraway, 2003: 8). Paying attention to how these ontological politics are done in practice can help us, first, to understand the emergence of this crucial, but generally hidden, aspect of power, and, second, to ask questions and propose answers about how it might be done differently.

Notes

Chapter 1

1 All names of people, places, institutions and so on have been anonymised to maintain confidentiality.

2 The Community Infrastructure Levy (CIL) is a charge paid by developers to LPAs after the grant of planning permission to help fund local infrastructure. Where a town/parish council has a neighbourhood plan in place, 25 per cent of the money raised by the charge in the neighbourhood area must be passed on to that council. Where there is not a neighbourhood plan, it will only receive 15 per cent, and that will be capped at a level of £100 per household. However, not all LPAs have a CIL schedule in place, so this benefit is not available to all potential NPGs.

3 Although in a book primarily oriented to neighbourhood planning in England, my readings of these other situations will necessarily be highly simplified.

Chapter 2

1 'Material considerations' is the term used to describe the issues that can be considered in planning decisions. It is a category that is at once absolute and pre-given (if a matter is cast as not being 'material', it simply cannot be considered to have any weight in planning terms), and ambiguous and fluid (there is no definitive list of material considerations – some things are ruled in and ruled out but there are substantial grey areas and policy and guidance are framed in such a way as to maintain that ambiguity and fluidity [Planning Portal, nd]).

2 A policy and practice briefing developed in collaboration with leading scholars and non-governmental organisations involved in neighbourhood planning, setting out recommendations for strengthening and improving neighbourhood planning through the planning reforms of the early 2020s can be found at https://eprints.lancs.ac.uk/id/eprint/161481/1/Levelling_Up_and_Neighbourhood_Planning_October_2021.pdf

3 See, for example, conflicts in Hackney (https://www.hackneycitizen.co.uk/2014/12/03/neighbourhood-forums-stamford-hill-rejected-hackney-council/) and Bermondsey (http://www.london-se1.co.uk/news/view/7803), and especially Rickmansworth (https://www.threerivers.gov.uk/egcl-page/rickmansworth-neighbourhood-forum), where the LPA chose first not to designate the area proposed by the incipient Neighbourhood Forum, but to designate a significantly larger area, and then rejected the group's application to be designated as a Neighbourhood Forum on the basis that they did not adequately represent the newly enlarged area.

4 For example, http://locality.org.uk/projects/building-community/, http://www.ourneighbourhoodplanning.org.uk/home and https://mycommunity.org.uk/take-action/neighbourhood-planning/

5 The Department for Communities and Local Government was the government department responsible for planning when neighbourhood planning was first introduced in 2011. It was superseded in 2018 by the Ministry for Housing, Communities and Local Government, which was in turn replaced in 2021 with the Department for Levelling Up, Housing and Communities.

6 In certain circumstances it is also possible for referendums to include, or be restricted to, businesses operating in the plan area.

7 The National Planning Policy Framework was revised and updated in 2018, 2019 and again in 2021, but the key policies continued to function broadly as described here,

except where I specifically note changes. In 2021 the government pledged a thorough review of the National Planning Policy Framework as part of the planning reform process triggered by the 2020 *Planning for the Future* White Paper, but at the time of writing the outcomes of this remain uncertain, and the 'radical' proposals promised in the White Paper appear highly unlikely to be carried through. Neighbourhood planning appears set to remain a significant part of the English planning system for the foreseeable future.

[8] The wording of and footnotes to this policy were updated in 2018, 2019 and 2021. The earlier changes more restrictively specified the policies that could be relied upon to restrict or refuse development, expanded the circumstances in which policies could be considered out of date, and incorporated a requirement to meet development needs which could not be met within neighbouring areas – that is, they further strengthened the pro-growth imperative. The 2021 update, in contrast, enhanced the sustainability element of the presumption in plan-making by requiring that plans promote a sustainable pattern of development, align growth and infrastructure, improve the environment, make effective use of land in urban areas, and mitigate and adapt to the effects of climate change. However, its broad effects remain the same since 2012.

[9] I have personally witnessed this in several examinations in which I was a participant. For example, during the Examination in Public for the Cheshire West and Chester Local Plan in 2014, nine 'objective assessments' were presented, with the highest more than 100 per cent greater than the LPA's own assessment: the LPA's assessment was accepted in the end. At a 'technical meeting' before the examination of the Cheshire East Local Plan, also in 2014, more than a dozen assessments were put forward, with the inspector eventually requiring the LPA to re-assess their assessment of need using different criteria, which resulted in an increase of around 33 per cent.

[10] In December 2016 the government introduced a measure to partially protect policies in neighbourhood plans from being declared out of date in this way. This covered cases where the plan had been formally adopted less than two years ago, allocated sites for housing, and the LPA had at least a three-year supply of land (Hansard, 2016). However, these criteria effectively exclude the majority of neighbourhood plans.

[11] 'Conservative' is here used in opposition to 'progressive', and is not intended to minimise the sometimes radical nature of the reforms.

Chapter3

[1] 'Affect' is essentially the capacity to affect and be affected by people or things. It has been variously described as 'visceral forces beneath, alongside, or generally other than conscious knowing' (Gregg and Seigworth, 2010), 'sensation that is registered but not necessarily considered in that thin band of consciousness that we now call cognition' (Thrift, 2009) and 'embodied meaning making' that is 'both discursive and pre-discursive' (Ahmed, 2004). It is not clearly defined or bounded in the literature, and I do not attempt to more precisely define it here. However, in keeping with the wider 'affective turn' in the social sciences, I recognise that affects are important to us, to our experience of the world and to the ways in which we understand the world as meaningful (Smith, 2009). They are crucial components of a sense of place, of how we know and value our surroundings and through which places and things become imbued with meaning and significance (Casey, 2001; Thrift, 2004; Duff, 2010). Indeed, 'the embedding of affect in place, is the primary means by which thin places are transformed into thick places' (Duff, 2010): the very notion of 'place' ceases to make sense if we do not recognise the affective, felt, relational experience of place (Soja, 1989; Thrift, 2008). The term 'affective' is often conflated with 'emotional', but it also invokes wider and deeper meanings (Pile, 2010). Where emotions are considered to be the

wholly subjective inner experiences of pre-existing atomistic individuals, affects are conceptualised as trans-personal flows (that is, neither wholly subjective nor objective) that emerge from the interactions of bodies and places (Massumi, 2002; Smith, 2009). These flows contribute to ongoing processes of subject formation, rather than simply being experienced by a pre-formed, complete subject (Massumi, 2002; Curti et al, 2011). Thinking in terms of affect therefore helps to de-centre the atomistic individual as the object of study and maintain a more relational focus (Dawney, 2011), as well as acknowledging that the 'forces' or 'sensations' of the affective register may manifest in ways not conventionally understood as 'emotional'.

[2] See, for example, Yearley (2005), Asdal et al (2007) and Felt et al (2016) for more thorough accounts of the de- and re-construction of the story of science and knowledge-making.

[3] Performativity is discussed in greater detail later in this chapter.

Chapter 4

[1] I take an expanded, sociological approach to identity, in contrast to the individualist and psychological perspectives that tend to dominate the Enlightenment imaginary (Lawler, 2008), with an additional material dimension to reflect the inextricable connections between meanings and the social and material assemblages that they are a part of (Symon and Pritchard, 2015).

[2] The idea of technologies of participation builds on previous descriptions of technologies of 'community' (Rose, 1999), 'elicitation' (Lezaun and Soneryd, 2007), 'democracy' (Laurent, 2011) and 'citizenship' (Inch, 2015).

Chapter 5

[1] Since then further guidance has been produced for examiners (NPIERS, 2018), and formal and informal guidance and advice for NPGs has proliferated, but the overall requirement to demonstrate meeting the four basic conditions based on unspecified evidence remains.

[2] This challenge was successful, and a second review was then conducted by external consultants using a different methodology. This situation could, perhaps, have been avoided by including stakeholders earlier to contribute to the process of producing evidence.

[3] In February 2016 this expectation was formalised in updated national guidance to say that where neighbourhood plans 'contain policies relevant to housing supply, these policies should take account of latest and up-to-date evidence of housing need' (DCLG, 2014b). This guidance was subsequently further revised to state that the 'National Planning Policy Framework expects most strategic policy-making authorities to set housing requirement figures for designated neighbourhood areas as part of their strategic policies' – however it is not clear that this expectation has been consistently fulfilled.

[4] This, alongside government guidance, was one of the key technologies of participation in the early days of neighbourhood planning, and a central means of legitimising other technologies and helping them to travel.

[5] As discussed later in this chapter, consultants and participants in both NPGs repeatedly describe the examiner as 'the inspector', which is suggestive of a more general interpretative conflation between the Examinations in Public of local plans (run by planning inspectors) and the independent examination of neighbourhood plans (run by examiners).

[6] In the end, Andrea persuaded the NPG that only two of these sites should be put forwards, on the basis that the others already had a degree of protection from local plan policies or other designations (and designating would therefore require a particularly strong justification), and/or that they were in private ownership and that designating them would therefore be especially difficult. This represented a typically conservative

approach (Parker et al, 2015), and did not meet the aspirations of the NPG, but by that point this issue had taken up so much time and effort and been the centre of so much difficulty and complication that they were unwilling to dedicate more energy to it and to conflict with their expert adviser.

[7] Sandercock, a prominent planning theorist who specialises in multicultural and community engagement, is here talking about planning documents in general, and the documents of neighbourhood planning have tended to follow this pattern.

[8] Some authors have suggested that, on the contrary, NPGs just need to become more professionalised and get better at producing technical evidence in order to resist developer challenges (Parker et al, 2016). There are good reasons for this – developers have attacked neighbourhood plans through the courts as well as at planning appeals, and they do need to be robust enough to withstand challenge. However, in the relatively few cases where NPGs and their plans have been censured (in examinations, appeals or courts) for not having adequate evidence, it has not been because they have attempted innovative forms of evidence production or presentation, but that they have attempted to reproduce technical, abstract forms of evidence and have made errors – which is not surprising, because they are not experts in producing technical information, but rather experts in the lived experience of place. That is their moral authority for acting and that needs to be more strongly acknowledged and foregrounded in the kinds of evidence that are produced and the ways in which they are presented. As Sturzaker and Gordon (2017) note, 'that the courts appear largely willing to avoid an excessively technical approach to the neighbourhood planning rules is significant'. Neighbourhood planners are at risk when they attempt to produce (or to 'fix') technical evidence beyond their technical competence, not when they try to produce experiential evidence which represents their qualifying competence.

Chapter 6

[1] A designation that protects small but valued areas of green space, that can be applied only through the making or reviewing of a local plan or neighbourhood plan.

[2] Although even more peripheral to these new centres (and therefore from the new arrangements of power) are those places and communities – the vast majority – that are not undertaking neighbourhood planning, and who are thus arguably disadvantaged by the generation of new centres of power from which they remain excluded.

[3] This reliance on plans that had passed examination as templates was common among neighbourhood planning consultants, as highlighted by the planner officer quoted earlier in this section: 'I have not yet seen a consultant that doesn't try to work to a template' (Bradley and Brownill, 2017b: 119).

[4] The LPA had employed two different sets of consultants, at different points in time, using different tools and templates, to conduct the assessments for (a) the AONB development plan and (b) the wider strategic local plan that covered the whole district. The NPG tended to rely on the templates of the consultants who had worked on the AONB development plan.

[5] Although see Rydin and Natarajan (2016) for discussion of the materiality of community consultation in neighbourhood planning.

Chapter 7

[1] Although it is also possible that this could result in some opinions and perspectives that were opposed to the general approach and trajectory of the NPG being suppressed. This is not something that I observed – but then, arguably, it would not be visible, unless dissent was explicitly encouraged as a key part of the process Tsouvalis and Waterton (2012).

[2] Although as indicated above, even within the NPG, relations with place were far from uniform.

[3] The Arts and Humanities Research Council's Connected Communities programme is designed to help understand the changing nature of communities in their historical and cultural contexts, and the role of communities in sustaining and enhancing quality of life. See https://connected-communities.org/

[4] The consultants for Oakley did eventually re-incorporate some community actions in the main body of the text, but some issues were lost and the ones that were included were not well-integrated – demonstrating that while this approach has the potential for better connection of issues it requires careful application. The examiner of the Wroston plan recommended placing community actions in a separate appendix, but in revising the plan on behalf on the NPG, and in discussion with the LPA, I was able to retain them in their context.

Chapter 8

[1] I have focused here on citizen collectives which act as intermediaries between communities and other actors, or which in some way, implicitly or explicitly, are considered to represent the interests, knowledge, values and experience of wider publics. However, those wider publics, and other actors such as governments, and their representatives, are also always in-the-making, and are enacted, reproduced and/or reconfigured through these processes, at the same time as they are being enacted in thousands of other multiple, overlapping processes.

References

Abram, S.A. (2000) 'Planning the public: some comments on empirical problems for planning theory', *Journal of Planning Education and Research*, 19(4): 351–357.

Agarwal, B. (1997) 'Environmental action, gender equity and women's participation', *Development and Change*, 28(1): 1–44.

Agnew, J.A. (2011) 'Space and place', in Agnew, J.A. and Livingstone, D.N. (eds) *The SAGE Handbook of Geographical Knowledge*, London: SAGE, pp 316–330.

Ahmed, S. (2004) *The Cultural Politics of Emotion*, Edinburgh: Edinburgh University Press.

Aitken, M. (2009) 'Wind power planning controversies and the construction of "expert" and "lay" knowledges', *Science as Culture*, 18(1): 47–64.

Allen, B.L. (2003) *Uneasy Alchemy: Citizens and Experts in Louisiana's Chemical Corridor Disputes*, Cambridge, MA: MIT Press.

Allen, C. and Crookes, L. (2009) 'Fables of the reconstruction: a phenomenology of "place shaping" in the north of England', *Town Planning Review*, 80(4/5): 455–480.

Allmendinger, P. and Haughton, G. (2012) 'Post-political spatial planning in England: a crisis of consensus?', *Transactions of the Institute of British Geographers*, 37(1): 89–103.

Aparicio, I.R. and Blaser, M. (2008) 'The "lettered city" and the insurrection of subjugated knowledges in Latin America', *Anthropological Quarterly*, 81(1): 59–94.

Appadurai, A. (2002) 'Deep democracy: urban governmentality and the horizon of politics', *Public Culture*, 14(1): 21–47.

Archer, D. and Dodman, D. (2015) 'Making capacity building critical: power and justice in building urban climate resilience in Indonesia and Thailand', *Urban Climate*, 14: 68–78.

Arnstein, S. (1969) 'A ladder of citizen participation', *Journal of the American Institute of Planners*, 35(4): 216–224.

Arthur, W.B. (1994) *Increasing Returns and Path Dependence in the Economy*, Ann Arbor: University of Michigan Press.

Asdal, K., Brenna, B. and Moser, I. (eds) (2007) *Technoscience: The Politics of Interventions*, Oslo: Oslo Academic Press.

Atia, M. (2019) 'Refusing a "city without slums": Moroccan slum dwellers' nonmovements and the art of presence', *Cities*, 125: 102284.

Atkinson, P., Coffey, A., Delamont, S., Lofland, J. and Lofland, L. (2007) *Handbook of Ethnography*, London: SAGE.

Aylett, A. (2010) 'Conflict, collaboration and climate change: participatory democracy and urban environmental struggles in Durban, South Africa', *International Journal of Urban and Regional Research*, 34(3): 478–495.

Bächtiger, A., Dryzek, J.S., Mansbridge, J., Warren, M., Strandberg, K. and Grönlund, K. (2018) *The Oxford Handbook of Deliberative Democracy* (1st edn), Oxford: Oxford University Press.

Bäckstrand, K. (2004) 'Scientisation vs. civic expertise in environmental governance: eco-feminist, eco-modern and post-modern responses', *Environmental Politics*, 13(4): 695–714.

Baeten, G. (2007) 'The uses of deprivation in the neoliberal city', in BAVO (ed) *Urban Politics Now: Re-imagining Democracy in the Neoliberal City*, Rotterdam: NAi Publishers, pp 44–57.

Bailey, N. (2010) 'Understanding community empowerment in urban regeneration and planning in England: putting policy and practice in context', *Planning Practice & Research*, 25(3): 317–332.

Bailey, N. (2017) 'Housing at the neighbourhood level: a review of the initial approaches to neighbourhood development plans under the Localism Act 2011 in England', *Journal of Urbanism: International Research on Placemaking and Urban Sustainability*, 10(1): 1–14.

Bailey, N. and Pill, M. (2015) 'Can the state empower communities through localism? An evaluation of recent approaches to neighbourhood governance in England', *Environment and Planning C*, 33(2): 289–304.

Baiocchi, G. and Ganuza, E. (2017) *Popular Democracy: The Paradox of Participation*, Redwood City: Stanford University Press

Baker, M., Coaffee, J. and Sherriff, G. (2007) 'Achieving successful participation in the new UK spatial planning system', *Planning Practice & Research*, 22(1): 79–93.

Balooni, K., Lund, J.F., Kumar, C. and Inoue, M. (2010) 'Curse or blessing? Local elites in joint forest management in India's Shiwaliks', *International Journal of the Commons*, 4(2): 707–728.

Barnett, J., Burningham, K., Walker, G. and Cass, N. (2012) 'Imagined publics and engagement around renewable energy technologies in the UK', *Public Understanding of Science*, 21(1): 36–50.

Barton, C. and Grimwood, G.G. (2021) *Calculating Housing Need in the Planning System (England)*, London: House of Commons Library.

Baum, H. (2015) 'Planning with half a mind: why planners resist emotion', *Planning Theory & Practice*, 16(4): 498–516.

Beals, F., Kidman, J. and Funaki, H. (2020) 'Insider and outsider research: negotiating self at the edge of the emic/etic divide', *Qualitative Inquiry*, 26(6): 593–601.

Beaumont, J. and Nicholls, W. (2008) 'Plural governance, participation and democracy in cities', *International Journal of Urban and Regional Studies*, 32(1): 87–178.

Beierle, T.C. (1999) 'Using social goals to evaluate public participation in environmental decisions', *The Review of Policy Research*, 16(3–4): 75–103.

Benford, R. (2005) 'The half-life of the environmental justice frame: innovation, diffusion and stagnation', in Pellow, D.N. and Brulle, R.J. (eds) *Power, Justice and the Environment: A Critical Appraisal of the Environmental Justice Movement*, Cambridge, MA: MIT Press, pp 37–54.

Benmergui, L. (2009) 'The Alliance for Progress and housing policy in Rio de Janeiro and Buenos Aires in the 1960s', *Urban History*, 36(2): 303–326.

Bhan, G. (2014) 'The impoverishment of poverty: reflections on urban citizenship and inequality in contemporary Delhi', *Environment and Urbanization*, 26(2): 547–560.

Bherer, L. and Breux, S. (2012) 'The diversity of public participation tools: complementing or competing with one another?', *Canadian Journal of Political Science*, 45(2): 379–403.

Bherer, L., Dufour, P. and Montambeault, F. (2016a) 'The participatory democracy turn: an introduction', *Journal of Civil Society*, 12(3): 225–230.

Bherer, L., Dufour, P. and Montambeault, F. (eds) (2016b) 'The participatory democracy turn [special issue]', *Journal of Civil Society*, 12(3).

Bickerstaff, K., Tolley, R. and Walker, G. (2002) 'Transport planning and participation: the rhetoric and realities of public involvement', *Journal of Transport Geography*, 10(1): 61–73.

Bishop, J. (2018) 'Neighbourhood plans in use', *Place Studio report* [online] Available from: https://placestudio.com/wp-content/uploads/2018/07/Plans-in-Use-Report-1.pdf [Accessed 21 October 2021].

Blackman-Woods, R. (2018) 'Planning should be about designing places that people want to live and work in', *Labour Party press release* [online] Available from: https://labour.org.uk/press/planning-designing-places-people-want-live-work-roberta-blackman-woods/ [Accessed 3 November 2022].

Blumer, H. (1954) 'What is wrong with social theory?', *American Sociological Review*, 19(1): 3–10.

Boddy, M. and Hickman, H. (2018) '"Between a rock and a hard place": planning reform, localism and the role of the planning inspectorate in England', *Planning Theory & Practice*, 19(2): 198–217.

Bødker, S., Dindler, C. and Iversen, O. (2017) 'Tying knots: participatory infrastructuring at work', *The Journal of Collaborative Computing and Work Practices*, 26(1): 245–273.

Bond, S. (2011) 'Negotiating a democratic ethos: moving beyond the agonistic – communicative divide', *Planning Theory*, 10(2): 161–186.

Boonyabancha, S. (2005) 'Baan Mankong: going to scale with "slum" and squatter upgrading in Thailand', *Environment and Urbanization*, 17(1): 21–46.

Boonyabancha, S. and Kerr, T. (2015) 'How urban poor community leaders define and measure poverty', *Environment and Urbanization*, 27(2): 637–656.

Bradley, Q. (2015) 'The political identities of neighbourhood planning in England', *Space and Polity*, 19(2): 97–109.

Bradley, Q. (2017a) 'A passion for place: the emotional identifications and empowerment of neighbourhood planning', in Brownill, S. and Bradley, Q. (eds) *Localism and Neighbourhood Planning: Power to the People?* Bristol: Policy Press, pp 163–180.

Bradley, Q. (2017b) 'Neighbourhood planning and the impact of place identity on housing development in England', *Planning Theory and Practice*, 18(2): 1–16.

Bradley, Q. (2017c) 'Neighbourhoods, communities and the local scale', in Brownill, S. and Bradley, Q. (eds) *Localism and Neighbourhood Planning: Power to the People?* Bristol: Policy Press, pp 39–56.

Bradley, Q. (2017d) 'The new normal: is a planning orthodoxy being imposed on neighbourhood plans?', *Critical Place blog* [online] Available from: http://criticalplace.org.uk/2017/01/31/the-new-normal-is-a-plann ing-orthodoxy-being-imposed-on-neighbourhood-plans [Accessed 1 July 2020].

Bradley, Q. (2018) 'Neighbourhood planning and the production of spatial knowledge', *Town Planning Review*, 89(1): 23–42.

Bradley, Q. (2020) 'The use of direct democracy to decide housing site allocations in English neighbourhoods', *Housing Studies*, 35(2): 333–352.

Bradley, Q. and Sparling, W. (2016) 'The impact of neighbourhood planning and localism on house-building in England', *Housing, Theory and Society*, 34(1): 106–118.

Bradley, Q. and Brownill, S. (2017a) 'Reflections on neighbourhood planning: towards a progressive localism', in Brownill, S. and Bradley, Q. (eds) *Localism and Neighbourhood Planning: Power to the People?* Bristol: Policy Press, pp 251–267.

Bradley, Q. and Brownill, S. (2017b) 'Voices from the neighbourhood: stories from the participants in neighbourhood plans and the professionals working with them', in Brownill, S. and Bradley, Q. (eds) *Localism and Neighbourhood Planning: Power to the People?* Bristol: Policy Press, pp 113–126.

Bradley, Q., Burnett, A. and Sparling, W. (2017) 'Neighbourhood planning and the spatial practices of localism', in Brownill, S. and Bradley, Q. (eds) *Localism and Neighbourhood Planning: Power to the People?* Bristol: Policy Press, pp 57–74.

Bradlow, B.H. (2015) 'City learning from below: urban poor federations and knowledge generation through transnational, horizontal exchange', *International Development Planning Review*, 37(2): 129–142.

Braun, K. and Schultz, S. (2010) '"… a certain amount of engineering involved": constructing the public in participatory governance arrangements', *Public Understanding of Science*, 19(4): 403–419.

Braun, K. and Könninger, S. (2018) 'From experiments to ecosystems? Reviewing public participation, scientific governance and the systemic turn', *Public Understanding of Science*, 27(6): 674–689.

Brown, G. (2015) 'Engaging the wisdom of crowds and public judgement for land use planning using public participation geographic information systems', *Australian Planner*, 52(3): 199–209.

Brownill, S. (2016) 'Assembling localism: practices of assemblage and building the "Big Society" in Oxfordshire, England', in Rydin, Y. and Tate, L. (eds) *Actor Networks of Planning: Exploring the Influence of Actor Network Theory*, London and New York: Routledge, pp 79–94.

Brownill, S. (2017a) 'Assembling neighbourhoods: topologies of power and the reshaping of planning', in Brownill, S. and Bradley, Q. (eds) *Localism and Neighbourhood Planning: Power to the People?* Bristol: Policy Press, pp 145–162.

Brownill, S. (2017b) 'Neighbourhood planning and the purposes and practices of localism', in Brownill, S. and Bradley, Q. (eds) *Localism and Neighbourhood Planning: Power to the People?* Bristol: Policy Press, pp 19–38.

Brownill, S. and Parker, G. (2010a) 'Same as it ever was? Reflections on a practitioner roundtable on participation in England', *Planning Practice & Research*, 25(3): 409–415.

Brownill, S. and Parker, G. (2010b) 'Why bother with good works? The relevance of public participation(s) in planning in a post-collaborative era', *Planning Practice & Research*, 25(3): 275–282.

Brownill, S. and Bradley, Q. (2017) *Localism and Neighbourhood Planning: Power to the People?* Bristol: Policy Press.

Brugnach, M. and Ingram, H. (2012) 'Ambiguity: the challenge of knowing and deciding together', *Environmental Science and Policy*, 15(1): 60–71.

Bruno, T. and Jepson, W. (2018) 'Marketisation of environmental justice: U.S. EPA environmental justice showcase communities project in Port Arthur, Texas', *Local Environment*, 23(3): 276–292.

Bryant, B. (2011) *Environmental Crisis or Crisis of Epistemology? Working for Sustainable Knowledge and Environmental Justice*, New York: Morgan James Publishing.

Bryant, B. and Mohai, P. (eds) (1992) *Race and the Incidence of Environmental Hazards: A Time for Discourse*, Boulder: Westview.

Bua, A. and Bussu, S. (2020) 'Between governance-driven democratisation and democracy-driven governance: explaining changes in participatory governance in the case of Barcelona', *European Journal of Political Research*, 60(3): 716–737.

Bulkens, M., Minca, C. and Muzaini, H. (2015) 'Storytelling as method in spatial planning', *European Planning Studies*, 23(11): 2310–2326.

Bullard, R.D. (ed) (1993) *Confronting Environmental Racism: Voices from the Grassroots*, Boston: South End Press.

Burchell, G., Gordon, C. and Miller, P. (1991) *The Foucault Effect: Studies in Governmentality*, Hemel Hempstead: Harvester Wheatsheaf.

Burkey, S. (1993) *People First: A Guide to Self-Reliant, Participatory Rural Development*, London: Zed Books.

Burningham, K., Barnett, J. and Walker, G. (2014) 'An array of deficits: unpacking NIMBY discourses in wind energy developers' conceptualizations of their local opponents', *Society and Natural Resources*, 28(3): 246–260.

Burns, L. and Yuille, A. (2018) *Where Next for Neighbourhood Plans: Can They Withstand the External Pressures?* London: National Association of Local Councils

Buser, M. (2013) 'Tracing the democratic narrative: Big Society, localism and civic engagement', *Local Government Studies*, 39(1): 3–21.

Bussu, S. (2019) 'Collaborative governance: between invited and invented spaces', in Elstub, S. and Escobar, O. (eds) *Handbook of Deomcratic Innovation and Governance*, Cheltenham, UK and Northampton, MA: Edward Elgar, pp 60–76.

Caldeira, T. and Holston, J. (2015) 'Participatory urban planning in Brazil', *Urban Studies*, 52(11): 2001–2017.

Calhoun, C.J. (1992) *Habermas and the Public Sphere*, Cambridge, MA: MIT Press.

Callon, M. (1999) 'Some elements of a sociology of translation: domestication of the scallops and the fishermen of Saint Brieuc Bay', in Biagioli, M. (ed) *The Science Studies Reader*, New York and London: Routledge, pp 67–83.

Callon, M. and Law, J. (2005) 'On qualculation, agency, and otherness', *Environment and Planning D*, 23(5): 717–733.

Callon, M. and Muniesa, F. (2005) 'Peripheral vision: economic markets as calculative collective devices', *Organization Studies*, 26(8): 1229–1250.

Callon, M. and Rabeharisoa, V. (2008) 'The growing engagement of emergent concerned groups in political and economic life: lessons from the French Association of Neuromuscular Disease Patients', *Science, Technology, & Human Values*, 33(2): 230–261.

Callon, M., Lascoumes, P. and Barthe, Y. (2009) *Acting in an Uncertain World: An Essay on Technical Democracy*, Cambridge, MA and London: MIT Press.

Cannon, J. (2020) 'The NPPF definition of "deliverable" is not a closed list', *Cornerstone Barristers briefing* [online] Available from: https://cornerstonebarristers.com/news/nppf-definition-lsquodeliverablersquo-not-closed-list/ [Accessed 1 November 2021].

Carman, M. (2015) 'Spokespeople for a mute nature: the case of the villa Rodrigo Bueno in Buenos Aires', in Isenhour, C., McDonogh, G. and Checker, M. (eds) *Sustainability in the Global City: Myth and Practice*, New York: Cambridge University Press, pp 238–259.

Carmona, M., Alwarea, A., Giordano, V., Gusseinova, A. and Olaleye, F. (2020) *A Housing Design Audit for England*, London: Place Alliance.

Casey, E.S. (2001) 'Between geography and philosophy: what does it mean to be in the place-world?', *Annals of the Association of American Geographers*, 91(4): 683–693.

Cass, N. (2006) *Participatory-Deliberative Engagement: A Literature Review (Working Paper 1.2)*, Manchester: School of Environment and Development, Manchester University.

Cass, N. and Walker, G. (2009) 'Emotion and rationality: the characterisation and evaluation of opposition to renewable energy projects', *Emotion, Space and Society*, 2(1): 62–69.

Catney, G., Frost, D. and Vaughn, L. (2019) 'Residents' perspectives on defining neighbourhood: mental mapping as a tool for participatory neighbourhood research', *Qualitative Research*, 19(6): 735–752.

Chambers, R. (1984) *Rural Development: Putting the Last First*, London: Longman.

Chambers, R. (1994a) 'Participatory rural appraisal (PRA): analysis of experience', *World Development*, 22(9): 1253–1268.

Chambers, R. (1994b) 'The origins and practice of participatory rural appraisal', *World Development*, 22(7): 953–969.

Chambers, R. (1997) *Whose Reality Counts? Putting the First Last*, London: Intermediate Technology Publications.

Chetwyn, D. (2013) *Neighbourhood Plans: Roadmap Guide*, London: Locality.

Chilvers, J. and Kearnes, M. (2016) *Remaking Participation: Science, Environment and Emergent Publics*, Abingdon and New York: Routledge.

Chilvers, J. and Kearnes, M. (2020) 'Remaking participation in science and democracy', *Science Technology & Human Values*, 45(3): 347–380

Church, A., Fish, R., Haines-Young, R., Mourato, S., Tratalos, J., Stapleton, L., et al (2014) *UK National Ecosystem Assessment Follow-on Work Package Report 5: Cultural Ecosystem Services and Indicators*, UK: LWEC. Available from: http://uknea.unep-wcmc.org/LinkClick.aspx?fileticket=l0%2FZh q%2Bgwtc%3D&tabid=82 [Accessed 23 March 2023].

Civic Voice (2015) 'Collaborative planning for all', *Civic Voice report* [online] Available from: http://www.civicvoice.org.uk/uploads/files/Collaborative _planning_1.pdf [Accessed 4 November 2022].

Clarke, N. and Cochrane, A. (2013) 'Geographies and politics of localism: the localism of the United Kingdom's coalition government', *Political Geography*, 34: 10–23.

Cleaver, F. (2001) 'Institutions, agency and the limitations of participatory approaches to development', in Cooke, B. and Kothari, U. (eds) *Participation: The New Tyranny?* London: Zed Books, pp 36–55.

CLG Select Committee (2014) *Operation of the National Planning Policy Framework: Fourth Report of Session 2014–15*, London: The Stationery Office.

Code, L. (2015) 'Care, concern, and advocacy: is there a place for epistemic responsibility?', *Feminist Philosophy Quarterly*, 1(1): 1–20.

Cole, L.W. and Foster, S.R. (2001) *From the Ground Up: Environmental Racism and the Rise of the Environmental Justice Movement*, New York: New York University Press.

Colomb, C. (2017) 'Participation and conflict in the formation of neighbourhood areas and forums in "super-diverse" cities', in Brownill, S. and Bradley, Q. (eds) *Localism and Neighbourhood Planning: Power to the People?* Bristol: Policy Press, pp 127–144.

Connelly, S. (2011) 'Constructing legitimacy in the new community governance', *Urban Studies*, 48(5): 929–946.

Connelly, S. (2015) 'The long march to collaborative democracy and open source planning: public participation in English local governance', conference paper presented at *Emerging Directions in Decentralized and Participatory Planning: Implications for Theory, Practice and Roles of the Planner, March 2011*, Annand, India: Institute of Rural Management.

Connelly, S., Richardson, T. and Miles, T. (2006) 'Situated legitimacy: deliberative arenas and the new rural governance', *Journal of Rural Studies*, 22(3): 267–277.

Conservative Party, The (2010) *Open Source Planning: Policy Green Paper No. 14*, London: The Conservative Party.

Cooke, B. and Kothari, U. (eds) (2001) *Participation: The New Tyranny?* London: Zed Books.

Coolsaet, B. (2020) *Environmental Justice: Key Issues*, London: Routledge

Corburn, J. (2005) *Street Science: Community Knowledge and Environmental Health Justice*, Cambridge, MA: MIT Press.

Cornwall, A. (2002) 'Locating citizen participation', *IDS Bulletin*, 33(2): i–x.

Cornwall, A. (2008) 'Unpacking "participation": models, meanings and practices', *Community Development Journal*, 43(3): 269–283.

Cornwall, A. and Coelho, V.S. (eds) (2007) *Spaces for Change? The Politics of Citizen Participation in New Democratic Arenas*, London and New York: Zed Books.

Cornwall, A. and Pratt, G. (2011) 'The use and abuse of participatory rural appraisal: reflections from practice', *Agriculture and Human Values*, 28(2): 263–272.

CPRE (2014) *Community Control or Countryside Chaos? The Effect of the National Planning Policy Framework Two Years On*, London: CPRE.

Craig, D. and Porter, D. (1997) 'Framing participation', *Development in Practice*, 7(3): 229–236.

Cresswell, T. (2015) *Place: An Introduction* (2nd edn), Oxford: Wiley Blackwell.

Cruikshank, B. (1999) *The Will to Empower: Democratic Citizens and Other Subjects*, Ithaca, NY: Cornell University Press.

Curti, G.H., Aitken, S.C., Bosco, F.J. and Goerisch, D.D. (2011) 'For not limiting emotional and affectual geographies: a collective critique of Steve Pile's "Emotions and affect in recent human geography"', *Transactions of the Institute of British Geographers*, 36(4): 590–594.

Daskalaki, M. and Kokkinidis, G. (2017) 'Organizing solidarity initiatives: a socio-spatial conceptualization of resistance', *Organization Studies*, 38(9): 1303–1325.

David, P.A. (1985) 'Clio and the economics of QWERTY', *The American Economic Review*, 75(2): 332–337.

Davies, A. (2001a) 'What silence knows', *Environmental Values*, 10(1): 77–102.

Davies, A. (2001b) 'Hidden or hiding? Public perceptions of participation in the planning system', *Town Planning Review*, 72(2): 193–216.

Davies, J. (nd) 'Evidence based planning and monitoring', *RTPI briefing* [online] Available from: https://www.rtpi.org.uk/media/5923/John-Davies.pdf [Accessed 24 September 2020].

Davies, J.S. (2008) 'Double-devolution or double-dealing? The Local Government White Paper and the Lyons Review', *Local Government Studies*, 34(1): 3–22.

Davoudi, S. (2006) 'Evidence-based planning: rhetoric and reality', *disP: The Planning Review*, 165(2): 14–24.

Davoudi, S. (2012) 'The legacy of positivism and the emergence of interpretive tradition in spatial planning', *Regional Studies*, 46(4): 429–441.

Davoudi, S. (2015) 'Planning as practice of knowing', *Planning Theory*, 14(3): 316–331.

Davoudi, S. and Cowie, P. (2013) 'Are English neighbourhood forums democratically legitimate?', *Planning Theory & Practice*, 14(4): 562–566.

Davoudi, S. and Madanipour, A. (2013) 'Localism and neo-liberal governmentality', *Town Planning Review*, 84(5): 551–561.

Davoudi, S. and Madanipour, A. (eds) (2015) *Reconsidering Localism*, New York: Routledge.

Davoudi, S., Raynor, R., Reid, B., Crawford, J., Sykes, O. and Shaw, D. (2018) 'Policy and practice spatial imaginaries: tyrannies or transformations?', *Town Planning Review*, 89(2): 97–124.

Dawney, L. (2011) 'The motor of being: a response to Steve Pile's "Emotions and affect in recent human geography"', *Transactions of the Institute of British Geographers*, 36(4): 599–602.

DCLG (2010) 'Planning power from town hall and Whitehall to local people', *DCLG press release* [online] Available from: https://www.gov.uk/government/news/planning-power-from-town-halls-and-whitehall-to-local-people [Accessed 12 May 2020].

DCLG (2012a) *National Planning Policy Framework*, London: Department for Communities and Local Government.

DCLG (2012b) 'Neighbourhood planning', *DCLG guidance* [online] Available from: https://www.gov.uk/government/publications/neighbourhood-planning [Accessed 15 March 2019].

DCLG (2013) *You've Got the Power: A Quick and Simple Guide to Community Rights*, London: DCLG.

DCLG (2014a) 'Housing and economics needs assessment', *DCLG national planning practice guidance* [online] Available from: https://www.gov.uk/guidance/housing-and-economic-land-availability-assessment [Accessed 15 August 2019].

DCLG (2014b) 'Neighbourhood planning', *DCLG national planning practice guidance* [online] Available from: https://www.gov.uk/guidance/neighbourhood-planning--2 [Accessed 15 September 2021].

De Geest, F. and De Nys-Ketels, S. (2019) 'Everyday resistance: exposing the complexities of participatory slum-upgrading projects in Nagpur', *Housing Studies*, 34(10): 1673–1689.

Dehon, E. and Fitzsimons, J. (2021) 'Legal challenges to neighbourhood plans and orders: the Supreme Court has the final word', *Local Government Lawyer article* [online] Available from: https://localgovernmentlawyer.co.uk/planning/318-planning-features/47154-legal-challenges-to-neighbourhood-plans-and-orders-the-supreme-court-has-the-final-word [Accessed 21 October 2021].

Deleuze, G. and Guattari, F. (1988) *A Thousand Plateaus: Capitalism and Schizophrenia*, London: Athlone Press.

Della Porta, D. (2013) *Can Democracy Be Saved? Participation, Deliberation and Social Movements*, Cambridge: Polity Press.

Denzin, N.K. and Lincoln, Y.S. (2008) *The Landscape of Qualitative Research* (3rd edn), Los Angeles: SAGE.

Department for Transport, Local Government and the Regions (2001) *Planning: Delivering a Fundamental Change*, London: DTLR.

Despret, V. (2004) 'The body we care for: figures of anthropo-zoo-genesis', *Body and Society*, 10(2–3): 111–134.

Deuskar, C. (2019) 'Clientelism and planning in the informal settlements of developing democracies', *Journal of Planning Literature*, 34(4): 395–407.

Devine-Wright, P. (2009) 'Rethinking NIMBYism: the role of place attachment and place identity in explaining place-protective action', *Journal of Community and Applied Social Psychology*, 19(6): 426–441.

Devine-Wright, P. (2015) 'Local attachments and identities', *Progress in Human Geography*, 39(4): 527–530.

Devine-Wright, P. and Clayton, S. (2010) 'Introduction to the special issue: place, identity and environmental behaviour', *Journal of Environmental Psychology*, 30(3): 267–270.

Diamond, L.J. (2015) 'Facing up to the democratic recession', *Journal of Democracy*, 26(1): 141–155.

DLP Planning (2014) 'Important recent appeal decision regarding neighbourhood plans', *DLP Consultants client briefing* [online] Available from: https://www.dlpconsultants.co.uk/wp-content/uploads/2016/04/185-Client-Briefing-Important-Recent-Appeal-Decisions-Regarding-Neighbourhood-Plans.pdf [Accessed 10 October 2021].

DLUHC (2022) 'Urban and deprived areas among those chosen for planning pilots', *DLUHC press release* [online] Available from: https://www.gov.uk/government/news/areas-selected-for-planning-pilots-for-deprived-communities [Accessed 25 April 2022].

Donnelly, M. (2016) 'High court quashes neighbourhood plan over "inadequate" evidence base', *Planning Resource article* [online] Available from: https://www.russell-cooke.co.uk/media/1039132/high-court-quashes-neighbourhood-plan-over-inadequate-evidence-base-russell-cooke-in-planning-resource.pdf [Accessed 21 October 2021].

Dovey, K., Shafique, T., van Oostrum, M. and Chatterjee, I. (2021) 'Informal settlement is not a euphemism for "slum": what's at stake beyond the language?', *International Development Planning Review*, 43(2): 139–150.

Duff, C. (2010) 'On the role of affect and practice in the production of place', *Environment and Planning D*, 28(5): 881–895.

Duggan, K. (2017) *Envisioning the Future Village: The Role of Digital Technology in Supporting More Inclusive Visions in the Neighbourhood Planning Process*, PhD Thesis, University of Brighton.

Dupont, V., Vaquier, D., Bautès, N., Gonçalves, R.S., Gomes, F.C.M., Fernandes, L.L., et al (2013) 'Slum demolition: impact on the affected families and coping strategies', in Saglio-Yatzimirsky, M.-C. and Landy, F. (eds) *Megacity Slums: Social Exclusion, Space and Urban Policies in Brazil and India*, London: Imperial College Press, pp 307–361.

Earle, L. (2013) 'Drawing the line between state and society: social movements, participation and autonomy in Brazil', *The Journal of Development Studies*, 49(1): 56–71.

Edwards, M. (2008) *Just Another Emperor? The Myths and Realities of Philanthrocapitalism*, New York: Demos and The Young Foundation.

Elster, J. (1998) *Deliberative Democracy*, New York: Cambridge University Press.

Elstub, S. and Escobar, O. (eds) (2021) *Handbook of Democratic Innovation and Governance*, Cheltenham, UK and Northampton, MA: Edward Elgar.

Ercan, S.A. and Hendriks, C.M. (2013) 'The democratic challenges and potential of localism: insights from deliberative democracy', *Policy Studies*, 34(4): 422–440.

Ercan, S.A. and Gagnon, J.-P. (2014) 'The crisis of democracy: which crisis? Which democracy?', *Democratic Theory*, 1(2): 1–10.

Escobar, A. (1995) *Encountering Development: The Making and Unmaking of the Third World*, Princeton: Princeton University Press.

Escobar, A. (2007) 'Worlds and knowledges otherwise: the Latin American modernity/coloniality research program', *Cultural Studies*, 21(2–3): 179–210.

Eurocities (2018) 'Mapping the future', *Eurocities participatory mapping tool* [online] Available from: https://citizens.eurocities.eu/mapping-the-future.html [Accessed 2 May 2022].

European Commission (2021) 'Competence centre on participatory and deliberative democracy', *European Commission resource* [online] Available from: https://knowledge4policy.ec.europa.eu/participatory-democracy_en [Accessed 7 October 2021].

Exeter St James Forum (2013) 'Exeter St James neighbourhood plan', *Exeter St James Community Trust* [online] Available from: https://www.exeterstja mes.org/about/ [Accessed 3 November 2022].

Eyre, J.S. (2021) 'Sefton MBC v Secretary of State EWHC (Admin) 1082. Case No: CO/2050/2020 & CO/2051/2020', *England and Wales High Court (Administrative Court)* [online] Available from: http://www.bailii.org/ ew/cases/EWHC/Admin/2021/1082.html [Accessed 27 February 2020].

Ezeh, A., Oyebode, O., Satterthwaite, D., Chen, Y.-F., Ndugwa, R., Sartori, J., et al (2017) 'The history, geography, and sociology of slums and the health problems of people who live in slums', *Lancet*, 389(10068): 547–558.

Faber, D. (2008) *Capitalizing on Environmental Injustice: The Polluter-Industrial Complex in the Age of Globalization*, Lanham: Rowman & Littlefield.

Faber, D. and McCarthy, D. (2001) 'The evolving structure of the environmental justice movement in the United States: new models for democratic decision-making', *Social Justice Research*, 14(4): 405–421.

Fals Borda, O. and Rahman, M.A. (eds) (1991) *Action and Knowledge: Breaking the Monopoly with Participatory Action Research*, New York: The Apex Press.

Fanon, F. (1965 [1961]) *The Wretched of the Earth*, London: McGibbon & Kee.

Farrell, M. and Tandon, R. (2016) 'A shifting paradigm: engendering the politics of community engagement in India', in Meade, R.M., Shaw, M. and Banks, S. (eds) *Politics, Power and Community Development*, Bristol: Policy Press, pp 121–138.

Farrington, J., Bebbington, A.J., Lewis, D.J. and Wellard, K. (1993) *Reluctant Partners? Non-Governmental Organizations, the State and Sustainable Agricultural Development*, London: Routledge.

Featherstone, D., Ince, A., Mackinnon, D., Strauss, K. and Cumbers, A. (2012) 'Progressive localism and the construction of political alternatives', *Transactions of the Institute of British Geographers*, 37(2): 177–182.

Felt, U. and Fochler, M. (2010) 'Machineries for making publics: inscribing and de-scribing publics in public engagement', *Minerva*, 48(3): 219–238.

Felt, U., Fouché, R., Miller, C.A. and Smith-Doerr, L. (2016) *The Handbook of Science and Technology Studies* (4th edn), Cambridge, MA and London: MIT Press.

Ferguson, J. (1990) *The Anti-Politics Machine: 'Development', Depoliticization, and Bureaucratic Power in Lesotho*, Minneapolis: University of Minnesota Press.

Field, M. and Layard, A. (2017) 'Locating community-led housing within neighbourhood plans as a response to England's housing needs', *Public Money & Management*, 37(2): 105–112.

Fiorino, D. (1990) 'Citizen participation and environmental risk: a survey of institutional mechanisms', *Science Technology & Human Values*, 15(2): 226–243.

Fischer, F. (2000) *Citizens, Experts, and the Environment : The Politics of Local Knowledge*, Durham, NC: Duke University Press.

Fischer, F. (2006) 'Participatory governance as deliberative empowerment: the cultural politics of discursive space', *American Review of Public Administration*, 36(1): 19–40.

Fischer, F. and Forester, J. (1993) *The Argumentative Turn in Policy Analysis and Planning*, Durham, NC: Duke University Press.

Fishkin, J.S. and Cran, W. (2009) *When The People Speak: Deliberative Democracy and Public Consultation*, Oxford and New York: Oxford University Press.

Foa, R.S., Klassen, A., Slade, M., Rand, A. and Collins, R. (2020) *The Global Satisfaction with Democracy Report 2020*, Cambridge: Centre for the Future of Democracy.

Foster, J. (1997) *Valuing Nature? Ethics, Economics and the Environment*, London and New York: Routledge.

Foucault, M. (1977) *Discipline and Punish: The Birth of the Prison*, London: Allen Lane.

Foucault, M. (1980) *Power/Knowledge: Selected Interviews and Other Writings, 1972–1977* (1st American edn), edited by C. Gordon, New York: Pantheon Books.

Franchina, V., Cagnazzo, C., Di Costanzo, A., Arizio, F., Frazzetto, A.M.E., Gori, S., et al (2020) 'Patient associations and clinical oncology research: how much does a patient's voice really matter?', *Expert Review of Pharmacoeconomics & Outcomes Research*, 21(3): 433–440.

Francis, P. (2001) 'Participatory development at the World Bank: the primacy of process', in Cooke, B. and Kothari, U. (eds) *Participation: The New Tyranny?* London: Zed Books, pp 72–87.

Freeman, R. (2017) 'Care, policy, knowledge: translating between worlds', *The Sociological Review*, 65(2_suppl): 193–200.

Freire, P. (1970) *Pedagogy of the Oppressed*, New York: Herder & Herder.

Frickel, S. (2004) 'Just science? Organizing scientist activism in the US environmental justice movement', *Science as Culture*, 13(4): 449–469.

Frickel, S., Gibbon, S., Howard, J., Kempner, J., Ottinger, G. and Hess, D.J. (2010) 'Undone science: charting social movement and civil society challenges to research agenda setting', *Science, Technology & Human Values*, 35(4): 444–473.

Fritzen, S.A. (2007) 'Can the design of community-driven development reduce the risk of elite capture? Evidence from Indonesia', *World Development*, 35(8): 1359–1375.

Fung, A., Wright, E.O. and Abers, R. (2003) *Deepening Democracy: Institutional Innovations in Empowered Participatory Governance*, London: Verso.

Gabrys, J. (2017) 'Citizen sensing, air pollution and fracking: from "caring about your air" to speculative practices of evidencing harm', *The Sociological Review*, 65(2_suppl): 172–192.

Gabrys, J., Pritchard, H. and Barratt, B. (2016) 'Just good enough data: figuring data citizenships through air pollution sensing and data stories', *Big Data & Society*, 3(2): 205395171667967.

Galis, V. and Lee, F. (2014) 'A sociology of treason', *Science, Technology & Human Values*, 39(1): 154–179.

Gallent, N. and Robinson, S. (2013) *Neighbourhood Planning: Communities, Networks and Governance*, Bristol: Policy Press.

Gaventa, J. and Cornwall, A. (2006) 'Challenging the boundaries of the possible: participation, knowledge and power', *IDS Bulletin*, 37(6): 122–128.

Geddes, M., Davies, J. and Fuller, C. (2007) 'Evaluating local strategic partnerships: theory and practice of change', *Local Government Studies*, 33(1): 97–116.

Gieryn, T.F. (1983) 'Boundary-work and the demarcation of science from non-science: strains and interests in professional ideologies of scientists', *American Sociological Review*, 48(6): 781–795.

Gieryn, T.F. (1995) 'Boundaries of science', in Jasanoff, S., Markle, G.E., Petersen, J.C. and Pinch, T. (eds) *Handbook of Science and Technology Studies* (revised edn), Thousand Oaks: SAGE, pp 393–443

Gieryn, T.F. (1999) *Cultural Boundaries of Science: Credibility on the Line*, Chicago: University of Chicago Press.

Gilbert, A. (2007) 'The return of the slum: does language matter?', *International Journal of Urban and Regional Research*, 31(4): 697–713.

Gilio-Whitaker, D. (2019) *As Long as Grass Grows: The Indigenous Fight for Environmental Justice, from Colonization to Standing Rock*, Boston: Beacon Press.

Gill, N., Singleton, V. and Waterton, C. (2017) 'The politics of policy practices', *The Sociological Review*, 65(2_suppl): 3–19.

Goffman, E. (1968) *Stigma: Notes on the Management of Spoiled Identity*, London: Penguin.

Gond, J.-P., Cabantous, L., Harding, N. and Learmonth, M. (2016) 'What do we mean by performativity in organizational and management theory? The uses and abuses of performativity', *International Journal of Management Reviews*, 18(4): 440–463.

González Rivas, M. (2014) 'Decentralization, community participation, and improvement of water access in Mexico', *Community Development*, 45(1): 2–16.

Goodchild, B. and Hammond, C. (2013) 'Planning and urban regeneration since 2010: a recipe for conflict and dispute?', *People, Place and Policy*, 7(2): 82–90.

Green, R., Lambert, E. and Du Feu, B. (2020) 'Planning law case update (part 2): November 2020', *Cornerstone Barristers briefing* [online] Available from: https://cornerstonebarristers.com/cmsAdmin/uploads/case-law-pt-2-rgelabdf_001.pdf [Accessed 1 November 2021].

Gregg, M. and Seigworth, G.J. (2010) *The Affect Theory Reader*, Durham, NC: Duke University Press.

Grimwood, G.G. (2018) *House of Commons Library Briefing Paper 05838: Neighbourhood Planning*, London: House of Commons Library.

Guimarães, E.F., Malheiros, T.F. and Marques, R.C. (2016) 'Inclusive governance: new concept of water supply and sanitation services in social vulnerability areas', *Utilities Policy*, 43: 124–129.

Habermas, J. (1996) *Between Facts and Norms: Contributions to a Discourse Theory of Law and Democracy*, Cambridge, MA: MIT Press.

Hacking, I. (1999) *The Social Construction of What?* Cambridge, MA: Harvard University Press.

Halseth, G. and Booth, A. (2003) '"What works well; what needs improvement": Lessons in public consultation from British Columbia's resource planning processes', *Local Environment*, 8(4): 437–455.

Hansard (2011) 'H.C. Localism Bill: Vol 521, Col 629, 17th January' [online] Available from: https://publications.parliament.uk/pa/cm201012/cmhansrd/cm110117/debtext/110117-0003.htm [Accessed 20 April 2021].

Hansard (2016) 'H.C.W.S. 346 Neighbourhood Planning: Written Statement' [online] Available from: https://www.parliament.uk/business/publications/written-questions-answers-statements/written-statement/Commons/2016-12-12/HCWS346/ [Accessed 20 April 2021].

Hansard (2017) 'H.C. Local Housing Need: Vol 628, Col 1010, 14th September' [online] Available from: https://hansard.parliament.uk/commons/2017-09-14/debates/308E35F7-5DE6-4427-A7B1-01FB92E39F7E/LocalHousingNeed [Accessed 20 April 2021].

Hansard (2022a) 'H.C. Neighbourhood Plans, 7th June 2022, Vol 715, Col 295WH' [online] Available from: https://hansard.parliament.uk/commons/2022-06-07/debates/22060730000001/NeighbourhoodPlans [Accessed 3 July 2022].

Hansard (2022b) 'H.C. Neighbourhood Plans, 7th June 2022, Vol 715, Col 296WH' [online] Available from: https://hansard.parliament.uk/commons/2022-06-07/debates/22060730000001/NeighbourhoodPlans [Accessed 3 July 2022].

Haraway, D. (1988) 'Situated knowledges: the science question in feminism and the privilege of partial perspective', *Feminist Studies*, 14(3): 575–599.

Haraway, D. (1989) *Primate Visions: Gender, Race, and Nature in the World of Modern Science*, New York: Routledge.

Haraway, D. (1991) *Simians, Cyborgs and Women: The Reinvention of Nature*, London: Free Association Books.

Haraway, D. (1997) *Modest_Witness@Second_Millenium.FemaleMan_Meets_OncoMouse*, London and New York: Routledge.

Haraway, D. (2003) *The Companion Species Manifesto: Dogs, People, and Significant Otherness*, Chicago: Prickly Paradigm Press.

Haraway, D. (2016) *Staying with the Trouble: Making Kin in the Chthulucene*, Durham, NC: Duke University Press.

Harding, S.G. (1986) *The Science Question in Feminism*, Milton Keynes: Open University Press.

Harrison, J.L. (2011) 'Parsing "participation" in action research: navigating the challenges of lay involvement in technically complex participatory science projects', *Society & Natural Resources*, 24(7): 702–716.

Harrison, J.L. (2016) 'Bureaucrats' tacit understandings and social movement policy implementation: unpacking the deviation of agency environmental justice programs from EJ movement priorities', *Social Problems*, 63(4): 534–553.

Harrison, J.L. (2017) '"We do ecology, not sociology": interactions among bureaucrats and the undermining of regulatory agencies' environmental justice efforts', *Environmental Sociology*, 3(3): 197–212.

Harrison, J.L. (2019) *From the Inside Out: The Fight for Environmental Justice Within Government Agencies*, Cambridge, MA: MIT Press.

Hastings, A. and Matthews, P. (2015) 'Bourdieu and the Big Society: empowering the powerful in public service provision?', *Policy & Politics*, 42(4): 545–560.

Haughton, G. and Allmendinger, P. (2013) 'Spatial planning and the new localism', *Planning Practice & Research*, 28(1): 1–5.

Haughton, G., Allmendinger, P. and Oosterlynck, S. (2013) 'Spaces of neoliberal experimentation: soft spaces, postpolitics, and neoliberal governmentality', *Environment and Planning A*, 45(1): 217–234.

Healey, P. (1997) *Collaborative Planning: Shaping Places in Fragmented Societies*, Houndmills and London: Macmillan.

Hernandez, B., Hidalgo, M.C., Salazar-Laplace, M.E. and Hess, S. (2007) 'Place attachment and place identity in natives and non-natives', *Journal of Environmental Psychology*, 27(4): 310–319.

Hickey, S. and Mohan, G. (eds) (2004) *Participation: From Tyranny to Transformation? Exploring New Approaches to Participation in Development*, London: Zed Books.

Hilder, P. (2006) 'Power up, people: double devolution and beyond', *Public Policy Research*, 13(4): 238–248.

Hildyard, N., Hegde, P., Wolvekamp, P. and Reddy, S. (2001) 'Pluralism, participation, and power: joint forest management in India', in Cooke, B. and Kothari, U. (eds) *Participation: The New Tyranny?* London: Zed Books, pp 56–71.

Hill, Z. (2017) 'Decision Letter on Application for Land at West Street, Coggeshall. PINS reference: APP/Z1510/W/16/3160474' [online] Available from: https://acp.planninginspectorate.gov.uk/ViewCase.aspx?CaseID=3160474&CoID=0 [Accessed 12 October 2019].

HM Government (2022) *Levelling Up the United Kingdom White Paper (CP 604)*, London: HM Stationery Office.

Hoch, C. (2006) 'Emotions and planning', *Planning Theory & Practice*, 7(4): 367–382.

Holifield, R. (2012) 'The elusive environmental justice area: three waves of policy in the US Environmental Protection Agency', *Environmental Justice*, 5(6): 293–297.

Holifield, R., Chakraborty, J. and Walker, G. (2018) *The Routledge Handbook of Environmental Justice*, Abingdon and New York: Taylor & Francis.

Holland, A. (1997) 'The foundations of environmental decision-making', *International Journal of Environment and Pollution*, 7(4): 483–496.

Holly, N. (2017) 'Accidental antagonism? Technical governance and local struggles over housing numbers in southern England', *Town Planning Review*, 88(6): 683–704.

Holston, J. (2009) 'Insurgent citizenship in an era of global urban peripheries', *City & Society*, 21(2): 245–267.

Home, R.K. (1991) 'Deregulating UK planning control in the 1980s', *Cities*, 8(4): 292–300.

Hoppe, R. (2010) *The Governance of Problems: Puzzling, Powering and Participation*, Bristol: Policy Press.

Horst, M. and Irwin, A. (2010) 'Nations at ease with radical knowledge: on consensus, consensusing and false consensusness', *Social Studies of Science*, 40(1): 105–126.

House of Commons (2011) The Localism Act, *UK Statutes* [online] Available from: https://www.legislation.gov.uk/ukpga/2011/20/contents/enacted [Accessed 4 May 2021].

Houston, D. and Vasudevan, P. (2018) 'Storytelling environmental justice: cultural studies approaches', in Holifield, R., Chakraborty, J. and Walker, G. (eds) *The Routledge Handbook of Environmental Justice*, Abingdon and New York: Taylor & Francis, pp 241–251.

Houtzager, P. and Gurza Lavalle, A. (2010) 'Civil society's claims to political representation in Brazil', *Studies in Comparative International Development*, 45(1): 1–29.

Huxley, V. (2000) 'The limits to communicative planning', *Journal of Planning Education and Research*, 19(4): 369–377.

Ianniello, M., Iacuzzi, S., Fedele, P. and Brusati, L. (2019) 'Obstacles and solutions on the ladder of citizen participation: a systematic review', *Public Management Review*, 21(1): 21–46.

Imparato, I. and Ruster, J. (2003) *Slum Upgrading and Participation: Lessons from Latin America*, Washington, DC: World Bank Publications.

Inch, A. (2015) 'Ordinary citizens and the political cultures of planning: in search of the subject of a new democratic ethos', *Planning Theory*, 14(4): 404–424.

Inch, A., Sartorio, F., Bishop, J., Beebeejaun, Y., McClymont, K., Frediani, A.A., et al (2019) 'People and planning at fifty', *Planning Theory & Practice*, 20(5): 735–759.

Ingold, T. (2000) *The Perception of the Environment: Essays on Livelihood, Dwelling and Skill*, London and New York: Routledge.

Ingold, T. and Vergunst, J.L. (2008) *Ways of Walking: Ethnography and Practice on Foot*, Aldershot: Ashgate.

Innes, J.E. and Booher, D.E. (2000) 'Collaborative dialogue as a policy making strategy', Working Paper 2000-05, Institute of Urban and Regional Development, University of California.

Innes, J.E. and Booher, D.E. (2004) 'Reframing public participation: strategies for the 21st century', *Planning Theory & Practice*, 5(4): 419–436.

Insole, P. and Piccini, A. (2013) 'Your place or mine? Crowdsourced planning, moving image archives and community archaeology', *Archäologische Informationen*, 36: 31–43.

Intercoopoeration (2005) *Participatory Monitoring and Evaluation: Field Experiences*, Hyderabad: SDC-IC NGO Programme Karnataka-Tamil Nadu.

Irvin, R.A. and Stansbury, J. (2004) 'Citizen participation in decision making: is it worth the effort?', *Public Administration Review*, 64(1): 55–65.

Irwin, A. (1995) *Citizen Science: A Study of People, Expertise and Sustainable Development*, London: Routledge.

Irwin, A. (2016) 'On the local constitution of global futures: science and democratic engagement in a decentred world', *Nordic Journal of Science and Technology Studies*, 3(2): 24–33.

Janner-Klausner, D. (2022) 'Neighbourhood planning: keeping the community engaged', *Commonplace blog* [online] Available from: https://www.comm onplace.is/blog/neighbourhood-planning [Accessed 4 May 2022].

Jasanoff, S. (1990) *The Fifth Branch: Science Advisers as Policymakers*, Cambridge, MA: Harvard University Press.

Jasanoff, S. (2003) 'Technologies of humility: citizen participation in governing science', *Minerva*, 41(3): 223–244.

Jasanoff, S. (2004a) *States of Knowledge: The Co-Production of Science and Social Order*, London and New York: Routledge.

Jasanoff, S. (2004b) 'The idiom of co-production', in Jasanoff, S. (ed) *States of Knowledge: The Co-Production of Science and Social Order*, London and New York: Routledge, pp 1–12.

Jasanoff, S. and Kim, S.-H. (2015) *Dreamscapes of Modernity: Sociotechnical Imaginaries and the Fabrication of Power*, Chicago: University of Chicago Press.

Javid, S. (2016) 'Decision letter on Application for land to the south of Ford Lane, Yapton. PINS reference: APP/C3810/A/14/2228260' [online] Available from: https://www.gov.uk/government/uploads/system/uplo ads/attachment_data/file/552556/16-08-13_DL_IR_Ford_Lane_A run_2228260.pdf [Accessed 12 October 2019].

Javid, S. (2017) 'Decision letter on Application made by Bellway Homes, Bellcross Co Ltd & Fosbern Manufacturing Ltd for land west of Castlemilk, Buckingham, PINS reference: APP/J0405/V/16/3151297' [online] Available from: https://www.gov.uk/government/uploads/system/uploads/attachment_data/file/630085/17-07-19_DL_IR_Castlemilk_Buckingham_3151297.pdf [Accessed 12 October 2019].

Jha, M.K. (2016) 'Community organising and political agency: changing community development subjects in India', in Meade, R.R., Shaw, M. and Banks, S. (eds) *Politics, Power and Community Development*, Bristol: Policy Press, pp 65–82.

Johnstone, P. and Stirling, A. (2015) 'Comparing nuclear power trajectories in Germany and the UK: from "regimes" to "democracies" in sociotechnical transitions and discontinuities', *Energy Research and Social Science* 59(101245): 1–27.

Jones, P., Layard, A., Speed, C. and Lorne, C. (2013) 'MapLocal: use of smartphones for crowdsourced planning', conference paper presented at *Using ICT, Social Media and Mobile Technologies to Foster Self-organisation in Urban and Neighbourhood Governance*, TU Delft, 16 May [online] Available from: http://resolver.tudelft.nl/uuid:83750788-a8e9-4630-803b-6f6a19ddb220 [Accessed 3 November 2022].

Jones, P., Layard, A., Speed, C. and Lorne, C. (2015) 'MapLocal: use of smartphones for crowdsourced planning', *Planning Practice & Research*, 30(3): 322–336.

Jöns, H. (2011) 'Centre of calculation', in Agnew, J. and Livingstone, D.N. (eds) *The SAGE Handbook of Geographical Knowledge*, London: SAGE, pp 158–170.

Kahila-Tani, M., Kytta, M. and Geertman, S. (2019) 'Does mapping improve public participation? Exploring the pros and cons of using public participation GIS in urban planning practices', *Landscape and Urban Planning*, 186: 45–55.

Kapoor, I. (2002) 'The devil's in the theory: a critical assessment of Robert Chambers' work on participatory development', *Third World Quarterly*, 23(1): 101–117.

Kapoor, I. (2005) 'Participatory development, complicity and desire', *Third World Quarterly*, 26(8): 1203–1220.

Kelty, C.M. (2020) *The Participant: A Century of Participation in Four Stories*, Chicago: University of Chicago Press.

Kenny, S. (2016) 'Changing community development roles: the challenges of a globalising world', in Meade, R.R., Shaw, M. and Banks, S. (eds) *Politics, Power and Community Development*, Bristol: Policy Press, pp 47–64.

Khan, E. (2020) 'Neighbourhood Watch: Three quarters of consultants say neighbourhood plans increase resistance to development', *Planning Resource article* [online] Available from: https://www.planningresource.co.uk/article/1701318/neighbourhood-watch-three-quarters-consultants-say-neighbourhood-plans-increase-resistance-development [Accessed 20 October 2021].

King, V. (2011) 'The Localism Bill: power to the people?', *BBC News*, 9 November [online] Available from: http://www.bbc.co.uk/news/uk-polit ics-15636272 [Accessed 29 August 2019].

Kisby, B. (2010) 'The Big Society: power to the people?', *Political Quarterly*, 81(4): 484–491.

Knez, I. (2005) 'Attachment and identity as related to a place and its perceived climate', *Journal of Environmental Psychology*, 25(2): 207–218.

Knorr-Cetina, K. (1981) *The Manufacture of Knowledge: An Essay on The Constructivist and Contextual Nature of Science*, Oxford and New York: Pergamon Press.

Koster, M. and Nuijten, M.C.M. (2012) 'From preamble to post-project frustrations: the shaping of a slum upgrading project in Recife, Brazil', *Antipode*, 44(1): 175–196.

Kothari, U. (2001) 'Power, knowledge and social control in participatory development', in Cooke, B. and Kothari, U. (eds) *Participation: The New Tyranny?* London: Zed Books, pp 139–152.

Kothari, U. (2005) 'Authority and expertise: the professionalisation of international development and the ordering of dissent', *Antipode*, 37(3): 425–446.

Kurtz, H.E. (2007) 'Gender and environmental justice in Louisiana: blurring the boundaries of public and private spheres', *Gender, Place and Culture*, 14(4): 409–426.

Kyamusugulwa, P.M. (2013) 'Participatory development and reconstruction: a literature review', *Third World Quarterly*, 34(7): 1265–1278.

Lafferty, W.M. and Eckerberg, K. (1998) *From the Earth Summit to Local Agenda 21: Working Towards Sustainable Development*, London: Earthscan.

Lambert, C. (2006) 'Community strategies and spatial planning in England: the challenges of integration', *Planning Practice & Research*, 21(2): 245–255.

Lane, S.N., Odoni, N., Landstrom, C., Whatmore, S.J., Ward, N. and Bradley, S. (2011) 'Doing flood risk science differently: an experiment in radical scientific method', *Transactions of the Institute of British Geographers*, 36(1): 15–36.

Latour, B. (1984) 'The powers of association', *The Sociological Review*, 32(1_ suppl): 264–280.

Latour, B. (1987) *Science in Action: How to Follow Scientists and Engineers Through Society*, Cambridge, MA: Harvard University Press.

Latour, B. (1993) *We Have Never Been Modern*, Cambridge, MA: Harvard University Press.

Latour, B. (1995) 'The "pedofil" of Boa Vista: a photo-philosophical montage', *Common Knowledge*, 4(1): 145–187.

Latour, B. (1999) *Pandora's Hope: Essays on the Reality of Science Studies*, Cambridge, MA: Harvard University Press.

Latour, B. (2004a) *Politics of Nature: How to Bring the Sciences into Democracy*, Cambridge, MA: Harvard University Press.

Latour, B. (2004b) 'Why has critique run out of steam? From matters of fact to matters of concern', *Critical Inquiry*, 30(2): 225–248.

Latour, B. (2005) *Reassembling the Social: An Introduction to Actor-Network-Theory*, Oxford: Oxford University Press.

Latour, B. and Woolgar, S. (1979) *Laboratory Life: The Social Construction of Scientific Facts*, Beverly Hills: SAGE.

Laurent, B. (2011) 'Technologies of democracy: experiments and demonstrations', *Science and Engineering Ethics*, 17(4): 649–666.

Law, J. (2004) *After Method: Mess in Social Science Research*, London: Routledge.

Law, J. (2007) 'Making a mess with method', in Outhwaite, W. and Turner, S. (eds) *The SAGE Handbook of Social Science Methodology*, Thousand Oaks: SAGE, pp 595–606.

Law, J. (2008) 'On sociology and STS', *Sociological Review*, 56(4): 623–649.

Law, J. (2009) 'Actor-network theory and material semiotics', in Turner, B.S. (ed) *The New Blackwell Companion to Social Theory* (3rd edn), Oxford: Blackwell pp 141–158.

Law, J. and Mol, A. (2002) *Complexities: Social Studies of Knowledge Practices*, Durham, NC: Duke University Press.

Law, J. and Urry, J. (2004) 'Enacting the social', *Economy and Society*, 33(3): 390–410.

Law, J. and Singleton, V. (2013) 'ANT and politics: working in and on the world', *Qualitative Sociology*, 36(4): 485–502.

Law, J. and Singleton, V. (2014) 'ANT, multiplicity and policy', *Critical Policy Studies*, 8(4): 379–396.

Lawler, S. (2008) *Identity: Sociological Perspectives*, Cambridge: Polity Press.

Layard, A., Milling, J. and Wakeford, T. (2013a) *Creative Participation in Place-making*, Swindon: AHRC.

Layard, A., Painter, J., Pande, R., Ramsden, H. and Fyfe, H. (2013b) 'Localism, narrative and myth', *AHRC Connected Communities project summary* [online] Available from: https://connected-communities.org/index.php/project/localism-narrative-myth/ [Accessed 4 November 2022].

Leach, M., Scoones, I. and Wynne, B. (2005) *Science and Citizens: Globalization and the Challenge of Engagement*, London: Zed Books.

Legacy, C. (2017) 'Is there a crisis of participatory planning?', *Planning Theory*, 16(4): 425–442.

Legacy, C., Metzger, J., Steele, W. and Gualini, E. (2019) 'Beyond the post-political: Exploring the relational and situated dynamics of consensus and conflict in planning', *Planning Theory*, 18(3): 273–281.

Lehoux, P., Daudelin, G. and Abelson, J. (2012) 'The unbearable lightness of citizens within public deliberation processes', *Social Science & Medicine*, 74(12): 1843–1850.

Leino, H. and Peltomaa, J. (2012) 'Situated knowledge – situated legitimacy: consequences of citizen participation in local environmental governance', *Policy and Society*, 31(2): 159–168.

Lerner, S. (2006) *Diamond: A Struggle for Environmental Justice in Louisiana's Chemical Corridor*, Cambridge, MA: MIT Press.

Levine, A. (1982) *Love Canal: Science, Politics, and People*, Lexington: Lexington Books.

Levitas, R. (2012) 'The just's umbrella: austerity and the Big Society in Coalition policy and beyond', *Critical Social Policy*, 32(3): 320–342.

Lewicka, M. (2011) 'Place attachment: how far have we come in the last 40 years?', *Journal of Environmental Psychology*, 31(3): 207–230.

Lezaun, J. and Soneryd, L. (2007) 'Consulting citizens: technologies of elicitation and the mobility of publics', *Public Understanding of Science*, 16(3): 279–297.

Lezaun, J., Marres, N. and Tironi, M. (2017) 'Experiments in participation', in Felt, U., Fouché, R., Miller, C.A. and Smith-Doerr, L. (eds) *The Handbook of Science and Technology Studies* (4th edn), Cambridge, MA and London: MIT Press, pp 195–222.

Lievanos, R.S. (2012) 'Certainty, fairness, and balance: state resonance and environmental justice policy implementation', *Sociological Forum*, 27(2): 481–503.

Lindblom, L.J. (2017) 'Barwood Strategic Land II LLP v East Staffordshire Borough Council & Secretary of State for Communities and Local Government EWCA (Civ) 893. Case No: C1/2016/4569', *England and Wales Court of Appeal (Civil Division)* [online] Available from: https://www.bailii.org/ew/cases/EWCA/Civ/2017/893.html [Accessed 27 February 2020].

Lindén, L. and Lydahl, D. (2021) 'Editorial: care in STS', *Nordic Journal of Science and Technology Studies*, 9(1): 3–12.

Lines, K. and Makau, J. (2018) 'Taking the long view: 20 years of Muungano wa Wanavijiji, the Kenyan federation of slum dwellers', *Environment and Urbanization*, 30(2): 407–424.

Locality (2017) 'Neighbourhood planning', *Neighbourhood planning guidance* [online] Available from: https://neighbourhoodplanning.org/about/neighbourhood-planning/ [Accessed 21 August 2017].

Lord, A. and Tewdwr-Jones, M. (2014) 'Is planning "under attack"? Chronicling the deregulation of urban and environmental planning in England', *European Planning Studies*, 22(2): 345–361.

Lord, A., Mair, M., Sturzaker, J. and Jones, P. (2017) '"The planners' dream goes wrong?": questioning citizen-centred planning', *Local Government Studies*, 43(3): 344–363.

Lovbrand, E. (2011) 'Co-producing European climate science and policy: a cautionary note on the making of useful knowledge', *Science & Public Policy*, 38(3): 225–236.

Lowndes, V. and Pratchett, L. (2012) 'Local governance under the coalition government: austerity, localism and the big society', *Local Government Studies*, 38(1): 21–40.

Ludwig, C. and Ludwig, G. (2014) 'Empty gestures? A review of the discourses of "localism" from the practitioner's perspective', *Local Economy*, 29(3): 245–256.

Lung-Amam, W.S. and Dawkins, C. (2020) 'The power of participatory story mapping: advancing equitable development in disadvantaged neighbourhoods', *Community Development Journal*, 55(3): 473–495.

Luyet, V., Schlaepfer, R., Parlange, M.B. and Buttler, A. (2012) 'A framework to implement stakeholder participation in environmental projects', *Journal of Environmental Management*, 111: 213–219.

Lynch, M. (1985) *Art and Artifact in Laboratory Science: A Study of Shop Work and Shop Talk in a Research Laboratory*, London: Routledge & Kegan Paul.

Mace, A. (2013) 'Delivering local plans: recognising the bounded interests of local planners within spatial planning', *Environment and Planning C*, 31(6): 1133–1146.

Macnaghten, P. and Urry, J. (2001) *Bodies of Nature*, London and Thousand Oaks: SAGE.

Mance, H. (2016) 'Britain has had enough of experts, says Gove', *Financial Times*, 3 June [online] Available from: https://www.ft.com/content/3be49 734-29cb-11e6-83e4-abc22d5d108c [Accessed 8 June 2019].

Mansuri, G., Rao, V. and World, B. (2013) *Localizing Development: Does Participation Work?* Washington, DC: World Bank.

Manuel, J. and Vigar, G. (2021) 'Enhancing citizen engagement in planning through participatory film-making', *Environment and Planning B*, 48(6): 1558–1573.

Manuel, J., Vigar, G., Bartindale, T. and Comber, R. (2017) 'Participatory media: creating spaces for storytelling in neighbourhood planning', in *Conference Proceedings of the ACM CHI Conference on Human Factors in Computing Systems*, 6–11 May, Denver, CO. pp 1688–1701.

Manzo, L.C. (2005) 'For better or worse: exploring multiple dimensions of place meaning', *Journal of Environmental Psychology*, 25(1): 67–86.

Marres, N. (2005) 'Issues spark a public into being: a key but often forgotten point of the Lippmann-Dewey debate', in Latour, B. and Weibel, P. (eds) *Making Things Public: Atmospheres of Democracy*, Cambridge, MA: MIT Press, pp 208–217.

Marres, N. (2012) *Material Participation: Technology, the Environment and Everyday Publics*, Houndmills and New York: Palgrave Macmillan.

Marres, N. and Lezaun, J. (2011) 'Materials and devices of the public: an introduction', *Economy and Society*, 40(4): 489–509.

Marris, C. and Rose, N. (2010) 'Open engagement: exploring public participation in the biosciences', *PLoS Biology*, 8(11): e1000549.

Martin, A., Viseu, A. and Myers, N. (2015) 'The politics of care in technoscience', *Social Studies of Science*, 45(5): 625–641.

Massey, D. and Thrift, N. (2003) 'The passion of place', in Johnston, R. and Williams, M. (eds) *A Century of British Geography*, Oxford: Oxford University Press, pp 275–299.

Massumi, B. (2002) *Parables for the Virtual: Movement, Affect, Sensation*, Durham, NC: Duke University Press.

Matthews, P., Bramley, G. and Hastings, A. (2015) 'Homo economicus in a big society: understanding middle-class activism and NIMBYism towards new housing developments', *Housing, Theory and Society*, 32(1): 54–72.

McDonnell, L. (2017) 'Work in progress', *Property Law Journal*, May [online] Available from: https://www.planninglawblog.com/work-in-progress/ [Accessed 4 November 2022].

McDonnell, L. (2018) 'Neighbourhood plans v housing', *Property Law Journal*, February [online] Available from: https://www.dentons.com/en/insights/articles/2018/february/14/neighbourhood-plans-v-housing [Accessed 21 October 2021].

McKee, K. (2015) 'An introduction to the special issue – the Big Society, localism and housing policy: recasting state-citizen relations in an age of austerity', *Housing, Theory and Society*, 32(1): 1–8.

McNeil, M. and Roberts, C. (2011) 'Feminist science and technology studies', in Buikema, R., Griffin, G. and Lykke, N. (eds) *Theories and Methodologies in Postgraduate Feminist Research: Researching Differently*, London: Routledge, pp 2–42.

McNeil, M., Arribas-Ayllon, M., Haran, J., Mackenzie, A. and Tutton, R. (2017) 'Conceptualizing imaginaries of science, technology and society', in Felt, U., Fouché, R., Miller, C.A. and Smith-Doerr, L. (eds) *The Handbook of Science and Technology Studies* (4th edn), Cambridge, MA and London: MIT Press, pp 435–464

Meade, R.R., Shaw, M. and Banks, S. (eds) (2016a) *Politics, Power and Community Development*, Bristol: Policy Press.

Meade, R.R., Shaw, M. and Banks, S. (2016b) 'Politics, power and community development: an introductory essay', in Meade, R.R., Shaw, M. and Banks, S. (eds) *Politics, Power and Community Development*, Bristol: Policy Press, pp 1–30.

Metzger, J. (2011) 'Strange spaces: a rationale for bringing art and artists into the planning process', *Planning Theory*, 10(3): 213–238.

Metzger, J. (2014a) 'Spatial planning and/as caring for more-than-human place', *Environment and Planning A*, 46(5): 1001–1011.

Metzger, J. (2014b) 'The subject of place: staying with the trouble', in Haas, T. and Olsson, K. (eds) *Emergent Urbanism: Urban Planning & Design in Times of Structural and Systemic Change*, Aldershot: Ashgate, pp 91–100.

Metzger, J., Soneryd, L. and Linke, S. (2017) 'The legitimization of concern: a flexible framework for investigating the enactment of stakeholders in environmental planning and governance processes', *Environment and Planning A*, 49(11): 2517–2535.

MHCLG (2020) *Planning for the Future White Paper*, London: HM Government.

MHCLG (2021) 'Two funds to support the uptake of neighbourhood planning', *MHCLG guidance* [online] Available from: https://www.gov. uk/government/publications/neighbourhood-planning-two-funds-to-support-greater-uptake/two-funds-to-support-the-uptake-of-neighbourh ood-planning [Accessed 8 October 2021].

Mignolo, W.D. (2011) *The Darker Side of Western Modernity: Global Futures, Decolonial Options*, Durham, NC: Duke University Press.

Millstone, E., Stirling, A. and Glover, D. (2015) 'Regulating genetic engineering: the limits and politics of knowledge', *Issues in Science & Technology*, 31(4): 23–26.

Miraftab, F. (2004) 'Invited and invented spaces of participation: neoliberal citizenship and feminists' expanded notion of politics', *Wagadu*, 1(1): 1–7.

Miraftab, F. (2006) 'Feminist praxis, citizenship and informal politics: reflections on South Africa's anti-eviction campaign', *International Feminist Journal of Politics*, 8(2): 194–218.

Miraftab, F. (2020) 'Insurgency and juxtacity in the age of urban divides', *Urban Forum*, 31(3): 433–441.

Mitlin, D. (2008) 'With and beyond the state: co-production as a route to political influence, power and transformation for grassroots organizations', *Environment and Urbanization*, 20(2): 339–360.

Mitlin, D. (2018) 'Beyond contention: urban social movements and their multiple approaches to secure transformation', *Environment and Urbanization*, 30(2): 557–574.

Mitlin, D. and Bebbington, A. (2006) *Social Movements and Chronic Poverty across the Urban-Rural Divide: Concepts and Experiences. Working Paper 65*, Manchester: Chronic Poverty Research Centre.

Mohai, P., Pellow, D. and Roberts, J.T. (2009) 'Environmental justice', *Annual Review of Environment and Resources*, 34(1): 405–430.

Mohan, G. (2001) 'Beyond participation: strategies for deeper empowerment', in Cooke, B. and Kothari, U. (eds) *Participation: The New Tyranny?* London: Zed Books, pp 153–167.

Mohan, G. and Stokke, K. (2000) 'Participatory development and empowerment: the dangers of localism', *Third World Quarterly*, 21(2): 247–268.

Mohanty, R., Thompson, L. and Coelho, V.S. (2011) *Mobilising the State? Social Mobilisation and State Interaction in India, Brazil and South Africa*, Brighton: Institute of Development Studies, University of Sussex.

Mol, A. (1999) 'Ontological politics: a word and some questions', *The Sociological Review*, 47(1_suppl): 74–89. doi: 10.1111/j.1467-954X.1999. tb03483.x

Mol, A. (2002) *The Body Multiple: Ontology in Medical Practice*, Durham, NC: Duke University Press.

Mol, A. (2010) 'Actor-Network Theory: sensitive terms and enduring tensions', *Kölner Zeitschrift für Soziologie und Sozialpsychologie. Sonderheft*, 50(1): 253–269.

Morgan, S. (2017) 'Neighbourhood planning in the high court', *Landmark Chambers briefing* [online] Available from: https://www.landmarkchamb ers.co.uk/wp-content/uploads/2018/08/SFM-Neighbourhood-Plann ing-1.pdf [Accessed 21 October 2021].

Moser, I. (2008) 'Making Alzheimer's disease matter: enacting, interfering and doing politics of nature', *Geoforum*, 39(1): 98–110.

Mosse, D. (1994) 'Authority, gender and knowledge: theoretical reflections on the practice of participatory rural appraisal', *Development and Change*, 25(3): 497–526.

Mouffe, C. (2005) *On the Political*, London: Routledge.

Mueller-Hirth, N. (2012) 'If you don't count, you don't count: monitoring and evaluation in South African NGOs', *Development and Change*, 43(3): 649–670.

Mukherjee, A. (2014) 'Participatory rural appraisal', in Coghlan, D. and Brydon-Miller, M. (eds) *The SAGE Encyclopaedia of Action Research*, London: SAGE, pp 606–608.

Mukherjee, F. (2015) 'Public participatory GIS', *Geography Compass*, 9(7): 384–394.

Mukherjee, N. (2002) *Participatory Learning and Action: With 100 Field Methods*, New Delhi: Concept Publishing.

Müller, M. (2015) 'Assemblages and actor-networks: rethinking socio-material power, politics and space', *Geography Compass*, 9(1): 27–41.

Murdock, E.G. (2020) 'A history of environmental justice: foundations, narratives and perspectives', in Coolsaet, B. (ed) *Environmental Justice: Key Issues*, London: Routledge, pp 6–17.

Murphy, M. (2015) 'Unsettling care: troubling transnational itineraries of care in feminist health practices', *Social Studies of Science*, 45(5): 717–737.

Nadin, V. (2007) 'The emergence of the spatial planning approach in England', *Planning, Practice & Research*, 22(1): 43–62.

Narayanasamy, N. (2009) *Participatory Rural Appraisal: Principles, Methods and Application*, Los Angeles: SAGE.

National Audit Office (2019) *Planning for New Homes*, London: House of Commons.

Newman, J. (2012) *Working the Spaces of Power: Activism, Neoliberalism and Gendered Labour*, London: Bloomsbury Academic.

Newman, J. (2014) 'Landscapes of antagonism: local governance, neoliberalism and austerity', *Urban Studies*, 51(15): 3290–3305.

Newton, D.E. (2009) *Environmental Justice: A Reference Handbook* (2nd edn), Santa Barbara and Oxford: ABC-CLIO.

Norgrove, S.D. (2017) 'Letter from Sir David Norgrove, Chair of the UK Statistics Agency, to Boris Johnson MP', *UK Statistics Authority* [online] Available from: https://uksa.statisticsauthority.gov.uk/wp-content/uplo ads/2017/09/Letter-from-Sir-David-Norgrove-to-Foreign-Secretary.pdf [Accessed 3 November 2020].

Norris, P. (2011) *Democratic Deficit: Critical Citizens Revisited*, New York: Cambridge University Press.

Novotny, P. (2000) *Where We Live, Work and Play: The Environmental Justice Movement and the Struggle for a New Environmentalism*, Westport: Praeger.

NPIERS (2018) 'Neighbourhood Planning Independent Examiner Referral Service: guidance to service users and examiners', *NPIERS guidance* [online] Available from: shorturl.at/cimW5 [Accessed 17 September 2021].

Ockwell, D. and Rydin, Y. (2006) 'Conflicting discourses of knowledge: understanding the policy adoption of pro-burning knowledge claims in Cape York Peninsula, Australia', *Environmental Politics*, 15(3): 379–398.

ODPM (2004) *Community Involvement in Planning: The Government's Objectives*, London: HMSO.

OECD (2001) 'Citizens as partners', *OECD handbook* [online] Available from: https://www.oecd-ilibrary.org/governance/citizens-as-partners_97 89264195578-en [Accessed 7 October 2021].

O'Faircheallaigh, C. (2010) 'Public participation and environmental impact assessment: purposes, implications, and lessons for public policy making', *Environmental Impact Assessment Review*, 30(1): 19–27.

Orme, J. (2010) 'Why are some campaigners calling the Localism Bill a NIMBY's charter?', *The Independent*, 17 December [online] Available from: http://www.independent.co.uk/property/house-and-home/why-are-some-campaigners-calling-the-localism-bill-a-nimbys-charter-2162 630.html [Accessed 29 September 2021].

O'Rourke, D. and Macey, G.P. (2003) 'Community environmental policing: assessing new strategies of public participation in environmental regulation', *Journal of Policy Analysis and Management*, 22(3): 383–414.

Ottinger, G. (2009) 'Epistemic fencelines: air monitoring instruments and expert-resident boundaries', *Spontaneous Generations: A Journal for the History and Philosophy of Science*, 3(1): 55–67.

Ottinger, G. (2013) *Refining Expertise: How Responsible Engineers Subvert Environmental Justice Challenges*, New York: New York University Press.

Ottinger, G. (2017) 'Reconstructing or reproducing? Scientific authority and models of change in two traditions of citizen science', in Tyfield, D., Lave, R., Randalls, S. and Thorpe, C. (eds) *The Routledge Handbook of the Political Economy of Science*, Abingdon and New York: Taylor & Francis, pp 351–363.

Ottinger, G. (2018) 'Opening black boxes: environmental justice and injustice through the lens of Science and Technology Studies', in Holifield, R., Chakraborty, J. and Walker, G. (eds) *The Routledge Handbook of Environmental Justice*, Abingdon and New York: Taylor & Francis, pp 89–100.

Ottinger, G. and Cohen, B. (2012) 'Environmentally just transformations of expert cultures: toward the theory and practice of a renewed science and technology', *Environmental Justice*, 5(3): 158–163.

Ottinger, G. and Sarantschin, E. (2017) 'Exposing infrastructure: how activists and experts connect ambient air monitoring and environmental health', *Environmental Sociology*, 3(2): 155–165.

Overdevest, C. and Mayer, B. (2008) 'Harnessing the power of information through community monitoring: insights from social science', *Texas Law Review*, 86(7): 1493–1526.

Parker, G. (2017) 'The uneven geographies of neighbourhood planning in England', in Brownill, S. and Bradley, Q. (eds) *Localism and Neighbourhood Planning: Power to the People?* Bristol: Policy Press, pp 75–91.

Parker, G. and Street, E. (2015) 'Planning at the neighbourhood scale: localism, dialogic politics, and the modulation of community action', *Environment and Planning C*, 33(4): 794–810.

Parker, G., Lynn, T., Wargent, M. and Locality (2014) *User Experience of Neighbourhood Planning in England*, London: Locality.

Parker, G., Lynn, T. and Wargent, M. (2015) 'Sticking to the script? The co-production of neighbourhood planning in England', *Town Planning Review*, 86(5): 519–536.

Parker, G., Salter, K. and Hickman, H. (2016) 'Caution: examinations in progress. The operation of neighbourhood development plan operations', *Town and Country Planning*, December: 516–522.

Parker, G., Lynn, T. and Wargent, M. (2017a) 'Contestation and conservatism in neighbourhood planning: reconciling agonism and collaboration?', *Planning Theory & Practice*, 18(3): 446–465.

Parker, G., Salter, K. and Hickman, H. (2017b) *Examining Neighbourhood Plans in England: The Experience So Far*, Reading: University of Reading.

Parker, G., Salter, K. and Dobson, M. (2018) *Neighbourhood Planning HIVE Report: Experiences of Participants*, Reading: Department of Real Estate and Planning, University of Reading.

Parker, G., Wargent, M., Salter, K., Lynn, T., Dobson, M., Yuille, A. and Bowden, C. (2020) *Impacts of Neighbourhood Planning in England*, London: MHCLG.

Parker, G., Sturzaker, J. and Wargent, M. (2022) 'Levelling up neighbourhoods: back to the very local future', *Town and Country Planning*, 91(3/4): 99–101.

Parry, C. (2020) 'Neighbourhood plans: challenging the unchallengeable', *Cornerstone Barristers blog* [online] Available from: https://cornerstonebar risters.com/news/neighbourhood-plans-challenging-unchallengeable/ [Accessed 21 October 2021].

Peirson, A.E. and Ziervogel, G. (2021) 'Sanitation upgrading as climate action: lessons for local government from a community informal settlement project in Cape Town', *Sustainability*, 13(15): 8598.

Perkins, C. (2007) 'Community mapping', *Cartographic Journal*, 44(2): 127–137.

Perkins, D.D. and Manzo, L.C. (2006) 'Finding common ground: the importance of place attachment to community participation and planning', *Journal of Planning Literature*, 20(4): 335–350.

Pestoff, V. (2006) 'Citizens and co-production of welfare services: childcare in eight European countries', *Public Management Review*, 8(4): 503–519.

Pestoff, V. (2009) 'Towards a paradigm of democratic participation: citizen participation and co-production of personal social services in Sweden', *Annals of Public and Cooperative Economics*, 80(2): 197–224.

Petts, J. (2005) 'Enhancing environmental equity through decision-making: learning from waste management', *Local Environment*, 10(4): 397–409.

Petts, J. and Brooks, C. (2006) 'Expert conceptualisations of the role of lay knowledge in environmental decisionmaking: challenges for deliberative democracy', *Environment and Planning A*, 38(6): 1045–1059.

Pickles, E. (2013) 'New step for localism as every regional plan has gone', *DCLG press release* [online] Available from: https://www.gov.uk/gov ernment/news/new-step-for-localism-as-every-regional-plan-has-gone [Accessed 18 September 2017].

Pieterse, J.N. (1998) 'My paradigm or yours? Alternative development, post-development, reflexive development', *Development and Change*, 29(2): 343–373.

Pile, S. (2010) 'Emotions and affect in recent human geography', *Transactions of the Institute of British Geographers*, 35(1): 5–20.

Pimentel Walker, A.P. (2016) 'Self-help or public housing? Lessons from co-managed slum upgrading via participatory budget', *Habitat International*, 55: 58–66.

Piper, L. and Von Lieres, B. (2015) 'Mediating between state and citizens: the significance of the informal politics of third-party representation in the global south', *Citizenship Studies*, 19(6–7): 1–18.

Planning Advisory Service (2013) 'Neighbourhood planning: a guide for councillors', *Planning Advisory Service advice* [online] Available from: https://www.local.gov.uk/pas/pas-topics/neighbourhood-plans/neighbourhood-planning-guide-councillors [Accessed 1 August 2016].

Planning Aid (nd) 'Material planning considerations', *Planning Aid advice* [online] Available from: https://studylib.net/doc/18118912/material-plann ing-considerations [Accessed 4 November 2022].

Planning Portal (nd) 'What are material considerations', *Planning Portal advice* [online] Available from: https://www.planningportal.co.uk/services/help/faq/planning/about-the-planning-system/what-are-material-considerations [Accessed 4 November 2022].

Polletta, F. (2016) 'Participatory enthusiasms: a recent history of citizen engagement initiatives', *Journal of Civil Society*, 12(3): 231–246.

Porter, L., Sandercock, L., Umemoto, K., Bates, L.K., Zapata, M.A., Kondo, M.C., et al (2012) 'What's love got to do with it? Illuminations on loving attachment in planning', *Planning Theory & Practice*, 13(4): 593–627.

Potter, J. (1996) *Representing Reality: Discourse, Rhetoric and Social Construction*, London and Thousand Oaks: SAGE.

Poverty Truth Network (2022) 'The distinctiveness of our work', *PTN website* [online] Available from: https://povertytruthnetwork.org/the-network/the-distinctives-of-our-work/ (Accessed 8 May 2022).

Preston City Council (2018) 'The community mapping toolkit', *Preston City Council toolkit* [online] Available from: https://qi.elft.nhs.uk/wp-content/uploads/2018/11/Community-Mapping-Toolkit-3.pdf [Accessed 13 March 2021].

Pretty, J.N. (1995) 'Participatory learning for sustainable agriculture', *World Development*, 23(8): 1247–1263.

Puig de la Bellacasa, M. (2011) 'Matters of care in technoscience: assembling neglected things', *Social Studies of Science*, 41(1): 85–106.

Puig de la Bellacasa, M. (2012) '"Nothing comes without its world": thinking with care', *Sociological Review*, 60(2): 197–216.

Puig de la Bellacasa, M. (2017) *Matters of Care: Speculative Ethics in More Than Human Worlds*, Minneapolis: University of Minnesota Press.

Pánek, J. and Pászto, V. (2020) 'Emotional mapping in local neighbourhood planning: four examples from the Czech Republic', in Nunes Silva, C. (ed) *Citizen-Responsive Urban E-Planning: Recent Developments and Critical Perspectives*, Hershey: IGI Global, pp 138–167.

Raco, M., Street, E. and Freire-Trigo, S. (2016) 'The new localism, anti-political development machines, and the role of planning consultants: lessons from London's South Bank', *Territory, Politics, Governance*, 4(2): 216–240.

Radil, S.M. and Anderson, M.B. (2019) 'Rethinking PGIS: participatory or (post)political GIS?', *Progress in Human Geography*, 43(2): 195–213.

Rambaldi, G., Corbett, J., McCall, M.K., Olson, R., Muchemi, J., Kyem, P., et al (eds) (2006) *Participatory Learning and Action 54 – Mapping for Change: Practice, Technologies and Communication*, London: International Institute for Environment and Development.

Rawles, K. and Holland, A. (1996) 'The ethics of conservation', *Thingmount Working Paper Series*, TWP 96-01, Department of Philosophy, Lancaster University.

Raynsford, N. (2018) 'Former housing minister warns of "a new generation of slum housing"', *IHBC NewsBlog* [online] Available from: https://news blogsnew.ihbc.org.uk/?p=20939 [Accessed 4 November 2022].

Raynsford, N., Ellis, H., Chang, M., MacRae, C., Mulligan, J., Pednekar, S., et al (2018) *Planning 2020: Raynsford Review of Planning in England*, London: TCPA.

Reed, M.S. (2008) 'Stakeholder participation for environmental management: a literature review', *Biological Conservation*, 141(10): 2417–2431.

Rhodes, R.A.W. (1996) 'The new governance: governing without government', *Political Studies*, 44(4): 652–667.

Ringquist, E.J. (2005) 'Assessing evidence of environmental inequities: a meta-analysis', *Journal of Policy Analysis and Management*, 24(2): 223–247.

Rittel, H. and Webber, M. (1973) 'Dilemmas in a general theory of planning', *Integrating Knowledge and Practice to Advance Human Dignity*, 4(2): 155–169.

Rolfe, S. (2018) 'Governance and governmentality in community participation: the shifting sands of power, responsibility and risk', *Social Policy and Society*, 17(4): 579–598.

Roosth, S. and Silbey, S. (2009) 'Science and technology studies: from controversies to posthumanist social theory', in Turner, B.S. (ed) *The New Blackwell Companion to Social Theory* (3rd edn), Oxford: Blackwell, pp 451–473.

Rose, N. (1996) 'The death of the social? Refiguring the territory of government', *Economy and Society*, 25(3): 327–356.

Rose, N.S. (1999) *Powers of Freedom: Reframing Political Thought*, Cambridge and New York: Cambridge University Press.

Roth, D., Köhne, M., Rasch, E.D. and Winnubst, M. (2021) 'After the facts: producing, using and contesting knowledge in two spatial-environmental conflicts in the Netherlands', *Environment and Planning C*, 39(3): 626–645.

Rowe, G. and Frewer, L.J. (2005) 'A typology of public engagement mechanisms', *Science, Technology & Human Values*, 30(2): 251–290.

Roy, A. (2009) 'Why India cannot plan its cities: informality, insurgence and the idiom of ubanization', *Planning Theory*, 8(1): 76–87.

Rozee, L. (2014) 'A new vision for planning: there must be a better way?', *Planning Theory & Practice*, 15(1): 1–15.

Rydin, Y. (2007) 'Re-examining the role of knowledge within planning theory', *Planning Theory*, 6(1): 52–68.

Rydin, Y. and Natarajan, L. (2016) 'The materiality of public participation: the case of community consultation on spatial planning for north Northamptonshire, England', *Local Environment*, 21(10): 1243–1251.

Rydin, Y., Natarajan, L., Lee, M. and Lock, S. (2018) 'Black-boxing the evidence: planning regulation and major renewable energy infrastructure projects in England and Wales', *Planning Theory & Practice*, 19(2): 218–234.

Sagoe, C. (2016) 'One tool amongst many: considering the political potential of neighbourhood planning for the Greater Carpenters neighbourhood, London', *Architecture_MPS*, 9(3): 1–20.

Saija, L., De Leo, D., Forester, J., Pappalardo, G., Rocha, I., Sletto, B., et al (2017) 'Learning from practice: environmental and community mapping as participatory action research in planning', *Planning Theory & Practice*, 18(1): 127–153.

Salter, K. (2017) 'Neighbourhood plan examinations: why they need to be tough' *RTPI blog* [online] Available from: https://www.rtpi.org.uk/brief ing-room/rtpi-blog/neighbourhood-plan-examinations-why-they-need-to-be-tough/ [Accessed 2 November 2019].

Samper, J., Shelby, J.A. and Behary, D. (2020) 'The paradox of informal settlements revealed in an ATLAS of informality: findings from mapping growth in the most common yet unmapped forms of urbanization', *Sustainability*, 12(22): 9510.

Samuels, I. (2012) 'Limits to localism', *Focus*, 9(1): 41–42.

San Martín, W. and Wood, N. (2022) 'Pluralising planetary justice beyond the North-South divide: recentring procedural, epistemic, and recognition-based justice in earth-systems governance', *Environmental Science & Policy*, 128: 256–263.

Sandercock, L. (2003) 'Out of the closet: the importance of stories and storytelling in planning practice', *Planning Theory & Practice*, 4(1): 11–28.

Sandercock, L. and Attili, G. (2010) *Multimedia Explorations in Urban Policy and Planning*, Heidelberg, London and New York: Springer.

Sandover, R., Moseley, A. and Devine-Wright, P. (2021) 'Contrasting views of citizens' assemblies: stakeholder perceptions of public deliberation on climate change', *Politics and Governance*, 9(2): 76–86.

Schlosberg, D. (2007) *Defining Environmental Justice: Theories, Movements, and Nature*, Oxford: Oxford University Press.

Schlosberg, D. and Collins, L.B. (2014) 'From environmental to climate justice: climate change and the discourse of environmental justice', *WIREs Climate Change*, 5(3): 359–374.

Scott, J.C. (1998) *Seeing Like a State: How Certain Schemes to Improve the Human Condition have Failed*, New Haven: Yale University Press.

Seale, C. (1999) 'Quality in qualitative research', *Qualitative Inquiry*, 5(4): 465–478.

Seebohm, F. (1968) *Report of the Committee on Local Authority and Allied Personal Social Services. Cm. 3703*, London: HMSO.

Seeliger, L. and Turok, I. (2014) 'Averting a downward spiral: building resilience in informal urban settlements through adaptive governance', *Environment and Urbanization*, 26(1): 184–199.

Shah, A. (2007) *Participatory Budgeting*, Washington, DC: World Bank.

Shapin, S. and Schaffer, S. (1985) *Leviathan and the Air-Pump: Hobbes, Boyle, and the Experimental Life*, Princeton: Princeton University Press.

Shaw, M. (2011) 'Stuck in the middle? Community development, community engagement and the dangerous business of learning for democracy', *Community Development Journal*, 46(S2): ii128–ii146.

Shilling, F.M., London, J.K. and Liévanos, R.S. (2009) 'Marginalization by collaboration: environmental justice as a third party in and beyond CALFED', *Environmental Science & Policy*, 12(6): 694–709.

Shove, E. (2012) *The Dynamics of Social Practice: Everyday Life and How It Changes*, London: SAGE.

Sibley-Esposito, C. (2014) 'Not out of the woods yet: spatial planning (de)regulation under the Coalition government', *Observatoire de la Société Britannique*, 15: 189–214.

Singleton, V. and Mee, S. (2017) 'Critical compassion: affect, discretion and policy–care relations', *The Sociological Review*, 65(2_suppl): 130–149.

Skeffington, A. (1969) *People and Planning: Report of the Skeffington Committee on Public Participation in Planning*, London: HMSO.

Smith, D.E. (1987) *The Everyday World as Problematic: A Feminist Sociology*, Boston: Northeastern University Press.

Smith, G. (2005) *Beyond the Ballot: 57 Democratic Innovations from Around the World*, London: Power Inquiry.

Smith, I., Lepine, E. and Taylor, M. (2007) *Disadvantaged by Where You Live? Neighbourhood Governance in Contemporary Urban Policy*, Bristol: Policy Press.

Smith, J., Tyszczuk, R., Lewis, K., Day, R., Goodbody, A., Whyte, N., et al (2016) 'Stories of change', *AHRC Connected Communities project* [online] Available from: https://storiesofchange.ac.uk/ [Accessed 4 November 2022].

Smith, L. and Rubin, M. (2015) 'Beyond invented and invited spaces of participation: the Phiri and Olivia Road court cases and their outcome', in Bénit-Gbaffou, C. (ed) *Popular Politics in South African Cities: Unpacking Community Participation*, Cape Town: HSRC Press, pp 248–281.

Smith, M. (2009) *Emotion, Place and Culture*, Farnham: Ashgate.

Soja, E.W. (1989) *Postmodern Geographies: The Reassertion of Space in Critical Social Theory*, London and New York: Verso.

Soneryd, L. (2016) 'What is at stake? Practices of linking actors, issues and scales in environmental politics', *Nordic Journal of Science and Technology Studies*, 3(2): 18–23.

Sorensen, A. and Sagaris, L. (2010) 'From participation to the right to the city: democratic place management at the neighbourhood scale in comparative perspective', *Planning Practice & Research*, 25(3): 297–316.

Star, S.L. (1990) 'Power, technology and the phenomenology of conventions: on being allergic to onions', *The Sociological Review*, 38(1_suppl): 26–56.

Stenmark, M. (1997) 'What is scientism?', *Religious Studies*, 33(1): 15–32.

Stewart, J. and Lithgow, S. (2015) 'Problems and prospects in community engagement in urban planning and decision-making: three case studies from the Australian Capital Territory', *Policy Studies*, 36(1): 18–34.

Stirling, A. (2006) 'Analysis, participation and power: justification and closure in participatory multi- criteria analysis', *Land Use Policy*, 23(1): 95–107.

Stirling, A. (2008) '"Opening up" and "closing down": power, participation, and pluralism in the social appraisal of technology', *Science, Technology & Human Values*, 33(2): 262–294.

Stirling, A. (2014) 'Transforming power: social science and the politics of energy choices', *Energy Research & Social Science*, 1(C): 83–95.

Stirling, A. (2015) 'Power, truth and progress: towards knowledge democracies in Europe', in Wilsdon, J. and Doubleday, R. (eds) *Future Directions for Scientific Advice in Europe*, Cambridge: Centre for Science and Policy, pp 135–153.

Stirling, A. (2016) 'Knowing doing governance: realizing heterodyne democracies', in Voß, J.-P. and Freeman, R. (eds) *Knowing Governance: The Epistemic Construction of Political Order*, London: Palgrave Macmillan, pp 259–289.

Stirrat, R. (1996) 'The new orthodoxy and old truths: participation, empowerment and other buzzwords', in Bastian, S. and Bastian, N. (eds) *Assessing Participation: A Debate from South Asia*, Delhi: Konark Publishers, pp 67–92.

Storey, A. (2014) 'Making experience legible: spaces of participation and the construction of knowledge in Khayelitsha', *Politikon*, 41(3): 403–420.

Strathern, M. (1996) 'Cutting the network', *Journal of the Royal Anthropological Institute*, 2(3): 517–535.

Strong, D. (1994) 'Disclosive discourse, ecology, and technology', *Environmental Ethics*, 16(1): 89–102.

Sturzaker, J. (2011) 'Can community empowerment reduce opposition to housing? Evidence from rural England', *Planning Practice & Research*, 26(5): 555–570.

Sturzaker, J. and Shaw, D. (2015) 'Localism in practice: lessons from a pioneer neighbourhood plan in England', *Town Planning Review*, 86(5): 587–609.

Sturzaker, J. and Gordon, M. (2017) 'Democratic tensions in decentralised planning: rhetoric, legislation and reality in England', *Environment and Planning C*, 35(7): 1324–1339.

Suchman, L. (2012) 'Configuration', in Lury, C. and Wakeford, N. (eds) *Inventive Methods: The Happening of the Social*, New York: Routledge, pp 48–60.

Swaine, J. (2017) 'Donald Trump's team defends "alternative facts" after widespread protests', *The Guardian*, 23 January [online] Available from: https://www.theguardian.com/us-news/2017/jan/22/donald-trump-kellyanne-conway-inauguration-alternative-facts [Accessed 26 October 2017].

Swyngedouw, E. (2005) 'Governance innovation and the citizen: the Janus face of governance-beyond-the-state', *Urban Studies*, 42(11): 1991–2006.

Swyngedouw, E. (2009) 'The antinomies of the postpolitical city: in search of a democratic politics of environmental production', *International Journal of Urban and Regional Research*, 33(3): 601–620.

Symon, G. and Pritchard, K. (2015) 'Performing the responsive and committed employee through the sociomaterial mangle of connection', *Organization Studies*, 36(2): 241–263.

Sze, J. and London, J.K. (2008) 'Environmental justice at the crossroads', *Sociology Compass*, 2(4): 1331–1354.

Taylor, C. (2004) *Modern Social Imaginaries*, Durham, NC: Duke University Press.

Taylor, D.E. (2000) 'The rise of the environmental justice paradigm: injustice framing and the social construction of environmental discourses', *The American Behavioral Scientist*, 43(4): 508–580.

TCPA (2017a) 'The Raynsford Review of Planning provocation paper 2: people and planning', *TCPA briefing paper* [online] Available from: https://tcpa.org.uk/wp-content/uploads/2022/03/Provocation-Paper-2-People-and-planning.pdf [Accessed 4 November 2022].

TCPA (2017b) 'The Raynsford Review of Planning background paper 2: the rise and fall of town planning', *TCPA briefing paper* [online] Available from: https://tcpa.org.uk/wp-content/uploads/2022/03/Background-Paper-2-The-rise-and-fall-of-town-planning.pdf [Accessed 4 November 2022].

TCPA (2021) 'Our fragile high streets – death by permitted development rights?', *TCPA research briefing* [online] Available from: https://tcpa.org.uk/wp-content/uploads/2021/11/fin_1_8_classe_with-maps.pdf [Accessed 4 November 2022].

Tesh, S.N. (2000) *Uncertain Hazards: Environmental Activists and Scientific Proof*, Ithaca, NY: Cornell University Press.

Tewdwr-Jones, M. (1998) 'Rural government and community participation: the planning role of community councils', *Journal of Rural Studies*, 14(1): 51–62.

Thevenot, L. (2007) 'The plurality of cognitive formats and engagements: moving between the familiar and the public.', *European Journal of Social Theory*, 10(3): 409–423.

Thiele, L. and Young, M. (2016) 'Practical judgment, narrative experience and wicked problems', *Theoria*, 63(148): 35–52.

Thrift, N. (2004) 'Intensities of feeling: towards a spatial politics of affect', *Geografiska Annaler: Series B, Human Geography*, 86(1): 57–78.

Thrift, N. (2008) *Non-Representational Theory: Space, Politics, Affect*, London: Routledge.

Thrift, N. (2009) 'Understanding the affective spaces of political performance', in Smith, M., Davidson, J., Cameron, L. and Bondi, L. (eds) *Emotion, Place and Culture*, Farnham: Ashgate, pp 79–98.

Throgmorton, J. (1996) *Planning as Persuasive Storytelling: The Rhetorical Construction of Chicago's Electric Future*, Chicago: University of Chicago Press.

Throgmorton, J. (2003) 'Planning as persuasive storytelling in a global-scale web of relationships', *Planning Theory*, 2(2): 125–151.

Traweek, S. (1988) *Beamtimes and Lifetimes: The World of High Energy Physicists*, Cambridge, MA: Harvard University Press.

Tritter, J.Q. and McCallum, A. (2006) 'The snakes and ladders of user involvement: moving beyond Arnstein', *Health Policy*, 76(2): 156–168.

Tsing, A.L. (2005) *Friction: An Ethnography of Global Connection*, Princeton: Princeton University Press.

Tsouvalis, J. (2016) 'Latour's object-orientated politics for a post-political age', *Global Discourse*, 6(1–2): 26–39.

Tsouvalis, J. and Waterton, C. (2012) 'Building "participation" upon critique: the Loweswater Care Project, Cumbria, UK', *Environmental Modelling and Software*, 36: 111–121.

Tuan, Y.-F. (1975) 'Place: an experiential perspective', *Geographical Review*, 65(2): 151–165.

Turley (2014) *Neighbourhood Planning: Plan and Deliver?* London: Turley Associates.

UNDP (1993) *Human Development Report*, New York: Oxford University Press.

UN-HABITAT (2003) *The Challenge of the Slums: Global Report on Human Settlements 2003*, London: Earthscan.

UN-HABITAT (2011) *Global Report on Human Settlements, 2011: Cities and Climate Change*, London and Washington, DC: Earthscan.

UN-HABITAT (2016) *Urbanization and Development: Emerging Futures. World Cities Report 2016*, Nairobi: United Nations Human Settlements Programme.

United Nations (1955) *Progress Through Community Development*, New York: United Nations Bureau of Social Affairs.

United Nations (2019) *World Urbanization Prospects: The 2018 Revision*, New York: United Nation Department of Economic and Social Affairs.

United Nations (2021) *UN Human Rights Council Resolution 48/13: The Human Right to a Safe, Clean, Healthy and Sustainable Environment*, New York: UN General Assembly.

Urry, J. (2004) 'The "system" of automobility', *Theory, Culture & Society*, 21(4/5): 25–40.

Urry, J. and Macnaghten, P. (1998) *Contested Natures*, London: SAGE.

US Executive Office of the President (2021) 'Executive Order 13990: Protecting Public Health and the Environment and Restoring Science to Tackle the Climate Crisis' [online] Available from: https://www.whitehouse.gov/briefing-room/presidential-actions/2021/01/20/executive-order-protecting-public-health-and-environment-and-restoring-science-to-tackle-climate-crisis/ [Accessed 4 November 2022].

Uysal, U.E. (2012) 'An urban social movement challenging urban regeneration: the case of Sulukule, Istanbul', *Cities*, 29(1): 12–22.

van Hulst, M. (2012) 'Storytelling, a model of and a model for planning', *Planning Theory*, 11(3): 299–318.

Verran, H. (1998) 'Re-imagining land ownership in Australia', *Postcolonial Studies*, 1(2): 237–254.

Verran, H. (2001) *Science and an African Logic*, Chicago: University of Chicago Press.

Vidal, T., Berroeta, H., Di Masso, A., Valera, S. and Pero, M. (2013) 'Place attachment, place identity, sense of community, and local civic participation in an urban renewal context', *Estudios De Psicologia*, 34(3): 275–286.

Vigar, G., Gunn, S. and Brooks, E. (2017) 'Governing our neighbours: participation and conflict in neighbourhood planning', *Town Planning Review*, 88(4): 423–442.

Villiers, T. (2022) 'Theresa Villiers: the government must not centralise control over planning', *Conservative Home column* [online] Available from: https://conservativehome.com/2022/06/14/theresa-villiers-the-government-must-not-centralise-control-over-planning/ [Accessed 24 June 2022].

Voß, J.-P. and Amelung, N. (2016) 'Innovating public participation methods: technoscientization and reflexive engagement', *Social Studies of Science*, 46(5): 749–772.

Walker, G. (2012) *Environmental Justice Concepts, Evidence and Politics*, Abingdon and New York: Routledge.

Walker, G., Cass, N., Burningham, K. and Barnett, J. (2010) 'Renewable energy and sociotechnical change: imagined subjectivities of "the public" and their implications', *Environment and Planning A*, 42(4): 931–947.

Walton, J.K. (2000) *The British Seaside: Holidays and Resorts in the Twentieth Century*, Manchester: Manchester University Press.

Wargent, M. (2021) 'Localism, governmentality and failing technologies: the case of neighbourhood planning in England', *Territory, Politics, Governance*, 9(4): 571–591.

Wargent, M. and Parker, G. (2018) 'Re-imagining neighbourhood governance: the future of neighbourhood planning in England', *Town Planning Review*, 89(4): 379–402.

Waterton, C. and Wynne, B. (1998) 'Can focus groups access community views?', in Barbour, R.S. and Kitzinger, J. (eds) *Developing Focus Group Research: Politics, Theory and Practice*, London and Thousand Oaks: SAGE, pp 127–143.

Waterton, C., Maberly, S.C., Tsouvalis, J., Watson, N., Winfield, I.J. and Norton, L.R. (2015) 'Committing to place: the potential of open collaborations for trusted environmental governance', *PLoS Biology*, 13(3): p.e1002081–e1002081.

Watson-Verran, H. and Turnbull, D. (1995) 'Science and other indigenous knowledge systems', in Jasanoff, S., Markle, G.E., Petersen, J.C. and Pinch, T. (eds) *Handbook of Science and Technology Studies* (revised edn), Thousand Oaks: SAGE, pp 115–139.

Weber, R. (2002) 'Extracting value from the city: neoliberalism and urban redevelopment', *Antipode*, 34(3): 519–540.

Wekesa, B.W., Steyn, G.S. and Otieno, F.A.O. (2011) 'A review of physical and socio-economic characteristics and intervention approaches of informal settlements', *Habitat International*, 35(2): 238–245.

Welsh, I. and Wynne, B. (2013) 'Science, scientism and imaginaries of publics in the UK: passive objects, incipient threats', *Science as Culture*, 22(4): 540–566.

Wenger, E. (1998) *Communities of Practice: Learning, Meaning, and Identity*, Cambridge and New York: Cambridge University Press.

Wesselink, A., Paavola, J., Fritsch, O. and Renn, O. (2011) 'Rationales for public participation in environmental policy and governance: practitioners' perspectives', *Environment and Planning A*, 43(11): 2688–2704.

White, S.C. (1996) 'Depoliticising development: the uses and abuses of participation', *Development in Practice*, 6(1): 6–15.

Wilcox, D. (1994) *Community Participation and Empowerment: Putting Theory into Practice*, York: Joseph Rowntree Foundation.

Williams, A., Goodwin, M. and Cloke, P. (2014) 'Neoliberalism, Big Society, and progressive localism', *Environment and Planning A*, 46(12): 2798–2815.

Williams, G. (2004) 'Evaluating participatory development: tyranny, power and (re)politicisation', *Third World Quarterly*, 25(3): 557–578.

Wills, J. (2016) 'Emerging geographies of English localism: the case of neighbourhood planning', *Political Geography*, 53: 43–53.

Wilson, J. and Swyngedouw, E. (2014) *The Post-Political and Its Discontents: Spaces of Depoliticisation, Spectres of Radical Politics*, Edinburgh: Edinburgh University Press.

Wilson, S., Wilson, O.R., Heaney, C.D. and Cooper, J. (2007) 'Use of EPA collaborative problem-solving model to obtain environmental justice in North Carolina', *Progress in Community Health Partnerships*, 1(4): 327–337.

Wilson, S., Aber, A., Wright, L. and Ravichandran, V. (2018) 'A review of community-engaged research approaches used to achieve environmental justice and eliminate disparities', in Holifield, R., Chakraborty, J. and Walker, G. (eds) *The Routledge Handbook of Environmental Justice*, Abingdon and New York: Taylor & Francis, pp 283–296.

Wittmer, H., Rauschmayer, F. and Klauer, B. (2006) 'How to select instruments for the resolution of environmental conflicts?', *Land Use Policy*, 23(1): 1–9.

Wolsink, M. (2006) 'Invalid theory impedes our understanding: a critique on the persistence of the language of NIMBY', *Transactions of the Institute of British Geographers*, 31(1): 85–91.

Woolgar, S. (1988) *Science, the Very Idea*, Chichester and New York: Tavistock Publications.

World Bank (1996) *The World Bank Participation Sourcebook*, Washington, DC: World Bank.

World Bank (2001) *World Development Report 2000/2001: Attacking Poverty*, New York: Oxford University Press.

World Bank (2014) *Strategic Framework for Mainstreaming Citizen Engagement in World Bank Group Operations*, Washington, DC: World Bank.

Wylie, S.A., Jalbert, K., Dosemagen, S. and Ratto, M. (2014) 'Institutions for civic technoscience: how critical making is transforming environmental research', *The Information Society*, 30(2): 116–126.

Wynne, B. (1982) *Rationality and Ritual: The Windscale Inquiry and Nuclear Decisions in Britain*, Chalfont St Giles: British Society for the History of Science.

Wynne, B. (1991) 'Knowledges in context', *Science, Technology & Human Values*, 16(1): 111–121.

Wynne, B. (1992) 'Misunderstood misunderstanding: social identities and public uptake of science', *Public Understanding of Science*, 1(3): 281–304.

Wynne, B. (1993) 'Public uptake of science: a case for institutional reflexivity', *Public Understanding of Science*, 2(4): 321–338.

Wynne, B. (1996) 'May the sheep safely graze? A reflexive view of the expert-lay knowledge divide', in Szerszynski, B., Lash, S. and Wynne, B. (eds) *Risk, Environment and Modernity: Towards a New Ecology*, London: SAGE, pp 44–83.

Wynne, B. (2007) 'Public participation in science and technology: performing and obscuring a political conceptual category mistake', *East Asian Science, Technology & Society*, 1(1): 99–110.

Wynne, B. (2016) 'Ghosts of the machine: publics, meanings and social science in a time of expert dogma and denial', in Chilver, J. and Kearnes, M. (eds) *Remaking Participation: Science, Environment and Emergent Publics*, Abingdon and New York: Routledge, pp 99–120.

Yan, X. and Xin, G. (2017) 'Reforming governance under authoritarianism: motivations and pathways of local participatory reform in the People's Republic of China', *Democratization*, 24(3): 405–424.

Yanow, D. (2000) *Conducting Interpretive Policy Analysis*, Thousand Oaks: SAGE.

Yearley, S. (2005) *Making Sense of Science: Understanding the Social Study of Science*, London: SAGE.

Yeh, E. (2016) '"How can experience of local residents be 'knowledge'?" Challenges in interdisciplinary climate change research', *Area*, 48(1): 34–40.

Young, C. and Burcher, J.C. (2014) 'Love thy neighbour: An update on neighbourhood plans'. *No 5 Chambers speech transcript* [online] Available from: https://www.no5.com/media/publications/love-thy-neighbour-an-update-on-neighbourhood-plans/ [Accessed 8 September 2020].

Young, K., Ashby, D., Boaz, A. and Grayson, L. (2002) 'Social science and the evidence-based policy movement', *Social Policy and Society*, 1(3): 215–224.

Yuille, A. (2021) 'Contradictory cares in community-led planning', *Nordic Journal of Science and Technology Studies*, 9(1): 39–52.

Yuille, A. (2022) 'Can the marooned flagship of local democracy in English planning be refloated? The case of neighbourhood planning', *Town Planning Review*, 93(4): 341–352.

Zapata Campos, M.J., Kain, J.-H., Oloko, M., Scheinshohn, M., Stenberg, J. and Zapata, P. (2022) 'Residents' collective strategies of resistance in Global South cities' informal settlements: space, scale and knowledge', *Cities*, 125: 103663.

Ziervogel, G. (2019) 'Building transformative capacity for adaptation planning and implementation that works for the urban poor: insights from South Africa', *Ambio*, 48(5): 494–506.

Ziervogel, G., Enqvist, J., Metelerkamp, L. and van Breda, J. (2021) 'Supporting transformative climate adaptation: community-level capacity building and knowledge co-creation in South Africa', *Climate Policy*, 22(5): 607–622.

Index

Page numbers in *italic* type refer to figures; those in **bold** type refer to tables. References to endnotes show both the page number and the note number (231n3).

citizens' assemblies 11, 13
citizens' juries 11
civic engagement 11
  see also participatory democracy
Clarke, N. 49
climate policy 9, 13
Clinton, B. 21
Coalition government (Conservative-Liberal
  Democrat), 2010–2015 28, 33, 46,
  48–49
Cochrane, A. 497
Code, L. 84, 104
'collaborative democracy' 49
collaborative governance 11
collective identity 240, 241, 242
Colomb, C. 91, 93
commercial buildings, conversion to
  residential use 44
Commonplace mapping tool 219
communicative action 49
community councils 11
community groups 9, 12
  see also community organising in
  informal settlements
Community Infrastructure Levy
  (CIL) 250n2
*Community Involvement in Planning: The
  Government's Objectives*, ODPM 29
community mapping 218
Community Organisers funding 51
community organising in informal
  settlements 15, 22–25, 237
  evidence 156–159
  expertise, agency and power 192–195
  identity and legitimacy 118, 121–123
Community Strategies 46
'community, the' 91–92, *92*, 233–234
'community-deficit' interpretation of
  experiential knowledge deficit 210
Competence Centre on Participatory
  and Deliberative Democracy,
  European Commission 9
Comprehensive Environmental Response,
  Compensation, and Liability Act 1980
  (Superfund), US 19
concern, matters of 27, 85, 112, 201, 210,
  211, 212, 214–215, 218, 222, 223, 225,
  227–228, 229, 234, 236
Connected Communities programme, Arts
  and Humanities Research Council 217
Connelly, S. 45, 95
consensus conferences 11
Conservative Party/governments 31, 32,
  45, 59
  *Open Source Planning: Policy Green Paper
  No.14* (2010) 14, 32, 47, 49, 164
  Planning for the Future White Paper
  2020 (planning reforms) 8, 34, 86,
  248, 251n7

see also Coalition government
  (Conservative-Liberal
  Democrat), 2010–2015
consultants 152, 160, 234
  Oakley NPG case study 103, 107, 110,
  142, 143–145, 148, 173–178, 179, 182,
  199, 207, 228
  Wroston NPG case study 5, 101, 106,
  134, 135–136, 137, 138, 179–180, 181,
  182, 183, 184–187, 216, 221, 235–236
Cooke, B. 18
co-production 11, 64, 79–81, 158
  see also participatory democracy
Cornwall, A. 13, 178–179
corporate capture of regulatory
  systems 192
Country Estates 167
COVID-19 pandemic 12
Cowie, P. 95
CPRE 44
craft-based knowledges 70
  see also knowledge
Creative Participation in Place-making 217
Cresswell, T. 228
Crookes, L. 111, 150
Cruikshank, B. 53
cultural change, in planning 226

D

Dakota Access Pipeline 20
Daskalaki, M. 123
Davies, A. 66, 131
Davoudi, S. 51, 69, 73, 95, 101, 128, 200
DCLG (Department for Communities and
  Local Government) 33, 36, 250n5
  'Housing and economics needs
  assessment,' *DCLG national
  planning practice guidance* (2014) 40
  National Planning Policy Framework
  (2012) 141, 211
  'Neighbourhood planning,' *DCLG
  guidance* (2012) 30
  'Neighbourhood planning,' *DCLG
  national planning practice guidance*
  (2014) 7, 36–37, 48, 71, 127,
  130, 252n3
  *You've Got the Power: A Quick and Simple
  Guide to Community
  Rights* 130
decentralisation 43
  community organising in informal
  settlements 196–197
decolonial perspective 15
Deep South Center for Environmental
  Justice 120
Deleuze, G. 75
deliberative democracy 11, 49
  see also participatory democracy
deliberative opinion polls 11